Supporting Polylingual EAL College Readers and Educators Through Multimodality:

AI-Powered Quest for Lingua Franca

Olga Gould-Yakovleva
State University of New York, USA

IGI Global
Scientific Publishing
Publishing Tomorrow's Research Today

Vice President of Editorial	Melissa Wagner
Director of Acquisitions	Mikaela Felty
Director of Book Development	Jocelynn Hessler
Production Manager	Mike Brehm
Cover Design	Jose Rosado

Published in the United States of America by
IGI Global Scientific Publishing
701 East Chocolate Avenue
Hershey, PA, 17033, USA
Tel: 717-533-8845
Fax: 717-533-7115
Website: https://www.igi-global.com E-mail: cust@igi-global.com

Library of Congress Cataloging-in-Publication Data

Names: Gould-Yakovleva, Olga author
http://id.loc.gov/authorities/names/n2025026920
http://id.loc.gov/rwo/agents/n2025026920
Title: Supporting polylingual EAL college readers and educators through multimodality : AI-powered quest for lingua franca / Olga Gould-Yakovleva.
Description: Hershey PA : IGI Global Scientific Publishing, 2026. | Includes bibliographical references and index. | Summary: "This book offers valuable insights for higher education students and instructors, focusing on the experiences of diverse, multilingual English as an Additional Language (EAL) students. It explores the role of multimodality in supporting struggling readers"-- Provided by publisher.

Identifiers: LCCN 2025016764 (print) | LCCN 2025016765 (ebook) | ISBN 9798337334264 hardcover | ISBN 9798337334271 paperback | ISBN 9798337334288 ebook
Subjects: LCSH: English language--Study and teaching (Higher)--Foreign speakers http://id.loc.gov/authorities/subjects/sh85043719 | English language--Rhetoric--Study and teaching (Higher) http://id.loc.gov/authorities/subjects/sh2009124990 | Multilingual persons--Education (Higher) | Reading (Higher education) http://id.loc.gov/authorities/subjects/sh85111680
Classification: LCC PE1128.A2 G666 2026 (print) | LCC PE1128.A2 (ebook) | DDC 428.0071/1--dc23/eng/20250624
LC record available at https://lccn.loc.gov/2025016764
LC ebook record available at https://lccn.loc.gov/2025016765

British Cataloguing in Publication Data
A Cataloguing in Publication record for this book is available from the British Library.

TO MY LOVED ONES

I dedicate this book to my very first teachers: my parents and grandparents whom I dearly love and respect for many a thing they have taught me.

To my father, Pyotr P. Yakovlev, a musician and an educator of a great inspirational power who used to reward me, if well deserved, with his highly uplifting praise, “Ausgezeichnet!” [“Excellent!”]. He also encouraged me to fearlessly stand for what is right.

To my mother, Alexandra I. Yakovleva, who set me off to each complicated assignment with the phrase, “The most important thing is to start. You just begin! A journey of thousand miles starts with one single step.” As a scientist, a physicist, my mother would reason, “Every effort produces an outcome. The stronger the effort is, the higher is a probability of achieving the coveted goal.”

To my paternal grandmother, Dana R. Yakovleva, who taught me to stand strong to any challenges. Dana empowered me with her moto, “At the times when one’s eyes fear, the hands still can do the job.”

To my maternal grandmother, Yulia G. Sherstkina, from whom I received the lessons of diligence. Yulia taught me, “Patience and perseverance make any task done.”

To my both grandfathers, I. S. Pankov and P. F. Jakovlev, who, due to their life controversies, I have never happened to meet.

To my husband, Stephen B. Gould who, along with a flock of our furry kids, survived through my busy absence or absence-like presence during the long years of my scholarly work.

BARB: TO MY HARDEST TEACHERS

That class was the most frustrating academic experience for me as a high-school student compared to my entire childhood and teenage years of schooling. The new teacher’s full name was Barbara, but the class called her Barb. Well, at those times, whichever name she would have, I would strongly dislike it. Unexplainably, her every feature disturbed me. I strongly disliked Barb’s clumsy manners, the hissing way she forced her fricatives out, her round red chicks, and her clothes, which almost burst on her apple-shaped figure.

Why did I dislike this aging woman in her close-to-retirement years, a single mom of an extremely funny looking doctoral student? Now, when I am an adult, the reason for my former acute nonacceptance of my teacher opened to me. – This was rejection of the new and unknown. Our class was suddenly "switched" from our loved and respected Literature and Writing teacher Ms Mary Gregory to this new Barb. None of us felt happy with that unexpected change. In a fruitless attempt to regain our lost happiness, a delegation of students-ambassadors consisting of the bravest class members visited our previous teacher and asked her to "please, take us back." Ms Mary smiled in response; she said she would be happy to serve as our teacher, but the decision was not of her own and not up to her role at the school to revert. The diplomatic mission returned to the class all disheartened and helpless.

So, Barb stayed in charge. She was hard and direct with no bedside manners. Her words struck; their aftertaste lasted. One of the classroom poetry recitations seems to have stayed with me forever. - My childhood best friend, then, got deeply bewitched and immersed in Block's poem; our entire class froze still while listening in bewilderment.

The boy mesmerizingly whispered,

Night, street, lantern, apothecary,
A senseless and feeble light.
Live for another quarter-century –
All will be so. No flight.
You'll die – you'll start it over again
And all will repeat, the old pattern:
Night, icy splashes of the waterway,
Apothecary, street, lantern. (Alexander Block, October 10, 1912, O. Gould-Yakovleva Trans. 2025)

In cold blood, Barb gave him a "B," and the reason for the unexpectedly low compared to the performance grade was that student's faint stuttering. My classmates' protests and advocacy produced no result; Barb sharply cut off, "He needs to fix it. It is possible. So, he can." She stood firm with her verdict; her face looking hard as a stony red round autumn apple. That notion flowed into Barb's nickname – the Autumn Apple. And this Apple was bitter and crisp in more than one way.

She mercilessly turned down my *close-to-ideal* essay, as I viewed my own work at my teen age. A student of excellence, seldom would I bring home a grade lesser than *A*. Barb, though, put it straight, "You started your talk with a moth-beaten old cliché. And your writing has a feel of following a sample." Hissing through all her fricatives, s's, sh's, and tch's, Barb almost spit her verdict into my shuttered being. The merciless Apple advised me to leave far behind all the school-taught composing. She set me to start from anew. With the stainless-steel force of a human-driven machinery, Barb excavated the soil of unknown before my bewildered mind and re-streamed my thinking and writing from the swamp of "what needs to be done for an *A*" to the channel of frank and sincere speech of my own, neither borrowed nor followed by many. Now, after years and decades of my scholarly work, I found the worth in all Apple's points.

Could it be not so hopelessly late, I would send Barb my thanks. Could time be reversed! Could I thank our Miss Barbara in person for her brave standing against the facelessness of a *grade A*-tailored rubric. Could I express my gratitude for this teacher's tireless efforts in helping me "wake up" and grow, look for, then unharness the voice of my own. I would also add, "I am sorry." I am sorry, Miss Barbara, for my not being ready then yet to look farther, beyond your autumn-apple looks, rigid manners, and straightforward talks. Sorry for my being stubborn and childish and valuing meaningless over the meaningful in a person, a context, or text.

Your teaching, Miss Barbara, brought me somewhat even farther than anyone would have expected those days. And, guess what, Miss Teacher? – I know, it was not just myself. We have made through this journey together, with you, thanks to you, and to all my "the hardest" teachers.

REFERENCES

Block, A. (2025). Ночь, улица, фонарь, аптека. [Night, street, lantern, apothecary] In *Избранное* [Collective works]. (Gould-Yakovleva, O., Trans.). Musaget. (Original work published 1912)

Table of Contents

Preface

WHERE IT STEMS. MOTIVE & BACKGROUND

Prior to proceeding with the major content of this book, it is imperative for me, as the researcher, educator, and author, to shed some light on the roots of my search for Lingua Franca. I am willing to share with my readers some information without which their understanding of the purpose of this book may not be complete.

Almost a century ago, this quest for a commonly understandable language was started by my multilingual and multicultural grandfather, P. F. Yakovlev [`Jækəv-lev]. Further, I will spell my grandfather's name the way it appears in his publications in the German and Esperanto languages, i.e., Jakovlev.

Pavel Feodorovich [Esperanto. Paŭlo Teodorovîĉ] Jakovlev was one of the most dedicated and passionate leaders and promoters of the Esperanto movement and one of the few esperantists who miraculously survived, but only shortly outlived his colleagues, the Esperanto speakers amidst Stalin's regime of dictatorship and repressions. Born in 1893 into the family of the autochthonous residents of the Russia's Northern Capital, the City of St. Petersburg, my grandfather grew up among the speakers of a variety of socially-contesting local languages and dialects (e.g., Äyrämöiset, Finnish, Ingrian, Izhorian, Karelian, Veps, etc.) in addition to more largely spoken Russian and German. This overwhelming multilingualism of the local environment moved Jakovlev towards the idea of finding or developing the linguistic means for barrier-free communication via using one, commonly understandable language. While being aware of the complex grammar of the German or Finnish languages as an insider in their linguistic aura, my grandfather well realized the need in such tongue, which might be easy to master and utilize by speakers of any world languages or dialects. So, being absorbed with his una-linguistic idea, Jakovlev focused on utilization and wide-spreading of the artificially developed language, Esperanto, which was initially created by Ludwig Zamenhof in 1873.

At the beginning of the 20th century, P. Jakovlev served as the President of the Soviet Esperantist Union (S.E.U.) (Radiolyubitel, 1925, 3, p. 2). Along with the cohort of the dedicated promoters of the Esperanto language, who were noted as "famekonataj esperantistoj" [celebrated esperantists] (1925, 3, p. 2), Jakovlev was tirelessly disseminating the ideas of enabling and establishing the international communication via the means of this learner-friendly and commonly understandable language, largely comprised of the internationally recognizable vocabulary words, the so-called *cognates*.

As the S.E.U. leader, my grandfather published his articles (e.g., Jakovlev, 1924a, 1924b) and gave series of radio-lectures and lessons in the German, Russian, and Esperanto languages while aiming to assist vast domestic and international audiences with their connecting with each other across the country borders without any tremendous linguistic barriers. At those times, Esperanto enthusiasts used the available to them technological affordances, such as their personal, self-constructed, home-bound radio-stations. So, the speakers of the Esperanto language all over the world could communicate efficiently in this language, regardless of the countries of their residence or location.

Interestingly, it was the WJS station in the United States, which on June 19th 1922 pioneered the very first radio program series in the Esperanto language. Later that same year, this trailblazing example was followed by London; then, in 1923, by Moscow, Montreal, and Rio de Janeiro; and in 1924, the estafette was taken by Paris and Helsinki (Vlasov, 2013, p. 154). In this way, Jakovlev's dream started coming into fulfillment. This dream might have allowed his multilingual country-fellow-men and women using a commonly understandable language for borderless communication.

Importantly, the quest for finding and implementing the commonly understandable language by Jakovlev was mentioned by the contemporary Esperanto researcher, D. V. Vlasov in his publications: *Journalism of the Russian Esperanto Movement in the XX Century: Tendencies of Development and Typological Specifics* (2014a) and the monograph book entitled *History of Implementation of Esperanto in Russia* (2014b). Particularly, Vlasov gave some extra weight to the fact that in 1924-1925, S.E.U. (then headed by Jakovlev as the President) initiated regular publications in the Esperanto language in the journals *Radiolyubitel* [Radio-Amateur] and *Internacia Lingvo* [International Language]. Following the powerful and enthusiastic start, the scale of these efforts resulted in organizing international conferences and congresses for Esperanto speakers in Russia's two capital cities: Moscow and St. Petersburg.

Most importantly, this work opened the door for international collaboration among the colleagues-esperantists in many European and American countries. As documented by Detlev Blanke (2008) in his book *Historio de la Laborista Esperanto-Movado* [History of the Working-Class Esperanto Movement], on August 7th, 1930, the Central Committee of the Esperantists of the Soviet Countries (CCESC) formed by Ernest K. Drezen, Pavel F. Jakovlev, Victor Ĵavoronkov, and Sergey Valentinov made the decision to establish the S.E.U.-owned publishing agency with its complete independence from the European ones. This event laid the start to the journal *Internaciisto* [Internationalist] headed by the József Batta as the editor-in-chief.

An interesting detail can be spotted in the 8th issue of the first volume of the 1924 *Radiolyubitel* journal on p. 114. There, one of the articles detailed the debate among the American radio-amateurs who were deciding on the choice of the commonly understandable language for international communication to be used for radio transmissions. Those discussants were struggling to choose between the Ido and the Esperanto languages; yet, gave prevalence to the latter one. And only a year later, in the first issue of the second volume of the above journal, the American radio-amateurs' preference of Esperanto, as the language of the international communication, was supported by their French counterparts (Radiolyubitel, 1925, p. 4).

All the above facts about the radio-broadcast programs and international communication via radio (not internet at those times yet) in the Esperanto language explained the connection between the S.E.U. and the journal *Radiolyubitel* [Radio-Amateur]. This publication not only provided details on radio-engineering and constructing private radio-stations for international communication, but also covered global affairs; particularly, concerning the language for the common communication for the world's radio-amateurs.

Apparently, Stalin's regime of authoritarianism and terror could not tolerate this growing global movement where Esperanto served as the language of common communication connecting vast audiences of its speakers on both sides of the Iron Curtain. As the result, all members of the CCESC and many from the S.E.U. were arrested and shortly executed in 1938 (Stepanov, 2013).

It was a miracle and the God's providence that in 1933, long before the above, disastrous and final for the S.E.U. events, Jakovlev, as a Graduate of St. Petersburg Mining University and a professional geologist, had travelled to the far East and out of reach for Stalin's NKVD. Due to the specifics of his profession, Jakovlev worked in the extremely remote locations within several geological expeditions to the Caucasus mountains, Kazakhstan steppes, Siberian Taiga, and the Arctic Circle Zone.

It was most devastating and simultaneously heroic that none of Jakovlev's colleagues at CCESC or S.E.U. mentioned his name during their arrests and interrogations by Stalin's investigators. In their desperate attempt to survive and prove their innocence, my grandfather's colleagues and friends shielded him and his family of six, one of whom was my father, then yet an infant. Thanks to his friends' selfless efforts, Jakovlev appeared out of Stalin's repression manipulations with millions of innocent lives. Moreover, due to his distant and longitudinal expeditions, my grandfather remained uninformed about the massive arrests of Esperantists in the capital and major regional cities.

Nevertheless, upon his return from one of his sequestered trips to the country center, Jakovlev happened to hear the radio broadcasting, which reported about numerous executions of the Soviet Esperantists. Filled with compassion and desperation, my young then yet grandfather suffered a heart attack and passed away within three days of torturous psychological and emotional devastation. Consequently, our family silenced the facts of my grandfather's activity for decades in their terror-fueled attempt to shield and to save us, the children, from the prosecutions under the later regimes.

Nowadays, nearly a century after those tragic events, I feel devoted to continue the work lead by my grandfather. Though I approach Jakovlev's ideas from a different angle, I remain dedicated to look for, find, and promote a commonly-understandable language, the tongue many peoples may use in addition to or, whenever possible, in the lieu of a verbal one. And the name of this additional and commonly understandable language is Multimodality.

ABOUT THE CONTENT OF THIS BOOK

My decision to disseminate the content discussed in this book was powered with thought about and care for those people for whom this work might be of great help. These might be college or university students who struggle with reading comprehension of dense course texts, many of whom are English as an Additional (Second, New, Foreign) Language learners. Another large category of readers who might strongly benefit from getting familiarized with the topics addressed in this book are school teachers, college instructors, and university professors in search of more efficient reading comprehension strategies.

Additionally, my writing is also purposed specifically for those beginning scholars who are preparing to engage with research. They might be working towards their Associate's, Bachelor's, Master's, or Doctoral degrees. Many of these young or midcareer scholars might have limited access to quality and in-depth research advisement or mentorship. As many students find themselves left to survive on their own in academe, some of them struggle with the very concept of research, while many might not even know where to begin, what to read, how to design, and conduct their studies.

If my readers happened to have found themselves unadvised, I am here with my writing to give them a hand. This tireless endeavor to help has been guided and torched by my unfadable memories of struggling myself. My blind-folded journey through self-education on the background of a chain of adversities, the most excruciating of which was loss of my parents, moved me towards appropriating the moto: Per Aspera Ad Astra! [Latin. Through Hardships to the Stars].

With the above thought, I wrote out every process involved in preparation to conducting research, developing major ideas, designing, and conducting a qualitative case study with all its parts and additions, where the major purpose was to find an Additional language to facilitate print-based reading. One more thought to conclude this section is to advise readers to either read sequentially this entire book or selectively choose some high-interest chapters. I will briefly address major points of each book chapter below.

Part I

In Part I titled "Preparing for my Research," I will detail on all preparation processes involved in developing a study. In the first chapter "Introduction. Silent Outcries for Help," I will expose the reading comprehension problems encountered by college and university students, many of whom are polylingual International or Domestic English as an Additional Language speakers. I will also pose my research questions and justify the need in this study based on the identified gap. Further, in the second chapter "Choosing and Umbrella," I will explain, which paradigms and theories underpinned this research. Importantly, I will explain how theories connect to practice. In the next chapter titled "Exploring Forerunners," I will present the results of my review of the seminal and most recent literature in the field of multimodality. This chapter will demonstrate the process of identifying the gap in research. Chapter IV "Delving Deeper" aims to invite readers onto a journey to the roots of research in the fields of semiotics and social semiotics. In this chapter, I will discuss the postulates by the founding fathers on these theories. Importantly, the input of these theorists into developing the field of multimodality may not be overlooked, as their findings and teachings are fundamental for understanding this field.

Upon having discussed the preparatory steps, which are made by researchers prior to beginning their studies, I will proceed with Chapter V "Designing the Study" where I detail every process in designing a qualitative research project, starting with selecting the method, securing the Institutional Review Board (IRB) approval, recruiting prospective participants, and deciding on the major research instruments and tools. In the final chapter of the first part of this book, Chapter VI, which is titled "Data Collection and Analysis," readers will find my detailed report on every process included in collecting data followed by explanation of how these data will be analyzed to answer research questions.

Conclusively, Part I of this book aims to help the beginning researchers to get thoroughly prepared to conduct their own projects. Though design, number of participants, the research topic, and purpose might most certainly differ, readers will get the idea of many steps in the process of the preparatory activity. Although some of these actions (e.g., the IRB approval) might not be required of investigators in some overseas countries, many of the discussed steps are an absolute must for the U.S. researchers, regardless of the domestic or international location of their project site and research participants.

Part II

In the second part entitled "Digging Through the Stratum of Unspoken," I will start presenting the findings of my study. First, I will introduce my research participants as reading personalities with their joys and struggles when reading academic texts or fiction both in their Native tongues and in the English language. These findings were based not only on the interview responses by my participants, but also on their responses to the researcher-developed surveys and questionnaires.

In Chapter VII titled "People Behind the Numbers," I will provide detailed information on the home countries and languages of the participating students. Besides giving each participant his or her reading characteristics, as per their own words, I will also share the results of my observations of these students' behaviors during reading.

Chapter VIII "Revealing the Hidden Struggle" is concerned with the research participants' revelations focused on their positive experiences with reading as well as their comprehension problems. Through their interviews, surveys, and questionnaires, students were asked to share about what exactly presented most serious obstacles for them and which strategies helped them most to cope with the comprehension tasks.

The following Chapter IX "So, What Helped?" will go even deeper into the details on implementation of diverse reading comprehension strategies, which apparently differed from unimodal text-based ones when multimodality was added to Shakespearean print-based texts used in this project. All findings with regards to the helpful meaning-making strategies discussed in this chapter, as well as in the entire second part of this book, might be interesting and helpful to both students and their instructors.

Conclusive portion of Part II, Chapter X titled "When Numbers Speak Louder Than Words" will present some numeric data from the participants' comprehension tests to the Shakesperean texts. These data serve to support the information obtained from the interviews with the participating students and allows the researcher to triangulate these research findings for their greater validity. Importantly, readers will be able to see the evidence in addition to and as an illustration to the textually narrated ideas.

Importantly, the interpretation of research results discussed in all PART II chapters might be of interest to schoolteachers and university professors, while students on all grade levels, specifically, college and university learners, might find this information useful for both their reading comprehension endeavors and practical test-taking.

Part III

The third part is titled "Nonchalant Accounts of AI." Regardless of the scandalous reputation of Artificial Intelligence (AI) gained due to its misuse by some dishonest or uninformed users, this portion of the book aims to show how technological software may be efficiently utilized for qualitative data analysis. More precisely, Chapter XI entitled "MAXQDA-Portrayed Speech" is comprised of the researcher's interpretations of the AI-developed images of the major ideas in each participant's interview speeches. These MaxQda portraits of Day 1 interviews were generated by the AI software for qualitative data analysis and were the results of processing interview transcripts with extraction of most important and most frequently used by each participant topics and themes. For a greater clarity, every visual MaxQda portrait is accompanied by the researcher's clarifications and multiple direct quotations from the participant's Day 1 interview speeches.

Chapter XII "AI and Day 1 Group Accounts" might be of high interest for both researchers and educators. AI utilized for developing whole group matrices allowed to identify some significant patterns and differences, for example, by gender, in the students' working with the texts and test questions. Information presented in this chapter might help instructors to select and implement more suitable reading strategies gender-wise.

Next Chapter XIII "More Truths Unveiled" will shed more light on the helpful strategies utilized by the research participants on Day 2, when they worked with multimodally supplemented texts and thus could implement not only text-based, but also diverse multimodal strategies. These findings might be of high significance for those language and content-area educators who seek some useful means to supplement their instruction to enhance their EAL students' reading comprehension and efficiency. The following Chapter XIV "Triangulating with AI: Day 2 Group Accounts" will touch on the significance of the process of triangulation of large amounts of data from multiple sources where AI might serve for presenting extensive evidence in a concise form. Overall, in this chapter, whole group data MaxQda-developed matrices based on Day 2 interviews will help readers to grasp the essence of students' speeches at a glance.

Part IV

Part IV entitled "How Multimodalities work" may draw interest of more than one kind of reading audience. This portion of the book contains two analyses, each presented in its own chapter. Both Chapter XV "Multimodal Analysis 1: Attempting to Understand Role, Position, and Significance of Visuals within Multimodal Ensembles" and Chapter XVI titled "Analysis 2: Visual Language Intermodal Relations Data Analysis" rest on rich description of the semiosis within the Shakesperean play texts and the multimodal ones available in Gian Franco Zeffirelli's 1968 movie production of *Romeo and Juliet.* Apparently, the purpose of both analyses was to attempt to understand how exactly observations of multimodal texts enable comprehension of the observable and audible events in presence and in absence of the verbal texts. Full transcripts of these analyses may be found in Part VI Appendices at the end of this book.

Part V

Part V titled "Quest for Lingua Franca" is the conclusive part of this publication. Chapter XVII "Jakovlev's Search for Lingua Franca" adds more details on how I furthered my grandfather's work aiming to identify and set into classroom implementation a commonly understandable language for all students. I illustrate my statements with unbeatable evidence presented both textually and visually. In the final Chapter XVIII titled "Post Scriptum," I express the idea of the need for reconceptualization of multimodality. Imperatively, in this portion of my book, I conclude my search for Lingua Franca and claim that the Multimodal language may and needs to be viewed and used in the college classrooms as a useful and helpful Additional language in service of better reading comprehension.

Part VI

I decided to make appendices a separate part of this book. Part VI "Appendices" contains three important pieces of information, which might be of great interest to my readers. In *Appendix A*, one can find the surveys and questionnaires used within this project. *Appendix B* presents all interview questions. And *Appendix C*, as I mentioned before, is comprised of the full-detailed transcripts of both *Multimodal Analyses 1* and *2*. Though I had to remove the images due to the copyright considerations, I provided my rich verbal descriptions of events in every snapshot. As Shakespeare never published his 1597 play of *Romeo and Juliet*, and the timeframes have long exceeded those established by the copyright regulations of "50 years after the author's life-time," some portions of the discussed excerpts will be made available for the readers' convenience. At the end of this book, readers may also find the list of all references used in this manuscript.

I truly hope diverse reading audiences find the ideas expressed by the study participants useful for themselves or for struggling readers. I also believe many beginning scholars as well as experienced educators will find my writing helpful, as that was the major purpose for this entire work.

Wishing my readers exciting discoveries and enjoyable reading.

Olga Gould-Yakovleva
State University of New York, USA

REFERENCES

Blanke, D. (1933, 1953). *Historio de la Laborista Esperanto-Movado*. [History of the working-class Esperanto Movement]. In A. Sidorov *Esperanto Wave* [Волна Эсперанто] (1983 Eds.). Moscow: Impeto. Retrieved from: https://lernolibro.ru/otrivki/blanke

Jakovlev, P. F. (1924a). Radio-kroniko Sovetlanda [Radio-chronicles of Soviet country]. *Radiolyubitel* [Radio-Amateur], *1*(4), p. 2. http://archive.radio.ru/web/1924/04/001/

Jakovlev, P. F. (1924b). Радиотелефония и международный язык [Wireless telephony and international language]. *Radiolyubitel* [Radio-Amateur], *1*(5), p. 71.

MAXQDA. (2021). MAXQDA 2022 [computer software]. Berlin, Germany: VERBI Software. Available from maxqda.com.

Shakespeare, W. (1597). *Romeo and Juliet*.

Stepanov, N. (2013). Esperanto en Rusio: История эсперанто в России и Советском Союзе. Биографии репрессированных эсперантистов, архивные материалы. [Esperanto in Russia: History of Esperanto in Russia and Soviet Union. Biographies of the repressed esperantists, archival materials]. *Historio* [History]. http://historio.ru

VERBI Software. (2021). MAXQDA 2022 [computer software]. Berlin, Germany: VERBI Software. Available from maxqda.com.

Vlasov, D. V. (2013). Эсперанто в Советском радио-эфире в 1920-1930-е годы. [Esperanto in the Soviets radio broadcast in the years of 1920-1930-s]. *Вестник Санкт Петербургского Университета* [St. Petersburg University Press], *9*(4), 154-161. https://jf.spbu.ru/upload/files/file_1399403466_3033.pdf

Vlasov, D. V. (2014a). *Журналистика российского эсперанто-движения в XX в.: Тенденции развития и типологические особенности*. [Journalism of the Russian Esperanto movement in the XX century: Tendencies of development and typological specifics]. Doctoral dissertation manuscript. St. Petersburg University. https://jf.spbu.ru/upload/files/file_1399403145_8952.pdf

Vlasov, D. V. (2014b). *История применения эсперанто в России: Печать, радиовещание, переписка, самиздат* [History of implementation of Esperanto in Russia: Press, broadcasting, correspondence, and self-publishing]. Impeto.

Zamenhof, L. L. (1887). *Международный языкъ: Предисловіе и полный учебникъ* [International language: Introduction and complete grammar]. Warsaw: Typolithography of H. Kelter.

Zeffirelli, F. (1968). *Romeo and Juliet.* Paramount Pictures. Retrieved from public domain: https://www.youtube.com/watch?v=VCe0nzdD76k

Acknowledgement

The author of this book would like to acknowledge the efforts of all the people involved in this project.

I would like to express my heartfelt gratitude to Nina Eddinger, IGI Global Scientific Publishing Book Development Editor for leading me through all stages of the book preparation processes.

I also deeply appreciate the insightful contributions from this book reviewers, whose expertise, time, and dedication helped enhance the rigor of my work.

Special thanks to the IGI-Global team: Melissa Wagner, Vice President of Editorial; Mikaela Felty - Director of Acquisitions; Lydia Lonie, Assistant Acquisitions Editor; Chris Shearer - Director of Publications; Kyle Frey, Parker Bender, DeannaJo Zombro, and Mahli Rupp - Production Assistants. Your timely provided insightful communication is greatly appreciated.

Thank you, dear All, for accompanying me on my way to getting this manuscript published.

Sincerely,

Olga Gould-Yakovleva, Ph.D.

SUNY, United States of America

Introduction

Before buying or borrowing a book from a library, readers naturally want to know whether and how they might benefit from the information it has to offer. In anticipation of this question, I am looking back at the times of my younger years and university studies. Thoughtfully shifting through my memories, I tried to address the topics of high significance for students and their educators. So, whether you are teaching or only preparing to teach, this book might be of great help to you.

Let us get acquainted. I will introduce myself at the start of this book. Allow me to guess now who you are, my dear reader. Are you a beginning researcher? – Keeping your possible questions in mind, I have thoroughly described all the steps involved in qualitative research, particularly a case study. From designing a project and elaborating the method, through recruitment and work with research participants, further, through data collection and their analysis, and reporting the findings, I detailed all this work in my writing aiming to give you the picture or a blueprint for your own future endeavors. So, read this book, then, dive into your own research, using my writing as Ariadne's thread, which lead this legendary person through the labyrinth of unknown.

Are you a school teacher of Reading, English Language Arts, or English as an Additional (Second, New, or Foreign) language? I was working on my projects aiming to help you in your struggles. Equipped with my shared through this book experience, see how you can help your struggling readers to achieve higher while being deeper engaged in reading and learning.

Are you an English language learner and a speaker of more than one language? Are you a curious mind who is willing to know how human brain reads the surrounding world? Are you eager to learn how humans make meaning from the pronounced or silenced words? Are you willing to know how, while being so different, we still can understand each other; sometimes, without words? Then, this book is for you and your hungry for knowledge mind. Enjoy your reading journey, and let your exploration be filled with discoveries.

Are you a college instructor or a university professor, just like myself? So many of our students are longing for help. See how helpful my students-research-participants found the multimodal approach and how they ranked their usage of helpful strategies.

My dear respected reader, are you more than I can imagine? Well, I am wishing you to spend a most enjoyable time while rediscovering this big and complex world via reading the profound ideas expressed by the experienced researchers, honorable educators, and well-known authors, as well as the highly educated, thoughtful, and intelligent research participants whose endeavors shaped this publication. Read and think what you can come out with. I am wishing you best of luck!

Olga Gould-Yakovleva
State University of New York, USA

Section 1
Preparing for Research

Chapter 1
Introduction:
Silent Outcries for Help

ABSTRACT

In this chapter, I will discuss the current state of things in the field of multimodalities. And in the very first subsection, I will try to explain why it is so important to help polylingual English as an Additional Language students in the United States colleges and universities and internationally. After having presented some statistical data on the numbers of EAL students in the U.S. higher education institutions, I will attempt to justify the purpose and significance of this book and the study behind it. Importantly, I will show the gap in the research with particularly this learner population. I will also pose the research questions, which stem from my practical teaching, research, and the years of my scholarship. To facilitate my readers from the out-of-field backgrounds, I will define some key-words and major concepts, which are widely used in the fields of semiotics, social semiotics, and multimodality, so my readers from practically any academic or professional sphere can read and enjoy this book without the need to research on the used terminology.

BIG KIDS – BIG PROBLEMS

For a caring and concerned parent of today, sending a child to school and waiting for them to return home with a bag full of textbooks and homework sheets seems like a fairy-tale of the *auld lang syne*. Back in 2012 yet, Miller and McVee issued a statement, which sounded almost as harsh as a verdict, "Over the past 20 years, the idea of literacy has changed dramatically" (Miller, & McVee, 2012a, p. 1).

Subsequently, these authors continued,

This change is particularly significant for our students, who have grown up surrounded and shaped by literacy practices related to computers, the Internet, mobile phones and other ubiquitous computing devices for communicating,

DOI: 10.4018/979-8-3373-3426-4.ch001

taking pictures and videos, playing music and games, searching for, and storing digital material. (Miller, & McVee, 2012a, p. 2)

The practices mentioned above are known as means of multimodality; though, multimodality is not limited to its digital forms. In modern day classrooms, multimodal representations, for example, digital videos and audios, can be effectively used by educators in their instruction in addition to conventional print-based texts with the purpose to assist students with their meaning making in the process of reading conventional print-based texts supported with the features of multimodality. Yet, often, teachers choose to use the above to merely entertain or motivate their reluctant learners.

So, why is multimodal support and assistance important in teaching and learning? The answer is straight: whenever students are struggling with making the meaning of complex academic texts, they need some support. And if early in the young children's educational paths, their loved ones find themselves able to help their offsprings with reading the traditional print-based books, which are often supplemented with some helpful meaning-making pictures or illustrations, things change in the upper grades. With the children's progress through middle and high school, it generally becomes increasingly harder for their family members to provide academic support. And when the growing students enroll in colleges and universities, complexity of their course readings may become overwhelming for too many.

As an educator, I became aware of this problem during the years of my practical teaching experiences and observations. Subsequently, the conclusion I have drawn is that some families cannot proudly boast with their young-age or college-age offsprings who never faced any academic challenges. Moreover, even the prominent students may struggle at times. As a matter of fact, when experiencing academic challenges, many students silence their need in help, guidance, and assistance. No wonder that many children, teenagers, and young people feel embarrassed when perceiving their own academic challenges as their lower aptitude compared to their classmates. In turn, in a desperate attempt to not lose their face, the other students around them also silence their problems, while comparing themselves to their peers through the lens of a mistaken assumption of the academic superiority of the surroundings compared to the struggling selves. In this closed-circle self-siege, students long for their educators' sensitivity, helpfulness, and skill. These struggling readers want their teachers to hear and discern their silent outcries for help.

It needs to be admitted though, that hearing these cries, a.k.a., knowing about the existing problems, does not mean yet being able to help. Most importantly, these useful and helpful teaching and learning strategies urge to be found and applied. So, the need in the means, which might help if not all, then many, brought me, as an educator and an educational researcher, to the necessity in researching and looking for some working solutions to help struggling readers in school classrooms on all grade levels, including university and college.

So, I set on my way. Prior to this current project, I designed a range of studies (e.g., Gould, 2015, 2016, 2017; Gould-Yakovleva, 2023a, 2023b) and conducted series of research on this topic, each time with a new group of participants, all of whom were polylingual English as Additional language speakers and Domestic or International college or university students. Though the design, method, and research processes differed in each of my previous studies, major focus of each was on studying how implementation of multimodalities might help students with their meaning making.

Here, as if pre-opening the curtain of the research discussed in this book, I will reveal that the research participants in my previously conducted studies (e.g., Gould-Yakovleva, 2017, 2023a, 2023b) found multimodal support beneficial for meaning making in the process of their reading conventional print-based texts supported by diverse means of multimodality present in digital videos chosen to accompany print-based text. Interestingly, these research-participants shared that they strongly relied on the non-verbal language.

It would be fair yet to admit that I was not the first investigator who researched the field of multimodality. Multiple researchers who conducted their studies in the United States found implementation of multimodality beneficial for student learning (e.g., Ainsworth et al., 2023; Ajayi, 2008; 2009, 2015; Brown & Eskildsen, 2024; Bruce, 2009a, 2009b; Bruce & Chiu, 2015; Lincoln & Rademacher, 2006; McVee, Bailey, & Shanahan, 2008a, 2008b; Miller, 2013; Nelson, 2008; Yusra et al., 2025). Importantly, many studies carried out in highly technologically developed countries found multiple positive effects from implementing multimodal texts on different aspects of learning outcomes (e.g., Archer & Price, 2021; Baildon & Damico, 2009; Binder & Kotsopoulos, 2011; Exley & Cotrell, 2012; Gould-Yakovleva, McVee, & Fronczak, 2020; Kitson, 2011; Kuo, Yu, & Hsiao, 2013; Liu & Qu, 2014; Mills, 2007; Molyneux & Godinho, 2012; Ntelioglou, 2011; Pantaleo, 2012a, 2012b; Saint-Georges, & Weber, 2013; Vincent, 2006; Yusra et al., 2025). Yet, many authors stressed the importance of further research in this field due to its high significance for both students and their educators (e.g., Archer, 2025; Giampapa, 2010; Huang, 2012; Kaur, et al., 2012; Lee et al., 2024; Shanahan et al., 2014; Włodarczyk et al., 2023).

JOYS AND CONCERNS WITH THE GROWING NUMBERS

Importantly, it needs to be clarified that researching and discussing the topic of multimodality for education became critical in the 21st century. Increasingly growing waves of migration have been continually bringing new EAL students to the American and overseas classrooms. Lack of political and economic stability in many countries changed the demographic composition of the American classrooms of today. Tragically unsafe and unstable situations in many international localities caused the demographics in many U.S. schools to dramatically shift from homogeneity to extreme diversity. Subsequently, the on-going influx of new students presented new challenges for educators. Continuously greater numbers of multicultural and polylingual students arrive in the American classrooms.

According to the U.S. Department of Education, National Center for Education Statistics (2024), the number of English as Additional Language (EAL) speaking students is dramatically growing in United States educational establishments on all grade levels (See *Figure 1* for the increase in numbers of EAL speaking student populations in the United Sates).

Figure 1. Number of English learner students as a percent of enrolment in the U.S. public schools (National Center for Education Statistics, 2024) and prediction of growth by 2025

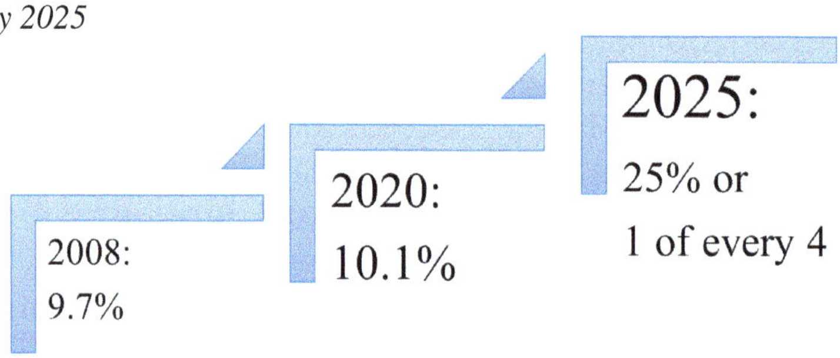

As shown in *Figure 1,* one of every 4 students in the 2025 classrooms from K through Grade 12 is a speaker of English as an Additional Language. Correspondingly, the numbers of International EL learners continue to grow in colleges and universities. According to the Open Door historical statistical data report, percentage of the international students in U.S. postsecondary institutions increased from 3.3 - 3.5% as registered in the first decade of the 21st century to 4.6 - 5.6% during the second and third decades with just slight fluctuation between different years. Translating the percentages into the numbers of people, as per the Department of Education, National Center for Education Statistics, the amounts of international students in American postsecondary institutions increased from 564,766 in 2005-2006 academic year to 723,277 in 2010-2011. Only one year later, this number went up to 819,644 of undergraduate and graduate international students. Further, according to the data of the Institute of International Education (Farrugia & Bhandari, 2016), in the 2014-2015 academic year, the number of international students that included EAL speakers in the United States stepped over 900,000. And in 2022-2023, this population peaked higher than one million, to be more exact, 1,057,188 people (See Figure 2 below for the growth of number of international students, including EAL speakers, in U.S. colleges and universities between 2000 and 2023).

Figure 2. Growing over decades number of international students in the U.S. colleges and universities from 2000 to 2023 academic year (Institute of International Education, 2024)

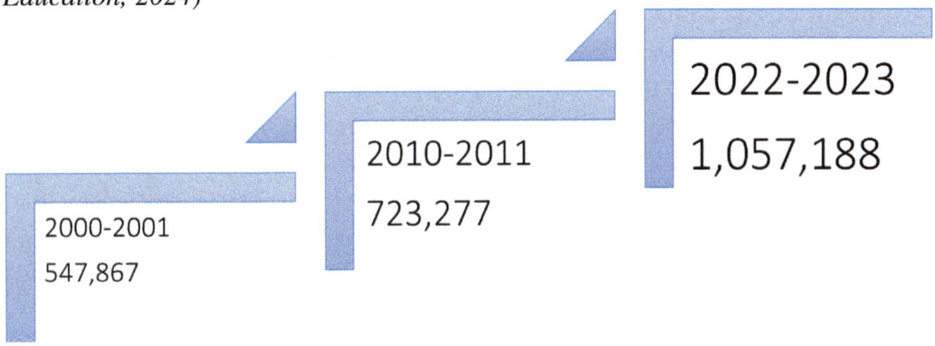

Though the American institutions of higher education celebrate the growing crowds of their international students in their welcoming tenets, the major concerns which alarm college and university educators is the inevitable and dramatically diverging English language proficiency levels in the extremely demographically and linguistically diverse international student populations. The above concerns move teachers-practitioners, college educators, and researchers to search for new and helpful ways to teach the incredibly different in multiple aspects EAL students, who need help with their meaning making; thus, need to be somehow assisted with gaining the understanding of the content of the readings on the background of the tremendous differences in their English language proficiency.

Thus, educators with help from educational researchers need to explore some more efficient ways for teaching and learning to better assist their diverse multicultural and polylingual students with their transitioning in between their home languages and mother tongues to English as their target language. Here my major claim comes into play, and it is that this transition may need to be efficiently facilitated with the help from the commonly understandable means of communication – the Additional Language of Multimodality.

LOOKING FOR LINGUA FRANCA

Knowing from inside about the passion for teaching intrinsically motivating educators, I recognize that teachers on all grade levels, including higher education, do continuously search, experiment, and test in their classrooms a plethora of classical, innovative, or, so-called, *their own* instructional methods, strategies, and techniques. The results of all the endeavors differ on a case-by-case basis, depending on every class linguistic and demographic composition. So, the search for that long-coveted panacea - *the Lingua Franca* continues and progresses. These days, it parallels to and is often intertwined with the development of the omniscient technologies. The latter inevitably leads to the use of technological multimodalities. Diverse positive effects of different modes of multimodality on students have been intensively studied and explored worldwide, as I mentioned before. Still, there persists a significant gap in the research on how multimodality may influence, alter, and alleviate the meaning making processes in the polylingual EAL speaking college students. (See *Figure 3* below for the number of studies by grade level).

Now, let us look at the need in research from the numeric perspective. Out of all the available literature I dug over prior to conducting this research, 53% publications reported their findings with the elementary age students, while 28% of the reports were concerned with middle and high school populations. Out of 19% of studies with the college students, only 6% were concerned with the higher education population in the United States, and 13% of research was conducted with the overseas EAL college students. Further, it was close to impossible to find literature on effects of resources of multimodal ensembles (when added to conventional print-based texts) on meaning making in polylingual EAL speaking college students.

Figure 3. Percentage of studies in the field of multimodality by grade level based on available literature

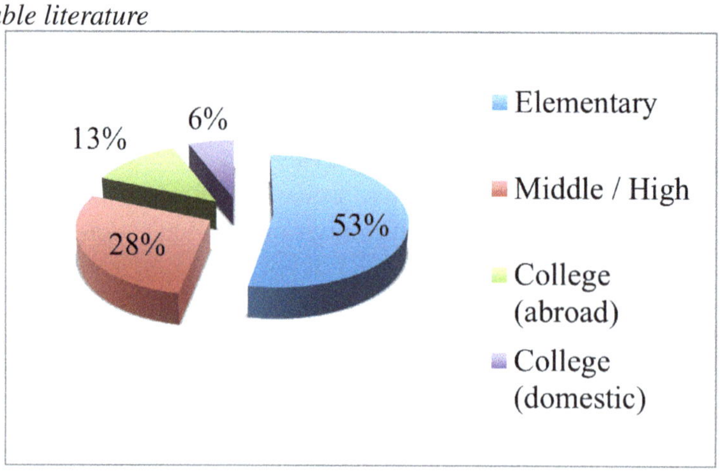

Figure 3 data imply the need in research on effects of multimodalities on college student populations, while the data on specifically Polylingual portion of this population is not present at all. Why so? The answer is simple: apparently, polylingualism in the American families and globally has been progressively increasing, as humankind are leaving behind the old generations' intercultural and international prejudices as well as the political, social, ethnical, religious or any kind of self-isolation practices. Obviously, the affordable and speedy international travel and the modern days' electronic means of communication make the processes of the growing social interconnectivity inevitable.

Conclusively, in the current chronotope (Bakhtin, 1981), using multiple languages for a range of different purposes and life scenarios presents a range of advantageous opportunities, rather than burdensome challenges. Thus, adhering to the multiplicity of the individually inherited or situationally acquired languages may be considered beneficial, rather than strenuous by the users of multiple tongues. Yet, the presence, usage, and mastery of one common language, understandable to majority of people might significantly simplify the processes of acquiring and sharing new information and knowledge. If only that equally omni-comprehensible inter-language could be identified and utilized.

JUSTIFYING THIS RESEARCH

Challenges of Language Learning

As I shared above, the knowledge of several languages offers their users multiple benefits. For example, polylingual people can broaden their perspectives while using the information from a multiplicity of primary sources compared to using just one by a monolingual person who should be concerned with the matter of trustworthiness, reliability, and unbiasedness of the available to them resources published or broadcast in that language. Even recognizing the possibility of exposure to different points of view in the speakers of that one language (L 1), we need to consider availability of even more diverse perspectives present and presented by carriers of other languages. Logically, the more languages, the more perspectives; that is the greatest advantage of polylingualism.

Nevertheless, the unbeatable truth is that mastery of practically any additional language, including English as the language of international communication, requires an extensive time and strong effort. Prior to being able to use the new language freely and comfortably, practically every student must invest lots of work and time. And the speed and efficiency of progress depends on multiple factors. For example, switching codes between different languages may present quite a challenge. Next, navigating between different alphabetical systems is a significantly more strenuous task rather than using the Latin-based ones. Yet, even the speakers of the European, Latin-based tongues may struggle with acquiring different grammar and so-called language logic. While switching between the hieroglyphic, Cyrillic, pictographic, or any other alphabetical systems presents more than one challenge. Additionally, a certain language speaker's ear, while being accustomed to discern within range of the known sounds and voice pitches might struggle recognizing and even hearing the ones of the new to them language.

Moreover, the thinking patterns, the cultural mentality, and the manner of expression may differ in different languages. The closer are the linguistic groups within their Native linguistic families, the easier or smoother may be the work of acquiring an additional language. Understandably, this work might feel more demanding when the owned and the new linguistic systems differ dramatically both in their oral and print-based forms. With the above explanations presented, it becomes more understandable that many polylingual EAL speaking students may experience serious difficulties with meaning making while reading texts in any Additional Language including English.

Taking into consideration the fast-growing number of the Polylingual EAL-learning student populations in U.S. schools and worldwide leads educators to the need in better accommodating these learners in terms of providing them with efficient language instruction. Thus, the American and international researchers and educators need to further research the field of language acquisition and look for some new, these days, technology-based ways to teach polylingual EAL-speaking students more efficiently. It is equally important to find the means which might help these students to study more efficiently at home, while learning individually and independently. So, via my research presented in this book, I sought to find some means that might powerfully assist reading comprehension in polylingual EAL-speaking college students. And my researcher assumption, based on the years of my practical teaching and research, allowed me to conclude that teaching polylingual EAL-speaking college students the multimodalities and multiliteracy skills has a great potential to assist these learners with their meaning making.

Struggles in College

Could my Native English-speaking readers only imagine the struggles and frustrations of the EAL-learning students who painstakingly strive to master the new to them English language, while having little to no help from their families, friends, and country-fellow men and women. Surprising to many newly-arrived to America international students, that English they studied and used in their home-countries has little in common with the English language they encounter once on the American shore. The American classmates, neighbors, and store cashiers all speak some *new* and *unusual* English, which the newcomers often find difficult to understand. Moreover, once in the classroom and equipped with the readings, in whichever field, be that the Medical or Biological Sciences or Civil or Space Engineering, the newly-arrived EAL learners face an exacerbating urge to simply decipher and understand the language of their academic readings, which is loaded with each field-specific vocabulary.

One might object saying that the Native English language speakers go through almost identical struggles with the new to them terminology and content. I would not oppose this argument. Nevertheless, studying the new vocabulary and content in a new or additional language is a significantly greater challenge. I am asking my readers to approach the idea of using a new language from the perspective of a traveler who goes overseas, not on a pleasure trip, but for the purpose of earning a degree in an overseas university or college. Just for an instance, consider the possibility for yourself or any American person to study such fields as Medicine, Quant Physics, Aircraft Engineering, or Biochemistry at a highly reputable university in Germany, France, or Sweden. Now, imagine these subjects taught in the official languages of these countries. Well, only the person who has been through the educational experiences in a language other than their mother tongue may have fully perceived and can fairly reflect on their studies in a new to them language and on the involved struggles.

Besides the linguistic struggles, the international students often experience shocking difficulties with the cultural aspects of everyday life in a new to them country and culture. While honoring the brave ones who made it through studies abroad, I question the need for their intellectual torments. As a solution, I would propose the Vygotskyan (1978, 1987) way, where a learner is being helped by some more experienced others. So, how can these learned others, the classroom instructors, assist their EAL college learners? Some strategies work, but are they helpful enough? The answer to the above question may only be given by the learners of English as an Additional language. How can their voices be heard? How can we gain the knowledge of their victories and struggles?

I view qualitative research as one of the most reliable ways to get to know every participant's ideas, hidden thoughts, frustrations, and reflections on success. Thus, it is highly significant to study effects of multimodality on postsecondary students, specifically, on the polylingual EAL college or university students who come from different linguistic, educational, cultural, historical, literary, and religious backgrounds. It is highly important to expose these students to different educational practices. Through the means of educational practice and research, it is possible to find best efficient teaching and learning tools for practically every learner in a highly diverse and inclusive American or international classroom. So, I have a good hope that the findings of my research may help educators make the strong positive change in their instruction via adjusting their curriculums and teaching approaches and practices to the needs of all their learners. I have special hope the needs of the polylingual EAL college students will be better addressed when the vast audiences of educators get the knowledge of how – how the meaning making of print-based texts may be supported with the features of multimodality.

Hopefully, now, my readers fully understand the sacred purpose which powered and propelled my study.

Research Questions

So, with my strong research- and practice-based trust in the power of multimodality, I posed the following questions for my new research project:

1) In what ways, if any, does inclusion of multimodal resources in combination with traditional print-based text assist polylingual EAL-speaking college students' reading comprehension?
2) What are polylingual EAL-speaking college students' perceptions of working with multimodal texts?
3) Which multimodal resources, if at all, do polylingual EAL-speaking college students find most helpful, moderately helpful, and least helpful in the process of reading texts supported by features of multimodality?

Additionally, I was greatly interested to investigate the role of the diverse resources of multimodal ensembles in the students' meaning making.

Prior to conducting this current study, I scrutinized the available to me seminal and most recent literature on the above or closely related topics in the field. My investigation confirmed the anticipated gap in the current research. For my readers' convenience, I will deliver the findings of my review of literature in the next chapter of this book with more details.

Gap in Research

Digging over literature in the field helped to confirm the gap in the research on the specific population of the Polylinguals and their struggles with meaning making of highly complex academic or fictional texts in the college or university settings. The studies conducted by the American and international research, including the studies in the field of multimodality in the first decades of the 21st century (e.g., Ajayi, 2009, 2015; Archer, 2025; Archer & Price, 2021; Breuer& Archer, 2016; Ericson & Häikiö, 2025; Jacobs, 2012; Lee et al., 2024; Maula & Awwalia, 2025;

McVee et al., 2008a, 2008b; Molle & Prior, 2008; Nelson, 2008; Rahmanu et al, 2020; Yusra et al., 2025; Zarobe & Querol-Julian, 2025) deserve highest praise and respect. Yet, the number of studies on effects of multimodality on diverse polylingual student populations in American higher education is still insufficient.

Though the United States has been moving towards closing this gap on multimodality studies, there remains still a cognitive abyss in the research on multimodality for the Polylingual postsecondary students. Moreover, I have not found any studies specifically on the effects of multimodality and the resources of multimodal ensembles on polylingual EAL-speaking college students' meaning making. Apparently, this population was left out. So, for the sake of closing this research chasm in the knowledge and helping the vast audiences of Polylingual EAL learning college students, I made my decision to delve into my new study. In this current book, I will reflect on the results of my search for the Lingua Franca as the means to facilitate meaning making to practically any diverse, polylingual, EAL learner.

Field Terms Clarified

As I anticipate, some of my readers might come from different fields, which might or might not be concerned with multiliteracies and multimodalities. Thus, with the purpose to facilitate my audiences with their reading and deeper understanding the topics discussed in this book, I will define some vocabulary specific to the field of my study as used in this book.

EALs: EAL speaking students are English as an Additional Language (EAL)-speaking students. This category of language users is different from those ones who are defined as *English as the Second Language speakers* since the English language is not necessarily their second language (L 2). It might be their third (L 3) or fourth (L 4) language, depending on the order in which these students acquired or studied the languages, including and starting off with their mother tongue(s), which may well exceed just one.

Polylingual: It would be appropriate to name the group of participants in this study *Polylingual*. As Cekaite and Evaldsson (2008) explained, "We use the term *polylingual* in describing how language users employ whatever linguistic features are at their disposal to achieve their communicative aims" (Cekaite & Evaldsson, 2008, p. 179). As follows from the above definition, the Polylinguals, compared to multilingual persons, find it more difficult switching codes in between using different languages. This is why the Polylinguals utilize a range of resources (for example, gestures, facial expressions, postures) to convey and make the meaning.

Multimodal: Multimodal texts or sites are defined by Duncum as the ones that "include a range of modalities, especially language, images, and sound" (Duncum, 2004, p. 253). This term is applicable to the print-based texts supported by visual, auditory, and other features of multimodality.

Multimodality: The term *multimodality* comprises a combination of several modes, such as auditory, tactical, visual, gestural, print-based etc. as defined by Kalantzis and Cope (2008). Murray (2013) similarly defined multimodality as a mixture of different modes (e.g., texts, sounds, visuals), which help to create meaning.

Meaning making: Making the meaning through the means of multimodality is defined by Ajayi (2008) as "a process by which learners gain critical consciousness of the interpretation of events in their lives in relation to the world around them" (p. 211). The above definition may be equally applied to making the meaning of the read texts. Saldaña (2015) defined meaning making as, "the individual's intertwined cognitive and emotional mental processing of something (a text, a piece of art, an experience, etc.) that stimulates personal interpretive relevance and generates personal understanding" (p. 60).

REFERENCES

Ainsworth, S., Griffiths, D., Macrory, G., & Pahl, K. (2023). *Multimodality and multilingualism: Towards an integrative approach.* Multilingual Matters.

Ajayi, L. (2008). Meaning-making, multimodal representation, and transformative pedagogy: An exploration of meaning construction instructional practices in an ESL high school classroom. *Journal of Language, Identity, and Education, 7*(3/4), 206–229. DOI: 10.1080/15348450802237822

Ajayi, L. (2009). English as a second language learners' exploration of multimodal texts in a junior high school. *Journal of Adolescent & Adult Literacy, 52*(7), 585–595. DOI: 10.1598/JAAL.52.7.4

Ajayi, L. (2015). Critical multimodal literacy: How Nigerian female students critique texts and reconstruct unequal social structures. *Journal of Literacy Research, 47*(2), 216–244. DOI: 10.1177/1086296X15618478

Archer, A. (2025). Multimodality and the affordances of co-presence for inclusion in higher education. *Designs for Learning, 16*(1), 1–8. DOI: 10.16993/dfl.230

Archer, A., & Price, C. (2021). Assessment, recognition and the contact zone: How much is 'enough'? *Education as Change, 25*, 1–18. DOI: 10.25159/1947-9417/8741

Baildon, M., & Damico, J. S. (2009). How do we know?: Students examine issues of credibility with a complicated multimodal web-based text. *Curriculum Inquiry, 39*(2), 265–285. DOI: 10.1111/j.1467-873X.2009.00443.x

Bakhtin, M. M. (1981). Discourse in the novel. In Holquist, M. (Ed.), *The dialogic imagination: Four essays by M. M. Bakhtin* (pp. 259–422). University of Texas Press.

Binder, M., & Kotsopoulos, S. (2011). Multimodal literacy narratives: Weaving the threads of young children's identity through the arts. *Journal of Research in Childhood Education, 25*(4), 339–363. DOI: 10.1080/02568543.2011.606762

Breuer, E., & Archer, A. (2016). *Multimodality in higher education.* Brill. DOI: 10.1163/9789004312067

Brown, A., & Eskildsen, S. W. (2024). *Multimodality across epistemologies in second language research.* Routledge. DOI: 10.4324/9781003355670

Bruce, D. L. (2009a). Reading and writing video: Media literacy and adolescents. In Christenbury, L., Bomer, R., & Smagorinsky, P. (Eds.), *Handbook of adolescent literacy research* (pp. 287–333). The Guilford Press.

Bruce, D. L. (2009b). Writing visual images: Examining the video composition processes of highs school students. *Research in the Teaching of English*, *43*(4), 426–450. DOI: 10.58680/rte20097073

Cekaite, A., & Evaldsson, A. (2008). Stating linguistic identities and negotiating monolingual norms in multiethnic school setting. *International Journal of Multilingualism*, *5*(3), 177–196. DOI: 10.1080/14790710802387588

Duncum, P. (2004). Visual culture isn't just visual: Multiliteracy, multimodality and meaning. *Studies in Art Education: A Journal of Issues and Research in Art Education, 45*(3), 252-264.

Ericson, K., & Häikiö, T. K. (2025). Visuality and multimodality as tools for learning in geography and art education. *Journal of Aesthetic Education*, *59*(2), 50–73. DOI: 10.5406/15437809.59.2.05

Exley, B., & Cottrell, A. (2012). Reading in the Australian curriculum English: Describing the effects of structure and organization on multimodal texts. *Engineers Australia*, *47*(2), 91–98.

Farrugia, C. A., & Bhandari, R. (2016). *Open doors 2016 report on International educational exchange*. Institute of International Education.

Giampapa, F. (2010). Multiliteracies, pedagogy and identities: Teacher and student voices from a Toronto elementary school. *Canadian Journal of Education*, *33*(2), 407–431.

Gould, O. (2015, December). *How multimodal features influence college-level International students' reading comprehension of traditional print-based texts.* Paper presentation at the 65th annual meeting of Literacy Research Association (LRA), San Diego, CA.

Gould, O. (2016, February). *How multimodal features influence polylingual EAL speaking college students' reading comprehension of traditional print-based texts.* Research Component paper presented at the12th Midwinter meeting of National Council of Teachers of English Assembly for Research (NCTEAR), University of Eastern Michigan, Ypsilanti, MI.

Gould, O. (June 12, 2017). *'Please, tell them!': Voices from university classrooms on the effects of multimodality on polylingual EAL speaking college students' meaning making.* (Doctoral dissertation). ProQuest LLC.

Gould-Yakovleva, O. (2023a). Seeking remedy for improving international college students' reading comprehension: A qualitative case study on using multimodality for English language learning. *International Journal of Higher Education Pedagogies*, *4*(4), 33–54. DOI: 10.33422/ijhep.v4i4.599

Gould-Yakovleva, O. (2023b). Voices from university classrooms on effects of multimodality on polylingual EAL college students' meaning making. *International Journal of Second and Foreign Language Education*, *2*(2), 1–19. DOI: 10.33422/ijsfle.v2i2.450

Gould-Yakovleva, O. (2024). Demystifying the notion of charisma: Micro-ethnography on a veteran-teacher's classroom practices. *The Qualitative Report*, *29*(4), 1192–1211. DOI: 10.46743/2160-3715/2024.6521

Gould-Yakovleva, O., & Liu, X. (2024). Mutualism as mutual trust: An ethnographic case study on an elementary-school teacher-team participation in a science PD program. *The Qualitative Report*, *29*(4), 915–938. DOI: 10.46743/2160-3715/2024.6440

Gould-Yakovleva, O., McVee, M., & Fronczak, D. (2020). "Ready-ready" to teach: The telling case of a reflective teacher-practitioner. *The Qualitative Report*, *25*(2), 306–319. DOI: 10.46743/2160-3715/2020.4040

Gould-Yakovleva, O., McVee, M., & Fronczak, D. (2020). "Ready-ready" to teach: The telling case of a reflective teacher-practitioner. *The Qualitative Report*, *25*(2), 306–319. DOI: 10.46743/2160-3715/2020.4040

Huang, Y. H. (2012). EFL students' views on writing with pictures, sound, and music. *English Teaching & Learning*, *36*(2), 79–123. DOI: 10.6330/ETL.2012.36.2.03

Institute of International Education. (2024). Enrollment trends. *Open doors.* https://opendoorsdata.org/data/international-students/enrollment-trends/

Jacobs, G. E. (2012). Developing multimodal academic literacies among college freshmen. *The Journal of Media Literacy Education*, *4*(3), 244–255.

Kalantzis, M., & Cope, B. (2008). *New Learning: Elements of a science of education.* Cambridge University Press. DOI: 10.1017/CBO9780511811951

Kaur, S., Ganapathy, M., & Sidhu, G. K. (2012). Designing learning elements using the multiliteracies approach in an ESL writing classroom. *Southeast Asian Journal of English Language Studies*, *18*(3), 119–134.

Kitson, L. (2011). Reconceptualising understandings of texts, readers and contexts: One English teacher's response to using multimodal texts and interactive whiteboards. *Engineers Australia*, *46*(3), 76–86.

Kuo, F. O., Yu, P. T., & Hsiao, W. H. (2013). Develop and evaluate the effect of multimodal presentation system on elementary ESL students. *The Turkish Online Journal of Educational Technology*, *12*(4), 29–40.

Lee, S. S. J., Siew, L. L., Tiong, N. D., & Ma, N. (2024). Multimodality in art teacher education in China. *Design*, *1*(1), 45–54. DOI: 10.36922/dp.4554

Lincoln, F., & Rademacher, B. (2006). Learning styles of ESL students in community colleges. *Community College Journal of Research and Practice*, *30*(5/6), 485–500. DOI: 10.1080/10668920500207965

Liu, X., & Qu, D. (2014). Exploring the multimodality of EFL textbooks for Chinese college students: A comparative study. *RELC Journal*, *45*(2), 135–150. DOI: 10.1177/0033688214533865

Maula, Q. I., & Awwalia, L. (2025). Scrutinizing teachers' practice of multimodality use in elementary English classroom. *KnE Social Sciences*, *10*(12), 69–79. DOI: 10.18502/kss.v10i12.18863

McVee, M. B., Bailey, N. M., & Shanahan, L. E. (2008a). Teachers and teacher educators learning from new literacies and new technologies. *Teaching Education*, *19*(3), 197–210. DOI: 10.1080/10476210802250216

McVee, M. B., Bailey, N. M., & Shanahan, L. E. (2008b). Using digital media to interpret poetry: Spiderman meets Walt Whitman. *Research in the Teaching of English*, *43*(2), 112–143. DOI: 10.58680/rte20086774

Miller, S. M. (2013). A research metasynthesis on digital video composing in classrooms: An evidence-based framework toward a pedagogy for embodied learning. *Journal of Literacy Research*, *45*(4), 386–430. DOI: 10.1177/1086296X13504867

Miller, S. M., & McVee, M. B. (2012a). *Multimodal composing in classrooms: Learning and teaching for the digital world*. Routledge.

Miller, S. M., & McVee, M. B. (2012b). Changing the game: Teaching for embodied learning through multimodal composing. In Miller, S., & McVee, M. (Eds.), *Multimodal composing in classrooms: Learning and teaching for digital world* (pp. 132–152). Routledge.

Mills, K. A. (2007). Access to multiliteracies: A critical ethnography. *Ethnography and Education*, *2*(3), 305–325. DOI: 10.1080/17457820701547310

Molle, D., & Prior, P. (2008). Multimodal genre system in EAP writing pedagogy: Reflecting on a need analysis. *TESOL Quarterly*, *42*(4), 541–566. DOI: 10.1002/j.1545-7249.2008.tb00148.x

Molyneux, P., & Godinho, S. (2012). "This Is My Thing!": Middle years students' engagement and learning using digital resources. *Australasian Journal of Educational Technology*, *28*(8), 1466–1486. DOI: 10.14742/ajet.782

Murray, J. (2013). Composing multimodality. In Lutkewitte, C. (Ed.), *Multimodal composition: A critical sourcebook* (pp. 323–350). Bedford / St. Martin's.

Nelson, M. E. (2008). Multimodal synthesis and the voice of the multimedia author in a Japanese EFL context. *Innovation in Language Learning and Teaching*, *2*(1), 65–82. DOI: 10.1080/17501220802158826

Ntelioglou, B. Y. (2011). 'But why do I have to take this class?' The mandatory drama-ESL class and multiliteracies pedagogy. *Research in Drama Education*, *16*(4), 595–615. DOI: 10.1080/13569783.2011.617108

Pantaleo, S. (2012a). Exploring grade 7 students' responses to Shaun Tan's "The Red Tree.". *Children's Literature in Education*, *43*(1), 51–71. DOI: 10.1007/s10583-011-9156-x

Pantaleo, S. (2012b). Meaning-making with colour in multimodal texts: An 11-year-old student's purposeful "doing.". *Literacy*, *46*(3), 147–155. DOI: 10.1111/j.1741-4369.2012.00664.x

Rahmanu, E. D., Altun, L., & Kariati, N. M. (2020). Case study on multimodality perception in the higher education classroom. *Journal Sosial dan Humaniora. Journal of Social Sciences and Humanities*, *10*(3), 1–11. DOI: 10.31940/soshum.v10i3.2091

Saint-Georges, I., & Weber, J.-J. (2013). *Multilingualism and multimodality: Current challenges for educational studies*. Brill Academic Publishing. DOI: 10.1007/978-94-6209-266-2

Saldaña, J. (2015). *Thinking qualitatively: Methods of mind*. Sage. DOI: 10.4135/9781071909782

Shanahan, L. E., McVee, M. B., & Bailey, N. M. (2014). Multimodality in action: New literacies as more than activity in middle and high school classrooms. In Ferdig, R. E., & Pytash, K. E. (Eds.), *Exploring multimodal composition and digital writing* (pp. 36–53). IGI Global. DOI: 10.4018/978-1-4666-4345-1.ch003

U.S. Department of Education, National Center for Education Statistics. (2024). *Digest of Education Statistics*. Retrieved from: https://nces.ed.gov/programs/digest/d22/tables/dt22_204.27.asp

Vincent, J. (2006). Children writing: Multimodality and assessment in the writing classroom. *Literacy*, *40*(1), 51–57. DOI: 10.1111/j.1467-9345.2006.00426.x

Vygotsky, L. S. (1978). *Mind in society: The development of higher psychological processes*. Harvard University Press.

Vygotsky, L. S. (1987). *The collected works of L. S. Vygotsky: Vol. 1. Problems of general psychology, including the volume thinking and speech* (R. W. Rieber & A. S. Carton, Eds., Trans. N. Minick). New York: Plenum.

Włodarczyk, M., Tyrkkö, J., & Adamczyk, E. (2023). *Multilingualism from manuscript to 3D: Intersections of modalities from medieval to modern times*. Routledge. DOI: 10.4324/9781003166634

Yusra, S. R., Hanifa, R., Wardana, A., & Fahmiati, M. (2025). Leveraging instructional multimodality for enhanced English grammar learning of undergraduate students: A higher education perspective. *International Journal of Information and Education Technology (IJIET), 15*(6), 1172–1181. DOI: 10.18178/ijiet.2025.15.6.2320

Zarobe, Y. R., & Querol-Julian, M. (2025). Multilingualism and multimodality in the CLIL/EMI classroom. *Journal of Multilingual and Multicultural Development, 46*(5), 1397–1415. DOI: 10.1080/01434632.2025.2482734

Chapter 2
Choosing an Umbrella

ABSTRACT

In Chapter 2, I will detail the process of selecting the right umbrella prior to conducting this research. First, I will provide an overview of the Multiliteracies theory coined by the New London Group (NLG, 1996) and furthered by Kalantzis and Cope (2008). Importantly, this theory underpins my study of multimodality. Importantly, these authors' approach to multimodal teaching and learning implies the idea of necessity of multiple literacies. The above notion will be thoroughly discussed. Subsequently, I will explore socio-cultural theory principles developed by Vygotsky (1978, 1987) and address the topics related to his Zones of Proximal Development (ZPDs) as used in education. Next, I will tie the Vygotskyan ideas to the findings by the NLG researchers and theorists. Further, I will also ponder about the postulates by the semioticians and social semiotics theorists, such as Franks and Jewitt and Kress and van Leeuwen, whose contribution to the field is truly invaluable; thus, is highly significant for this study.

INTRODUCTION

As a qualitative researcher and a life-long educator, I strongly believe in importance of selecting and adhering to a precise umbrella, a paradigm, and a theory or a combination of such prior to the start of each project, be that research or practical teaching. As a devoted follower of socio-cultural constructivism, I trust and adhere to the approaches and methods postulated by the famous theorists, for example Mikhail Bakhtin (1981), Yuri Bronfenbrenner (1979, 1993), and Lev Vygotsky (1978, 1987). Studying these theorists' ideas in connection to the field of multimodality in the digital age led me to realization of mega-importance of multiliteracy. The latter term may be understood as acquisition or mastery of several types of literacy (e.g., alphabetical, technological, digital, social, emotional, cultural, etc.) These days, being literate in a range of fields or being multiliterate has become the

DOI: 10.4018/979-8-3373-3426-4.ch002

only condition for successful teaching, learning, and performing one's professional functions in the modern days' chronotope (Bakhtin, 1981).

DEFINING MULTILITERACIES

Prior to exploring the phenomenon of multiple literacies, I am inviting my readers on a quick journey back through time with the purpose to help them compare and reconsider the notion of literacy and being literate as it was viewed in different millennia, centuries, or even the recent decades. Back in the olden days, they considered a literate person the man (or, less often, a woman) who was able to read, good if also write, memorize, and reproduce information obtained from the oral or written texts. According to Lankshear and Knobel (2003), literacies are "...socially recognized ways of communication through the medium of encoded texts..." (p. 4). Nowadays, as noticed by Moore-Russo and Shanahan, literacies cannot any longer be viewed as a meager ability "to read and write using alphabetic code" (2014, p. 527). Literacy of today needs to be multifaceted, multidimensional, and multimodal. To be more exact, one needs to acquire and master multiple literacies and become multiliterate. Being multiliterate means having multiple literacy skills in combination with a wide range of knowledg**es,** which allow the actor1 to read, understand, and reuse the print-based or digital texts, as well as the messages encoded in sounds and visuals. The word *multiliteracies* was first coined by the New London Group (NLG) in 1996. The very prefix of this term, *multi,* implies the idea of existence of multiple forms of literacy, which includes mastery of usage of multiple modes of multimodality.

Confirming this idea, the prominent NLG members, Kalantzis and Cope, wrote in their 2008 book *New Learning: Elements of the Science of Education* that the phenomenon of multimodalities includes more than one mode. Just as in case with multiliteracies, the *multi* part of this word implicitly conveys the idea of existence of multiple modalities and multiple modes. According to Kalantzis and Cope (2008), "The 'multiliteracies' theory suggests that learner activities should involve a wide variety of representational modes" (p. 203). Further, in chapter 8 Pedagogy and Curriculum, these authors named and described several modes of multimodalities, such as: written and oral language, visual, auditory, tactile, gestural, and spatial representations (Kalantzis & Cope, 2008, pp. 203-204). These authors delivered to wide educational audiences their message of high importance of research in the promising field of multimodalities and new literacies, which have the potential to globally change educational approaches in the era of the *Digital Turn* (Mills, 2010; NLG, 1996). Their claims sound logical in the epoch where the speedy development of digitalities strongly affected and continue invading the field of education. Most importantly, the digitalities are shaping the new generations of learners. Thus, the approaches and methods of teaching and learning quest to be changed in the modern days' classrooms.

VYGOTSKYAN THEORIES

When talking about technology in education, it is highly important to keep in mind that modern days' students often own some technological and digital literacy from a very young age. New generations are born to reside in the midst of the ever-evolving technologies. Yet, how they will be directed towards learning is dependent only on humans, i.e., these children's parents and teachers. In connection to the above, another theory asks to come into play to underpin this study. This theory should be concerned with the human nature of education, yet, in the digital age. For instance, the New London Group grounded their works in Vygotsky's (1978, 1987, 2000) socio-cultural constructivism. In connection to their discussion on new literacies, the NLG attracted attention of wide academic and professional audiences to the dramatic increase of social and cultural diversity at the schools of today. So, where did the NLG see the connection between the new multiliteracies, multimodalities, and Vygotsky's socio-cultural constructivism?

This Russian philosopher and educational psychologist Lev Semyonovich Vygotsky lived only 38 years, of which his creative work took a half of his life. This prominent thinker and experimenter wrote his works at the start of the 20th century, but was first published in his mercilessly censoring homeland more than 20 years after his death, in 1956. Vygotsky's works were translated into English even later, in 1978. Nevertheless, the Vygotskyan postulates contemplated by this great mind longer than a century ago are still relevant to the modern days' teaching and educational research.

One of the most important and influential findings by Vygotsky (1978, 1987) is the one that details the role of mediation, which needs to be provided to a learner by a more experienced and knowledgeable other. A more learned peer, parent, or professional educator can mediate a student through his or her Zone of Proximal Development (ZPD). A ZPD is an area where the learner has little to no experience, no knowledge, and, at times, not even a single exposure. Struggling on their own, students might or might not achieve a mastery level. Yet, the mediated learning was found by Vygotsky more efficient compared to independent and individual studies by a student. To provide just some examples, envision a child or an adult without prior exposure to playing a musical instrument, for instance the piano. Letting this unexperienced learner decipher the music scores and transfer those print-based signs onto the piano keyboard would inevitably present a long-lasting challenge accompanied with frustration. Nevertheless, when mediated or taught by a more experienced other, the beginning musician might master the piano skills significantly faster and reach a higher mastery level.

So, Vygotsky (1978, 1987) advocated in favor of mediation in any field. Specifically, the detailed on implementation of mediational tools, appropriately selected for each content area. For example, poetry writing involves teaching the concept of the rhythm and rhyme; while teaching musicianship may start with exploring the rhythms and pitches. As for studying an additional language, diverse means and modes of multimodality might be used as mediational tools, which teachers may use to facilitate students with their progressing through ZPDs.

While talking about learning an additional language, especially in multicultural and multilingual or polylingual classrooms of today it is important to consider Vygotsky's (1978, 1987) view on meaning making. According to this philosopher, humans construct the meaning of oral, print-based, or non-verbal texts while basing their comprehension work on their individual historical, cultural, and socio-cultural prior knowledge. So, representatives of different countries or cultures, each with their diverging prior experiences may make different meaning from reading the same text. Thus, it is of high significance for educators in the modern-days' American or international classrooms on all grade levels, including university or college, to understand the essence of Vygotsky's (1978) principles of his socio-cultural constructivism theory and their applicability to the current chronotope. Today's educators need to possess the mediational tools, which help the diverse learners from highly diverging backgrounds to equally grasp the essence of the read texts.

With the above understanding of the diversity and multiplicity of the sociums from which Polylingual EAL speaking students arrive to the American educational institutions, educators and researchers of today are searching such mediational tools, which might efficiently assist all their students with their meaning making, regardless of the differences in their historically and socio-culturally constructed background knowledge. Understandably, in an American or international language-learning classroom, usage of only print-based texts would not solve the problem with meaning making. Thus, there arises the need in an alternative or an additional way to communicate the meaning and alleviate the process of meaning making. These new mediational tools need to be helpful to every student, despite their dramatically diverging cultural backgrounds and educational traditions and histories. This coveted by the language educators tool needs to have the power to assist all learners with deeper and more efficient meaning making.

The phenomenon of making the meaning was explored by Vygotsky from the position of an educational psychologist. Aiming to explain the phenomena of thinking, which occur in a human mind, Vygotsky created a metaphoric verbal portrait of the process of meaning making. This psychologist compared the work of processing the "mosaic" details or bits of information and developing a whole mental "picture" to the atoms, which combine to form the universe. In his effort to help educators to deeper understand the nature of brain work, Vygotsky created even a more visualizable model of the psychological process of meaning making. This psychologist compared the work of a human mind to a mason's work. Just as a mason adds new rows of building blocks to the previously built ones to construct an object, humans add new to them knowledge to the pre-existing combinations in their minds.

The Vygotskian (1978, 1987) ideas were furthered by many of his followers. For example, Connery, John-Steiner, and Marjanovic-Shane (2010) wrote that, "Signs, including gestures, movements, words, and visual symbols, provide an efficient means of mediating generalizations" (p. 87). Further, these authors clarified, "As building blocks of meaning, independent signs are organized into codes for easy conveyance. Semiotic codes are then interwoven into systems to produce cultural texts" (p. 88). Conclusively, these authors suggested usage of independent semiotic signs, which humans can read from different modes of multimodality, i.e., visual images, gestures, body movements, facial expressions, auditory sounds, etc. When used as "building blocks," these researchers conveyed, these multimodal signs may assist readers with their meaning making, be they added to the print-based texts.

At this point, Vygotskian (1978, 1987) theoretical postulates, supported by Connery et al. (2010) findings, intertwine with the principles of social semiotics. Thus, it is the right time and place in this book to explain the logical interconnectedness between these closely related theories, which helped shape the research discussed in this book.

SOCIAL SEMIOTICS AND ITS RESOURCES

Usage of the verbal, oral or written, language is the luxury available exclusively to humans. The science of using the verbal language has been extensively studied. Yet, besides the oral or written verbal communication, humans largely utilize the non-verbal or semiotic language. This aspect of delivering and comprehending ideas involves many enticing and enigmatic aspects. The field of social semiotics has been actively explored since the end of the 19th and beginning of the 20th century by such prominent thinkers as Ferdinand de Saussure (1959) and Michael Halliday (1978). The findings by these theorists were furthered by the modern days' researchers in the field of multimodality, Anton Franks, Carey Jewitt, Gunther Kress, and Theo van Leeuwen. Their major theoretical works included such publications as *A Social Semiotic Approach to Contemporary Communication* by Kress (2011), *Introducing Social Semiotics* by van Leeuwen (2004), *The Meaning of Action in Learning and Teaching* by Franks and Jewitt (2001), and more on the closely related topics. It is important to touch at least some major aspects of social semiotics theory, as discussed by the above authors, in connection to the Vygotskyan socio-cultural constructivism. This conversation will further explain the role and significance of social semiotics theory to my current research.

Both Kress (2011) and van Leeuwen (2004) studied the phenomena of semiotic modes, resources, signs, and symbols, which humans use for communicative purposes in addition or, sometimes, in the lieu of the verbal communication. Interestingly, many non-verbal means of communication, including but not limited to facial expressions, signs, and symbols, may be equally understandable to the speakers of different languages in the absence of a commonly shared tongue. So, according to Kress and van Leeuwen (2002), these communicative modes and resource can be produced physiologically, (i.e., via vocal sounds, gestures, face work, or body language) or with the help from some means of technology; for example, by using a pen, a computer, software, fabric, tools, instruments, or building materials.

Before I proceed with discussion of usage of the semiotic resources for meaning making, I will interpret some terminology. For instance, it is important to understand the difference between *signs* and *symbols* of communication. Signs are informative. For example, a frown on one's face can be viewed as a sign of disapproval, according to van Leeuwen (2004). Colors can also be read as signs. According to Kress (2011), reds can be used to express aggression, while the black of an attire in many European settings is situationally associated with mourning and grief. So, purposeful choice of color is often utilized by artists and designers with the intention to convey certain meanings, such as mood, for example, through the art they create.

Symbols are signs that stand for something else. For example, a symbol of a cross is strongly associated with and imperatively symbolizes Christianity; while such symbols as a hexagram, a six-pointed star, or a lyre have a strong connotation with Judaism. Additionally, the signified meaning may be conveyed by or through the observable forms of actions, symbolic objects, or words, which are called signifiers as stated by van Leeuwen (2004).

Importantly, it needs to be noticed that understanding signs and symbols might also be culturally shaped. And this is the crossing point where social semiotics and Vygotskyan socio-cultural constructivism need to be equally considered by educational researchers and educators in their work on developing mediational tools for making the meaning.

Framing

Another important notion to consider when talking about social semiotics is the phenomenon of framing, which was deeply explored by Theo van Leeuwen (2004). Human ideas, expressed through verbally uttered or non-verbally conveyed communicative means, are rich in subtleties. The meaning of the clearly expressed or implied idea within a certain situation might change with the change in its framing. The very phenomenon of framing has its own rules for carrying the meaning; these rules may be applied to usage of physical space, verbally or orally-produced text, an image, or their combinations. All entities, (e.g., objects, subjects, textual messages, and images) can be "re-shuffled" and re-positioned with the usage of visible and invisible means of framing. All the above changes may be done to convey or alter the meaning. I will illustrate the above statements with an example explaining how and which entities might serve humans as meaning-forming or meaning-changing frames. Physical frames are easy to visualize; these can be walls, barriers, or empty spaces. The invisible borders, such as human distancing, for example, though imaginative, still can serve as non-tresspassable frames. Skillfully and thoughtfully arranged framing may strongly affect human activity. A group of co-workers might strongly benefit from individualized framing in their working room. This might be using substantial shelving units for dividing the shared space into individual cubicles, which may enhance the employees' focus on their individually and independently performed tasks. On the contrary, removing or minimizing the physical frames in an office might be used to foster collaborative effort and simplify participation of all workers in a joint venture.

Same rules of framing may be applied by educators with the purpose to influence their students' learning processes. Moreover, thoughtful framing of multimodal means of communication may be used by teachers for enhancing comprehension of the print-based, auditory, or visual texts in learners.

The above idea needs to be furthered. Van Leeuwen (2004) assigned the names to different elements of framing. For instance, *segregation* may be used to divide space, objects, or human groups in parts by constructing physical barriers such as walls. Next element, *separation* is division by empty spaces between groups. Separation still allows members of a group to communicate. *Integration*, viewed as integrating an object or a subject into a new space. Some examples of integration may be placing an object or a human into a physical space, or inserting an image into a print-based text, or adding some text to an image. As per van Leeuwen, frames may be porous. For example, a room with a door is a re-frameable space; people can lock or unlock the door, or keep it wide open; and this may strongly affect the non-verbally communicated meaning through restricting or inviting possible communication acts. So, framing actions may influence the character of interactions between different people or groups of actors. Same rules of framing may be applied to the print-based and multimodal texts, where an overlap of text and image can create the feeling of interconnectedness, which is referred by semioticians as *permeability*.

Two other important elements of framing described by von Leeuwen are *rhyme* and *contrast*. A *rhyme* is being understood as having some qualities in common; for example, color, shape, or texture of different objects within a space or in texts, or images. A *contrast* suggests availability of two or more elements that differ by any qualities or features. All the above carry the meaning and may produce the change in the meaning in a real-life situation, in a print-based, or multimodal text.

Another powerful semiotic phenomenon is *typography*. Making changes in a text's *typography* may strongly affect or alter its meaning.

Semiotics of the Print

Interestingly, the verbal print-based language may also have its non-verbal meaningful aspects. Both Kress (2011) and van Leeuwen (2004) agreed on the point that such attributes of print as font, size, color have the potential to convey meanings. Some changes made to typography of a text may also change the meaning of its context. For example, usage of different types of typography may change the meaning of a neutral phrase of politeness, "It was a pleasure meeting with you." This simple and polite expression may gain a different meaning if designed with a purpose in mind. This phrase, when written with the help of italics for the word *pleasure*, as "It was a *pleasure* meeting with you," may assign to this phrase the emotionally-loaded meaning, which, most likely, is well comprehensible to the actors, this meeting's participants. Though individual perceptions of the readers without the knowledge of the circumstances may differ; yet, the visible differences in typography might prompt a reader to question and try to interpret and understand the purpose of the changes and the meaning behind it. Oftentimes, the ideas implied by the means of framing may be correctly understood.

I will also provide an example from the field of musicianship. Some of my readers might chuckle while reading the print-based, yet multimodally framed text in *Figure 1* below. Apparently, this example demonstrates how efficiently the changes in topography may mirror the variations in music dynamics or the intensity of the sound as used in the musical scores (See *Figure 4* below for some examples of usage of different typography).

Figure 1. Examples of different types of typography

Music symbol	Italian term	Translation	Font size-assisted representation
Ppp	pianississimo	very, very quiet	Pianississimo
Pp	pianissimo	very quiet	pianissimo
P	piano	Quiet	piano
mf	mezzo forte	moderately loud	mezzo forte
F	forte	Loud	forte
Ff	fortissimo	very loud	fortissimo
	crescendo	growing/increasing sound	crescendo
	diminuendo	diminishing sound	diminuendo

While people with their prior knowledge in music may smile just from having one glance at this intentionally re-framed text, I will explain the terminology used within it for my readers without the music education. The musical terms are often used in the original language they were created, the Italian language. Just like the road signs, these musical terms and their abbreviations or symbols are added by composers to the created by them musical scores. This work is needed to provide the performing musicians with directions, so they could play and precisely express the authentic ideas by the composer. These symbols or abbreviated terms might indicate the dynamics, i.e., speed or the force of the sound. As shown in *Figure 1* above, the first on the top abbreviation in the smallest print size, *ppp*, which stands for the Italian word *pianississimo,* means that a musician, an ensemble, or an orchestra need to play *very, very soft*, with the lowest possible, subtle sound. The right-most column in *Figure 1* includes the font-size assisted representation of the word *pianississimo* printed in the smallest font-size to visually indicate how very, very quiet this sound needs to be played.

The next to the top sign *pp* stands for the term *pianissimo*, which means in Italian *very softly* and is depicted in the next to the smallest print in the right-hand column. This slight increase in this *term's* print size signifies the need in a slight increase in the sound compared to the triple *ppp*. After that, there follows the single letter *p,* which symbolizes *playing piano* and means "play softly." A little bit stronger increase in its print size signifies the direction to produce a slightly louder, rather than the previous *ppp* and *pp* sounds. Subsequently, the terms *mezzo forte* (*mf*), *forte* (*f*), and fortissimo (*ff*), with the increase in their font sizes, each signify the rise in the sound strength starting from half-strong (*mf*), through strong (*f*), and ending with a very loud sound (*ff*). The increase in the font size, as shown in the rightmost column correspondingly allows to read the rising intensity in the sound via the increasing size of the font for each of these terms.

Next, such words as *crescendo* and *diminuendo* each have their specific angled symbols, each of which opens in left or right direction. The corresponding increase and decrease in the font size for each of these terms signifies gradual, progressive magnification (*cres*cendo) or weakening (*diminuendo*) of the dynamic of the sound.

All the above are just some examples of how the meaning may be changed with the help of the affordances of typographic; in particularly, via changing the size or shape of the font.

Language of Objects

Imperatively, not only print, but the objects have the power to convey the meaning. Kress (2011) and van Leeuwen (2004) related their findings in the field of social semiotics not only to the texts and images, but also to the physical objects, such as attire worn by humans, decorations of interiors or exteriors sites, design of the working spaces, structure and architectural detailing of buildings, layout of cities, and many more. Drawing on Bogatyrev's (1971) research on semiotic language of dress, van Leeuwen (2004) furthered the notions of *denotations* and *connotations.* The term *denotation* stands for the visible information, the readable exterior elements, while the word *connotations,* specifically used in plural, underlines a composite of multiple additional implied semiotic meanings. Both notions are used with the purpose to convey information while shaping the non-print-based visual texts via the means of patterns (in clothing), building materials (in architecture), or decorative elements (in design).

Kress (2011) and van Leeuwen (2004) noticed that all denotations and connotations form visual texts, designed by their creators for conveying the meaning to their potential readers. These theorists also recognized that social semiotics operates by its own rules. I would conclude that the rules of semiotics shape the grammar of the non-verbal texts.

Semiotic Rules

I caution my readers to get prepared to some unusual and unexpected turns in the flow of the semioticians' thought. Van Leeuwen and Kress believed that social semiotics established its own rules of communication. To be more precise, these authors reflected on the phenomena of personal and interpersonal authority, conformity, role-modeling, and expertise in communication. I will briefly explain these rules, which, just as textual one, help to convey and make the meaning. *Personal Authority* rule often forces people to abide by the directions or laws dictated by one powerful person or a group of people in their unshakeable leadership positions. The rule of *Interpersonal Authority* is a code of unwritten conventions, which are traditionally followed within a larger society as well as in its smaller social formations. Next rule, the *Rule of Conformity* suggests that all individuals within a group need to abide by the same rules accepted and followed by everyone within their social culture. In brief, this rule reads, "No one shall stand out." A failure to conform may lead to ostracism as everyone needs to behave "like everybody else around." Next rule, the rule of *Role Modeling* has a strong potential to shape the external ways in which people look, speak, act, or behave. However, this rule fails to control the internal intellectual prowess. Finally, *The Rule of Expertise* comes into play when large populations trust in an external, final opinion of a presumably more knowledgeable personality, an expert.

The above findings by the social semioticians, van Leeuwen and Kress, strongly intertwine and support the "marriage" between the greater semiotics, social semiotics, and Vygotskyan socio-cultural constructivism. The major condition for this "marriage" is the fact that all those semiotics rules have been *invented* and established by humans while, per Vygotsky, any knowledge has been socially and culturally constructed. As, practically no human being, with some extremely rare exceptions, has ever existed in a total isolation, torn off any human society, the rules of social semiotics, shared among humankind need to be attended to in the process of reading all verbal and non-verbal texts for making the meaning of the combinations of both.

Functionalism in Linguistics and Semiotics

Besides the above, highly significant for meaning making aspects, the founding fathers of semiotics also attended to the question of functions of language. While Gunther Kress (2011) outlined three major metafunctions of language, such as *representation*, *interaction*, *composition*, Theo van Leeuwen (2004) generally agreed with the ideas by his predecessor in the field, Roman Jakobson on the classification of language functions.

As early as in 1960, Jakobson (also found in 1981; and in 2004, in van Leeuwen, p. 77) identified 6 functions of language. The first, *referential function*, applies to the content of a message. Next, the *emotive function* refers to a speaker's attitude to the topic of the speech. Another one, the *conative function*, shows that things are done to or for an addressee. Interestingly, the *phatic function* is concerned with communicating with the purpose to avoid silence. The fifth, the *metalingual function* refers to the need between an addresser and his/her addressee to check whether they understand each other. And Jakobson's final, the *poetic function* is concerned with the choice of words, which sound better when pronounced together.

Conclusively, the postulates by Kress (2011) and van Leeuwen (2004) were coherent with and added to the ones previously coined by Jakobson (1960, 1981). The very idea of functions of language is of high significance for a deeper understanding of the linguistic phenomena used in communication for conveying and making the meaning.

CONNECTING THEORIES AND PRACTICE

As this publication aims to bridge theory, research, and practice, the discussion needs to return to the practical implementation of the findings by the semioticians in the classrooms. Primarily, usage of multimodalities by teachers-practicians on all grade levels, including university or college, may be viewed as usage of mediational tools for helping learners progress through their ZPDs, just as proposed by Vygotsky. The highest purpose of this practice is in assisting the learners with meaning making in the process of their reading conventional print-based texts supported by rich in semiotic means of multimodality. Thanks to the richness and expressiveness of the means of multimodality, the non-verbal multimodal language may serve as an educational intermediary used by educators for assisting their students with more efficient meaning making of the verbal texts. Yet, the knowledge in students seldom derives from observations. This means, instructors need to first master themselves, then teach to their students the multiple aspects of the multimodal language as well as the socio-culturally constructed rules of semiotics.

More, delving deeper in the studies of the non-verbal language, EAL educators may help their diverse learners to make a deeper meaning of highly complex academic texts when supplementing those with the means of multimodality. Usage of multimodality has a powerful potential to help the divers EAL-speaking students enhance their reading comprehension as much of the non-verbal communication in their mother tongues may be translated into their communication and mastering comprehension in English, as an additional language.

REFERENCES

Bogatyrev, P. (1971). *Voprosy teorii narodnogo iskusstva*. Iskusstvo.

Bronfenbrenner, U. (1979). *The ecology of human development: Experiments by nature and design*. Harvard University Press. DOI: 10.4159/9780674028845

Bronfenbrenner, U. (1993). Ecological models of human development. In Gauvan, M., & Cole, M. (Eds.), *Readings on the development of children* (pp. 37–43). Freeman.

Connery, M. C., John-Steiner, V. P., & Marjanovic-Shane, A. (2010). *Vygotsky and creativity: A cultural-historical approach to play, meaning making, and the arts*. Peter Lang. DOI: 10.3726/978-1-4539-0060-4

de Saussure, F. (1959). *Course in general linguistics*. Philosophical Library.

Franks, A., & Jewitt, C. (2001). *The meaning of action in learning and teaching*. British Educational Research Journal, 27(2), 201-218.

Halliday, M. A. K. (1978). *Language as social semiotic: The social interpretation of language and meaning*. University Park Press.

Jakobson, R. (1981). "Linguistics and poetics" (1960): Poetry of grammar and grammar of poetry. *Selected Writings*, *3*, 18–51.

Jewitt, C., & Oyama, R. (2001). Visual meaning: A social-semiotic approach. In van Leeuwen, T., & Jewitt, C. (Eds.), *Handbook of visual analysis* (pp. 134–156). Sage.

Kalantzis, M., & Cope, B. (2008). *New Learning: Elements of a science of education*. Cambridge University Press. DOI: 10.1017/CBO9780511811951

Kress, G. (2011). *Multimodality: A social semiotic approach to contemporary communication*. Routledge.

Kress, G., & van Leeuwen, T. (1996). *Reading images: The grammar of visual design*. Routledge.

Kress, G., & van Leeuwen, T. (2002). Colour as a semiotic mode: Notes for a grammar of colour. *Visual Communication*, *1*(3), 333–354. DOI: 10.1177/147035720200100306

Lankshear, C., & Knobel, M. (2003). *New literacies: Changing knowledge and classroom learning*. Open University Press.

Mills, K. A. (2010). A review of the "Digital Turn" in the New Literacy studies. *Review of Educational Research*, *80*(2), 246–271. DOI: 10.3102/0034654310364401

Moor-Russo, D., & Shanahan, L. (2014). A broader vision of literacy: Including the visual with the linguistic. *Journal of Adolescent & Adult Literacy, 57*(7), 527–532. DOI: 10.1002/jaal.282

New London Group. (1996). A pedagogy of multiliteracies: Designing social futures. *Harvard Educational Review, 66*(1), 60–92. DOI: 10.17763/haer.66.1.17370n67v-22j160u

New London Group. (2000). A pedagogy of multiliteracies: Designing social futures. In Cope, B., & Kalantzis, M. (Eds.), *Multiliteracies: Literacy learning and design of social futures* (pp. 9–38). Macmillan.

Van Leeuwen, T. (2004). *Introducing social semiotics.* Routledge. DOI: 10.4324/9780203647028

Vygotsky, L. S. (1978). *Mind in society: The development of higher psychological processes.* Harvard University Press.

Vygotsky, L. S. (1987). *The collected works of L. S. Vygotsky: Vol. 1. Problems of general psychology, including the volume thinking and speech* (R. W. Rieber & A. S. Carton, Eds., Trans. N. Minick). New York: Plenum.

Vygotsky, L. S. (2000). *Psychology.* EKSMO-Press.

ENDNOTES

1. It is important to understand the usage of the word actor in this book. The term *actor,* if not in a theatre, needs to be understood as a person who participates in an action or an event.

Chapter 3
Exploring Forerunners

ABSTRACT

With my strong belief in the power of multimodal reading, writing, teaching, learning, and communication, I explored the findings by my predecessors, the researchers developing the field of multimodality. I searched the online libraries, dug through my own professional literature collection, and dug over the available to me hard-copy archives. With a great emphasis on the seminal literature, for a reason, which will be further addressed, I scrutinized most recent publications, such as books and articles in the academic scholarly peer-reviewed journals. Additionally, I also considered conference presentations and full-text proceedings. In the search boxes of the digitalized resources, I entered the words multimodality, EAL, polylingual, college or university students, reading comprehension, and meaning making. Additionally, I utilized a so-called snowball technique, where references in the newly identified articles led me further to discovering increasingly more studies conducted by the Domestic and International researchers in the field of my study.

MORE THAN ONE BENEFIT

Pre-opening the curtain of my personality as a reader, I am eager to share with my audiences my excitement and curiosity about the findings by the other researchers investigating the field of multimodality. In this chapter, I will share the fruit of the work by my predecessors in this field. Moreover, I will elicit their research findings, conclusions, and implications. Particularly, seminal literature evoked my special interest as at the dawn of the era of multimodality, research sought to understand precisely how multimodalities worked, even in the era preceding the one of the Global Digitalization.

Targeting the information on the effects from multimodalities on the diverse student populations, I confirmed my initial researcher's assumption: the research reports by my predecessors indicated multiple positive effects from usage of multi-

DOI: 10.4018/979-8-3373-3426-4.ch003

modalities on multiple aspects of student learning and academic achievement (e.g., Archer, 2025; Baildon & Damico, 2009; Binder & Kotsopoulos, 2011; Breuer & Archer, 2016; Ericson & Häikiö, 2025; Hasty & Fain, 2014; Hegelheimer, 2006; Huang, 2012, 2023; Molle & Prior, 2008; Ntelioglou, 2011; Pahl, 2007; Pantaleo, 2012a; Shih, 2014; Stein, 2008; Stone, 2012; Zarobe & Querol-Julian, 2025). Yet, my curiosity drove me to further explore how multimodal support works for students on different grade levels. To my great satisfaction, the literature I examined supported the findings in my own studies conducted with adult college or university students (e.g., Gould-Yakovleva, 2023a, 2023b).

Further, the studies with middle- and high-school, and higher education students also indicated multiple benefits of multimodality to students of the corresponding ages (e.g., Ajayi, 2008, 2009, 2015; Archer & Price, 2021; Baildon & Damico, 2009; Lee et al., 2024; Maula & Awwalia, 2025; Rahmanu et al. 2020; Zarobe, & Querol-Julian, 2025). Just as one would expect, the research with elementary school students, whose teaching and learning materials were predominantly colorful and multimodal compared to the upper grades, confirmed significant positive effects of multimodality for the young and the youngest of learners (e.g., Giampapa, 2010; Kuo et al., 2013). Interestingly, many researchers not only in the United Stated, but also overseas found strong positive influences from the means of multimodality on diverse students' academic achievement (e.g., Bruce, 2009a; 2009b; Bruce & Chiu, 2015; Kaur et al., 2012; McVee et al., 2008a; Pietikainen & Pitkanen-Hunta, 2013; Unsworth, 2006; Usra et al., 2025).

My professional curiosity of a devoted Vygotskyan was heated by the report of the study by Lincoln and Rademacher's (2006) who identified some patterns in the ways the learners from different cultural and ethnic backgrounds utilized and perceived helpfulness of multimodal texts. Moreover, Lincoln found some variations by gender. Studying 69 adult English as a Second Language (ESL) learners in the age group between 23 and 45 in seven adult education centers in northwest Arkansas, Lincoln and Rademacher (2006) found that the female research participants preferred auditory and multimodal learning styles. Additionally, Lincoln and Rademacher (2006) found some distinct variations by ethnicity in male research participants. While both Hispanic males and females preferred note-taking and kinesthetic learning styles, these authors' ANOVA results demonstrated that Hispanic males did not choose the auditory styles, but Hispanic females valued the aural styles significantly over the visual ones. Another portion of Lincoln and Rademacher's (2006) research found that Asian males strongly relied on aural learning and note-taking.

Importantly, the findings in Lincoln and Rademacher's (2006) study may open before the researchers in the field of multimodality new horizons for exploration, as there have been found significant variations by gender, culture, and ethnicity in participants' perception and utilization of means of multimodality for learning purposes. So, the findings by Lincoln demonstrated how diverse populations selectively used different modes of multimodality. Though the research participants in Lincoln and Rademacher's (2006) study preferred different modalities, they did not reject them in favor of a conventional print-based text. On the contrary, all of them preferred using different modes, in addition to the print-based text. The above findings by Lincoln and Rademacher completely support the findings in my previously conducted studies (Gould-Yakovleva, 2023a, 2023b).

GLOBAL INTEREST

Notably, the field of multimodality was researched globally. With my focus on college or university students and in my strong attempt to help them succeed academically, I was also extremely interested in exploring the research with younger students on different grade levels. Amazingly, the researchers investigating the multimodality and its effects on young learners (e.g., Giampapa, 2010; Kaur et al., 2012; Kuo et al., 2013) while independently working in different world localities, with different numbers and genders of ethnically diverse students, came out with similar and highly positive results. For example, Giampapa (2010) studied one Canadian fourth grade teacher and his 29 students. Kaur et al. (2012) studied 37 Chinese ELL secondary school students in Penang, Malaysia. Kuo's et al. (2013) research involved 134 fifth-grade English Language learners in Taiwan. Regardless of all the ethnic, national, international, gender, and other differences between these projects' participants, these studies found that usage of multimodalities was beneficial to the participating students.

Some of the explored by myself qualitative research focused on only one participant. For instance, Lenters (2015) conducted her qualitative case study with one eleven-year-old student participant over the period of five months in Canada. This researcher aimed to understand how this participant engaged in the in-school and out-of-school multimodal literacy practices. This investigator also focused on the so-called "seemingly off-task activities" performed by her project participant. These observations occurred when the student in the focus of this research was simply over-writing the existing print-based texts with his own drawings accompanied with inscriptions. Based on her observations, Lenters (2015) suggested that educators underestimated and often misinterpreted the investigated by herself literacy practices employed by her focus student. Countering the educators who would probably view this student's multimodal activity as a game or indication of boredom, Lenters noticed that employment of multimodality allowed her student-participant to interact with the multimodal texts he read or created; thus, allowed this student to get deeper engaged with those texts. Contemplating about the usage of multimodalities, Lenters (2015) concluded, "Children and youth worldwide are discovering and exploring textual terrains in their homes, communities, and classrooms, and too often educational systems misrecognize this exploration" (p. 313). This author provided her implications for further research and recognized that, "We can extend our conception of the myriad ways young people come to be literate and provide important new avenues for pedagogical exploration" (2015, p. 313). Conclusively, Lenters implied the idea about the field of multimodal literacies as not being quite sufficiently researched yet.

Continuing traditions of the qualitative research, the American researchers Lysaker and Nie (2017) conducted their study grounded in the transactive theory with one fourth-grade participant. These researchers aimed to understand how students make the meaning of multimodal texts. Another purpose of their study was to investigate the differences between the student's unaided and illustration-aided retellings of texts. This research found that the participant produced 15 messages during unaided text retelling, while when the same student retold multimodally supported texts, he composed 65 messages, where this participant was noticed making intertextual connections. So, Lysaker and Nie (2017) concluded that, "Because the intertextual connections of picture-book reading involve the evolution of readers' understandings of characters, intertextuality often draws on social imagination to recontextualize prior understanding of the inner realities of characters in a 'new' text" (p. 63). These authors stated that addition of multimodal features to print-based texts might assist readers with their reengagement with the text via the affordances of color and visual representations. Additionally, these researchers also found that visual aids might assist students with their faster retrieval of certain specific aspects of information about the readings from their memory storage. Many researchers explored not only consumption but also reproduction of the multimodal language (e.g., Kuo et al., 2013). This researcher also found some correlation between the usage of multimodalities and students' satisfaction with their learning. The Canadian researcher Pantaleo (2012a) also noticed beneficial effects of multimodality on student engagement. These findings support the ones by the American researchers in the field of multimodality (e.g., McVee et al. 2008a, 2008b, 2012; Miller, 2013; Miller & McVee, 2012a, 2012b; and Shanahan et al., 2014). The work by the above researchers' teams deserves a special conversation and will be attended further in this chapter.

RESEARCH IN MY ALMA MATER

The State University of New York (SUNY) researchers-conducted studies by David Bruce, Ming Ming Chiu, Mary McVee, Suzanne Miller, and Lynn Shanahan, which were carried out in the United States of America, found that multimodal video composing (as the multimodal text reproduction) was one of the most effective means for many learners to get highly engaged in the academic processes, which, otherwise, many of them did not find attractive. In the studies by these researchers, the participating students not only demonstrated their deeper understanding of the meaning of texts through the visual means, but did it with a significantly higher engagement.

Issues with student satisfaction, engagement, and motivation have concerned educators and researchers throughout the history of education. Having studied the field of multimodal composing, Miller stressed in her large-scale 2013 metasynthesis the importance for teachers to "engage students in purposeful activities of transmediating for multimodal composing" (p. 422). Further in this publication, Miller conveyed, "A central finding in the metasynthesis was the importance of expanding the available resources for making meaning – from text to also images, sounds, movements, and gestures" (p. 422). So, summarizing Miller's (2013) findings, one can conclude that the means of multimodality, including but not limited to their visual, auditory, spatial, and gestural modes, have the potential to assist students with their meaning making when added to a print-based text.

I will detail on a very interesting study conducted by the American researchers of State University of New York, Mary McVee, Nancy Bailey, and Lynn Shanahan. One of their research projects took place in 2008 and was conducted at a Northeastern university in the United States over a period of a semester within a 15 week-long course. Participants in this research were a group of students, which included pre-service and beginning in-service teachers. McVee et al. (2012) insightfully investigated their participants' perceptions of their working with technology in the process of creating multimodal video-compositions based on pieces of poetry. This researchers team stressed in their publication that multimodality in the form of technology might be implemented in classrooms with the purpose to motivate the adult students in learning. Yet, just as in the previously discussed study by Jimenez and Meyer (2016), the SUNY researchers found that, "Motivational edge alone is not enough" (McVee et al., 2012, p. 29). This finding by McVee et al. corresponded with the conclusion drawn by Ajayi (2015) who pointed out that multimodalities had often been studied in terms of looking for possible ways to engage students and get them interested in classroom learning processes. Nevertheless, as the above authors concluded, the increase in motivation and engagements is not the only benefit of multimodal instruction.

To further the above thought, it is important to report that McVee et al. (2012) found more meaningful aspects of employment of multimodalities, rather than just their potential to motivate uninterested and disengaged learners. To support their statements, these authors included in their publication some quotes from their interview with their research participants. For instance, upon having created a multimodal text, one of the participating students reflected on the changes that occurred in her understanding of the use of technology for teaching and learning purposes. This participant confessed, "Now I see that technology is not just a tool, but a way to find and create the meaning" (McVee et al., 2012 p. 27).

Another participant in this study suggested that employment of multimodality may be beneficial to learners in multiple aspects of learning. Contemplating on multimodal interpretation of poetry, this student clarified that this type of activity "allows students to be involved in: rereading text, making connections, discovering meaning, questioning the writer's intentions…" (McVee et al., 2012, p. 29).

The findings by McVee, Bailey, and Shanahan also powerfully supported the idea that multimodality has the potential to assist students with meaning making. Not only the two cited above participants, but also the other subjects in these researchers' team studies confirmed that thanks to employment of multimodality within this project, they gained a deeper understanding of poetry of which they previously had little to no appreciation (2012). A deeper understanding of the content and the meaning of the poems used within this project allowed its participants to develop appreciation of poetry. Importantly, some of them marked their newly gained perceptions of the beauty and value of poetry as their achievement.

Upon completing their study, McVee et al. concluded that, "It is our [educators'] mission to take students beyond mere interest and engagement toward passionate construction of knowledge" (2012, p. 29). So, these researchers not only envisioned, but also confirmed multiple benefits from multimodalities to many aspects of teaching and learning.

Another researcher from the State University of New York, David Bruce (2012), independently or in collaboration with Chiu (2015), developed the idea of necessity to not only employ multimodality in the form of diverse educational technologies in classrooms, but also teach students visual framework and video grammar. This author suggested that students need to be taught how to read, understand, and write multimodal texts. Mere exposure to video materials (e.g., videos, movies) would not contribute to development of visual literacy skills in learners, unless teachers put their strong effort in explaining to their student the rules of multimodal language. This finding by Bruce strongly correlates with that postulated by Kress and van Leeuwen (1996, 2002), which had been previously discussed in this publication.

Further, Bruce (2012) delineated how reading and writing processes are strongly interconnected. This researcher developed an intricate method of *video deconstruction*, which he described in his 2012 publication. As not only a researcher, but an educator, this author described some exercises he offered to his students, "The idea behind it is for the reader to become aware of a film clip's structural components and how those components are woven together to create a narrative scene" (p. 36). According to Bruce, studying multimodalities involves multiple aspects, including reading visual texts critically. As the result of teaching multimodal literacy skills to students, including teaching deconstructing visual texts, students recognized that, "Learning video grammar has foundationally changed the way in which they perceived narrative video" (Bruce, 2012, p. 41). Bruce concluded his article with a powerful statement, "If we want our students to use video as a composition tool, they need a language to help them read it as well" (Bruce, 2012, p. 42). As one can perceive, the State University of New York researchers stepped significantly farther in their research, rather than simply looking for ways to engage bored and unmotivated learners.

Another example of research on effects from multimodality was the study by Lynn Shanahan conducted with an elementary classroom teacher and her fifth-grade learners in 2012 at a Northeastern public school district. Shanahan's research focused on multimodal composing by students in their science classroom. Just as her SUNY colleagues, Shanahan went further beyond the study of engagement and pointed out to multiple positive aspects of multimodal learning, such as cognitive, affective, and aesthetical. Based on this research finding, it is important for educators to include teaching multiliteracies in their curriculums with the purpose to allow students to "move beyond writing as print-based" towards intertwining multiple modes of communication and "layering the meaning between sign systems" (Shanahan, 2012, p. 112). This author concluded her publication with the statement, "This change in definition [of writing] assumes a multimodal semiotic approach to reading and writing where visual, linguistic, audio, and gestural design elements can be essential information mediums that engage readers cognitively and aesthetically" (Shanahan, 2012, p. 112).

Another powerful work on Embodied Learning authored by the State University of New York researchers Suzanne Miller and Mary McVee totally debunked the myths created about multiliteracies spread around within educational communities. These myths, as described by these authors, often positioned students as "*Digital Natives*" and teachers as "*Digital Immigrants*." The above notions are a pure misconception as per these authors. Yet, to debunk these myths, educators need to employ multimodalities more actively in their classroom instruction. One of the most important conditions of effective employment of new literacies and multimodalities, as found by the above researchers, was developing a *New Literacies stance* by teachers. This idea by Miller and McVee (2012) supported the findings by the other researchers and theorists (e.g., Bailey, 2012; Bruce, 2012; McVee et al., 2012; Wertsch, 1991) who viewed technology as a tool which may be used by educators in a multiplicity of creative ways for teaching and learning purposes.

Further, drawing on Bailey's (2012) research, Miller and McVee confirmed that the great potential of multimodality is not only in its use for student engagement. In addition, students may learn to re-discover the meanings hidden behind the signs and symbols that have been surrounding them in real-life situations, in their classrooms, and in multimodal texts they read or write. Studying multimodalities may lead learners to gaining new meaning, or deepening the meaning they had had prior to engaging with multimodal reading practices. This finding by Miller and McVee (2012) supported the ideas expressed by the other researchers in the discussed field (e.g., Ajayi, 2015; Bruce, 2012; Shanahan, 2012).

Nevertheless, as stated by Bruce (2012), it is not just the usage, but thoughtful planning and selection of multimodal teaching materials that matters. The need in the above becomes even more dramatic when it goes about teaching culturally diverse student populations. With regards to this idea, special attention should be given to the 2008 publication by the South-African researcher Pippa Stein. Stein dedicated her multiple research projects to studying specifically culturally diverse learners. This researcher focused in particular on "the forms of representation through which students make their meanings" (2008, p. 1). This researcher attracted attention of wide educational audiences to the fact that students make the meaning based on the sets of knowledge they possess in their individual "cultural worlds." Once again, the findings by this researcher strongly correlate with the Vygotskyan postulates of socio-culturally constructed knowledge.

AUSTRALIAN INPUT

Yet, while honoring the American researchers, it is fair to recognize that our colleagues in Australia have tremendously contributed to the field of multimodality. My readers might have a flashback to the Semiotics section of this book and recollect or briefly scan its portion on typography. The ideas by the world-renowned semioticians found reflection in the book by Jon Callow (2014) *The Shape of Text to Come: How Image and Text Work*. Callow offered his detailed suggestions on usage of multimodal texts, where he viewed a multimodal text as a combination of several multi-and unimodal ones. To get a better picture of the above notion, the readers may try to envision some print-based text performed in different fonts, colors, or typeface. Interestingly, Callow believed that even print alone may be viewed as a visual text, which contains and delivers the encoded meaning via affordances of the font type, its size, and the shape of the printed texts. This researcher further asserted that while purposefully changing the criteria above, an author may change the meaning of the entire message. Having encountered the changes in size, type, and shape of the print within a text, readers may also make or reconstruct the meaning of the verbal text in accordance with the visual representation of the message. The above findings by Callow strongly correlated with the ones made by the semioticians Kress and van Leeuwen.

Further, while contemplating about communication between human beings, Callow (2014) explained that, "All types of texts, from early manuscripts and children's illustrated picture books to film, video, and interactive media, have some type of visual elements present. Even spoken texts, when performed or delivered, have a certain 'visuality, depending on context'" (p. 3). Thus, multimodal reception of information is highly natural and habitual for humans. In a real-life situation, spoken text may be accompanied by additional non-verbal multimodal features (e.g., gestures, tones of the voice, intonations, and facial expressions). All these additional features serve the purpose to help a speaker to deliver his/her ideas with more precision, while their audience or addressees use the same visual features in addition to the verbal text with the purpose to make the meaning.

Most importantly, Callow attempted to further the idea of the visual nature of texts. This researcher suggested that visual texts, for example, still images, strongly appeal to humans' emotionality; thus, they may help viewers to get closer connected to the multimodal, rather than unimodal texts. As the result, this effect may more efficiently motivate readers in constructing the meaning while connecting the new to their prior knowledge and affective experiences.

Further, Callow (2014) explained that just as grammar of a verbal language, the grammar of the visuals needs to be taught to students for them to be able to read visual texts correctly, where *correctly* is the key word. Callow not only emphsized the need in educating students in terms of usage of multimodality, but also provided explicit examples on how to teach learners to read, decode, and understand multimodal texts comprised of both print-based and visual means.

Yet, similarly to many researchers who propel the field of multimodality and social semiotics (e.g., Norris, 2004; Serafini, 2011, 2014; Stein, 2008), Callow (2014) recognized importance of *all* semiotic signs and *all* modes. This author pointed out importance of reading both: salient and accompanying signs and modes within a multimodal ensemble. For example, when reading visual information in the form of a still image or a video, readers need to pay attention to main actors (*tenors*), the quality of their actions (how the tenors' actions line up), and the surrounding setting, colors, and layout of the visual features. According to Callow, additional meaning may be made while analyzing how actors (tenors) relate to each other and interact.

Positions of objects in an image or on a screen, carry the meaning and have the power to affect readers' perceptions elicited from the observable information. To provide just some examples, low angle or high angle view of an object or a person involves power in the relationship between a viewer and the viewed image. While looking upwards from a lower angle, viewers have less power over the image or an actor, compared to an instance when they look at it from a higher angle or from above. Another example would be facing the direct gaze of an actor straight at the reading audience. This moment would also involve the power and the so-called demand issued to the viewers and prompting them to take part in the observed situation, which is developed on a page or on the screen.

So, via his highly multimodal, rich in images publications, Callow clearly explained that watching a multimodal text is practically never a passive observation. Considering active engagement with and personal involvement of readers in multimodal readings, this author stated, "Multimodal texts, with their powerful mix of images and words, can be a highly engaging resource for students" (Callow 2012, 2014, p. 99). Thus, one of the major implications of Callow's research is that teachers need to actively employ multimodal texts in addition to or in combination with the print-based ones. This might help both: to stronger motivate students in learning, but, most importantly, to allow them to get deeper engaged with the content of the readings; thus, help them to make the meaning of these readings more precisely. This idea by Callow (2014) supports the ones expressed by Miller in her 2013 metasynthesis. Yet, one of the major conditions for successful decoding of multimodal texts, as found by Callow, is painstaking and thoughtful teaching learners how to understand semiotic signs and symbols, modes, and other aspects of visual grammar.

More, thanks to the results of their research studies, multimodality was embedded in public school curricula in Australia. Prior to this decision, several Australian researchers had explored the effects from the means of multimodality on public school student populations on all grade levels. Multiple studies with the Australian elementary school students ages eight through eleven found that multimodalities, including the computer-based ones, were beneficial for students' reading comprehension (e.g., Callow & Zammit, 2012; Cloonan, 2011; Mills, 2011; Molyneux & Godinho, 2012; Vincent, 2006; Walsh, 2008). Importantly, Vincent's study found that "five out of 26 ten-year-old participants (which is nearly twenty percent) needed computers as the only means for them to compose meaningful text" (Vincent, 2006).

All the above studies implied the idea of importance of visuals. Interestingly, an international researchers' team of Baildon and Damico (2009) echoed the idea on Media Literacy. These authors stated that children were more likely to believe, trust, and rely on multimodally presented information, rather than print-based one. Thus, visuals have a powerful effect on children and youth. With the above concluded, these researchers conveyed the idea of high importance of visual literacy. This idea strongly corresponds with the ones by the semioticians, previously discussed in this book. Baildon and Damico stated that in the age of web-based information, its visual means are trusted more compared to the print-based ones. It needs to be understood though that the publications by Baildon and Damico (2009) as well as the one by Kitson (2011) no way diminished the need in and the importance of the multimodal instruction. However, these researchers appealed to the wide educational and academic audiences and attracted their attention to the high importance of thoughtful curriculum development and instruction planning in terms of usage of means of multimodally presented information. Most importantly, they promoted the idea of necessity of a new type of literacy, the visual or multimodal ones.

CONCLUSIVE IDEAS

With my great respect to the authors of the reviewed above literature, whose findings and postulates paved my way into research of multimodality, I am also willing to honor the most recent works in the field (e.g., Breuer & Archer, 2016; Ericson & Häikiö, 2025; Lee et al., 2024; Mora et al., 2025; Pütz & Mundt, 2018; Włodarczyk et al., 2023). With my heartfelt gratitude to my colleagues – the researchers in the fields of multimodality who substantially contributed to the research with the bilingual or multilingual populations and multimodality (e.g., Ainsworth et al., 2023; Brown & Eskildsen, 2024; Reyes-Torres et al. 2025; Saint-Georges & Weber, 2013; Sidoni; 2023; Yusra et al., 2025; Zarobe & Querol-Julian, 2025), I must conclude that there is the population type, whose problems have not been addressed nor substantially researched yet, the polylingual EAL-speaking university students. According to the evidence-based definition by Cekaite & Evaldsson (2008), the Polylinguals are the EAL-learners whose academic struggles and problems require urgent researchers' and educators' attention and support due to their extreme translanguaging practices between all available to them verbal and non-verbal languages. Thus, I claim there is an urgent need in research with this specific population. Particularly, there is a high necessity to find more efficient multimodal support strategies to assist the polylingual EAL university students with their reading comprehension of highly complex academic and feature texts. Hopefully, this publication contributes to narrowing the existing abyss in the studies and literature as well as in the practical implementation of their findings in the university classrooms.

REFERENCES

Ainsworth, S., Griffiths, D., Macrory, G., & Pahl, K. (2023). *Multimodality and multilingualism: Towards an integrative approach*. Multilingual Matters.

Ajayi, L. (2008). Meaning-making, **multimodal** representation, and transformative pedagogy: An exploration of meaning construction instructional practices in an ESL high school classroom. *Journal of Language, Identity, and Education*, *7*(3/4), 206–229. DOI: 10.1080/15348450802237822

Ajayi, L. (2009). English as a second language learners' exploration of multimodal texts in a junior high school. *Journal of Adolescent & Adult Literacy*, *52*(7), 585–595. DOI: 10.1598/JAAL.52.7.4

Ajayi, L. (2015). Critical multimodal literacy: How Nigerian female students critique texts and reconstruct unequal social structures. *Journal of Literacy Research*, *47*(2), 216–244. DOI: 10.1177/1086296X15618478

Archer, A. (2025). Multimodality and the affordances of co-presence for inclusion in higher education. *Designs for Learning*, *16*(1), 1–8. DOI: 10.16993/dfl.230

Archer, A., & Price, C. (2021). Assessment, recognition and the contact zone: How much is 'enough'? *Education as Change*, *25*, 1–18. DOI: 10.25159/1947-9417/8741

Baildon, M., & Damico, J. S. (2009). How do we know?: Students examine issues of credibility with a complicated multimodal web-based text. *Curriculum Inquiry*, *39*(2), 265–285. DOI: 10.1111/j.1467-873X.2009.00443.x

Bailey, N. M. (2012). The importance of a new literacies stance in teaching English Language Arts. In Miller, S., & McVee, M. (Eds.), *Multimodal composing in classrooms: Learning and teaching for digital world* (pp. 44–62). Routledge.

Binder, M., & Kotsopoulos, S. (2011). Multimodal literacy narratives: Weaving the threads of young children's identity through the arts. *Journal of Research in Childhood Education*, *25*(4), 339–363. DOI: 10.1080/02568543.2011.606762

Breuer, E., & Archer, A. (2016). *Multimodality in higher education*. Brill. DOI: 10.1163/9789004312067

Brown, A., & Eskildsen, S. W. (2024). *Multimodality across epistemologies in second language research*. Routledge. DOI: 10.4324/9781003355670

Bruce, D. L. (2009a). Reading and writing video: Media literacy and adolescents. In Christenbury, L., Bomer, R., & Smagorinsky, P. (Eds.), *Handbook of adolescent literacy research* (pp. 287–333). The Guilford Press.

Bruce, D. L. (2009b). Writing visual images: Examining the video composition processes of highs school students. *Research in the Teaching of English, 43*(4), 426–450. DOI: 10.58680/rte20097073

Bruce, D. L. (2012). Learning video grammar: A multimodal approach to reading and writing video texts. In Miller, S., & McVee, M. (Eds.), *Multimodal composing in classrooms: Learning and teaching for digital world* (pp. 32–43). Routledge.

Bruce, D. L., & Chiu, M. M. (2015). Composing with new technology: Teacher reflections on learning digital video. *Journal of Teacher Education, 66*(3), 272–287. DOI: 10.1177/0022487115574291

Callow, J. (2012). The rules of visual engagement: Images as tools for learning. *Screen Education*, (65), 72–79.

Callow, J. (2014). *The shape of text to come: How image and text work*. PETAA.

Callow, J., & Zammit, K. (2012). "Where lies your text?" ("Twelfth Night" act I, scene V): Engaging high school students from low socioeconomic backgrounds in reading multimodal texts. *Engineers Australia, 47*(2), 69–77.

Ericson, K., & Häikiö, T. K. (2025). Visuality and multimodality as tools for learning in geography and art education. *Journal of Aesthetic Education, 59*(2), 50–73. DOI: 10.5406/15437809.59.2.05

Giampapa, F. (2010). Multiliteracies, pedagogy and identities: Teacher and student voices from a Toronto elementary school. *Canadian Journal of Education, 33*(2), 407–431.

Gould-Yakovleva, O. (2023a). Seeking remedy for improving international college students' reading comprehension: A qualitative case study on using multimodality for English language learning. *International Journal of Higher Education Pedagogies, 4*(4), 33–54. DOI: 10.33422/ijhep.v4i4.599

Gould-Yakovleva, O. (2023b). Voices from university classrooms on effects of multimodality on polylingual EAL college students' meaning making. *International Journal of Second and Foreign Language Education, 2*(2), 1–19. DOI: 10.33422/ijsfle.v2i2.450

Gould-Yakovleva, O. (2024). Demystifying the notion of charisma: Micro-ethnography on a veteran-teacher's classroom practices. *The Qualitative Report, 29*(4), 1192–1211. DOI: 10.46743/2160-3715/2024.6521

Gould-Yakovleva, O., & Liu, X. (2024). Mutualism as mutual trust: An ethnographic case study on an elementary-school teacher-team participation in a science PD program. *The Qualitative Report*, *29*(4), 915–938. DOI: 10.46743/2160-3715/2024.6440

Hasty, M. M., & Fain, J. G. (2014). Emergent understandings: Multilingual fourth grade students generating close readings as multimodal responses to global and informal texts. *Perspectives on Urban Education*, *11*(2), 10–20.

Hegelheimer, V. (2006). Helping ESL writers through a multimodal, corpus-based, online grammar resource. *CALICO Journal*, *24*(1), 5–32. DOI: 10.1558/cj.v24i1.5-31

Huang, Y. (2023). Open learning environment for multimodal learning based on knowledge base technology. *International Journal of Emerging Technologies in Learning*, *18*(11), 38–51. DOI: 10.3991/ijet.v18i11.39397

Huang, Y. H. (2012). EFL students' views on writing with pictures, sound, and music. *English Teaching & Learning*, *36*(2), 79–123. DOI: 10.6330/ETL.2012.36.2.03

Jimenez, L. M., & Meyer, C. K. (2016). First impressions matter: Navigating graphic novels utilizing linguistic, visual, and spatial resources. *Journal of Literacy Research*, *48*(4), 423–447. DOI: 10.1177/1086296X16677955

Kaur, S., Ganapathy, M., & Sidhu, G. K. (2012). Designing learning elements using the multiliteracies approach in an ESL writing classroom. *Southeast Asian Journal of English Language Studies*, *18*(3), 119–134.

Kress, G., & van Leeuwen, T. (1996). *Reading images: The grammar of visual design*. Routledge.

Kress, G., & van Leeuwen, T. (2002). Colour as a semiotic mode: Notes for a grammar of colour. *Visual Communication*, *1*(3), 333–354. DOI: 10.1177/147035720200100306

Kuo, F. O., Yu, P. T., & Hsiao, W. H. (2013). Develop and evaluate the effect of multimodal presentation system on elementary ESL students. *The Turkish Online Journal of Educational Technology*, *12*(4), 29–40.

Lee, S. S. J., Siew, L. L., Tiong, N. D., & Ma, N. (2024). Multimodality in art teacher education in China. *Design*, *1*(1), 45–54. DOI: 10.36922/dp.4554

Lenters, K. (2016). Riding the lines and overwriting in the margins: Affect and multimodal literacy practices. *Journal of Literacy Research*, *48*(3), 280–316. DOI: 10.1177/1086296X16658982

Lincoln, F., & Rademacher, B. (2006). Learning styles of ESL students in community colleges. *Community College Journal of Research and Practice*, *30*(5/6), 485–500. DOI: 10.1080/10668920500207965

Lysaker, J. T., & Nie, A. Y. (2017). Social and relational aspects of comprehending in one fourth grader's unaided and illustration-aided picturebook retellings: Retelling as co-authoring. *Journal of Literacy Research, 49*(1), 38–67. DOI: 10.1177/1086296X16684583

Maula, Q. I., & Awwalia, L. (2025). Scrutinizing teachers' practice of multimodality use in elementary English classroom. *KnE Social Sciences, 10*(12), 69–79. DOI: 10.18502/kss.v10i12.18863

McVee, M. B., Bailey, N. M., & Shanahan, L. E. (2008a). Teachers and teacher educators learning from new literacies and new technologies. *Teaching Education, 19*(3), 197–210. DOI: 10.1080/10476210802250216

McVee, M. B., Bailey, N. M., & Shanahan, L. E. (2008b). Using digital media to interpret poetry: Spiderman meets Walt Whitman. *Research in the Teaching of English, 43*(2), 112–143. DOI: 10.58680/rte20086774

McVee, M. B., Bailey, N. M., & Shanahan, L. E. (2012). The artful deception of technology integration and the move toward a new literacies mindset. In Miller, S., & McVee, M. (Eds.), *Multimodal composing in classrooms: Learning and teaching for digital world* (pp. 13–31). Routledge.

Miller, S. M. (2013). A research metasynthesis on digital video composing in classrooms: An evidence-based framework toward a pedagogy for embodied learning. *Journal of Literacy Research, 45*(4), 386–430. DOI: 10.1177/1086296X13504867

Miller, S. M., & McVee, M. B. (2012a). *Multimodal composing in classrooms: Learning and teaching for the digital world.* Routledge.

Miller, S. M., & McVee, M. B. (2012b). Changing the game: Teaching for embodied learning through multimodal composing. In Miller, S., & McVee, M. (Eds.), *Multimodal composing in classrooms: Learning and teaching for digital world* (pp. 132–152). Routledge.

Mills, K. (2011). "I'm making it different to the book": Transmediation in young children's multimodal and digital texts. *Australasian Journal of Early Childhood, 36*(3), 56–65. DOI: 10.1177/183693911103600308

Molle, D., & Prior, P. (2008). Multimodal genre system in EAP writing pedagogy: Reflecting on a need analysis. *TESOL Quarterly, 42*(4), 541–566. DOI: 10.1002/j.1545-7249.2008.tb00148.x

Molyneux, P., & Godinho, S. (2012). "This Is My Thing!": Middle years students' engagement and learning using digital resources. *Australasian Journal of Educational Technology, 28*(8), 1466–1486. DOI: 10.14742/ajet.782

Mora, R. A., Tian, Z., & Harman, R. (2024). *Translanguaging and multimodality as flow, agency, and a new sense of advocacy in and from the global south*. Routledge.

Norris, S. (2004). *Analyzing multimodal interaction: A methodological framework*. Routledge. DOI: 10.4324/9780203379493

Ntelioglou, B. Y. (2011). 'But why do I have to take this class?' The mandatory drama-ESL class and multiliteracies pedagogy. *Research in Drama Education, 16*(4), 595–615. DOI: 10.1080/13569783.2011.617108

Pahl, K. (2007). Creativity in events and practices: A lens for understanding children's multimodal texts. *Literacy, 41*(2), 86–92. DOI: 10.1111/j.1467-9345.2007.00462.x

Paivio, A. (1969). Mental imagery in associative learning and memory. *Psychological Review, 76*(3), 241–263. DOI: 10.1037/h0027272

Pantaleo, S. (2012a). Exploring grade 7 students' responses to Shaun Tan's "The Red Tree.". *Children's Literature in Education, 43*(1), 51–71. DOI: 10.1007/s10583-011-9156-x

Pietikainen, S., & Pitkanen-Hunta, A. (2013). Multimodal literacy practices in the indigenous Sami classroom: Children navigating in a complex multilingual setting. *Journal of Language, Identity, and Education, 12*(4), 230–247. DOI: 10.1080/15348458.2013.818471

Pütz, M., & Mundt, N.-F. (2018). *Expanding the linguistic landscape: Linguistic diversity, multimodality and the use of space as a semiotic resource*. Multilingual Matters.

Rahmanu, E. D., Altun, L., & Kariati, N. M. (2020). Case study on multimodality perception in the higher education classroom. *Journal Sosial dan Humaniora. Journal of Social Sciences and Humanities, 10*(3), 1–11. DOI: 10.31940/soshum.v10i3.2091

Reyes-Torres, A., Brisk, M. E., & Lacorte, M. (2025). *Multiliteracies, multimodality, and learning by design in second language learning and teacher education*. Routledge. DOI: 10.4324/9781032620497

Saint-Georges, I., & Weber, J.-J. (2013). *Multilingualism and multimodality: Current challenges for educational studies*. Brill Academic Publishing. DOI: 10.1007/978-94-6209-266-2

Serafini, F. (2011). Expanding perspectives for comprehending visual images in multimodal texts. *Journal of Adolescent & Adult Literacy, 54*(5), 342–350. DOI: 10.1598/JAAL.54.5.4

Serafini, F. (2014). *Reading the visual: An introduction to teaching multimodal literacy*. Teachers College Press.

Shanahan, L. E. (2012). Lessons in multimodal composition from a fifth-grade classroom. In Miller, S., & McVee, M. (Eds.), *Multimodal composing in classrooms: Learning and teaching for digital world* (pp. 97–113). Routledge.

Shanahan, L. E., McVee, M. B., & Bailey, N. M. (2014). Multimodality in action: New literacies as more than activity in middle and high school classrooms. In Ferdig, R. E., & Pytash, K. E. (Eds.), *Exploring multimodal composition and digital writing* (pp. 36–53). IGI Global., DOI: 10.4018/978-1-4666-4345-1.ch003

Shih, Y. C. (2014). Communication strategies in a multimodal virtual communication context. *System*, *42*, 34–47. DOI: 10.1016/j.system.2013.10.016

Sindoni, M. (2023). *Multimodality and translanguaging in video interactions*. Cambridge University Press.

Stein, P. (2000). Rethinking resources in the ESL classroom. Rethinking resources: Multimodal pedagogies in the ESL classroom. *TESOL Quarterly*, *34*(2), 333–336. DOI: 10.2307/3587958

Stein, P. (2008). *Multimodal pedagogies in diverse classrooms: Representations, rights and resources*. Routledge.

Stone, P. (2012). Learners performing tasks in a Japanese EFL classroom: A multimodal and interpersonal approach to analysis. *RELC Journal*, *43*(3), 313–330. DOI: 10.1177/0033688212463287

Unsworth, L. (2006). Toward a metalanguage for multiliteracies education: Describing the meaning-making resources of language-image interaction. *English Teaching*, *5*(1), 55–76.

Vincent, J. (2006). Children writing: Multimodality and assessment in the writing classroom. *Literacy*, *40*(1), 51–57. DOI: 10.1111/j.1467-9345.2006.00426.x

Walsh, M. (2008). Worlds have collided and modes have merged: Classroom evidence of changed literacy practices. *Literacy*, *42*(2), 101–108. DOI: 10.1111/j.1741-4369.2008.00495.x

Wertsch, J. V. (1991). *Voices of the mind*. Harvard University Press.

Włodarczyk, M., Tyrkkö, J., & Adamczyk, E. (2023). *Multilingualism from manuscript to 3D: Intersections of modalities from medieval to modern times*. Routledge. DOI: 10.4324/9781003166634

Yusra, S. R., Hanifa, R., Wardana, A., & Fahmiati, M. (2025). Leveraging instructional multimodality for enhanced English grammar learning of undergraduate students: A higher education perspective. *International Journal of Information and Education Technology (IJIET)*, *15*(6), 1172–1181. DOI: 10.18178/ijiet.2025.15.6.2320

Zarobe, Y. R., & Querol-Julian, M. (2025). Multilingualism and multimodality in the CLIL/EMI classroom. *Journal of Multilingual and Multicultural Development*, *46*(5), 1397–1415. DOI: 10.1080/01434632.2025.2482734

Chapter 4
Delving Deeper

ABSTRACT

Chapter 4 aims to make a deeper dive into semiotics and social semiotics as per the postulates by such well-known semioticians as Franks, Jewitt, Kress, and van Leeuwen. Further, in this chapter, I will engage in my analysis of the research in the field of multimodal teaching and learning in connection with and as explained by the social semiotics theory. Specifically, I will address such aspect of the function of multimodalities as transmediation as developed by Norris. Simultaneously, the findings by the international researchers will be discussed. For instance, Serafini's grammar of visual text will be addressed, which will help readers to gain a deeper understanding of how the theoretical findings may be applied in practical teaching. Moreover, in this chapter, I will shed some light on the findings from some brain research studies on the topics of multimodal reading. I will conclude this chapter narrating about how all the above work helped me identify the existing gap in the research.

ENGAGING WITH SEMIOTICS

Keeping in mind the speedy globalization processes, it was interesting to me as an educator and a researcher to peek inside the international classrooms. So, my attention was attracted to the studies by Lasisi Ajayi (2015). This researcher conducted his qualitative case study with three female focus participants selected from a sample of 38 high-school students in a Nigerian high school setting. The data were collected from multiple sources, for example, in-school and out-of-school participant observations, student-created artifacts (e.g., multimodal, print- and image-based texts, digital multimodal student-developed texts, media posts), and interviews with the participants. Upon having analyzed the data, Ajayi (2015) drew the conclusion that the participating students got deeper engaged in reading practices, where multimodality helped them to reconsider the content of the read texts,

DOI: 10.4018/979-8-3373-3426-4.ch004

and develop their own, reconceptualized understanding of the problems discussed in the readings. According to this researcher, when working with the multimodal texts, her study participants demonstrated higher level employment of their critical thinking in the process of learning. Thus, one of the major implications of Ajayi's (2015) study was that, "The critical issue for teachers is to understand how in-school literacy can recruit students' outside school literacies to leverage literacy learning" (p. 238). The findings by this researcher also indicated that teachers need to relate their instruction to their students' interests, while multimodality can be highly helpful for teaching, learning, and engagement purposes. Conclusively, the findings by this American researcher supported the ones made in the research conducted in many other overseas countries (e.g., Callow & Zammit, 2012; Molyneux & Godinho, 2012; Pantaleo, 2012a, 2012b).

Another quite interesting study on the upper-grade and older teenage students was conducted by Jimenez and Meyer (2016) and went beyond exploring student motivation. These researchers engaged in multiple-case studies with teenagers ranging between ages 15 to 20. Later, Jimenez and Meyer focused primarily on two female and two male participants in their sample of 27. Although research on motivation was trending during the time of their project, Jimenez and Meyer (2016) indicated it was important for them to understand mechanisms and strategies employed by readers of multimodal texts. Per Jimenez and Meyer's conclusion, teachers did not always have the knowledge nor understanding of the effects from multimodality. Thus, not too many of them supported the classroom readings with multimodal features during their teaching. As per Jimenez and Meyer, the reason behind the multimodal instruction deficiency was that many teachers had been raised and educated in predominantly print-based academic traditions. Jimenez and Meyer's (2016) study found that each of their four participants employed his or her individual approach to reading multimodal texts. In particularly, the readers who were lower proficient at reading print-based texts, initially attended to multimodal information, then, proceeded to the print-based parts of the texts supported by multimodalities. Finally, these low-proficient readers synthesized both: unimodal and multimodal types of texts to make the meaning. The findings by Jimenez and Meyer (2016) imply the idea that employment of multimodal texts may simplify reading comprehension to lower-proficient teenage readers in addition to increasing their motivation in reading.

Focusing on college and university population as a researcher, I should mention how excited I felt to explore the literature on the research conducted with my target population. It needs to be said that significantly fewer studies in the field of multimodality were conducted specifically with the college or university students in the United States and overseas. Yet, the reports from these studies indicated multiple beneficial effects from multimodality on this category of learners. For example, the studies with college students in the United States, Europe, and Asia found that the participants who received multimodal instruction demonstrated higher academic results and were also more efficient in their working processes, which resulted for them in better learning outcomes in contrast to those students who received unimodal print-based reading (e.g., Gellevij et al., 2002; Huang, 2012, 2023; Jacobs, 2012; Wang, 2011, 2022).

Regardless of every student's or a group of students' mother tongue(s) or their spoken language(s), Stein (2008, 2012) pointed out the limits of the solely verbal language. This scholar, just as Miller (2013), encouraged educators to expand meaning-making opportunities for learners from the verbal to multimodal ones (e.g., usage of visual means, bodily practices).

I will provide here some more details on Stein's (2008) longitudinal study. Starting in 1980, this South African researcher sought to identify some alternative pedagogies to benefit her students. Eventually, this educator and researcher found that the multimodal pedagogies may be viewed as most effective ones due to their being natural and close to the way people operate in real-life world, including a classroom. Drawing on the ideas of theorists in the field of semiotics (Jewitt & Kress, 2003), Stein (2008) clearly stated, "All acts of communication in classrooms are multimodal: there is no monomodal communication" (p. 121). This thought-provoking statement confirmed once again that in the naturally multimodal world, the instruction needs to be multimodal as well.

Importantly, Stein (2008) attempted to understand how exactly students engaged in meaning making processes. As the result of her 2008 study, this researcher developed her own understanding and definition of meaning making, which needs to be viewed as "a multi-semiotic, material social practice in which children as 'sign-makers' recruit the semiotic sources they need to communicate" (p. 11). Additionally, Stein attempted to analyze how students and teachers used different modes. This author contemplated,

> *Mapping how teachers and students actively work with modes and multimodality in their classrooms gives us a better understanding of the relationship between modes, pedagogy, knowledge, and learning. It enables us to examine what multimodality has to offer as a pedagogic resource and how it can be used to improve learning (Stein, 2008, p. 121).*

Conclusively, upon having discussed benefits from multimodal approach in education, Stein (2008) pointed out to the aspect of *multi-perspectivity* (p. 139), as an opportunity for students to regard an issue from multiple points of view or from different perspectives. This finding by Stein (2008) might be especially useful in diverse and inclusive classrooms, where students from different social, cultural, and academic backgrounds are attempting to learn new to them language and culture, including but not limited to English as an Additional Language.

Stein was one of the first authors who stressed the importance of studying the processes via which diverse students must daily translate multiple texts from one verbal language to another and from abstract phenomena to real-life ones. This scholar viewed the success in "translation" or correct meaning-making in students' ability to proficiently operate the sign systems they must read. Drawing on Millard (2006), Stein concluded that, "Signs are always only partial representations of the object which is being represented, students' texts, as signs, have to be seen as multimodal to acquire their full meaning" (p. 146). Furthering Stein's (2008) ideas, it is possible to suggest that based on the notion above, students need to be both: 1. exposed to multimodal texts and 2. taught how to read them. Stein (2008) referred to multimodality as one of the forms of knowledge.

NORRIS'S TRANSMEDIATION

The above idea about extending students' knowledge and meaning making via mediational and transmediational affordances of multimodality was also explored by Sigrid Norris (2004) in her book *Analyzing Multimodal Interaction: A Methodological Framework.* Imperatively, Norris's (2004) publication might be used for preparing future teachers to not only implement multimodal methods, techniques, and approaches in their classrooms, but also for preparing them to teach students how to correctly read multimodal texts, how to convey the meaning though affordances of multiple resources of multimodality, and how to read multimodal texts formed by diverse modes (e.g., visual, auditory, spatial, digital).

Quite innovatively for that time, Norris (2004) explained that observable, thus, potentially readable actions might be categorized as *lower-level* actions and *higher-level* ones. The lower-level actions are the smallest units of meaning, while the higher-level ones are comprised of multiple small units (p. 11). Norris also came out with the idea that the "higher-level actions, which are entailed in material objects" may be called "*frozen actions*" (2004, p. 11). According to this researcher, teaching students how to break higher-level units into several lower-level, smaller and easily readable, and understandable ones, has the potential to develop a set of useful multimodal reading skills and habits in learners, which might assist them with their meaning making.

Norris's way to study multimodality deserves to be called a scientific approach. Regarding an action as a physical movement through the space, but not only, Norris suggested usefulness of reading information via observing proxemics between actors in a situation. This author provided detailed explanation of how reading proxemics behavior might help a reader to construct the meaning about the actors, the situation, and the nature of interactions within that situation, be that friendship, affection, tension, or aggression.

Another unit of visually readable information, as per Norris (2004), might be the actors' body posture and head position. It is possible to assume that students, while reading multimodal texts, can make correct guesses about some of these observable behaviors, based on their personal previous experiences or previously observed similar actions or situations. Nevertheless, students may achieve a higher proficiency in reading visual texts on condition they were taught all *how to* by experienced and learned educators. This finding by Norris also strongly corresponds with Vygotsky's (1978, 1987) beliefs in scaffolded instruction for helping students more efficiently progress through their ZPDs, the zones of knowledge where these students do not have either expertise or, oftentimes, even exposure.

Another multimodal skill, as proposed by Norris, is teaching students how to read gestures. Though some gestures may differ by culture, teachers might choose to teach their students how to read and understand those gestures, which are most frequently used to accompany the verbal language within their surrounding culture or internationally. For example, in the United States public-school setting, teachers might teach their International or Domestic EAL students how to understand the gestures habitually used in our country.

It might be highly helpful to EAL students to learn to distinguish between different types of gestures. As proposed by McNeil (1992), there are four types of gestures. The *iconic gestures* are the ones that aim to describe certain objects. For example, a very popular gesture, when a person makes a shape of a heart bringing together the tips of the thumbs pointing down and the forefingers, forming the upper contour of the iconic heart shape. The other type, the *deictic gestures,* are frequently utilized to point with the index finger to some object or person with the purpose to attract one's attention to that object or person. The *beat gestures* can be used to accompany one's speech just like beating musical rhythms. *Metaphoric gestures* are often used by people to help them express some abstract ideas. This culture-bound knowledge of the meaning or the purpose of gesticulation might be of great service to the EAL learners who are new to the English language and the surrounding culture. According to Norris (2004), her idea of reading units of physical actions, such as movement through the space, positioning towards other actors, gestures, etc. might apply to spoken language as well.

Additionally, when relying on auditory means of multimodality, the key to figuring out the precise meaning would be in the correct understanding of intonation, tone of the voice, pitch of speech in combination with reading verbal and / or auditory texts. It is possible to admit that some intonations and tones of voice might be naturally understandable to practically all learners. For instance, quiet, friendly, warm, and soft speech would be, most probably, understood as such. Nevertheless, teaching students to distinguish between some subtle or culture-specific types of audible information would give them significantly more advantages in reading the meaning of those utterances correctly.

In addition to the verbal and non-verbal audible text, Norris (2004) addressed the issues with reading information from facial expressions and gazes of actors. It needs to be recognized that these types of visual texts may be also culture-specific. Nevertheless, it is highly significant to teach diverse students, including but not limited to the polylingual EAL speakers how to read and understand correctly the meaning of different facial expressions and gazes, which can be frequently observed within the culture, the language of which they endeavor to master.

SERAFINI'S GRAMMAR OF VISUAL TEXT

The ideas of multimodality as emotional literacy developed by Norris (2004) found support in the book by Franks Serafini (2011, 2014) *Reading the Visual: An Introduction to Teaching Multimodal Literacy*. Serafini (2014) confirmed the idea that multimodality needs not only to be utilized in classrooms (e.g., illustrated books, video, digital texts), but also thoughtfully taught. This scholar directly stated students need to be instructed on how to read multimodal texts. According to this author, learners need to be taught which modes they might use for encoding and decoding the meaning via visual texts. This author pinpointed the issues with decoding multimodal texts as "the discovery of the obvious" (Serafini, 2014, p. 15).

Similarly to Stein's (2008) notion of classroom events as being always multimodal and never monomodal, Serafini (2014) wrote about multimodal nature of *all* texts and communication. Nevertheless, regardless of multimodal nature of communication, education is primarily based on print-based texts, as noted by Serafini (2014) who found it unfortunate, since unimodal, print-based reception of information is not a natural way for humans to receive and deliver information on everyday basis.

To clarify his ideas for educators, Serafini categorized learning materials as textually dominant (e.g., essays, lectures, novels), visually dominant (e.g., photography, painting, sculpture), and blended structures (e.g., picture books, webpages, newspapers) (2014, p. 17). As in the modern days, mass media-based information becomes increasingly visually dominated, Serafini (2014) suggested that new literacies, including but not limited to visual literacy, need to be included in a classroom instruction. This author explained, "A visually literate person is able to discriminate and make sense of visual objects and images, create visuals, comprehend and appreciate the visuals created by others, and visualize objects in their mind's eye" (p. 22). Serafini delved in a deep exploration of the effects from multimodality on students and distinguished between several foundational processes, such as *perception*, *representation*, and *interpretation* of the visual information. This author recognized that in today's world, many societies increasingly deliver and receive information in multimodal ways via affordances of media. So, the idea of significance of Media Literacy as one of the forms of Multiliteracy was brought to the table and accentuated by this researcher. Notably, Serafini's ideas echoed the ones sounded in the publication by Baildon and Damico (2009). These authors also issued an alarming note related to the above topic and cautioned the wide educational and academic communities about the acute-standing necessity of teaching students how to verify credibility of media-based multimodal and textual resources.

Talking about Serafini as a passionate educational researcher, it needs to be noticed that this author conveyed multiple theoretical and practical ideas while targeting teachers as the primary audience for his publication. This researcher actively advocated for usage of multimodal materials, such as historical picture books, graphic novels, films, etc. in classroom instruction. Imperatively, he stressed that the major purpose for his publications was "to help teachers and students develop new strategies and practices that foster a different way of seeing, a more intentional way for students to navigate, interpret, and analyze visual images and multimodal ensembles" (p. 167). These ideas by Serafini (2014) strongly confirmed and correlated with the ones expressed by Pippa Stein and Jon Callow.

BRAIN AND MIND WORK

Importantly, Dale (2004, 2008, 2019) in her book *Learning Theories: And Educational Perspective*, which outlived its 8 editions, pointed out not only to the effects from visuals on humans' meaning making, but also found them being highly beneficial to the memorization processes. Schunk explored the idea of using *mental imagery* by people. This author defined mental imagery as "mental representations of visual / spatial knowledge including physical properties of the objects or events represented" (Schunk, 2008, p. 175). This scholar suggested that usage of imagery has the potential to increase learning outcomes in students. This researcher found that visual representations of objects or events in the form of images can be more efficiently transferred to the long-term memory by learners. Schunk also found that people are also more likely to store images longer in their long-term memory in contrast to storing the verbal texts.

Further, Schunk (2008) stated that for adult students, utilization of mental imagery works faster and more effectively, rather than for young learners. This scholar explained that the only step adult learners need for recollecting some parts of visual information stored in their long-term memory is to access that mental storage. According to Schunk, younger learners operate with imagery in a different way: they need to scan the image, which has been stored in their long-term memory to verify the information they need to retrieve. So, as one may conclude, usage of visuals and imagery in classroom instruction with adult students may be highly effective.

Moreover, drawing on Paivio (1971), Schunk (2008) identified two means of representing knowledge; those are "a verbal system incorporating knowledge expressed in language and an imaginal system storing visual and spatial information" (p. 178). Schunk (2008, 2019) stressed how both systems were interrelated. This author clarified that, "A verbal code can be converted into an imaginal code and vice versa but important differences exist. The verbal system is suited for abstract information, whereas the imaginal system is used to represent concrete objects or events" (p. 178). Schunk (2008) directly stated that, "Using concrete materials and pictures enhances memory" (p. 179). Thus, this author's implication for educators consists in the visuals, which need to be implemented in classrooms for students to be able to memorize the content, place, and store it in their long-term memory. Most importantly, usage of visuals enables more efficient retrieval of the sought parts of information from the long-term memory for practical usage.

The ideas similar to the ones detailed by Schunk (2008) were later expressed by Benjamin Bergen (2012) in his book *Louder than Words: The New Science of How the Mind Makes Meaning*. This author attempted to understand how human mind works and operates with verbal and non-verbal elements of a language. Bergen (2012) contemplated about ability of a human brain to make meaning practically instantaneously on every-day basis. Bergen (2012) recognized the role of the verbal language. Yet, it needs to be noticed that Schunk did not underestimate it either. While Schunk referred to still images of objects or events, Bergen developed the idea of utilization by humans of *motoric images*, and *motor* and *auditory imagery* (2012, p. 36) when people imagine actions, movements, or speech of others via imagining those of their own. Bergen (2012) provided examples where modern technologies (e.g., functional magnetic resonance imaging or fMRI) allowed scientists to see how several zones in human brain under investigation get activated while working on these tasks.

Regardless of different types of images and visuals discussed, both Schunk (2008) and Bergen (2012) recognized the positive effects of images on people's engagement, meaning making, and memorization processes. Bergen stated that seeing or imagining a picture comprised of multiple objects or phenomena would be easier and faster to remember, rather than attempting to memorize the same set of things in their verbal representations. Recognizing close interconnectedness between the verbal and non-verbal forms of communication, Bergen (2012) put strong emphasis on the role of visuals in meaning making. This scholar supported the above statements explaining that,

Vision is the main way we collect information from the world, so it's fitting that vision is also the sense we most closely associate with the internal life of our minds. We even encode it directly in our language – when we talk about meaning, and about understanding, we actually use language about sight. (Bergen, 2012, p. 49)

So, drawing support to his ideas from neurosciences, Bergen (2012) explained why reading multimodal texts results in faster and more efficient meaning making by humans. This author clarified that,

When people read sentences, they construct visual detailed simulations of the objects that are mentioned. When the picture they subsequently see matches the visual details of their embodied simulation … they are able to respond faster because what they see and what they're mentally simulating are more similar. (Bergen, 2012, p. 54)

Having made the above statement, Bergen (2012) added that it was important for readers to be exposed to exact visual representations of the textual verbal information, for the readers to be able to construct the meaning correctly based on both types of information representations.

One of the major implications suggested by Bergen that might be appropriated by educators is that reading verbal and visual texts in their intercombination is not passive, but active. It engages and involves readers or viewers in active meaning making via activating the brain zones, which are responsible for the actions mentioned in the read and viewed texts. This finding in the field of neurosciences detailed by Bergen (2012) found support in the ideas expressed by Callow (2014).

RESEARCH GAP FOUND

The major conclusion I have drawn from the readings I reviewed above is that the findings by the researchers developing the field of multimodality are strongly intertwined in between themselves, regardless, of the localities, distances, national, or cultural settings, their research participants' ages, genders, and many other factors. Moreover, the authors of the reviewed studies found powerful support in the theories, which are fundamental for my current research as well, i.e., Vygotsky's socio-cultural constructivism and semiotics and social semiotics by Kress and van Leeuwen (1996, 2002).

Nevertheless, I could not find any literature which would detail on the effects from the resources of multimodal ensembles on the Polylingual EAL-speaking college or university students' meaning making. Thus, this review of literature confirmed the anticipated by myself gap in the research and, subsequently, in the literature on possible effects from inclusion of multimodal features in addition to conventional print-based texts on the polylingual EAL speaking college students meaning making. As follows, my review of literature only strengthened my decision to conduct my new research study in the field of multimodality with these learners who are in need of academic support. Moreover, it brought me to realization of an urgent need in research, which targets this large and diverse layer of Domestic and International students, who habitually strive to utilize any available to them forms of language for one simple and sacred goal: to understand and be understood.

Additionally, my literature review empowered my idea about using different modes and ensembles of resources of multimodality as an additional commonly understandable language, that coveted *Lingua Franca* sought by my polylingual grandfather (Jakovlev, 1924b) in the beginning of the previous century. Thanks to the findings by my predecessors in the field of multimodality, which I discussed in this chapter, I understood that beneficial effects from multimodalities on the research participants in the studies by my predecessors may also apply to the polylingual EAL college learners. Thus, it became imperative for me to confirm my guesses, hypothesis, and assumptions via my new research.

REFERENCES

Ajayi, L. (2015). Critical multimodal literacy: How Nigerian female students critique texts and reconstruct unequal social structures. *Journal of Literacy Research*, *47*(2), 216–244. DOI: 10.1177/1086296X15618478

Baildon, M., & Damico, J. S. (2009). How do we know?: Students examine issues of credibility with a complicated multimodal web-based text. *Curriculum Inquiry*, *39*(2), 265–285. DOI: 10.1111/j.1467-873X.2009.00443.x

Bergen, B. K. (2012). *Louder than words: The new science of how the mind makes meaning*. Basic Books.

Callow, J. (2014). *The shape of text to come: How image and text work*. PETAA.

Callow, J., & Zammit, K. (2012). "Where lies your text?" ("Twelfth Night" act I, scene V): Engaging high school students from low socioeconomic backgrounds in reading multimodal texts. *Engineers Australia*, *47*(2), 69–77.

Gellevij, M., van der Meij, H., de Jong, T., & Pieters, J. (2002). Multimodal versus unimodal instruction in a complex learning context. *Journal of Experimental Education*, *70*(3), 215–239. DOI: 10.1080/00220970209599507

Huang, Y. (2023). Open learning environment for multimodal learning based on knowledge base technology. *International Journal of Emerging Technologies in Learning*, *18*(11), 38–51. DOI: 10.3991/ijet.v18i11.39397

Huang, Y. H. (2012). EFL students' views on writing with pictures, sound, and music. *English Teaching & Learning*, *36*(2), 79–123. DOI: 10.6330/ETL.2012.36.2.03

Jacobs, G. E. (2012). Developing multimodal academic literacies among college freshmen. *The Journal of Media Literacy Education*, *4*(3), 244–255.

Jakovlev, P. F. (1924b). Радиотелефония и международный язык [Wireless telephony and international language]. *Radiolyubitel* [Radio-Amateur], *1*(5), p. 71. http://archive.radio.ru/web/1924/05/008/

Jewitt, C., & Kress, G. R. (2003). *Multimodal literacy*. P. Lang.

Jimenez, L. M., & Meyer, C. K. (2016). First impressions matter: Navigating graphic novels utilizing linguistic, visual, and spatial resources. *Journal of Literacy Research*, *48*(4), 423–447. DOI: 10.1177/1086296X16677955

Kress, G., & van Leeuwen, T. (1996). *Reading images: The grammar of visual design*. Routledge.

Kress, G., & van Leeuwen, T. (2002). Colour as a semiotic mode: Notes for a grammar of colour. *Visual Communication, 1*(3), 333–354. DOI: 10.1177/147035720200100306

McNeill, D. (1992). *Hand and mind: What gestures reveal about thought.* University of Chicago Press.

Millard, J. (May *2006*). *eUSER conceptual and analytical framework.* Part D: e-Government, a deliverable of the European Commission financed eUSER project.

Miller, S. M. (2013). A research metasynthesis on digital video composing in classrooms: An evidence-based framework toward a pedagogy for embodied learning. *Journal of Literacy Research, 45*(4), 386–430. DOI: 10.1177/1086296X13504867

Molyneux, P., & Godinho, S. (2012). "This Is My Thing!": Middle years students' engagement and learning using digital resources. *Australasian Journal of Educational Technology, 28*(8), 1466–1486. DOI: 10.14742/ajet.782

Norris, S. (2004). *Analyzing multimodal interaction: A methodological framework.* Routledge. DOI: 10.4324/9780203379493

Paivio, A. (1969). Mental imagery in associative learning and memory. *Psychological Review, 76*(3), 241–263. DOI: 10.1037/h0027272

Pantaleo, S. (2012a). Exploring grade 7 students' responses to Shaun Tan's "The Red Tree.". *Children's Literature in Education, 43*(1), 51–71. DOI: 10.1007/s10583-011-9156-x

Pantaleo, S. (2012b). Meaning-making with colour in multimodal texts: An 11-year-old student's purposeful "doing.". *Literacy, 46*(3), 147–155. DOI: 10.1111/j.1741-4369.2012.00664.x

Schunk, D. H. (2008). *Learning theories: An educational perspective* (6th ed.). Pearson.

Schunk, D. H. (2019). *Learning theories: An educational perspective* (8th ed.). Pearson.

Serafini, F. (2011). Expanding perspectives for comprehending visual images in multimodal texts. *Journal of Adolescent & Adult Literacy, 54*(5), 342–350. DOI: 10.1598/JAAL.54.5.4

Serafini, F. (2014). *Reading the visual: An introduction to teaching multimodal literacy.* Teachers College Press.

Stein, P. (2008). Rethinking resources in the ESL classroom. Rethinking resources: Multimodal pedagogies in the ESL classroom. *TESOL Quarterly*, *34*(2), 333–336. DOI: 10.2307/3587958

Stein, P. (2012). *Multimodal pedagogies in diverse classrooms: Representations, rights and resources*. Routledge.

Vygotsky, L. S. (1978). *Mind in society: The development of higher psychological processes*. Harvard University Press.

Vygotsky, L. S. (1987). *The collected works of L. S. Vygotsky: Vol. 1. Problems of general psychology, including the volume thinking and speech* (R. W. Rieber & A. S. Carton, Eds., Trans. N. Minick). New York: Plenum.

Wang, M. (2011). Using multimodal presentation software and peer group discussion in learning English as a Second Language. *Australasian Journal of Educational Technology*, *27*(6), 907–923. DOI: 10.14742/ajet.920

Wang, M. (2022). The cultivation of students' multiple practical ability under the multimodal blended teaching mode. *International Journal of Emerging Technologies in Learning*, *17*(12), 106–120. DOI: 10.3991/ijet.v17i12.32087

Chapter 5
Designing the New Study

ABSTRACT

In this chapter, I will provide my detailed report on the processes involved in designing my study. So, I will not only detail the qualitative method, which I used for designing and conducting this current project, but will also reflect on many aspects accompanying this work. To be more specific, I will describe my role as a researcher, the site I selected for my study, recruitment of participants, and the further research processes. I will explain how I collected data and which exactly data was of high importance for this study. Besides explaining the method and design used for this study, I will outline and describe the major tasks, which the participants were offered to perform. Most certainly, I will address the principles according to which I analyzed the collected data. I will also mention the publications by the founding fathers of the qualitative methods, whose work I used as guidance to ensure trustworthiness of my findings, and the steps I undertook to avoid possible biases and ensure reliability of my study.

CHOICE OF METHOD

Though I stated my research questions in the introductory chapter of this book, I will help my readers to recollect them. The first question I aimed to answer via my research was: In what ways does inclusion of multimodal resources in combination with traditional print-based text assist polylingual EAL speaking college students' reading comprehension? The second question was concerned with the participants perceptions: What are polylingual EAL speaking college students' perceptions of working with multimodal texts? The third research question was concerned with the choice of resources by students. So, I wondered which multimodal resources do polylingual EAL speaking college students find most helpful, moderately helpful, and least helpful in the process of reading the text supported by features of multimodality? I also posed an additional question of my researcher interest; it was concerning the

DOI: 10.4018/979-8-3373-3426-4.ch005

role of the diverse resources of multimodal ensembles in the participants' meaning making. Striving to answer my research questions, I designed and conducted a qualitative case study according to the qualitative research traditions proposed and established by the iconic authors in the field (i.e, Creswell, 2007; Ely et al., 1994; Glesne, 2010; Glesne & Peshkin, 1992; Seidman, 2013; Spradley, 1980).

As soon as I secured the Institutional Review Board (IRB) approval, I started recruiting my prospective subjects. According to my plan, I set the goal to involve in this new project several brand new to my studies polylingual EAL speaking college students, the ones who had never taken part in my previous projects. For this purpose, I developed colorful and informative flyers and pinned them to the bulletin boards in all campus buildings at one public university in a Northeastern state in the United States. The flyer briefly detailed my project's major purpose and its expected benefits to the generations of learners. It also explained that I sought to recruit in my study either Domestic or International Polylingual English as an Additional language university students. My flyer also contained information on the time to be spent in this project, my contact email address, and a note on incentives for the participants.

As this research was far not my first qualitative case study concerning effects from multimodality, but one in a series of such, I will cite below an excerpt from my previously published article where I detailed on sampling,

> *According to Creswell (2007), it is oftentimes irrelevant to the study objectives to recruit and sample numerous participants while aiming to reach saturation. Purposeful sampling may be considered complete once the diversity of subjects in the sample has been achieved, thus, may result in the maximum variation. (Gould-Yakovleva, 2023a, p. 39)*

My sampling activity resulted in recruitment of eleven highly diverse university students all of whom were EAL speakers with high proficiency in the English as an Additional language. Each student in this sample reported different levels of proficiency in other languages they studied, could speak, or understand. Though I received some more emails from the students who were willing to take part in this project, I decided to pause the recruitment activity when, as per Creswell (2007), saturation was achieved.

According to my research design, I aimed to collect data from multiple sources, such as artifacts in the form of hard copies of the researcher-developed surveys and reflective questionnaires, semi-structured individual participant interviews and the hard copies of comprehension assessments, which my participants were supposed to complete upon having read the texts I selected to use in this project. I also collected data via taking different types of notes (e.g., field notes, site and participant observation notes, analytic memos). Further, in this book, I will describe all my research processes in the following chapters. Meanwhile, I will describe my role as the researcher.

RESEARCHER'S ROLE

Importantly, I was the primary investigator and the only researcher in this study. Thus, I took all roles to perform in this project: I selected the topic and theme to investigate, identified the research gap, developed research questions, designed, and create research instruments, i.e., interview questions, surveys, and questionnaires. Later, I selected and evaluated artifacts for this study. No one else was involved in data collection where, per Creswell's guidelines, I assembled all my artifacts (i.e., copies of comprehension tests, surveys, and reflective questionnaires, transcripts of the interviews, field notes, and memos, and the notes from my site and participant observations).

Further, I need to detail that I wrote analytic memos and observation notes with fidelity throughout the entire study. Meticulously and thoughtfully, I planned, organized, and conducted all my research processes. I tried to take care of every detail, starting from the IRB protocol, and all the involved consent forms, recruitment conversations, administration of every project task, interviewing participants, audio-recording and transcribing the interviews, and surveying the participating students. Being wholeheartedly immersed in my work, I tried to stay sharp as a hawk to not miss any slightest detail. For example, the coded data were stored securely at a specific location, and the master codes with the personal numbers and pseudonyms assigned to every participant were coded in such way that even if hacked, the coded information would not be understandable to anyone, but myself. For this purpose, I utilized all available to me languages in their intercombination and abbreviated forms. Additionally, I used signs, symbols, color-codes, and other signifiers developed for this research, with their meaning known exclusively to myself. All private, personal, and official names provided in the artifacts, interviews, surveys, and observation notes have been most definitely changed for pseudonyms or numbers. All this work was done for my participants' peace of mind as well as their identity security purposes.

The fact that years ago, during the times of my undergraduate and, subsequently, graduate studies, I was a part of the investigated population of polylingual English as an Additional Language speakers, helped me, as the researcher and interviewer to get closer connected with my study participants. Most certainly, was I aware of the problems of this type of student population, as I, once upon a time, was an insider of this learner group.

Subsequently, though, the above fact might have resulted in some biases, which would be highly undesirable. Thus, it was extremely important for me to guard against any possible biases and subjectivities as cautioned by Corrine Glesne (2010) and Johnny Saldaña (2013); so I did.

RECRUITING PARTICIPANTS

Though I had briefly mentioned my target research population, I will detail some more on my recruitment activity. For this project, I aimed to recruit exactly polylingual EAL speaking university students. This is why I had to reject the applications to participate in my project from some recent graduates. Neither could I accept any prospective students who had no university or college experiences yet. One of the conditions was that all participants in this study needed to be above the age of 18 years old. As the result, out of all people who showed interest in participating in this research, I selected eleven polylingual EAL speaking university students, who came from different educational and cultural backgrounds. Importantly, I aimed for the population of students with sufficient English Language proficiency, so that all participants were able to understand the language of the consent form, the texts and the test questions, audio- and video-materials, as well as the survey, reflective questionnaires, and interview questions. To ensure sufficient level of the English language proficiency, I targeted predominantly the students who got their Graduate Assistant positions at the university or domestic undergraduate or graduate students in good academic standing. The fact of obtaining a graduate assistantship at the university and maintaining good academic standing served as an indicator of a sufficient level of proficiency in the English language.

Initially, I tried to share the information on my prospective project by word of mouth. Yet, spreading the flyers or the information sheets, which included my invitation to participate in this research and provided general information on its purpose, significance, and expected benefits, helped the most. The university students could see the bright and attractive flyers on practically every billboard, so many of them reached out to me quite fast. When contacted, I talked and provided more clarifications to my potential research participants who showed interest to participate and wanted to learn more about this study. According to my principles, which read, "Every work needs to be acknowledged," I offered each research participant some compensation in the form of a gift card to one of the local restaurants in the amount of ten dollars per every hour of their work in my project. All hours combined might allow each participant to go out for lunch or dinner to a reputable restaurant and even take a friend with them if desired. Most importantly, I explained to my potential participants their rights within this project. Following the IRB Human

Subjects protocol, I let the students know they could choose to withdraw from this study at any time with no questions asked, but would still be compensated for their time spent working on this project's tasks.

PROJECT TASKS

I anticipate my readers, just like my research participants, may be eager to learn what work needed to be done within this research. Overall, the project, as planned, took two days for each individual participant, excluding the day(s) when I engaged potential participants in informal dialogues with the purpose to understand whether they might qualify and be interested to participate in my study. I marked the recruitment day as Day 0 and did not count it is a day within the project due to the unofficial and exploratory nature of my conversations with the recruited students. Potential recruits were not compensated for this initial conversation with the researcher. Here is the breakout of the research tasks by day:

Day 0 - Recruitment Day

1) Listen to investigator's explanations of the goals and procedures of this project
2) When decided to participate, read and sign the Consent Form in the presence of at least one witness, who will sign this form too
3) Ask any questions about this project
4) Schedule the days and times for Day 1 and Day 2 procedures.

Day 1

1) Receive a copy of the Consent Form signed by self as the participant, by the investigator, and one witness
2) Complete the brief Demographic Informational Survey in writing
3) Read a traditional print-based text, Text 1 (Prologue and an excerpt from Act I Scene I from *Romeo and Juliet* by Shakespeare (1597)) without any multimodal support, and attempt to answer comprehension questions to the Text 1
4) Reflect on the working processes in writing via answering *After Reading Text 1 Reflective Questions*
5) Read a traditional print-based text, Text 2 (Act II Scene II from *Romeo and Juliet* by Shakespeare), listen to the audio-recording of the Text 2, attempt to answer comprehension questions to the Text 2
6) Reflect on the working processes in writing via answering After Reading Text 2 Reflective Questions

7) Give an individual interview to the investigator about your perceptions of working with the text with audio support versus the one without any support.

Day 2

1) Read Text 3 (Act I Scene IV from *Romeo and Juliet* by Shakespeare), watch a video with sound (Zeffirelli, 1968) to the text, and try to answer comprehension questions to this Text 3
2) Reflect on the working processes in writing via answering *After Reading* Text 3 *Reflective Questions*
3) Give an individual interview to the investigator about your perceptions of working with the Text 3 with video and audio support. (See *Table 1* below for a concise overview of the tasks to be performed by research participants within this project).

Table 1. Tasks performed by research participants within this project

Name of Instrument/Artifact	To be used on	Mode
0. Consent Form	Day 0	Written
1. Demographic Informational Survey	Day I	Written
2. Text I (no support), Comprehension Questions	Day I	Written
3. After Reading Text 1 Reflective Questions	Day I	Written
4. Text II (Audio support), Comprehension Questions	Day I	Written
5. After Reading Text 2 Reflective Questions	Day I	Written
6. First Interview	Day I	Oral
7. Text III (Video support), Comprehension Questions	Day II	Written
8. After Reading Text 3 Reflective Questions	Day II	Written
9. Second Interview	Day II	Oral

"WHAT'S FIRST, WHAT'S NEXT?"

As there were multiple tasks to perform on each day within this project, I anticipated possible confusion in participating students about the sequence and flow of the tasks. I did not believe it might be effective to provide my participants with a hard copy of the table with research tasks shown above (See Table 1 above for the overview of the project tasks). Most likely, it would take students some additional time and effort for reading and discerning through the content of Table 1, which might have resulted in asking even more questions, and seeking further clarifications on what exactly and how tasks needed to be done. And when clarified, it might still be a problem for students to memorize all the information on all steps in the process at the first exposure.

Yet, my primary task was to not overwhelm my research participants with the lengthy detailed description of all the tasks to be performed by them within this study. It was equally important for me to formulate the directions to students in such a way that they could grasp the essence of the message with full understanding of the work load for them to anticipate. Least of all would I want to perplex the participating students. So, I aimed to make it easy for my research participants to comprehend and memorize the steps and the tasks they needed to complete in this project. With this purpose, I paraphrased the information about the work to be done and put it in easy and simple words.

Prior to exposing each participant to each of the texts, I orally provided brief and easily understandable directions. Please, see Table 2 below for the directions given to participants; yet, do not misunderstand: the listed are only the steps to follow, but not my exact speeches addressed to the students. I talked in a quiet and friendly tone, while my speech was slightly slowed done. I also assured the students that I would be providing guidance to them on the go, so they were able to smoothly transition from one task to another without fearing to forget what to do first and how to proceed next. And, certainly, I did assist my participants with catering all the working materials in a non-intrusive, quiet, and timely manner.

Table 2. Directions given to participants

Text 1 Without Any Support	Text 2 with Audio Support	Text 3 with Video and Sound Support
Pre-read	Pre-read	Pre-read
	Listen	Watch
Re-read	Re-read	Re-read
Answer comprehension questions to the text	Answer comprehension questions to the text	Answer comprehension questions to the text
Complete survey	Complete survey	Complete survey
Take a break and proceed to Text 2	Give interview	Give interview

Upon having received my directions, most students asked with a combination of surprise and relief in their voice tones, "That's it?" I heard this phrase from practically all the participants prior to the start of their working. The ease with which the students asked me to validate their understanding of the work to be done indicated that they clearly understood the amount and the nature of work to be completed for this project.

As I mentioned above, I chose to follow Creswell's (2007) guidelines, while collecting the data from multiple sources. For obtaining some numeric information on my participants' comprehension levels, I relied on the hard copies of print-based texts accompanied with comprehension tests. While for a deeper insight in my participants' perceptions, I took into consideration their answers to the questions in the surveys and questionnaires. Yet, my participants' sincerity and the emotional side of their perceptions were revealed to me during the semi-structured individual interviews. When conversing with each participant, I tried to keep eye contact with each of them and help their speeches flow. Simultaneously, I jotted down different types of notes (e.g., field notes, analytical memos, site, and participant observation notes) to help save every important moment.

My readers are probably curious to learn about the readings and multimodal materials students read when in this project. In the following section of this chapter, I will describe in detail the texts I offered to my research participants to read and decipher.

TEXTS

In this subsection, I will provide more details about the texts used in this project. First, I selected three texts from Shakespeare's play *Romeo and Juliet* to be used for this research. Text 1, which was offered to participants to read without any multimodal support was an excerpt from Act II Scene II. Text 2, which was supported with an audio recording of this very text was a portion from Act I Scene IV. And Text 3, which was supported with a video and sound was Act I Scene I. I found multimodal support for Text 2 and Text 3 in Zeffirelli's (1968) movie production of *Romeo and Juliet* filmed after this play by Shakespeare.

My readers might ask what moved me to choose the texts from a Shakespearian play. Here is the deal: I chose these readings since the texts in the English language of the 15-16th centuries would be, most probably, equally difficult for practically all participants. In my previously conducted studies, all participants stated they struggled with the Shakespearean English due to their having no prior exposure to the Shakespeare's works. Besides struggling with the language, the EAL students often shared with me they felt more confident with the contemporary expository or narrative texts. Yet, it was harder for them to make the meaning of the unpredictably developing interpersonal dialogues. In particular, the participants in my previously conducted studies shared it was puzzling to them to sequence or anticipate reactions of each conversation member. The insights from my previously conducted studies, confirmed my choice of Shakespearian texts as the ones equally new and complex for all participants.

There was also another important factor which supported my choice of the selected texts. As I anticipated, the topics raised by Shakespeare in his *Romeo and Juliet* were of high significance and of great interest to the young people. The very romantic theme of pure and devoted love topped the list of the other inherent to human beings topics of conflict, feud, compassion, helpfulness, resilience, rejection, standing for one's own, to name just a few. I anticipated my project participants might be able to closely relate to the problems discussed in the story of Romeo and Juliet; thus, they might be higher motivated in reading and understanding the selected excerpts from this play. Most of the students had superficial familiarity with just some major highlights of the story in this play. Some students heard before that it was a story of love between two young people, whose families were strongly against their relationship. Thus, this type of a story, as I hoped, might hook my participants' interest and desire to understand each of the read fragments in depth. So, regardless of the difficulty of the language, the above factors had the potential to contribute to the participants' engagement with this project's tasks.

Another important factor I considered while selecting the readings was presence of challenge. My major objective for this project's task was to send my participants on a quest, i.e., to challenge them with the highly complex to them readings. The very factor of ease would not have served the purpose of this project, which was to find the means to assist polylingual EAL college-level students with their deeper reading comprehension of challenging texts.

One more factor asks to be clarified. As one could imagine, each of the participating students might have had their individual background knowledge in their specific fields of study, for example, Medical Sciences, Physics, Space Engineering, Biology, or Ecology, etc. So, to ensure equal complexity level of the readings for all participants, I had to prevent the research tasks from being more familiar to some of the subjects, while new to some others. This thought shaped my final decision to select the classical texts, written in the dialogic genre, in the 15-16th century Shakespearean English.

There was yet another condition to take in consideration: Shakespeare's plays were not quite intended for reading. Initially, the works by this playwright were meant for performing by actors on the theatre stage. This historic and literary fact allowed my participants to employ their imagination when reading Shakespearian texts. Additionally, these students might find enjoyment in listening to the audio and watching the video recordings of some scenes from *Romeo and Juliet*; thus, my participants might develop a stronger interest in comprehending the meaning confined in Shakespearean texts.

READABILITY LEVELS

To ensure maximal similarity of the complexity of the texts used in this project, I checked their readability levels. I utilized Flesh Reading Ease Test (Flesh, 1949) and Flesh-Kincaid Grade Level Test (Kincaid et al., 1975). Flesh Reading Ease Test was used to identify reading ease of the three texts used in this study, while Flesh-Kincaid Grade Level Test was performed to identify the grade level of each of the three texts. Both tests measured average length of sentences and average number of syllables in the words within each of the three texts (See *Table 3* below for comparison of the results of the Reading Ease and Flesh-Kinkaid Grade Level tests).

Table 3. Results of reading ease and readability tests of text 1, text 2, and text 3 used in this project

	Text 1 Act II Scene II	**Text 2 Act I Scene IV**	**Text 3 Act I Scene I**
Sentences per Paragraph	1.0	1.2	1.3
Flesh Reading Ease	96.8	92.5	91.0
Flesh-Kincaid Grade Level	1.8	1.9	2.0

In this way, I identified that all three texts had approximately equal number of sentences per a paragraph. The reading ease coefficient of each of them was within a very close range, which was between 91 and 96.8. While the grade-level coefficient of average syllables per word equaled 1.8-2.0, which indicated that all three texts were on very close and practically similar readability levels.

REFERENCES

Creswell, J. W. (2007). *Qualitative inquiry and research design: Choosing among five traditions*. Sage Publications.

Ely, M., Anzul, M., Friedman, T., Garner, D., & Steinmetz, A. M. (1994). *Doing qualitative research: Circles within circles*. The Palmer Press.

Flesh, R. (1949). *The art of readable writing*. Harper.

Glesne, C. (2010). *Becoming qualitative researchers* (4th ed.). Longman.

Glesne, C., & Peshkin, A. (1992). *Becoming qualitative researchers: An introduction*. Longman.

Gould-Yakovleva, O. (2023a). Seeking remedy for improving international college students' reading comprehension: A qualitative case study on using multimodality for English language learning. *International Journal of Higher Education Pedagogies*, *4*(4), 33–54. DOI: 10.33422/ijhep.v4i4.599

Kincaid, J. P., Fishburne, R. P., Rogers, R. L., & Chissom, B. S. (1975). *Derivation of new readability formulas (automated readability index, fog count, and Flesch reading ease formula) for navy enlisted personnel.* (PDF)*(Report). Naval Air Station Memphis: Chief of Naval Technical Training. Research Branch Report 8–75.* Retrieved March 15, 2024.

Saldaña, J. (2013). *The coding manual for qualitative researchers*. Sage Publications.

Seidman, I. E. (2013). *Interviewing as qualitative research* (4th ed.). Teachers College Press.

Shakespeare, W. (1597). *Romeo and Juliet.*

Spradley, J. P. (1980). *Participant observation*. Holt, Rinehart and Winston.

Zeffirelli, F. (1968). *Romeo and Juliet.* Paramount Pictures. https://www.youtube.com/watch?v=VCe0nzdD76k

Chapter 6
Data Collection and Analyses

ABSTRACT

In this chapter, I will provide my detailed report on the data collection processes and their analyses. I will start with description of the materials offered to participants within this project, such as texts for unimodal and multimodal reading, researcher-developed surveys and questionnaires, audio- and video-materials, and interview structure. Following this information, I will clarify importance of thoughtful site selection and describe my endeavors to accommodate my research participants. I will also provide a detailed picture of all my observational and note-taking work and explain its importance. Further, in the sections on the data analysis, I will detail on every type of my analytical work, where the data from multiple sources were needed for triangulation purposes. Next, I will explain why and how I decided to use the affordances of the Artificial Intelligence (AI) for analyzing the interview data. Apparently, the report of the findings from the interviews, as performed by a machine intellect, can be considered fully unbiassed.

COMPREHENSION TESTS

Each of the above texts was followed by comprehension assessment, which was one of the major measurement instruments in this project. Every test was followed by six comprehension test questions the purpose of which was to evaluate how well (or not well) each student-participant understood the content of the text. Each set of predominantly inferential questions were based on the content of the corresponding text. While selecting the readings for this research, I evaluated them for logical comprehensibility and made sure it was possible to answer the comprehension questions to these texts via making the meaning from the content of these readings, without having any prior exposure to or any knowledge of this Shakespearian (1597)

DOI: 10.4018/979-8-3373-3426-4.ch006

play, i.e., without having read the play or watched the *Romeo and Juliet* production (Zeffirelli, 1968). Still, as I anticipated, the comprehension questions to the texts might have presented a serious challenge for my culturally diverse polylingual EAL speaking research participants.

Importantly, collecting numeric data in the form of the test scores was of an immense value for this study. As per Maxwell (2004), quantitative data helps researchers to adequately present evidence, which is imperative for supporting interpretation of findings (p. 479).

SURVEYS

Another significant instrument in this study were my researcher-developed Demographic Informational Surveys (See the questions from the Demographic Informational Surveys in *Appendix A*). These surveys were offered to participants to complete in the print-based hard copies. Students needed to fill in these The Demographic Informational Surveys by hand, individually, and independently. The initial demographic survey was planned as the before-reading task and contained 11 questions. Importantly, participants were offered a choice: to provide their brief or extended answers to the survey questions. Additionally, students were explained that they had an option to omit any answers to any of the survey questions if they did not feel comfortable to discuss some parts of their demographic information (e.g., home country, mother tongue, or their reading habits).

QUESTIONNAIRES

Next significant instrument in this study were the developed by myself After-Reading Reflective Questionnaires (See the questions from the After-Reading Reflective Questionnaires in *Appendix A).* These post-reading reflections were planned to be administered to participants in writing as well. Participants were to read these questionnaires and respond individually and independently. These post-reading assessments were scheduled for after-reading activity, to be completed after reading the print-based Text 1, and after working with the audio-supported print-based Text 2, as well as after reading and watching video with sound, which supported the print-based Text 3.

I will touch the bases of the questions, which the participants needed to answer. Questionnaire 1 contained three multiple choice questions, where the last one prompted the students to select from 19 unimodal, i.e., printed text-based reading and test-taking strategies. Students were asked to mark only those strategies which they utilized while working on print-based Text 1, which had no support. They also needed to answer some comprehension test-questions to this text. Participants were explained that they might add some more strategies to the existing list on condition they used those additional strategies when working on this project's tasks.

Subsequently, Questionnaires 2 and 3 included two more question sets each, which were concerned with working with multimodal texts. Thus, students were supposed to mark not only the print-based, unimodal strategies they used during reading and making the meaning of Texts 2 and Text 3, but also the multimodal ones, as Text 2 was supported with an audio recording, while Text 3 was accompanied with a video and the soundtrack.

INTERVIEWS

Yet, the major instruments in this qualitative case study were two semi-structured interviews. Every participant was interviewed independently and individually (Seidman, 2013). Within this project, every person gave the interview twice. The first interview took place on Day 1, as the final task for the first day's work in this project, while the second interview took place at the end of the entire project work for each of my research participants on Day 2. Every interview consisted of two sections, Section A and Section B (See interview questions in *Appendix B*), where all interview questions were open-ended to foster critical thinking.

Overall, Interview 1 contained 16 open-ended questions. The first interview included some ice-breaking questions about participants' home countries and their educational experiences in the U.S. and abroad. Those initial questions were followed by the ones concerned with participants' reading habits, preferences, and skills. Importantly, Section A of Interview 1 had several questions, which were specifically concerned with participants' perceptions of their working with Text 1 (no support). Section B of Interview 1 contained questions about participants' perceptions of their working with Text 2 supported with an audio and answering comprehension test questions to this text.

The second interview consisted of 12 questions. Nine of them in Section A of Interview 2 were concerned with participants' perceptions of their working with Text 3, which had video with sound support. Subsequently, these questions were extended by asking students to compare and or contrast all their experiences working with the video-with-sound-supported Text 3, audio-supported Text 2, and Text 1, which had no support at all. The purpose of this investigation was to identify most helpful means of multimodality and reading strategies, which assisted the students the most with their meaning making of the print-based texts supported by features of multimodality and answering comprehension test questions to the texts within this project. Section B of Interview 2 had three questions about the participants' digital and print-based reading habits, skills, and preferences.

Upon having conducted all interviews, I transcribed the participants' speeches, and analyzed the data from participants' revelations as suggested by Creswell (2007), Glesne (2010), and Glesne and Peshkin (1992). I will further address my data analysis processes in the Data Analysis Processes section of this chapter. Meanwhile, I will detail on my collection of the observational data, which was accompanied by note-taking and memoing in accordance with Miles & Huberman (1984) advice.

OBSERVATIONS AND NOTES

Though my research design included quite a collection of artifacts, importance of note-taking for qualitative research cannot be overlooked. So, I collected the data via observing and taking notes throughout this entire project. These were Field Notes and Site Observation Notes, Marginal Notes, and *Analytical Memos*, just as advised by the founding fathers of the qualitative method (e.g., Creswell, 2007; Miles & Huberman, 1984; Spradley, 1980). So, why was this portion of my researcher's work so significant? – The answer to this question may be of high significance and great help to beginning researchers. The fact is, it is close to impossible to retain in the long-term memory and be able to retrieve that enormous amount of information, which may be visually observed, heard, caught by the corner of the researcher's eye, sensed intuitively, or inferred from all the above. Thus, note-taking skill and endeavor is crucially important for qualitative research.

Thus, I started taking my Field Notes at the very start of this project and continued this field work during the entire period. I jotted down my memos even when I attempted to recruit potential participants for my study. Additionally, I often implemented the mental note-taking (Lofland & Lofland, 1995) during this study. This work was performed at the times when it seemed not appropriate to be note-taking while conversing with people as this action might have disrupted or even ruined a dialogue. Importantly, as per Bakhtin (1981), a dialogue is a genuine and sincere conversation; if not, it may change to a meager verbal exchange. At those moments, I strongly relied on my memorization skills and tried to save in my memory every meaningful detail, such as tone of voice, facial expressions, postures, positions of the head, and in the space. All this audible and visual information helped me to deeper understand the personalities of my interlocutors, their intentions, motivation, as well as the levels of their individual language mastery, and many other important to this research aspects. Later, I jotted down my mental notes by hand or digitally and reflected in my researcher's journal on the details of my informal conversations with my potential participants. I continued utilizing this mental note-taking method when in the active phase of my project as well.

GRAND TOURS

In addition to these highly valuable participant observations, I conducted three Grand Tour Observations as recommended by Spradley (1980). During and shortly after each of the three tours, I wrote my Descriptive Notes (Glesne, 2010). This work helped me outline some specific features of my research site. The purpose of the Research Site Observation Notes was for me to select most appropriate locations within the university, where my research participants might feel comfortable to engage in this projects' tasks as well as in interviews and conversations with the researcher. For this purpose, I walked through most of the campus buildings and took pictures with my iPhone with the subsequent data transfer to my mac for storage. It was important to not capture any people who were passing by or sitting in the multiple work or relaxation areas inside these buildings. So, in the sake of these persons' peace of mind, I made sure my phone camera did not focus on them. And, of course, I avoided overly crowded and noisy spaces. In this way, I built-up my Researcher-Created Visual Data (Glesne, 2010, p. 80).

Later, at the serenity of my home office or university office, I described in pen or digitally all the observed mini-sites within the larger research site. Then, I matched my descriptive notes with the photos I took. Based on the above data, I had to regretfully decline some of the architecturally splendid or artistically designed settings, which might have been highly attractive for my future participants to visit. Yet, some of those settings were extremely popular among the university students; thus, they were crowded or looked like high-traffic passages. So, I considered all those data, reflected in my Researcher-Created Visual Data and Site Observation Notes when planning on the spots with the minimal distracting factors for my potential research participants.

I will also shed some light on another important aspect of arranging meetings with each research participant. Based on my Researcher-Created Visual Data and Site Observation Notes, I had to refuse from my initial idea to conduct my study in one of the multiple university libraries. After having conducted my second Grand Tour, I concluded that some of my participants might become excited or vocal during interviews. Some might express their emotions or laugh; and I needed to arrange for them this freedom of expression. I also had a similar concern about playing the audio and the video during this research. Some participants might ask to increase the sound. So, based on my second Grand Tour data, I identified some potential risks of interruption from the library workers. Quite understandably, the loud sounds might disrupt the library operations. And the perspective for my subjects to be interrupted and restricted might equally disrupt my research processes. Eventually, my endeavors in the third Grand Tour reflected in the new round of the Site Observation Notes allowed me to identify some close-to-ideal sites for this project.

SELECTED SITES

As the result of the three Grand Tours, I selected several half-enclosed reading areas, which had some soft and comfortable chairs or sofas and side tables or desks. These areas were available on practically every floor in every building. There was also an option to reserve an office for certain hours to ensure that no intrusion could possibly interrupt my conversations with my participants or their speeches during interviews. Yet, there was one significant factor to consider; it was each participant's comfort level. The above idea prevented me from scheduling individual sessions with each of my research participants in an isolated and enclosed space. Intuitively, I understood that being confined in an unknown to a person closed space, one on one with a researcher might have affected my participants, interfere with, and reflect on their work.

My concern deserves to be further explained. For this purpose, I ask my readers to try to envision selves in the shoes of my subjects. Most of the students who volunteered to participate in my study were new to the United States. Their lack of familiarity with our country and people might bring them to a feeling and state of uncertainty and apprehension. So, I realized that the frames of a small office space might have led them to feeling uncomfortable.

As a caring researcher, I had to be very careful to not stress my research participants. So, upon having conducted my three Grand Observational Tours, I selected for my project a large office with multiple rooms and cubicles. When visiting that office, a new comer would notice some people: the university professors or their Graduate Assistants working at their computer stations in different cubicles and enclosures within that large office space. Additionally, that site included a large, centrally located, and commonly accessible area. So, the entire office presented a spacious, "inhabited" quarters with laterally-located semi-enclosed spaces. Several ceiling-height dividers separated the large common area and the smaller individual rooms. Comparably, this layout strongly reminded me of a structure of a traditional Japanese home interior where some privacy is a possibility, but complete isolation is out of question. So, the cubicle I occupied opened into the hallway leading to the adjacent work spaces. This half-openness also reduced the impression of being "caged" within an enclosed and limited space. Thus, my participants' awareness of the presence of other workers on the site might help with eliminating of a potential feeling of isolation discomfort.

Most certainly, I prepared all my equipment and printed the research materials prior to every participant's arrival to this site. I arranged all my assets on two large desks and moved in two soft chairs. Before every participant's arrival, I organized their work place: I sorted, numbered, and lined up in order all working copies papers on the participant's desk. I brought in my recording devices, computer, and speakers. All this work kept me immersed in the caring researcher stance, so I went even further: I fetched some soft drinks and snacks, just in case, if my students-participants missed their lunch. To sum up the above, I tried my best in arranging my prospective research site, especially the student work station. I wanted to send my participants the message, "Everything is prepared. If you are ready, let us start working."

PARTICIPANT OBSERVATIONS

Importantly, besides Field Notes and *Site Observation Notes*, the Participant Observation Notes present a highly significant portion in this study's data collection process. Whenever possible, I took my notes; yet, predominantly, in the absence of my research participants. When in their presence, I aimed to closely watch my research participants' faces and postures during their communicating with me or working with the print-based or multimodal texts: Text 1 (print-based only, with no support), Text 2 (print-based text with audio support), and Text 3 (print-based text with video and audio support). Observing the students' behaviors while their answering comprehension test questions to the texts was equally important. During my observations and in the process of taking my post-observational notes, I attempted to read and memorize the data collected from the visual information, so I could use it long after the students' departure from the research site.

While in communication with my participants, I had to control my own looks and behaviors as it was important for me to not disclose to my participants my internal analytical thinking processes. So, I tried to not stare directly at the students during their working on the project assignments. Rather than that, I tried to observe them in a covert and non-invasive manner. Most positively, it was important for me to not ruin my professional relationship with the participants. So, it is highly important for a researcher to develop, take, and immerse oneself into this respectful and non-intrusive observational stance, which should be one of the primary tasks of a caring investigator.

Moreover, I developed and appropriated my near-parental stance to both: my research and my study participants. Similarly to a mother who protects her children's sound sleep or their deep engagement in their homework or reading, I cared to prevent and eliminate any possible distractions to my research participants' work for my project. Specifically, I aimed to avoid writing my notes by hand or typing them on my technological devices in between or during observing the participating students' work on answering survey questions and filling-in the after-reading reflective questionnaires (Find Survey questions and After-reading Reflective Questionnaires in *Appendix A*). Instead, I had to rely on my researcher's skills of Mental Note Taking (Lofton & Lofton, 1995) as well as my memorization abilities.

Focused Observations

Talking about observations, it is worth connecting using multimodality as a tool for observing and observational note-taking. Observing participants' emotions, which reflected in their facial expressions and postures was a great tool for me. As a caring researcher, I was prepared to step in the situation and help my participants be a trace of an internal disturbance reflected on their faces. Those could, for example, include test-taking anxiety or rising frustration with the highly complex for some of them tasks. Were that the case, I would try my best to help my participants to mentally relax. The above can be done with the help of some easy questions, which might decrease or eliminate the internal tension at its early stage. In addition to the emotional support, I was ready to remind my participants of a possibility for them to pause working, take a break, or even leave this project. Yet, they would still receive my sincere gratitude for their attempt to participate in my research along with the monetary compensation for the time they spent in this project.

Yet, my major task of an observer was to conduct the Focused Observations (Spradley, 1980). So, I focused on multimodal observing of the non-verbal body language and face-work in my participants. Via these focused multimodal observations, I attempted to understand the information about working habits and skills of each student. Additionally, I tried to evaluate their engagement levels, presence or lack of motivation, and the strength of their efforts. So, I observed and memorized as much as I could. Later, after each encounter with every participant, I wrote down in every detail all the information, which I had observed; so I could analyze it, look for patterns in each individual student's behaviors, or, possibly, patterns in the behaviors by the entire group of my study participants (Glesne, 2010).

Importantly, when writing my notes, I tried to avoid any potential biases and judgmental descriptions of the events, processes, verbal, and non-verbal interactions, and behaviors of the participating students. At all times, I was extremely cautious about not jumping on any assumptions prior to analyzing and triangulating the data collected from multimap sources. Yet, I aimed to write down the observable and audible data; so, I observed without evaluating the people and the events (Glesne, 2010, p. 73). I added my conclusive thoughts and analytic memos to my collection of notes in accordance with Miles and Huberman's (1984) and Saldaña's (2013) principles. Eventually, I collected all my notes in a voluminous binder, my Fieldwork Journal (Spradley, 1980).

DATA ANALYSIS

In contrast to my previously conducted studies, where I analyzed the research data while utilizing researcher-created manual data analysis or used different software for the qualitative data analysis, I implemented a combination of different ways to analyze my data for this current project. As my data collection was quite extensive, I had to break it into portions and scrutinize every part separately prior to triangulating the whole set. Every step in these processes will be described in detail in the Findings section of this book. Nevertheless, in this section of the methodology chapter, I will provide at least some major highlights.

Data Analysis Processes

Upon having completed my data collection, I coded my data using, primarily, the Values Coding proposed by Johnny Saldaña in his 2013 publication *The coding Manual for Qualitative Researchers.* The Values Coding, as viewed by Saldaña is "the application of codes onto qualitative data that reflect a participant's values, attitudes, and beliefs, representing his or her perspectives or worldview" (2013, p. 110). Additionally, I employed the thematic coding proposed by this methodologist. I was looking for recurring themes and patterns in my research participants' interviews. Miles and Huberman (1984) memoing was of great help for me for my re-reading all the interview transcripts and leaving my memos in their margins. I analyzed the data, synthesized the findings (e.g., Ely et al., 1994; Creswell, 2007; Glesne, 2010; Seidman, 2013), and provided implications for researchers and educators. For my readers convenience, I will provide more detailed information on each step in my data analyses while breaking all my data into the sets by the type of collection.

Analyzing Notes and Artifacts

As my data collection started with note-taking, the analysis of these data will be discussed first. So, aiming to answer my research questions, I delved into the, literally, myriads of notes I had taken. I dug over through the Field Notes, Site, and Participant Observation Notes in my Field Journal. I put side by side my notes taken on different days to confirm the results of my observations. The purpose for this type of data analysis was to identify recurring patterns in each of the participant's behaviors as well as in the behavioral characteristics, which, as demonstrated by several of my research participants, they had in common.

So, the above work helped me to better understand the correlation between my subjects' words and my conclusions drawn from my observations. I painstakingly studied the notes, which documented the observable non-verbal language of the subjects and compared them with the notes, where I reflected on their audible oral speeches. My extreme focus on the non-verbal, visible, and audibly readable behaviors, consciously or subconsciously produced by my participants allowed me to draw a conclusion about the sincerity and openness of these students' revelations. This work was extremely important for my study, as I did not want my participants to cater to my research, but expected them to speak out their minds honestly and openly. As one can perceive, honesty and frankness are of a great value for a qualitative researcher who listens to understand the hidden.

From analyzing the observable non-verbal behaviors, I extended my analysis to scrutinizing the audible data, such as tones of the voice, intonations, and some non-verbal sounds in their simultaneous combination with the concurring visual information. Later, I triangulated the visual data recorded in the form of my observational notes with my marginal notes about the audible data, and the data provided by participants in their Demographic Informational Surveys and After-Reading Reflective Questionnaires. This triangulation allowed me to gain a deeper understanding of each participant's inner world as a person, a reading personality, a student, a polylingual, an EAL speaker, and in many more aspects. So, I developed an entire psychological, linguistic, and academic portrait of every subject. The results of this work were highly important for this qualitative case study, which aimed to hear an individual and unique voice of every participant.

Subsequently, I immersed myself in all the data via repetitive re-readings of each individual artifact. While doing so, I matched every individual subject's data set with the rest in the sample. I used this recursive process to gain a deeper understanding of my participants' perceptions, qualities, and characteristics. Was that redundant? – My answer is an absolute No. – Due to my having developed the *solicitudinal stance* (Gould-Yakovleva, 2023a, p. 35), I mutually connected to my participants in my genuine effort to help this student population via my research. So, I put my strongest effort in retaining in my long-term memory every data set, which contained lots of essential for this research information about each of the participants, their work habits and styles, and the reading and working strategies and methods, which they reportedly found beneficial and helpful. After having internalized as much information as possible, I could think and mentally process and reprocess across all these data without the need to constantly check with my dense notes.

As follows, I developed some visual representations of my mental research picture. For this purpose, I created some digital graphic displays of my data. This work not only allowed me to physically see my collection of all data sets, but also verify the findings and the products of my data analyses while making it more efficient and reliable. Besides, the visibility helped to ensure trustworthiness of my concussions, which, otherwise, would need to be blindly trusted, but could not be visually read, verified, and confirmed. So, I summarized the bulk data from the artifacts in tabled form (Creswell, 2007), which allowed me to simultaneously visualize and, importantly, demonstrate both: the information about every participant and the data about the whole sample. I also created visual representations of the data from the After-Reading Reflective Questionnaires in the form of charts and figures. These digital graphic representations of the data allowed me to speed the triangulation processes since all my data were readily available to me in their concise and easy-to-read visual forms.

I did the same with the data collected from the three comprehension tests to Text 1 (no support), Text 2 (audio support), and Text 3 (video with sound support), which were also placed in tables. This work allowed me to see correct and incorrect answers provided by every individual participant on each of the tests. Additionally, each of the three tables displayed the total test scores. Separately, I created a table with the means of correct and incorrect answers to the comprehension test questions to get a whole picture about the performance by the whole group of participants. The results of this work were of the highest importance for this research as they allowed me to triangulate the written and oral data provided by the participants in their interviews, surveys, and questionnaires, via displaying the evidence of the said / heard, observed, and numerically documented.

Analyzing the Interviews

Within this project, I planned to conduct two semi-structured individual interviews with each research participant. I transcribed all audio-recorded interview data using Macintosh transcribing software for audio-recordings. When this machine-work was completed, I proofread and manually corrected every transcript, wherever needed. When finished, I listened to the audio-recordings of my interviews with participants multiple times and manually highlighted in the hard-copy transcripts any changes in each student's intonations, tone of their voice, fluctuations in its pitch, and other non-verbal signifiers. Subsequently, I typed in **bold** the words, phrases, or sentences my interviewees stressed during their speeches. The above work was important for a deeper understanding of the meaning conveyed through the multiple affordances of a human voice in addition to the one comprehensible through the verbal means of their speech. In this way, I analyzed all 22 interviews.

Then, with the purpose to display and be able to more efficiently analyze the bulk multipage data (Miles & Huberman, 1984), which were obtained from the two sets, eleven interviews-strong each, I decided to utilize MAXQDA software (courtesy of MAXQDA - The Art of Data Analysis: Professional Software for Qualitative & Mixed Methods Research. © Verbi Software - Consult - Sozialforshung GmbH - Berlin, Germany. Web: www.maxqda.com).

Through the affordances of this software for qualitative data analysis, I color-coded every new theme with a specific color within the body of every transcribed interview and ran the color-coded transcripts through the MaxQda system. This qualitative data analyzing software allowed me to track the recurring themes, patterns, and values, as perceived and externalized by my participants, in multiple ways. For example, the MaxQda program enabled me to verify whether certain themes (e.g., "multimodality may assist students with memorization" or "multimodality enhances interest in students") and topics (e.g., "exposure to multimodalities activates several brain zones" or "multimodality assists with comprehension") were addressed by each participant only once or multiple times. The above work was important for this research as it allowed me to draw conclusions on significance of every theme to each of my participants. Importantly, this software allowed me to identify whether the themes and topics stressed by one participant were also discussed and marked as important by some other students. The above work simplified my analysis via allowing me to track the frequency of usage of each topic by the participating students.

Next important step in my data analyses was usage of the MaxQda software for visualizing the importance of each of the themes and values for every research participant. With the help of this software, I created visual representations of the time slots, during which each interviewee focused on each of the topics, which they found especially significant for selves. Additionally, via affordances of MaxQda, I was able to develop graphic representations of interview contents in the form of the interview portraits and matrices, which served me as the solid evidence in support of my mental pictures. It also allowed me to draw conclusions on frequence of the major topics, themes, and ideas delivered by participants during their interviews.

Imperative for me as a passionate researcher, usage of MaxQda software helped me to better control against any possible biases and subjectivities, as utilization of the artificial intellect for the data analyses fully excluded the possibility for the machine to be biased. All the above in their intercombination provided me with the alternative means of analysis via the software-created visual representations of the data. Later, in this book, my readers will have multiple chances to read and view all the evidence, which I am discussing in this section.

Multimodal Artifact-Based Analyses

On top of working with all the collected data as I described above, I decided to make an additional step and gain a deeper understanding of the polylingual EAL speaking college students' perceptions and their thinking processes during their reading the multimodal resources, which were added to the traditional print-based Text 2 in the form of an audio and Text 3 in the form of a video with the sound. For this purpose, I conducted two multimodal analyses. The first one I titled *Multimodal Analysis 1: Attempting to Understand Role, Position, and Significance of Visuals within Multimodal Ensembles*. This self-reflective analysis aimed to help me as an analyst to gain a more profound understanding of the role of visuals, which form multimodal ensembles. Next, I conducted the second analysis and titled it *Analysis 2: Visual Language Intermodal Relation Data Analysis*. The purpose of this second analysis was to understand the intermodal relations within multimodal ensembles. As it most often and naturally occurs, viewers or multimodal readers are exposed to whole ensemble, rather than single separate modes of it. These two analyses were of great help to me as a researcher and analyst and of high significance for this research as they enabled me developing a deeper understanding of the effects from multimodalities on meaning making processes in polylingual EAL speaking university students.

Triangulating Across All Data Sets

My deep respect to as well as my profound knowledge of the traditions developed by Creswell (2007), Ely et al. (1994), Glesne (2010), Glesne and Peshkin (1992), and Saldaña (2013) helped me to propel the strenuous work of triangulating large amounts of the collected data. These data collected from the site and participant observations, multiple artifacts, and participant interviews and transcripts, MaxQda-developed visual representations, etc. formed a bulk load, which could be organized only through the prowess of a human intellect, i.e., my own intellectual endeavor. I could not rely on, nor did I have any knowledge of any software, which could dismiss a researcher and complete all his or her analytical work. So, after having synthesized all my data, which was the most demanding and significant task, I started reflecting on all my work in my research report. This was a multi-year work, I should confess. This book is the result of all the above endeavor.

Trustworthiness

One more important note needs to be added before I proceed with reporting my findings. In this section, I will reflect on the matter of trustworthiness. Without this message, my discussion of the methodology would not be complete. To ensure trustworthiness of my research, I made my best effort to follow the postulates by Creswell (2007) and Ely et al. (1994). The latter group of authors, including Margot Ely, Margaret Anzul, Teri Friedman, Dianne Garner and Ann McCormack Steinmetz et al. wrote in their book *Doing Qualitative Research: Circles within Circles,*

> *This concern [with trustworthiness] begins before the first word is written and does not end until the research is completed. The quest is to make the research project credible, produce results that can be trusted, and establish findings that are, to use Lincoln and Guba's phrase, 'worth paying attention to.' (Ely et al., 1994, p. 156)*

So, being strongly dedicated to ensure trustworthiness of my study and to reach the above recommended state, I continuously monitored my own subjectivities and guarded against any potential biases (Glesne, 2010; Glesne & Peshkin, 1992). Zealously I engaged in seeking feedback from my peer scholars at several National and International conferences in the United States and overseas where I presented on different topics and portions of my study. I asked my colleagues and my former professors at my university to read my writings, as recommended by Creswell (2007) and provide me with their honest and merciless feedback, which they did. In response to my requests, I received only positive and supportive feedback, peer-reviews, and comments. My post-presentational conversations and correspondence with my conference audiences also helped me to better guard against possible biases. To my great satisfaction, I have not received any negative or alarming messages from my reviewers. All the above served as solid evidence of my moving in the right direction. So, all the highly valued feedback from my peer-reviewers helped me avoid biases and subjectivities and guided me with ensuring trustworthiness (Glesne, 2010).

Concluding Part I of my book, I need to say that I tried my best to detail every process involved in my study design processes. Now, in the following part of this publication, I will not only report but, most importantly, let my audience read and visualize many steps in my research through the affordances of their multimodal representations. Let multimodality of my current report serve as evidence to how and in what ways this phenomenon may be used for communicating ideas.

REFERENCES

Bakhtin, M. M. (1981). Discourse in the novel. In Holquist, M. (Ed.), *The dialogic imagination: Four essays by M. M. Bakhtin* (pp. 259–422). University of Texas Press.

Creswell, J. W. (2007). *Qualitative inquiry and research design: Choosing among five traditions*. Sage Publications.

Ely, M., Anzul, M., Friedman, T., Garner, D., & Steinmetz, A. M. (1994). *Doing qualitative research: Circles within circles*. The Palmer Press.

Glesne, C. (2010). *Becoming qualitative researchers* (4th ed.). Longman.

Glesne, C., & Peshkin, A. (1992). *Becoming qualitative researchers: An introduction*. Longman.

Gould-Yakovleva, O. (2023a). Seeking remedy for improving international college students' reading comprehension: A qualitative case study on using multimodality for English language learning. *International Journal of Higher Education Pedagogies*, *4*(4), 33–54. DOI: 10.33422/ijhep.v4i4.599

Lofland, J., & Lofland, L. (1995). *Analyzing social settings: A guide to qualitative observation and analysis*. Wadsworth.

MAXQDA. (2021). MAXQDA 2022 [computer software]. Berlin, Germany: VERBI Software. Available from maxqda.com.

Maxwell, J. A. (2010). Using numbers in qualitative research. *Qualitative Inquiry*, *16*(6), 475–482. DOI: 10.1177/1077800410364740

Miles, M. B., & Huberman, A. M. (1984). *Qualitative Data Analysis: A sourcebook of New Methods*. Sage Publications.

Saldaña, J. (2013). *The coding manual for qualitative researchers*. Sage Publications.

Seidman, I. E. (2013). *Interviewing as qualitative research* (4th ed.). Teachers College Press.

Shakespeare, W. (1597). *Romeo and Juliet*.

Spradley, J. P. (1980). *Participant observation*. Holt, Rinehart and Winston.

VERBI Software. (2021). MAXQDA 2022 [computer software]. Berlin, Germany: VERBI Software. Available from maxqda.com.

Zeffirelli, F. (1968). *Romeo and Juliet*. Paramount Pictures. Retrieved from public domain: https://www.youtube.com/watch?v=VCe0nzdD76k

Section 2

Digging Through the Stratums of Unspoken

Chapter 7
People Behind the Numbers

ABSTRACT

It is highly important to understand that most important actors in this research report are the people whose opinions, contemplations, feelings, and ideas matter the most. In Chapter VII, I will introduce the group of students who took part in my research. I will also attempt to show each of them as a scholar and a reading personality. Every participant will be shown as an English language learner and as a reader. As an intermediary, I will let the participating students share with my audiences about their home countries and home-used languages. These students will also detail about their educational paths and plans. Importantly, participants will disclose their reading abilities and preferences, as they view them through the lens of self-assessment.

DEMOGRAPHIC CHARACTERISTICS OF PARTICIPANTS

I will start with introducing my research participants as International students and polylingual EAL speakers. All these students differed by multiple characteristics, including but not limited to the countries of their origin, gender, ethnicity, languages spoken, tongues they were able to understand or studied over their lifetime period, etc. There were five female and six male participants in this sample. As shown in *Table 4* below, there were two female students from China, four males and one female from different geographic and administrative regions of India, one female from Japan, one female from Korea, one male from Saudi Arabia, and one male U.S. citizen, who came originally from Vietnam. Importantly, all participants were born outside of the United States. One male student was brought to this country by his family in his childhood. He was schooled in the United States in grades Kindergarten (K) through college. The rest of the participants arrived in the United States in their

DOI: 10.4018/979-8-3373-3426-4.ch007

college years with the purpose to get advanced education in American universities (See *Table 1* below for number of research participants by country of their origin and mother tongue).

Table 1. Number of research participants by country of origin and mother tongue

Country	**China**	**Japan**	**India**		**Saudi Arabia**	**South Korea**	**Vietnam**
Gender	2 females	1 female	4 males	1 female	1 male	1 female	1 male
Mother	2 Mandarin[2]	1 Japanese	2 Telugu	1 Konkani	1 Arabic[3]	1 Korean	1 Vietnamese
Tongue			1 Hindi				
			1 Malayalam				

It needs to be recognized that all my research participants were highly proficient in the English language. Further on, throughout this paper, I will provide both: participants' names (pseudonyms) and their individual numbers with gender identification, where the letter *f* stands for *females* and *m* stands for *males* (for example, *Anjali #9f* or *Sanjay #1m*). These features might allow readers to match the participants' names in the narrative text within this paper with the abbreviated data placed in figures, tables, and charts.

As shown in *Table 4* above, the participants' mother tongues were: Arabic (Faiz, #11m), Hindi (Prem, #2m), Japanese (Miyuki, #5f), Konkani (Anjali, #9f), Korean (Eun, #8f), Malayalam (Kumar, #6m), Mandarin (Ting, #4f and Mei, #7f)), Telugu (Sanjay, #1m and Vijay, #3m), and Vietnamese (Sang, #10m). When questioned, the Native Mandarin[2] speakers Ting and Mei indicated they did not use the other language spoken in China, the Cantonese language; although, this latter one is being widely spoken in the region they came from and shares some cognates with the Mandarin. So, the Cantonese could not count as an additional language for these students due to their minimal use of it. Yet, I informally considered these persons' exposure to more than one Native language at their home country.

It also needs to be noticed that three participants: two males, Sanjay, #1m and Vijay, #3m and one female, Anjali, # 9f who came from the same administrative unit of India named different languages as their mother tongues. Sang, #10m, the male participant born in Vietnam was raised and educated in the United States. As stated by this person, he perceived himself as a Native American English language speaker. Yet, he had some foreign accent. English was his additional language, which he learned in the United States, while his first language and his mother tongue, which he acquired from his birth in Vietnam was Vietnamese.

I found some variations in terms of when in their life course each of the participants started studying the English language. For example, Faiz, #11m, the male student from Saudi Arabia reported that some English was taught to him starting off his middle school in his home country. Yet, he considered that the profound studies of the English language started for him at the time he got his scholarship and came to study at a college in the United States. Just as in the case with Ting, #4f and Mei, #7f and their linguistic environments, the life-story of the Native speaker of Arabic[3], Faiz, #11m with his minimal exposure to some other languages did not allow to count it towards his linguistic bank in the frames of this research, though might be informally considered.

Notably, the four female students from Asia, Eun, #8f from Korea, Miyuki, #5f from Japan, and two students from China, Ting, #4f and Mei, #7f had English as a Foreign Language since their elementary grades in their home countries. Slightly earlier than in the cases of the above four females, all students from India: Sanjay, Prem, Vijay, Kumar, and Anjali (consecutively, # 1m, 2m, 3m, 4m, & 9f) had English as one of the school subjects required by the program in their country from Grade 1, the first year of their schooling.

The story of Sang, #10m differed from the rest of the participants in this sample. Initially, this student was taught some basic skills of reading and writing in his mother tongue, Vietnamese, during his first year of schooling in his home country. Following the year when Sang started his school in Vietnam, he moved to the United States together with his family. Though he continued speaking and writing in his Vietnamese mother tongue when in the new to him country, Sang reported he soon developed the language skills in the American English on the level of native proficiency.

In addition to the above linguistic differences, my research participants' educational histories differed as well. As shown in *Table 2 below*, I found some variations by education level and field of studies.

Table 2. Participants' education and language history

#Gender Name	Degrees by country	Current program in the U.S. university		Languages4			
1 Male Sanjay	HS Bachelor's / India	Master's in Electrical Engineering	Telugu	Hindi	English		
2 Male Prem	HS Bachelor's Master's / India	Ph. D. in Electrical Engineering	**Hindi**	Marwari	English		
3 Male Vijay	HS Bachelor's / India	Master's in Chemical Engineering	**Telugu**	Hindi	English		
4 Female Ting	HS Bachelor's / China	Master's in TESOL	**Mandarin**	English	*German*	*Japanese*	
5 Female Miyuki	HS Bachelor's / Japan; Master's / USA	Ph. D. in Teaching Foreign or Second Languages	**Japanese**	English	*German*	*French*	*Thai*
6 Male Kumar	HS Bachelor's MBA / India	Master's in Electrical Engineering	**Malayalam**	Hindi	Tamil	English	*German*
7 Female Mei	HS Bachelor's / China; Master's / USA	Ph. D. in Early Childhood Education	**Mandarin**	English			
8 Female Eun	HS Bachelor's/ South Korea; Master's / USA	Ph. D. in Second Language Education	**Korean**	English	*Russian*		
9 Female Anjali	HS Bachelor's / India	Master's in Electrical Engineering / Photonics	**Konkani**	Hindi	Marathi	English	
10 Male Sang	HS / USA	Bachelor's in Business Administration	**Vietnamese**	Hindi	*Spanish*		
11 Male Faiz	HS Bachelor's / Saudi Arabia; Master's / USA	Ph. D. in Special Education	**Arabic**	English			

Language[4] in bold print indicates the participant's first mother tongue (e.g., **Mandarin**). Words printed in regular font indicate the languages habitually spoken and understood by participants (e.g., Hindi). The italicized words indicate languages attempted by students in a formal or informal learning setting (e.g., *Spanish*).

At the grounds of the American university, five of these students selected different concentrations in the field of Education (Ting, #4f; Miyuki, #5f; Mei, #7f; Eun, #8f; & Faiz, #11m). At the time of this project, three female participants: Ting,

#4f from China, Miyuki, #5f from Japan, and Eun, #8f from Korea were enrolled in graduate programs at the School of Education. Ting, #4f was working towards completion of her Master's program, while Mei, #5f and Eun, #8f were Ph. D. students with concentration in English for Speakers of Other Languages (ESOL). One female participant from China, Mei, #7f was enrolled in a Ph. D. program in Early Childhood Education. Faiz, #11m, the male student from Saudi Arabia was enrolled in Ph. D. program in Special Education, after having earned his Bachelor's degree is his home country and his Master's degree from a university in the United States. Four of these participants: Miyuki, Mei, Eun, and Faiz had initially earned their Bachelor's degrees from the educational institutions in their home-countries and their Master's degrees from a university in the USA.

Next four participants, the students from India: Sanjay, Vijay, Kumar, and Anjali were enrolled in different Master's and doctoral level science programs. Three students from India, including two males: Sanjay, #1m, and Kumar, #6m, and one female, Anjali, #9f were working towards their Master's degrees in Electrical Engineering. Anjali, #9f, the female participant, focused on Photonics, in particular. Vijay, male participant #3m from India was enrolled in Master's level program in Chemical Engineering, and Prem, #2m, male participant from India worked towards completion of his Ph. D. program in Electrical Engineering after having earned his Master's degree in his home country. Kumar, #6m male participant from India was studying towards his second Master's degree in Electrical Engineering at this American university, after having earned his first Master's in the same field in his home country.

Interestingly, almost all students, including Sanjay, #1m, Prem, #2m, Vijay, #3m, Ting, #4f, Miyuki, #5f, Kumar, #6m, Mei, #7f, Eun, #8f, Anjali, #9f, and Faiz, #11m indicated they came to the United States with the purpose to get the world-renowned high-quality American Higher Education. Sang, #10m, the American-schooled male participant born in Vietnam who was brought to the USA as a child and, later, was granted American citizenship, participated in this study as a Domestic student. Sang was enrolled in his Master's level program in Business Administration after having completed the elementary, middle, and high school programs at public schools in the United States. This student had had his prior experiences with studying Humanities at a private American college before he transferred to his current university and enrolled in the undergraduate program in Business Administration.

So, English was not the first language, but an Additional Language for all the participants. For six people, Ting, #4f, Miyuki, #5f, Mei, #7f, Eun, #8f, and Faiz, #11m, it was their second language. For the other three people, Sanjay, #1m, Prem, #2m, and Vijay, #3m, English was their third language. For one of the participants, Anjali, #9f, it was her fourth language after the three native tongues she learned from her immediate family members since her birth time. The other three people,

Mei, #7f, Eun, #8f, and Faiz, #11m, shared they did not have a chance to study more than two languages in their past histories and were active users of the two languages they mastered by the time of this research study.

As shared by Ting, #4f and Sang, #10m, though they tried to study some Foreign Languages, i.e., German and Japanese (Ting) and Spanish (Sang), these students reported that those languages remained on the level of the attempted foreign languages to them for the reason of low usage and lack of the further exposure to those foreign languages in their personal and academic lives. On the contrary, the five participants from India: Sanjay, #1m, Prem, #2m, Vijay, #3m, Kumar, #6m, and Anjali, #9f shared they were active users of all the languages they learned since their birth time and when in schools. Interestingly, Miyuki, #5f participant from Japan reported she was obligated to learn the official languages of the countries where she used to work in the past, which were Taiwan, Germany, and Japan. This person also felt these languages remained in her perception on the level of the attempted foreign languages, while she was an active user of mostly two of her languages: her native tongue, Japanese, and the English language.

Being friends with a Slavic-languages speaker, Eun, participant #8f, though declared herself as a speaker of only two languages, also attempted to learn from her friend two closely related Slavonic languages, Russian and Ukrainian.

Overall, my research participants appeared to be a highly diverse group in terms of their demographic and linguistic properties. This diversity made me extremely excited and fascinated as both a researcher and EAL educator.

CHARACTERISTICS OF PARTICIPANTS AS READERS

Unanimously, all eleven participants indicated having their special interest in the English language as the pathways language that could assist them with pursuing their academic and professional goals and professional opportunities in the United States and worldwide. Yet, studying a language is unavoidably connected with reading. So, *Table 3* below shows my participants as reading personalities and outlines their reading habits and preferences. Though these people were asked some questions about their reading habits, skills, and preferences in any language, including their mother tongue, and the languages other than English, it was explained that their perceptions needed to be focused on the English language within this project (See *Table 3* below for the data from participants' responses about their reading habits, skills, and preferences with regards to reading in the English language).

Table 3. Participants' habits and preferences in reading in English

Name # gender	Reads daily	Enjoys reading	Struggles with reading	Areas of reading problems	Reads Academic literature	Reads Fiction	Reads Non-fiction	Reads Internet sources
Sanjay #1m	Yes	Yes	Sometimes	Sophisticated vocabulary	Yes			Yes
Prem #2m	Yes	Yes	No	N/A	Yes	Yes	Yes	Yes
Vijay #3m	Yes	Yes	Sometimes	Unknown vocabulary	Yes			Yes
Ting #4f	Yes	Only when interested	Yes	Research articles	Yes			Yes
Miyuki #5f	Yes	Yes	Yes	Out-of-field publications	Yes			Yes
Kumar #6m	Yes	Yes	Sometimes	Poetic language / cultural texts	Yes	Yes	Yes	Yes
May #7f	Yes	Not in English	Yes	Professional terminology	Yes			Yes
Eun #8f	No	Yes	Sometimes	Cultural texts	Yes			Yes
Anjali #9f	3-4 days a week	Yes	Sometimes	Unknown vocabulary	Yes	Yes		Yes
Sang #10m	Yes	Yes	No	None	Yes	Yes	Yes	Yes
Faiz #11m	Yes	Yes	Sometimes	Out-of-field & cultural texts	Yes	Yes	Yes	Yes

Naturally, all participants recognized they had to read a lot of academic literature when at the university. However, two participants (Eun, #8f and Anjali, #9f) shared they did not read every single day when in college. Anjali, #9f expressed her fascination with reading overall, but this student shared she read only three to four days a week. Both cases may be explained with the above students' need in running jobs and making their own living.

Amazingly, most participants shared they truly enjoyed reading. Nevertheless, Ting, #4f noticed she felt enjoyment only when she was highly interested in the topic of her readings. Mei, #7f shared she could not fully enjoy reading in the English language yet. As this student believed, the above occurred since she did not possess the Native knowledge of the highly diverse vocabulary used in the readings on different topics. In accord with the above, Faiz, #11m also recognized that his insufficient knowledge of the specific social and cultural issues hindered the flow of the reading process for him; thus, reduced his reading enjoyment.

The other six people, Sanjay, #1m, Vijay, #3m, Kumar, #6m, Eun, #8f, Anjali, #9f, and Faiz, #11m, stated they struggled with reading on some topics sometimes. It was especially frustrating for them when they knew it was important to get to the root of the problems discussed in the literature. These participants also indicated that the lack of background knowledge in the field of the Christian religion and culture- or sub-cultures-specific knowledge presented a strong obstacle for them when they tried to read texts and desired a full understanding. All the above hindered their reading processes and prevented them from enjoying the readings.

Notably, the rest of the sample reported they developed the ability to skip some unknown to them vocabulary or parts of texts on condition that their understanding of the topic discussed in that piece of writing was not significantly affected. These students also shared that they had gained the ability to read without slowing the pace of reading or changing the flow of their reading regardless of some gaps in the vocabulary knowledge. When needed, as these students reported, they would return to some previously highlighted by themselves places of interest in their readings with the purpose to re-read and get a clearer idea and a deeper understanding of those parts of the read texts.

Controversially to my expectations, these students did not perceive themselves as struggling readers, but they believed they experienced some difficulties. As these readers perceived, they had to omit some hard for them parts of the texts, so that later they could return and re-read those complicated text portions. Yet, the above facts indicated that these students did struggle and experienced significant difficulties with reading comprehension. Importantly, their usage of the avoidance strategy cannot be considered the best solution to the problems with the reading comprehension.

As anticipated, the words by some of my study participants served as the evidence in support of my researcher's assumption, which was based on my life-long teaching experiences. When questioned about the causes of their problems with reading, two participants, Vijay, #3m and Anjali, #9f, reported that the new and unknown to them vocabulary was the major obstacle that hindered them with their reading comprehension.

Another participant, Sanjay, #1m, openly complained about his struggle with the overly sophisticated vocabulary and writing styles. This student believed that some authors purposefully employed unnecessary complicated language for crafting their publications towards a more sophisticated style. Instead, Sanjay, #1m suggested these authors should pursue the writing style which helps make their ideas precise, reader-friendly, and clearly delivered. Another four participants, Miyuki, #5f, Kumar, #6m, Eun, #8f, and Faiz, #11m, shared they had no difficulties comprehending the texts in the field of their study; yet, they experienced problems with understanding out-of-field literature, such as culture-specific poetry or fiction.

Importantly, Ting, #4f reported having problems with comprehending the language of research articles, while Mei, #7f had difficulties due to her problems with memorization, especially of the professional vocabulary in large amounts, for example, in the field of psychology. Overall, practically all participants in this sample in this study perceived themselves as eager readers. None of them reported adverse reaction or negative attitude to any kind of reading in any of known to them tongues, though reading in the English language was primarily in the focus of investigation.

Later, my data triangulation between the surveys, interviews, and participant observations, which I will further discuss in this book, allowed me to conclude that all research participants in this study made an informed decision to study at an American university. They were fully aware of the volume of the readings and the extent of the academic load within their programs. Nevertheless, the necessity to read extremely much for their programs did not discourage any of these students. On the contrary, all participants stated they were highly motivated to keep pursuing their educational and future career goals.

Moreover, these participants were also committed to continuing their schooling and advancing their studies. For example, the undergraduate and Master's level students expressed their interest in applying for doctoral programs upon completion of their current programs. For the above purpose, besides reading the program texts required by their professors, all students indicated they were looking for additional support texts online. Unfortunately, many students mentioned they had little to no time left for reading fiction while at the university. Nevertheless, five participants: four males, Prem, #2m, Kumar, #6m, Sang, #10m, and Faiz, #11m and one female, Anjali, #9f shared their interest in reading fiction for enjoyment. Almost all of them, except for Anjali, #9f, found some time in their busy schedules for reading non-fiction literature for enjoyment, while Anjali, #9f assigned her disconnect from reading for enjoyment to her being extremely busy when in college.

Importantly, my data analysis of the interviews with the participants confirmed the impression they produced during my participant observation phase in this project. To be more exact, my participants showed themselves as internally-motivated readers who were oriented towards their academic and professional success. Imperatively, all of them stated they would prefer some help with their reading comprehension, but did not receive any support in terms of understanding the course readings while in their programs. Triangulation of my observations with the speeches of my subjects and their written responses confirmed my decision to include all the data in my final, major data analysis. Thus, I proceeded with analyzing all eleven data sets. Yet, I will try now to help my readers envision each of my participants via describing their observed behaviors.

OBSERVABLE BEHAVIORS DURING THE READING PROCESSES

In this section, I will share the results of my observations, which were conducted in the traditions developed by Creswell (2007) and Spradley (1980). I documented in my observational notes the observable behaviors during the reading processes performed by my research participants. Later, I jotted down my researcher's reflections and added my analytical memos (Miles & Huberman, 1984; Saldaña, 2013). To ensure equality and fairness, I will describe each of the students in the order they arrived to participate in my study; so I numbered them accordingly.

Male Participant #1 Sanjay

Participant #1, Sanjay, a male Master's student in the field of Electrical Engineering earned his Bachelor's degree from a university in his home country, which was India. Sanjay was a speaker of three languages, where English was his language number three. Interestingly, when reading the texts within this project, Sanjay whispered the lines he was reading and slightly, but repeatedly pulled on his mustache or rubbed his cheek. These types of unconscious gestures in participant #1 indicated his feeling nervous. They intensified while he was working on *Text 1*, but were less intense when this student read *Text 2*. Noticeably, Sanjay's nervousness reduced when he attended to *Text 3*.

There was a distinctly observable change in Sanjay's behavior on Day 2 in this project. Notably, this participant did not touch his face, he also looked overall more confident and relaxed while working with *Text 3*. The final interview with this student unveiled this behavioral change enigma to me. During the second interview, Sanjay shared that it was easier for him to work with the print-based text supported by the features of multimodality in the form of a video with the sound, where multimodal resources were plentiful. While multimodally assisted, Sanjay shared, he received more clues useful for his meaning making and reading comprehension as he was offered both types of multimodal support: visual and auditory modes in their intercombination. Overall, the interview and the observations data allowed to conclude that Sanjay approached this research task as a very diligent student, who was determined to perform and complete the hard assignments at the highest level possible.

Male Participant #2 Prem

Prem, participant #2, was a male doctoral student with his Bachelor's and Master's degrees earned from a university in his home country, India. This participant studied the field of Electrical Engineering, just as Sanjay #2m. Prem was a speaker of three languages, including English as his third tongue. As a mature-age doctoral student with his rich academic, working, and life experiences, Prem took this current project extremely seriously. Prior to starting his work on the project's tasks, Prem asked multiple questions about the purpose of this study, my intentions as the investigator, and possible future steps and directions this study might have taken. Upon having received the sought answers, Prem became observably more confident. Yet, his paced and self-assured behavior as well as his confidence might also be explained with this student's being several years older and more academically experienced in comparison to Master's and Bachelor's level participants in this project.

One fact from Prem's academic history added an interesting note to my observations of this person's behaviors as a participant in my study. As a Ph. D. student, who had recently conducted and presented the results of his own research, this scholar found the new to him role of a *research subject*, which was contrary to his previously appropriated identity of an investigator. Nevertheless, when working on the assigned reading tasks, Prem was extremely determined to succeed as a student.

During reading, this participant was sitting straight in his chair; he was slightly leaning backwards, while remaining cross-legged and cross-armed. Prem's look was serious and observably focused, which showed that he was concentrated on and immersed in this project's tasks. Quite often, this participant tightened his lips, which showed a greater effort to comprehend the texts and answer the test questions correctly. Importantly, the final interview with this participant confirmed my conclusions drawn from these observations. All the combined data sourced from this participant confirmed that Prem took these research tasks as a responsible, serious, well-versed, and self-confident scholar who was determined to succeed.

Male Participant #3 Vijay

The next person who volunteered to participate in this study was Vijay, a male student from India and a speaker of three languages. This person was acquainted with Sanjay, but had never met before with his country-fellow-man, Prem. Vijay, participant #3 studied the field of Chemical Engineering on Master's level after having earned his Bachelor's degree from a university in his home country. Knowing about friendship between Sanjay and Vijay, I scheduled their visits to the research site back-to-back, so they did not have time to meet and discuss this project's aspects ahead of attempting them.

While observing Vijay's facial expressions, I received an impression that this research assignment appeared to be quite hard for this student. Oftentimes, Vijay looked lost. At such moments, his face perspired and reddened. At some other moments, this student got pale through his tan during reading. Having noticed that and doing my best as a caring researcher, I provided some clarifications to this student in between two tasks on Day 1. Specifically, I explained to Vijay in a light-tuned and non-invasive manner that I selected the hard texts for this project with a certain purpose, i.e., to equally challenge all my students, from any field of study with quite complex reading tasks. Offering students easy reads would not present a challenge; thus, would not be relevant for this project's objectives. I also clarified that this study aimed to investigate perceptions of students while they worked with extremely hard texts. Importantly, the purpose of this strenuous work consisted in finding some new, efficient ways to assist large populations of EAL students in colleges and universities with their deeper reading comprehension of the highly complex texts.

According to my further observations, my above explanations and encouragements helped this participant to reduce his internal tension. Not only did Vijay understand the importance of this study, but he became also able to embrace the importance of his struggles with this project's tasks. So, the significance of this intellectual sacrifice seemed to have invigorated this struggling reader.

Later, in the interview with this participant, Vijay confirmed my researcher's assumptions by revealing that, initially, he had felt apprehensive, challenged, overwhelmed, and almost combating with the first day's task. Subsequently, after our mid-way conversation, this student found himself feeling more confident. Overall, the combined data from multiple sources showed that Vijay was determined to do his best on this project's tasks, regardless of their complexity level, in the sake of the future generations of struggling EAL readers.

Female Participant #4 Ting

Ting, a female participant #4 from China had a very positive, talkative, and outgoing disposition. She enrolled in the university studies within the program of Teaching English to Speakers of Other Languages on Master's level. This student arrived in the United States after having earned her Bachelor's degree from a university in China. Prevalently, Ting was a speaker of two languages, Mandarin and English, but she had also studied German and Japanese during her high-school years back at home. Overall, this participant produced an impression of being an academically curious personality with her great interest in the new educational experiences. Additionally, Ting expressed her zest to explore the world via traveling.

Regardless of this student's easy-going manner, positive disposition, and smiley appearance, Ting worked on the texts with full responsibility. This participant often pressed her lips tight, which indicated her making a strong endeavor to deeper understand the print-based texts. During reading, this student slightly hunched over the paper, and when working on the comprehension questions to the texts, Ting was sitting with her ankles crossed and pulled tightly back under her chair. This student held her elbows tight to her body, so I concluded that her behaviors indicated her hidden internal tension. Amazingly, Ting did not allow herself to relax. Later, she confessed that she perceived this project's tasks as quite hard. Nevertheless, this person's posture and head position gave out her being internally engaged with the readings as well as being strongly concentrated. During the interviews with Ting, the data from this participant's observations found confirmation in her speeches: Ting appeared to be highly motivated to deeper comprehend the texts used in this research.

Female Participant #5 Miyuki

Participant #5 Miyuki was a female Ph. D. student from Japan who came to the USA to study the field of Second and Foreign Language Acquisition. Miyuki had had her rich and diverse academic and working experiences prior to her getting enrolled with her current university program in the United States. She was a speaker of five languages, three of which she had had to study and use for her professional assignments in the countries where she used to have jobs. Prior to enrollment with her current university program, Miyuki had earned her Bachelor's degree in her home-country and her Master's degree from another university in the United States. When in this project, Miyuki demonstrated an unusual combination of quite contradicting character features. At the first sight, this participant employed a very soft voice and her nice, cat-like manners. Yet, at times, through these externally exhibited features, there showed Miyuki's iron-strong will, her unbreakably-formed logic, and fossilized traditional convictions, which she openly expressed in her interviews and informal conversations with the researcher. As I understood, Miyuki's external behaviors and reasoning could not be approached from the position of traditional European psychology. Amazingly, it did not take this participant too long to finish reading and complete each of the three comprehension tests.

Subsequently, my conclusions drawn from the observational data found confirmation during the interviews, where this student shared about a strict set of conventional behavioral norms in the society where she was raised. For example, some of the norms described by Miyuki included multiple situation-appropriate gestures, postures, positions of legs, head, and arms, which were supposed to be situation-appropriate. For example, a person's speeches and behaviors were expected to be appropriately different in a range of diverse academic, professional, or personal-life contexts. Miyuki was less readable to an observer due to her habit to follow the strict behavioral cultural norms accepted and maintained by her society. Yet, her focused and serious gaze gave out her deep concentration at the instances when she was reading the texts or attempting to find the correct answers to the comprehension test questions. Overall, the entire data set on this participant allowed me to conclude that Miyuki was quite a philosopher with her solidly-shaped social position and the firm academic points of view, which this person was not inclined to trade.

Male Participant #6 Kumar

Kumar, a male participant #6 with his Bachelor's and Master of Business Administration (MBA) degrees from a university in his home-country, India, was working on his second Master's degree, this time in Electrical Engineering at the American university. This participant was a speaker of five languages, among which English was his language number four.

Kumar's working style at this current project's tasks appeared to be different from the other research subject's participatory practices. Later, in his first interview, this student revealed the fact that he had had absolutely no background knowledge on the content or topics of the three texts offered within this study. This student's internal struggle with his attempts to comprehend any of the three texts observably reflected in his appearance. Kumar's posture gave out this student's struggle, as well as his endeavor to overcome this challenge and understand the content of the texts. This participant was strongly stooping over the papers with the print-based texts. He was squinting his eyes and squirming his lips while working on all the assignments within this project.

When off task or between different tasks, Kumar became visibly relaxed, friendly, and talkative. These observable changes in this participant's behavior from relaxation to strong concentration indicated his intention to complete the project assignments at his best. Overall, Kumar was found a responsible worker. And the data from the interviews with this student fully supported the findings from my observations: this participant struggled a lot due to his having no background knowledge on Shakespeare and his works.

Female Participant #7 Mei

Mei, a female participant #7 from China had earned her Bachelor's degree from a university in her home country and, subsequently, gained some educational experiences in America. To be more exact, Mei earned her Master's degree from a U.S. university, then she enrolled with her current Ph.D. program in Early Childhood Education.

This student repeatedly complained about her problems with memorization, which she often experienced throughout her educational history. During her work with this study's tasks, Mei also shared she found it hard to memorize the content of the texts and the test questions offered within this project. This student frequently went back and forth between each text and the comprehension test questions.

Though Mei's face muscles did not show any significant signs of internal strain and strong concentration, the signs of her frustration with herself were visibly observable in the gaze of her eyes, her tensed position, nervous movements of her head, and her unsteady breathing pattern. Not only did Mei produce long and slow sighing sounds, but she also attempted to suppress her breath, which gave out her internal struggle with comprehension. This person appeared to be self-trained with hiding or at least attempting to hide the signs of her internal tension.

During her work with *Text 3* supported by video with the sound, Mei looked more relaxed and seemed to be greatly interested in the content of the video. Her breathing eased; she also showed less of internal distress when working on the multimodally assisted tasks. During the interviews, Mei's sincere and genuine revelations confirmed the above data obtained from my observations.

Female Participant #8 Eun

Eun, participant #8 was a female Ph. D. student from Korea. First, this student earned her Bachelor's degree from a university in her home-country, then she completed her Master's degree at a university in the United States. Upon having earned her Master's, Eun proceeded with her current doctoral program in Second Language Education. Though Eun considered herself a speaker of mostly two languages, where English was her second language and Korean was her mother tongue, I also knew from my unofficial conversation with this student that she attempted to study two closely-related Slavonic languages thanks to communicating with her friends.

From the very start, Eun revealed that she did not like reading. If so, this participant demonstrated her strong self-discipline when in this project. She was painstakingly working with all the texts in this project: unimodal, print-based ones, and the multimodal readings without any complaints. Obviously, Eun's lack of reading enjoyment did not stop her from focusing on this project's texts. When trying to understand the meaning of the content of the readings and attempting to answer the comprehension test questions, this participant was sitting crossed-legged in her chair while slightly swaying her right leg. My conclusion about this behavior as the one indicating anxiety, found support in Eun's interviews, where she described herself as a not very eager reader.

Nevertheless, when working, Eun's facial expression was very serious. Her behavior did not produce any signs of boredom. Further, in her interview, Eun, as a straightforward speaker, disclosed that though she did not enjoy reading, she was highly internally motivated in studying and completing all the academic tasks she needed to perform. Eun shared that she was raised, educated, and self-trained to work hard and overcome any possible academic challenges and difficulties. The interview data with this participant served as the evidence in confirmation of the data from my observations.

Female Participant #9 Anjali

Participant #9, Anjali was a female student from India who earned her Bachelor's degree from a university in her home country and was currently working on her Master's degree in Electrical Engineering / Photonics in a U.S. university. For Anjali, English was her fourth language, after the three tongues that she had mastered and was habitually using on daily basis at home, with her family, at school with her classmates, teachers, and friends. The case with Anjali was quite interesting for this study since initially, at the time of being a child, she had never been a self-motivated reader. Then, unexpectedly for herself, this person became hooked on non-fiction. This metamorphose occurred during her being a high-school student.

When in this project, Anjali worked on each of the tasks very diligently. This participant completed reading texts and answering the comprehension questions much faster than most of the other research participants. Anjali promptly finished all the assignments and swiftly left. Though, it needs to be clarified that this participant did not hurry through this project's work. On the contrary, Anjali got deeply engaged with the readings. Her focused behavior indicated her strong intention and serious attitude to the performed work.

Male Participant #10 Sang

The case with participant #10, Sang, the only undergraduate student in this project was quite unique and of high interest for this study. At first glance, Sang might have been considered a Domestic student, though of an International descent. Yet, this student started his schooling in his home country, which was Vietnam. As Sang was subsequently schooled in the United States, from Kindergarten through college, this student's speaking skills were well-developed. Additionally, as per Sang's confession, this project's tasks did not seem extremely hard for him because of his prior exposure to some other Shakespearean works. Visibly, Sang remained bright, engaged, and motivated during his entire time within this project.

When listening to the audio text, which was offered in support of the print-based *Text 2*, Sang visibly indulged in the beauty of the Shakespearean language. He noticeably immersed in listening to the actors' voices without tracking nor even looking into the print-based *Text 2*. As per his interview statements, Sang truly enjoyed the listening part. He also revealed his appreciation of poetry. Additionally, Sang confessed that in terms of comprehension, he benefited from listening the most. Sang also shared that when he was answering the comprehension questions to the third text, which was supported with the video with sound, this helped him the most. Importantly, Sang completed every project assignment quite fast compared to some other participants in this sample.

Male Participant #11 Faiz

Participant #11, Faiz was a male doctoral student with his initial Bachelor's degree earned from a university in his home country, Saudi Arabia, and his Master's degree from a university in the United States. When at home, Faiz had an opportunity to study predominantly in his mother tongue, while the English language education at his previously attended schools had only some basic and introductory character. It needs to be said that this was another outstanding case within the sample of this project's participants. It was quite late in his life that Faiz's studies went beyond the knowledge of alphabet and some basic words and phrases in English. This student started his intensive acquisition of the English language only upon his arrival in the United States, where this student enrolled in his Master's program. At the time of this project, Faiz was successfully moving towards completion of his Ph. D. studies in Special Education.

Observing this participant's behavior, I concluded that the texts presented a challenge for this student. Later, Faiz shared that he had had no previous exposure to the Old English language of the 15th-16th centuries. Though, it deserved attention that Faiz revealed himself as a highly self-motivated person who made his best effort to introduce himself to some Shakespearean works. For the above purpose, Faiz attended several open-air performances of Shakespeare's plays given by the local theatre companies every summer in the city parks. Importantly, Faiz's interest in Shakespeare started and developed independently and long before this project's start.

Nevertheless, when working within this study, Faiz's face showed astonishment with the high complexity of the print-based texts. This participant expressed his surprise verbally, yet, it was also showing in his behaviors. For example, this scholar half-opened his mouth and pulled the air in slowly while his eyes opened wider and his eyebrows slowly moved upwards. All these movements and facial expressions along with the "frozen" gaze in his eyes indicated that Faiz had not expected the texts to be so hard for him to comprehend.

On Day 1 in this project, Faiz decided to not pre-read *Text 2* prior to listening to the audio recording. On Day 2, this participant expressed his regret about his refusal from pre-reading the print-based *Text 2* prior to listening to the audio in support of that text. When reading and looking for answers to comprehension test questions to *Text 3*, Faiz physically vigorously switched back and forth between the texts and the test questions. At some instances, I, as the researcher worried this participant might not be willing to continue his work and would leave this project. Of course, as per my researcher's obligations, I had explained to all participants, including Faiz, that they had this option to withdraw from my project at any time with the monetary compensation still be granted to them. Yet, I strongly wished to collect the data from the participants who struggled with this project's tasks the most.

Regardless of my internal and never expressed apprehension, Faiz shared his firm intention to complete all the tasks. Moreover, he also confirmed and demonstrated his motivation and high interest in understanding these excerpts from Shakespeare's plays. Faiz revealed in his interview that he purchased some tickets to performances by both professional and amateur actors for the current Shakespearean season. So, his intention to comprehend the Shakespeare's English appeared to be genuine.

Later, when Faiz reflected on his working experiences with *Text 3*, which had multimodal video and audio support, he explained that he perceived this task as less strenuous compared to his working with the unimodal text. He also believed that he was more productive on the multimodal text and test.

Overall, my observations appeared to be highly useful for my research purpose. They allowed me to observably read more stories about my participants in addition to the ones they shared with me during our conversations and interviews. Importantly, there was no indication preventing me from trusting my research participants' words, which I will share with my readers in the next chapter.

REFERENCES

Creswell, J. W. (2007). *Qualitative inquiry and research design: Choosing among five traditions*. Sage Publications.

Saldaña, J. (2013). *The coding manual for qualitative researchers*. Sage Publications.

Spradley, J. P. (1980). *Participant observation*. Holt, Rinehart, and Winston.

Chapter 8
Revealing the Hidden Struggle

ABSTRACT

In Chapter 8, I will further discuss the findings in my research. To be more exact, this chapter will reveal my participants' perceptions of their working processes on the tasks within this project as they shared in their surveys. Importantly, the multimodal representations of the students' perceptions will allow my readers to not only textually read my report, but also promptly grasp the picture from colorful, multimodal shapes. Each figure, while consisting of larger and smaller layers represents a larger or smaller number of participants who shared identical or similar perceptions of their experiences in working with this project's unimodal and multimodal texts. Then, I will reflect on the data from the researcher-developed reflective questionnaires. I will let my reading audiences imaginatively listen to my participants' utterances. In this way, my readers may gain a deeper understanding of the ideas, feelings, and perceptions shared by each participating student.

PARTICIPANTS' PERCEPTIONS OF THEIR WORKING WITH TEXTS

As my readers may remember, I collected the data from multiple sources. Some of them were surveys and after-reading reflective questionnaires. This data set was highly important for a deeper understanding of the participants' ideas. The matter is that the spoken or orally uttered ideas might differ from the unspoken ones. Further, silently written down thoughts, i.e., a person's internal speeches, may also present quite an unexpected reading full of new ideas compared to the same human's orally

DOI: 10.4018/979-8-3373-3426-4.ch008

externalized thoughts. I was very curious to have a peek into my participants' inner world and reasoning via the affordances of the print-based surveys and questionnaires.

With regards to this project's readings, the three Shakespearean texts (1597), it was natural that each individual student differently perceived complexity level of each of the three texts offered within this project. As discussed above in this book's Chapter VI, all three texts were assessed with the help of the readability tests (Flesh, 1949; Kincaid et al., 1975) and were apparently on practically the same level. Yet, each text's complexity was perceived differently by the participating students. Interestingly, there were also found some commonalities in participants' perceptions, which I will not only discuss below, but will also show in the form of figures and tables. For example, none of the participants marked any of the texts as *"no work at all"* in their reflective questionnaires (See *Table 1* below for participants' perceptions of complexity level of their working with *Texts 1* (no support), *Text 2* (audio support), and *Text 3* (video with sound support).

Table 1. Participants' perceptions of complexity level of working with texts 1, 2, and 3

Text #	No work at all	Pretty easy	Not hard	A bit hard	Hard	Very Hard
1	0	1	1	2	4	3
2	0	2	3	3	3	0
3	0	4	5	1	1	0

As it was found later, in the process of the individual interviews, when questioned about complexity level of the texts, students were not always able to keep the focus on solely the difficulty level of the texts. They just could not discuss the question about the texts separately from sharing their perceptions of some other aspects of their experiences within this project. For example, a lot of discussions centered on reading the comprehension test questions and looking for the answers. Initially, most of the participants were generally addressing all their working processes, which included their reading and trying to comprehend the print-based *Texts 1, 2*, and *3*, attempting to make the meaning from the comprehension test questions, listening to, or watching the multimodal support in the form of an audio to *Text 2* or a video with the sound to *Text 3*. Eventually, every student reflected on their struggles with searching the answers to the test questions in the texts.

Notably, there was significantly more clarity in the participants' answers, which they provided in the questionnaires and surveys. Subsequently, I developed the visual representations, where the students' answers are shown numerically and marked in different colors. So, Figure 1 below visually represents participants' reactions on complexity level of print-based Text 1, which had no support, where none of the participants selected the option "It was no work at all" (See, Figure 1 below for students' perceptions of complexity level of their working with the print-based *Text 1*).

Figure 1. Participants' perceptions of working with text 1 (no multimodal support)

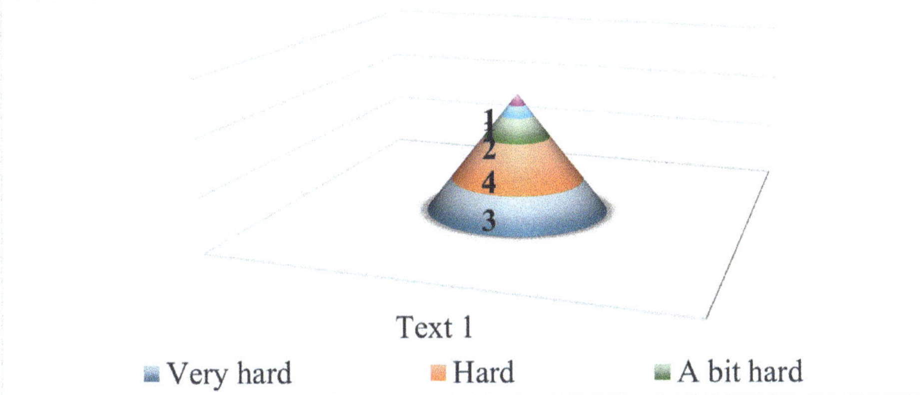

One student in each category (9%) found working with *Text 1 "pretty easy"* or *"not hard."* Two students (18%) found working with *Text 1 "a bit hard."* Four other participants (36%) stated it was *"hard"* for them to work with *Text 1* without any support. The remaining three people (27%) characterized working with *Text 1* as *"very hard."*

It needs to be stressed that when participants received multimodal support in the form of an audio to the print-based *Text 2*, none of them perceived working processes with this text as *"very hard"* versus *Text 1* (Revisit Figure 5 above then see Figure 2 below for participants' perceptions of working with *Text 2* (Audio support).

Figure 2. Participants' perceptions of working with text 2 (audio support)

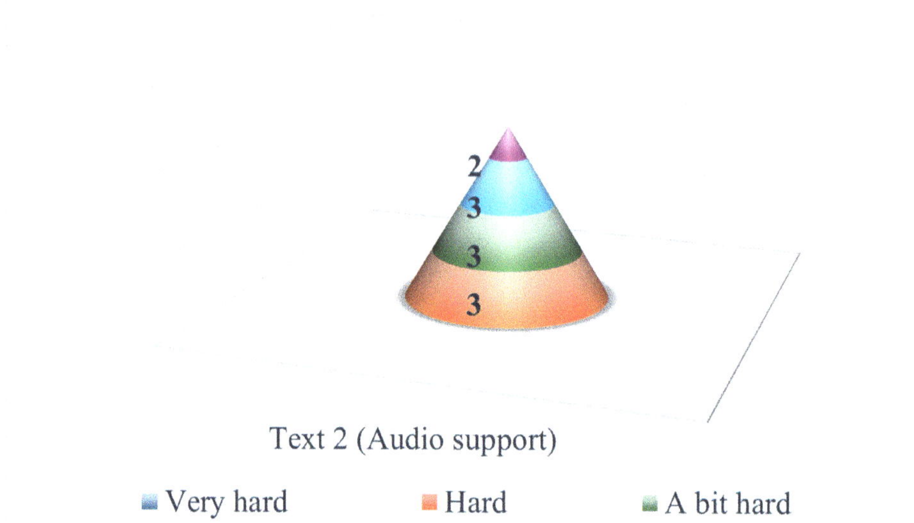

Imperatively, the data obtained from the reflective questionnaires supported the data collected from participants' interviews, i.e., two students (18% of the sample) perceived their working with the audio-supported *Text 2* as *"pretty easy."* The other three people (27%) characterized working with the audio-supported *Text 2* as *"not hard," "a bit hard,"* and *"hard."* Yet, nobody perceived the audio-supported *Text 2* as *"very hard."* Importantly, none of the students considered working with the audio-supported *Text 2* as "*no work at all.*" So, it can be concluded that all participants experienced some kind of challenges in this task.

Interestingly, working with *Text 3,* which was supplemented by a video with the sound, was not perceived by any of the research participants as *"very hard."* Nor did these students perceive that working with this text felt like "*no work at all.*" Only one person (9% of the sample) found working with *Text 3 "hard"* while another one believed it was *"a bit hard."* A significantly greater number of people found working with this text *"pretty easy"* (four students – 36% of the sample) or *"not hard"* (five students – 45%), which totaled nine out of eleven people or 82%. And that was one of the most important findings in this study, which supported the notion of helpfulness of means of multimodality (See Figure 7 below for participants' perceptions of their working with *Text 3*, which had video and audio support).

Figure 3. Participants' perceptions of working with text 3 (video and audio support)

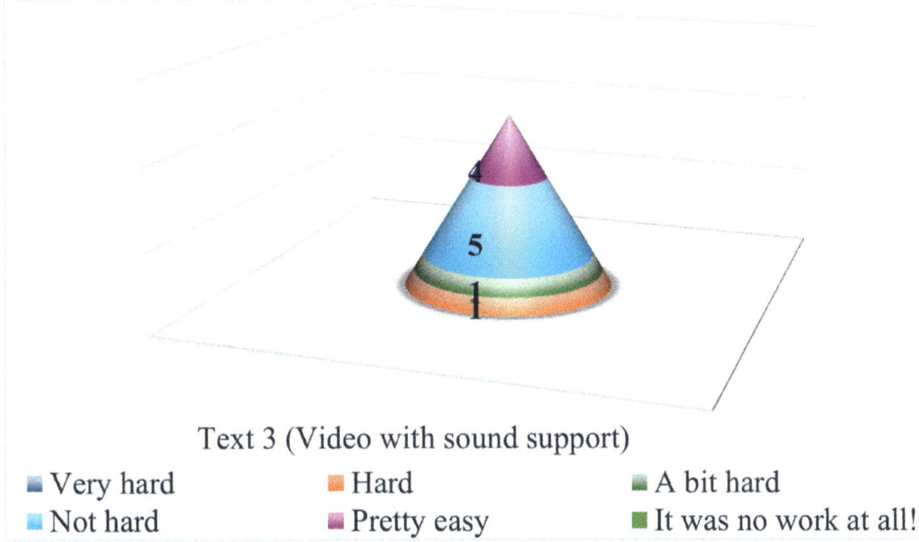

To envision a whole picture of my participants' perceptions of complexity levels of all three texts, I developed a figure where the visual representation of each of the three texts can be viewed next to and in comparison with each other. Figure 4 below serves the above purpose while comparatively depicting my participants' perceptions of their working with *Text 1* with no multimodal support, *Text 2* supported with an audio, and *Text 3* supported by a video with the sound (See Figure 4 below for participants' perceptions of working with the three texts).

Figure 4. Participants' perceptions of working with the three texts

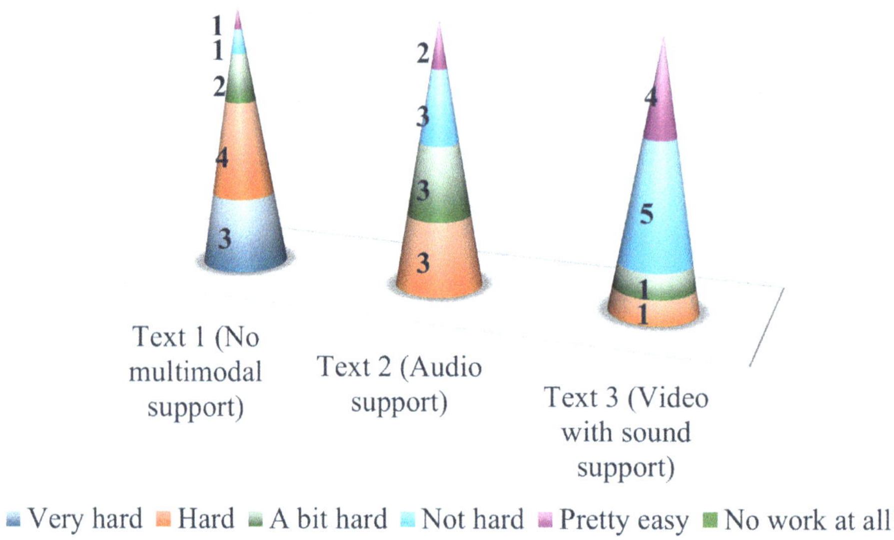

I will add some words to further my ideas with regards to the above representations. The top two parts of each column, which represent my participants' perceptions of easiness (*"pretty easy"* and *"not hard"*) show significant increase in volume exactly due to addition of greater number of multimodal resources in support of the print-based *Texts 2* and *3*, while the same two upper-most areas in the column 1 standing for *Text 1*, which had no support, look tiny as all students struggled to understand that solely print-based text. As the participants shared, addition of auditory support helped them to better understand *Text 2*, while the visual and auditory resources in their inter-combination, significantly simplified their working processes.

Now, I offer my readers to have another look at the above Figure 8 and examine areas 3 and 4 in each cone. These areas show decrease of the zones marked as "*hard.*" The lowest bottom section representing participants' perception of their greatest struggle working with each of the texts disappears in the right-most figure, which represents students' perceptions of their working with *Text 3* supported by features of multimodality in the form of a video with the sound. Importantly, my final triangulation process resulted in an important conclusion. Id est, the data from participants' questionnaires supported the ones obtained from their interviews, i.e., additional multimodal resources significantly eased the processes of the students' working with the print-based *Text 3*. This phenomenon can be explained with the fact that the students received support from a whole ensemble of multimodal resources, which they found most helpful to them compared to support from only one, auditory mode, added to the print-based *Text 2*. Later, in Part IV of this book titled "How Multimodalities Work," I will address these phenomena in a greater detail.

WHAT WAS EASY WITH THAT "EASY"?

As I described in the section above, my research participants experienced some initial confusion when asked to separate their perceptions of the complexity level of a text alone from their perceptions of all working processes involved in each task. Yet, upon my clarifications, the students were able to address these two diverging topics separately. Based on the above results, it became crucially important for me to understand whether my research participants considered *Text 3* easy by itself, as a unit of a print-based reading, or they found *Text 3* equally difficult to comprehend compared to the first two texts, *Text 1* and *Text 2*.

Imperatively, the notion I attempted to understand was whether the students perceived their working processes with *Text 3* easier thanks to the multimodal support in the form of a video with the sound. This finding might have supported or annihilated my initial researcher's hypothesis. Were my ideas proven wrong, it would be a hard bullet or even a blow to me as a long-time researcher of multimodality. Yet, I had to verify and test my assumptions, as this understanding was critically important for my research.

So, I delved deeper into my participants' perceptions of complexity or easiness of Text 3 alone versus the same notions but with regards to the added multimodal support. As it is shown in Figure 5 below, my participants' perceptions of complexity level of print-based Text 3 significantly differed from their perceptions of their working with the same text when it was supported by features of multimodality in the form of a video with the sound (See Figure 5 below for participants' perceptions of the print-based *Text 3* versus their perceptions of working with the same text).

Figure 5. Participants' perceptions of complexity level of the print-based text 3 versus their perceptions of working with the same text 3 with video and sound support

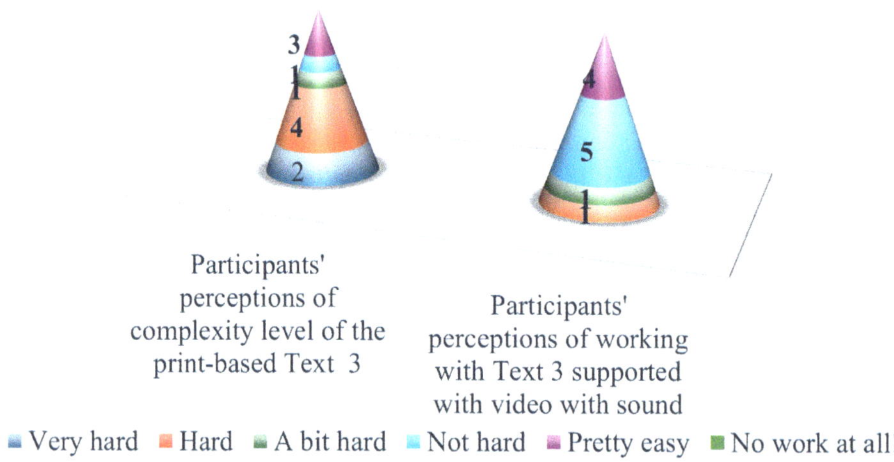

As it is seen in the left-hand column in Figure 5 above, none of the participants found that print-based *Text 3* presented *"no work at all."* Thus, a zone, which would represent this response is completely missing in this figure. Three people (27%) found the print-based *Text 3* "pretty easy," and one person (9%) found it "not hard." Prior to receiving multimodal support, a half of participants (55% of the sample) identified this print-based *Text 3* as "hard" (36%), or "very hard" (18%), while one person (9%) perceived it as "a bit hard." This finding confirmed my idea that the print-based *Text 3* by itself was not perceived as an "easier" reading compared to *Text 1* and *Text 2*. Nevertheless, working with *Text 3* was perceived by the participants as an easier task compared to the first two texts. Imperatively, the students unanimously assigned this easiness to addition of multimodal support from multiple modes of multimodality present in the video with the sound.

PREFERENCES OF VISUALS

Having a deeper insight in my participants' perceptions of multimodality added some more details to my research mosaic. Those findings need to be brought to the spotlight. Later in this project, during the interviews, all the students expressed their appreciation of multimodal support in the form of a video with sound added to the conventional print-based *Text 3*. All of them stated they would prefer this type of multimodal support in addition to any print-based texts, which they needed to read within their university programs. Prior to the interviews, in the questionnaires, students also shared about their appreciation of the effects of multimodalities during their working within this project's tasks (See Table 2 below for participants' preferences of type of multimodal support they would like to have in addition to the print-based texts to better understand the text).

Table 2. Numeric and percentage data on participants' preferences of type of multimodal support they would like to have in addition to print-based texts in order to deeper understand the texts

Type of multimodal support	Text 1	Text 2	Text 3
Video	3 – 27%	3 – 27%	2 – 18%
Audio	1 – 9%	1- 1 - 9%	1 – 9%
Both	7 – 64%	7 – 64%	8 – 73%
None of the above	0	0	0

To clarify the numeric data in Table 8 above, I am explaining that this table contains the information about the expressed by the participants preferences in having one or another type of multimodal support to each of the texts they read within this project. To be more exact, most participants (8 people, which is 73% as shown in the third from the top row in Table 8 above) stated they would prefer having support in the form of a video with an audio. Only one student, Sang, #10m (9% of the sample, as shown in the second from the top row in Table 8) confirmed that auditory support might work best for him for certain kinds of readings and, of course, for all three texts in this project. So, this student wished he could follow the auditory text while tracking the print-based one with his eyes. When prompted, this participant contemplated in doubt whether he might rely on his auditory skills higher than on his ability to read visual non-verbal texts. Upon having considered different scenarios in his think-aloud speech, Sang came out with his final choice, which appeared to be made in favor of a video with the sound, rather than an audio alone.

Some students, as shown in the upper numeric row in Table 8 above (2 or 3, 18 and 27% correspondingly) believed it would be more helpful to them to "see the whole picture" to be able to correctly make the meaning of the print-based text supported by a video. During the interviews, these participants confirmed the above idea and explained that their expression "*whole picture*" referred to the Bakhtinian chronotope, i.e., the setting, time, space, epoch, surroundings, environment etc., which could be only visually recognized in the process of watching a video.

Interestingly, one person, Mei, #7f, claimed she would not need any audio component at all. This participant believed she would be able to correctly read and understand the non-verbal visual language were it provided to support any print-based text. Mei stated she habitually used in her daily life this skill of reading information from facial expressions, gazes, gestures, postures, and movements of actors in real-life situations.

Based on the data from the interviews, most of participants initially did not discriminate between a video only and a video with the sound when they were answering questions in their questionnaires. Yet, during the interviews, the students confirmed that they would prefer to have both: the auditory and visual modes.

To help my readers visualize the whole picture of my participants' choices and preferences of the modes of multimodality, I have developed a visual representation of these data (See Figure 6 below). Just to clarify, these data were obtained via reflective questionnaires, and, further, triangulated with the data from my participant observations, and the data from their interviews. As a result, I noticed some variations in the preferences of types of multimodal support, although all students stated in their interviews, they would prefer both: video and the sound. As one can see, the upper section of each column in Figure 10 is dramatically larger than the middle and the bottom parts. This display allows to visualize the idea that a majority of participants clearly stated they would prefer to be exposed to both: video and audio support (See Figure 6 below for visual representation of the data on participants' preferences of type of multimodal support they would like to have in addition to the print-based texts to better understand the text).

Figure 6. Participants' preferences of type of multimodal support they would like to have in addition to print-based texts in order to better understand the texts

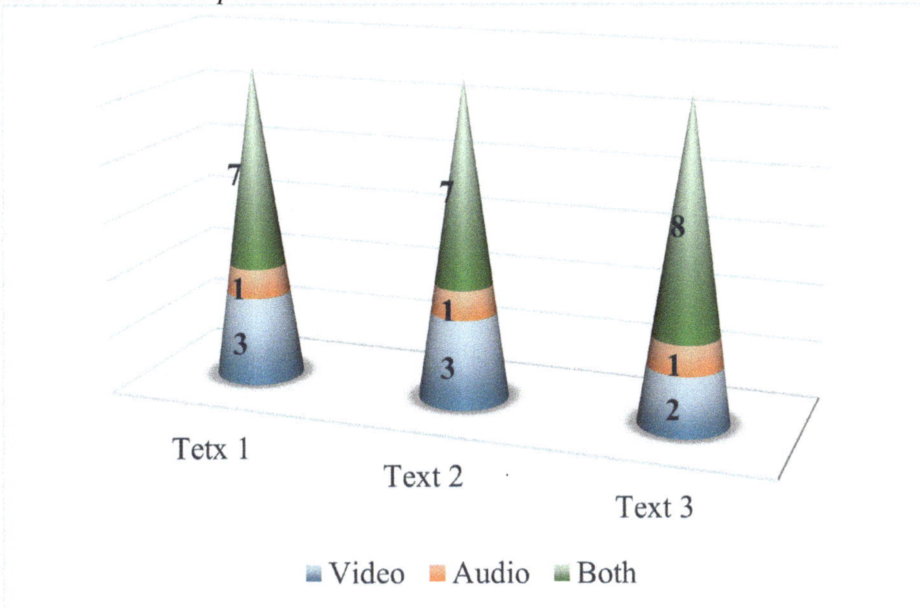

Contrary to the larger lower and the largest upper sections, the middle section of each of the three columns represents the opinion by one participant (Sang, #10m). This person shared at some points of his interviews that his auditory skills do him the best service with reading comprehension of some types of multimodal readings, as audio support allows him to read the print-based text while simultaneously listening to the audio.

There was an interesting moment during the interviews when Sang (participant #10m) expressed some uncertainty when asked to confirm whether he would prefer solely an audio support for gaining a deeper understanding of print-based texts. As per the results of this participant observations, Sang found it difficult to choose between an audio support only or a video with the sound. Prior to providing his final decision, this student asked for some extra thinking time to be able to contemplate his perceptions. Finally, Sang took back his initial statement about his preference of solely auditory support. As there was no certainty in Sang's preference of a type of multimodal support, it becomes important to consider his opinion about existence of an auditory type of learner population. I observed emotional manifestations reflecting in the facial expressions and speeches by this student, which indicated an intense internal conflict about prevalence of benefits of visual or auditory resources of multimodality. For this reason, the data on this student's preferences was marked as *"audio support"* preferred.

To ensure transparence of these research processes and, in this way, add to its trustworthiness, I need to disclose that some students were not fully positive in their self-evaluation of their ways of reading the world. This finding, most likely, may be explained with the fact that some people strongly belong to a specific category of learners/readers and can be characterized as, for example, strongly visual or predominantly auditory. Nevertheless, some others might represent the population of mixed-type learners, i.e., the ones who need a combination of means (e.g., kinetic, or visual) to be able to read the world. These findings correspond with the ones by Gardner (1993).

My above idea was confirmed during the interviews with participants. For example, Mei, participant #7f, stated several times during both interviews, on *Day 1* and *Day 2* that she read people and situations visually. This participant believed she was able to correctly understand the situation from reading exactly the non-verbal visual language. Moreover, Mei clearly stated she would *not* rely on the actors' speech to understand their implied ideas. Instead, as this student explained, she needed to see the speaker(s) to be able to correctly understand whether they were genuine, honest, and sincere and whether she could trust the verbal information these interlocutors shared with her in a dialogue.

Mei was not alone in her need of the visual language. There were two more people, Ting, #4f and Eun, #8f, who perceived the visual mode as most helpful to them in the process of meaning making of any real-life situations. Independently from each other, each of these students shared that they developed a strong and useful to them habit to read and easily understand any non-verbal visual texts (e.g., still images, videos). They both shared they were comfortable with reading some visually displayed information, which contained no verbal texts at all (e.g., videos with music, advertisements).

DEGREE OF HELPFULNESS

It was important for me to investigate and understand the degree of helpfulness of different types of multimodal support, as perceived by my participants. When questioned whether multimodality helped them to deeper understand the print-based texts offered within this project, none of the participants selected the available to them in the questionnaires reply, *"Quite the opposite! It did not help at all."* The other answer options given to the students were "*Not that much*," "*It helped a very,*

very small amount," "*Helped at some moments,*" "*Was pretty helpful,*" and "*Helped a lot!*"

Figure 7 below was developed to assist with visualization of the data obtained from the participants' reflective questionnaires. Overall, participants believed that addition of video with sound helped them to a greater degree rather than the audio support (See Figure 7 below for participants' perceptions of degree of helpfulness of multimodal support).

Figure 7. Participants' perceptions of the degree of helpfulness from addition of different types of multimodal support to print-based texts 2 and 3; the data obtained from reflective questionaries

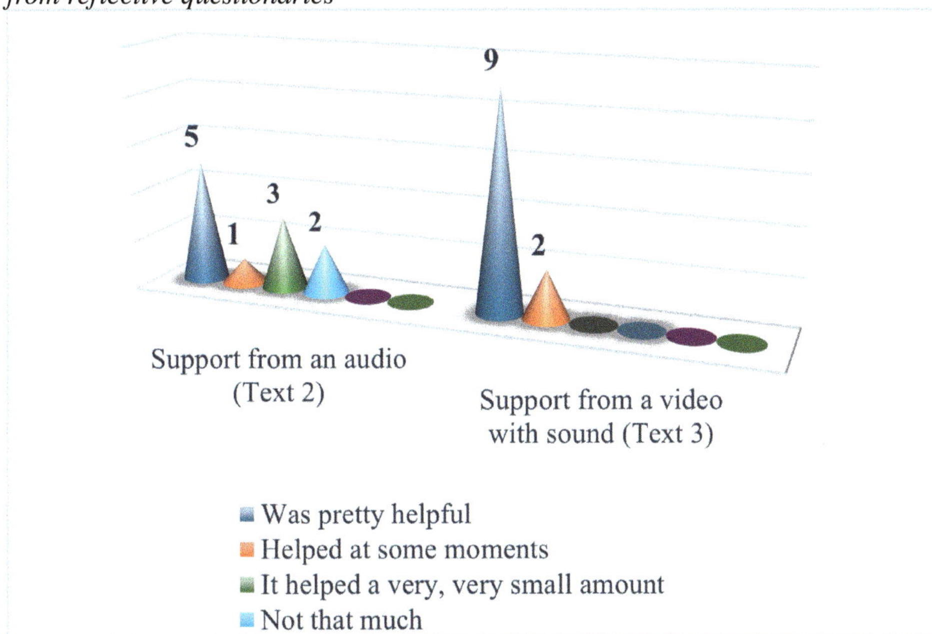

As one can see in Figure 7 above, there were some variations found in the process of the data triangulation. Yet, all students clearly stated in their interviews that multimodality was of great help. And the flat circles in this figure signify that no one chose the corresponding notion.

So, in the whole sample, five participants (45% of the sample) considered that addition of audio was "*pretty helpful*" and substantially helped them with understanding the print-based *Text 2*. The other two students (18% of the sample) indicated that addition of the audio to the print-based *Text 2* helped them, but "*not that much.*" Three more students (27%) believed that addition of the audio to *Text*

2 "helped a very, very small amount." One student (9%) believed the audio only *"helped at some moments."*

Importantly, there was noticed a significantly greater appreciation of multimodality in the form of a video with an audio. Addition of a video with the sound to the print-based *Text 3* produced more positive responses in favor of the video in combination with the audio support. None of the participants said that the video with the sound *"helped a very, very small amount"* or helped but *"not that much."* Nobody selected the option, *"Quite the opposite! It did not help at all!"* either. On the contrary, all participants indicated that addition of video with the sound to the print-based *Text 3* was *"pretty helpful"* (82%), while 2 people (18%) believed that video with the sound support *"helped at some moments,"* according to the data obtained from participants' reflective questionnaires.

Subsequently, during the interviews, all participants reflected more generously on potential benefits of a video with sound, which contributed to their meaning making. All students shared how beneficial it appeared to them in this study when support in the form of a video with the sound was provided to them in addition to the print-based *Text 3.* All students stressed how helpful this type of multimodal support was for their meaning making of the print-based *Text 3.* For example, Sanjay, #1m explained that what helped him to understand *Text 3* better was the opportunity to read the actors' emotions via their facial expressions, postures, and positioning in the space. Exactly same idea about benefits from the visuals was also expressed by Vijay, #3m.

Ting, #4f shared that the provided video support was of great help to her, as it was exactly the visual texts that helped her to make the correct meaning of those parts of the print-based text with which she had struggled prior to watching the video. Ting also clarified that the video helped her to closer relate to the events in the text, so that she got deeper engaged with the reading. This participant also noticed that her motivation in meaning making significantly increased thanks to the video.

Another female participant, #5f Miyuki, pointed out that she had a hard time figuring out the relationships between the characters and the pronouns used in the print-based text. This participant illustrated her words with the following example, "This text says, '*They whisper.*' But who are ***they*** (stressed with Miyuki's voice), I am not sure."

Further, Miyuki explained that there were more moments like the one she described above, when she could make the meaning correctly *only after* watching the video. This student also confirmed the idea expressed by other research participants about helpfulness of the actors' emotions in the video, which assisted her with a deeper comprehension of the meaning of the text. Kumar, #6m also shared that observing the actors' emotions helped him to better understand the text and to answer the comprehension questions to the video-supported *Text 3*. This participant stated, "Emotions were very helpful in answering the questions."

Mei, #7f also explained that the video was very helpful to her for verifying her initial guesses and assumptions, which she made during her pre-reading the print-based *Text 3*. This student clarified her ideas and provided some examples from her previous academic experiences. She shared,

> *I like interaction with real people. That is why I have never taken an online class before. I am so nervous about just reading and trying to get it from just the text. The first one, that text [Text 1 with no support] was the most challenging for me. I think in that case, it would be really* **very, very** *[stressed twice by her voice] helpful if I had a video. (Mei, #7f)*

Another female participant, Eun, #8f, suggested that it was much easier for her to memorize the events in the form of a visual text with the sound, rather than in its print-based form. Additionally, this student shared that the opportunity to better memorize the text was very helpful to her when she was working on the comprehension tests. Comparing both types of the same text, the conventional print-based one and the visual plus audible one, Eun recognized, "The text was still difficult to understand, so watching the video clip helped me understand all…" This participant also reflected on the engaging and motivational aspects of a video, which strongly contributed to her meaning-making processes.

Besides helpfulness with motivation and engagement, Anjali, #9f also pointed out that a video might assist viewers with more efficient sequencing the events in the text. As if in support of Eun's words, Anjali shared that the visual information made memorization of the events and facts in the story more efficient. This participant believed that the above factors made the reading-comprehension and test-taking tasks easier for her; thus, it might work the same way for the others.

Anjali also shared that she identified several information gaps in the print-based texts, which she read within this project. This participant believed this occurred due to these texts being non-narrative but dialogic by genre. According to Anjali, the video with sound helped her the most with filling-in the information gaps due to availability of multiple additional resources she could use; in particular, the setting, the actors' facial expressions, and the tone of the characters' voices, which were heavily loaded with emotions.

The ideas expressed by Anjali about the information gaps in the dialogic texts found support in the ideas shared by Sang, #10m. This participant provided the following example in support of his words on the benefits of video support for filling-in information gaps in non-narrative, dialogic texts. Talking about Juliet, Sang said,

> *The video showed that she [Juliet] didn't know, who he [Romeo] was. And then, she [Juliet] found out, who he [Romeo] was. Then, she [Juliet's nurse] came back and shocked Juliet too. So, that was something I didn't get from the text. (Sang)*

Similarly to the other participants in this study, Sang recognized that observing the actors' emotions via their facial expressions significantly helped him with his meaning making of *Text 3*.

Faiz, #11m also expressed his ideas on beneficial effects from the video with the sound, which assisted him with reading comprehension of *Text 3*. This participant shared,

I did not get that idea from the text [print-based Text 3] first. But when she [the actress in the role of Juliet] explained it with her facial expressions, it gave me a better sense of what's written in the text. (Faiz)

When asked to share more about which exactly resources in the video with sound he relied on for meaning making, this student explained, "I was trying to understand emotions in the text, the emotions of the people in the play, the facial expressions of the characters, their movements."

Though none of the participants selected "helped a lot" as an answer, this fact can be well-explained and understood. Regardless of availability of multimodal support, the texts offered within this project were written in the 15th-16th century Shakespearean language; thus, they presented quite a complex task for my culturally diverse polylingual EAL speaking research participants who had had little to no prior exposure to these type of readings in their past educational histories.

Nevertheless, the findings from the *After-Reading Reflective Questionnaires* confirmed the ones from the participants' interviews. In both cases, all students expressed their appreciation of the additional multimodal features with a significantly greater emphasis on the visuals. To be more exact, the support from the visual and auditory modes in their combination was strongly preferred by these students for their meaning making of the text and also answering the comprehension test questions.

ANY DISTRACTIONS?

Yet, after having confirmed with my participants their strong preferences of the visual multimodal support, I still considered important to investigate another of my researcher's assumptions; i.e., I needed to understand whether addition of features of multimodality to print-based texts might distract students from being focused on their reading the print-based texts. So, with the purpose to deeper understand whether my participants experienced any distractions from the multimodal features added to the print-based *Texts 2* and *3*, I posed several specific questions in the reflective questionnaires. Later, I also followed-up on this topic during the interviews.

As the result of the above investigation, I found that none of the participants said that addition of multimodal features to the print-based *Texts 2* and *3 "was extremely distracting!"* Yet, one person said that audio *"was pretty distracting"* to him. Two other two people perceived that the audio "distracted them at some moments." Majority of the sample (73%) believed that addition of the audio to the print-based *Text 2* either *"did not distract them that much"* (3 people, which was 27%) or *"did not distract them at all"* (4 people or 36%), while one person noticed, *"Quite the opposite! It* [the audio] *kept me focused."*

This picture changed when the conversation focused on *Text 3*. As for addition of the video with the sound to this print-based *Text 3*, almost all people in the sample (10 of 11 students – 91%) believed that additional multimodal visual and auditory features in the video *"did not distract them that much"* (4 people – 36%) or *"did not distract them at all"* (3 people - 27%) from staying focused on the content of the print-based *Text 3*. And three more people (27%) said, *"Quite the opposite! It kept me focused."*

I hope that the above data, when visually represented in Figure 8 below, allow my readers to better visualize the issue with the assumed distractions. Though there were some minor distractions from multimodalities, as perceived by some of the students, these instances were perceived as minimal and insignificant by participants in this study (See Figure 8 below for visual representation of the data on participants' perceptions of distraction level).

Figure 8. Participants' perceptions of distraction level from the multimodal features added to the print-based texts 2 and 3

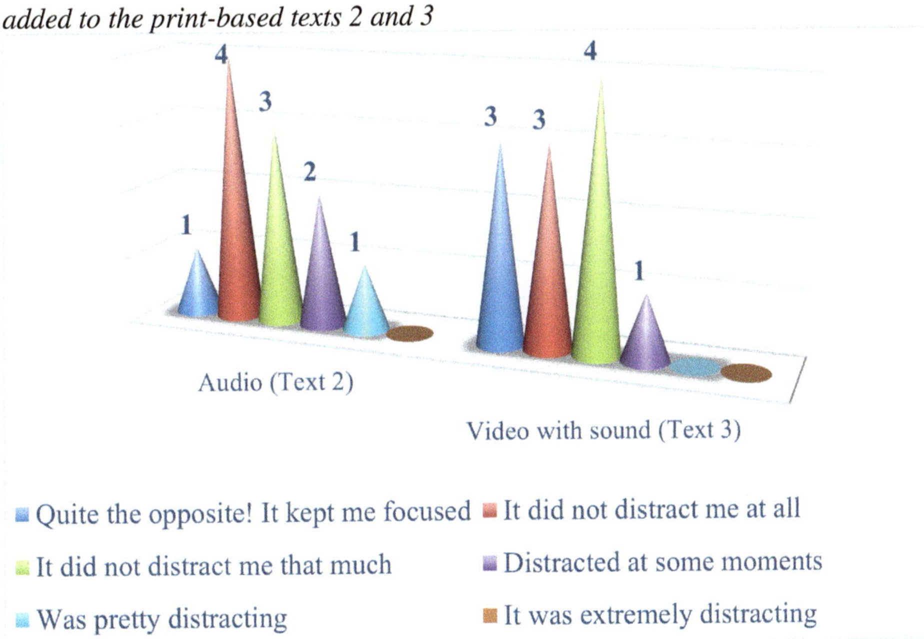

It can be clearly seen that the column marked as "*It was extremely distracting*!" is completely flat, which means none of the students considered this answer. Another column marked as *"It was pretty distracting"* is quite small and is present only in that part of the graph, which represents perceptions of distractions from addition of the audio. Importantly, this category is completely missing from the second graph, which represents perceptions of addition of video plus sound to the print-based *Text 3*. Importantly, it is visible that the positive perceptions of addition of multimodal features prevailed in both cases.

REFERENCES

Flesh, R. (1949). *The art of readable writing*. Harper.

Gardner (1993). *Multiple intelligences: The theory in practice*. New York, NY: Basic Books.

Kincaid, J. P., Fishburne, R. P., Rogers, R. L., & Chissom, B. S. (1975). *Derivation of new readability formulas (automated readability index, fog count, and Flesch reading ease formula) for navy enlisted personnel*. (PDF)*(Report). Naval Air Station Memphis: Chief of Naval Technical Training. Research Branch Report 8–75.* Retrieved March 15, 2024.

Shakespeare, W. (1597). *Romeo and Juliet*.

Chapter 9
So, What Helped?

ABSTRACT

In Chapter 9, I will discuss which exactly strategies these research participants found most helpful while working with this project's texts. Main purpose of this chapter is to give a hand to the educators who are searching for the means to help their struggling readers via offering them some working strategies. It is important to keep in mind that though these students struggled with comprehending of the unimodal print-based Text 1 without any support, they still utilized some reading comprehension strategies. Further, I will share my participants' perceptions of helpfulness of the different types of multimodal support to Texts 2 and 3. Apparently, multimodality was of great service to these struggling readers. Thus, the students were questioned about what exactly assisted them the most in their meaning making of the same texts, but multimodally supported.

COMPREHENSION AND TEST-TAKING STRATEGIES

Regardless of my findings discussed above, I could not stop at the achieved. It was particularly important to investigate what strategies my participants were implementing while working with each of the three texts and comprehension test questions. Most definitely, the findings in this investigation have a great potential to open the gate for utilizing those helpful comprehension strategies for significantly larger populations of instructors and their students. So, I decided to proceed with the study of the textual and multimodal strategies which my participants implemented to gain a deeper understanding of the content and the context of this project's texts, three excerpts from Shakespeare's 1597 play *Romeo and Juliet*, and the comprehension test questions to these readings.

DOI: 10.4018/979-8-3373-3426-4.ch009

Text 1. Unimodal Strategies

Through my further investigation of the above topic, I found that when working with the print-based *Text 1,* which had no support at all, and comprehension test questions to this text, all participants used only some print-based strategies. There was a total of 54 cases of usage of the reading comprehension strategies per the whole sample, as it followed from the participating students' responses marked in their reflective questionnaires.

When reading the unimodal *Text 1,* most often the students utilized the following reading comprehension and test-taking strategies: *Key-word Matching* (100%); *Making Predictions* (64% of the sample); *Identifying the Main Idea* (55%); *Using Context Clues, Making Inferences*, and *Sequencing the Events* (45% in each of these three categories); *Text Features*, and *Compare and Contrast* (34% for each of these two categories).

Some other strategies listed in the reflective questionnaires were used by the participants less often in the process of their working with the print-based *Text 1. Cause and Effect* and *Text Marking* strategies were implemented only by two students (18%) in each of these two categories. *Organizing Information Graphically, Summarizing*, and *Associating Oneself with the Character While Reading the Text* strategies were used by only one participant (9%) in each of the cases listed above.

Text 2. Audio-Based Strategies

A significant increase in the number of utilized strategies was found via the students' responses in their reflective questionnaires, which were concerned with the print-based *Text 2*, which was supported with an audio. As a whole sample, the participants utilized reading comprehension and test-taking strategies in 73 cases. There were 19 more cases of utilization of different reading strategies, which was 35% more versus working with the print-based *Text 1,* which did not have any multimodal support. Importantly, this increase in implementation of diverse reading strategies can be explained by the fact that the participants received the opportunity to implement some auditory multimodal strategies in addition to the previously used, unimodal, print-based ones.

When working with *Text 2* supported by an audio, the students most frequently used the following strategies: *Listening to the Characters' Speeches* and *Evaluating the Characters' Emotions* (73% in each of these two categories); *Key-word Matching* and *Using Context Clues* (64% in each case); *Making Predictions, Identifying the Main Idea, Making Inferences, Understanding Intonations of the Speakers* (55% in each of these four categories), *Text Features* (45%), *Text Marking* strategy, *Sequencing the Events*, and *Associating Oneself with a Character while Reading and*

/ or listening to the Text (27% each). Less often, the students utilized such strategies as *Summarizing* (18%); *Compare and Contrast*, *Cause and Effect*, *Organizing the Information Graphically* (9% in each of these four categories).

Text 3. Combinations of Multimodal Strategies

While working with *Text 3*, which was supported by many more features of multimodality in the form of a video with the sound, the participants implemented reading comprehension and test-taking strategies in **106** cases, which was *33 cases more* than they used while working with the print-based *Text 2* supported by an audio and *52 cases more* than they utilized while working with print-based *Text 1* with no multimodal support. This sudden increase in cases of utilization of different reading strategies between the audio-supported *Text 2* and *Text 3* supported by the video with the sound appeared to be **45%.**

Figure 1. Increase in number of strategies used by the whole sample in the process of their working with three texts and test questions within this project

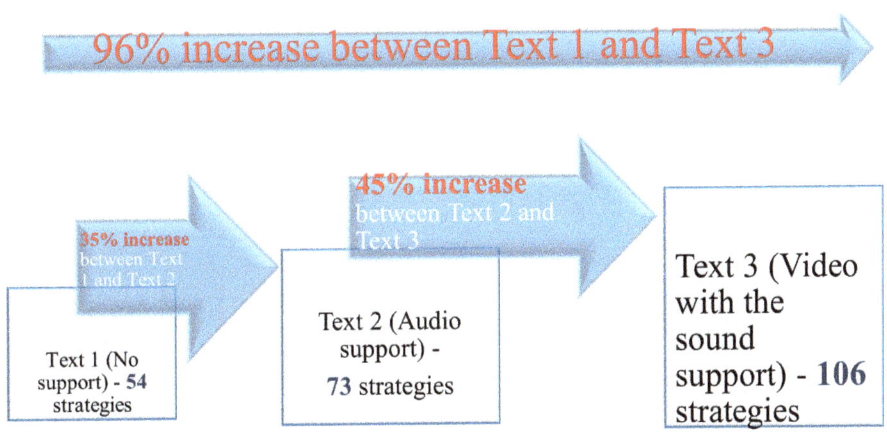

Imperatively, the increase in cases of usage of different reading strategies between *Text 1* (without any support) and Text 3 (video with the sound support) appeared to be as high as **96%.** Figure 1 above allows for a better visualization of these numeric data (See Figure 1 above for the increase in the usage of the reading strategies by the participants).

Overall, the students most frequently utilized the following reading comprehension and test-taking strategies while working with the print-based *Text 3* supported by a video with the sound: *Observing the Characters' Actions* and *Evaluation the*

Characters' Emotions (100% in each of these two categories); *Identifying the Main Idea* (91%); *Observing the Facial Expressions;* and *Observing Movements and Gestures of the Characters* (73% in each of the two categories above); *Using Context Clues* and *Listening to Characters' Speeches* (64% in each of the two categories); *Key-word Matching, Making Inferences, Sequencing Events* (55% in each of these three categories); *Making Predictions, Summarizing, Listening to the Characters' Speeches* (45% in each of these three categories); *Text Features* (27%); *Compare and Contrast*; *Cause and Effect*; *Text Marking* strategies, *Associating Oneself with a Character while Reading the Text and / or Watching and Listening* (18% in each of these four categories). For some reason, none of the participants used *Organizing Information Graphically.* As the students explained, this option was eliminated due to their having the visual support to the print-based *Text 3.*

To give my readers a visually represented picture, I organized all the above data on implementation of the strategies by my research participants in Figure 2, where every text is represented in a particular color. The columns representing the unimodal *Text 1* are shown in blue, the audio-supported *Text 2* is represented by the red-color columns, while *Text 3* with video and audio support is shown in light green (See Figure 2 below for visualization of utilization of reading comprehension and test-taking strategies by the whole group).

Figure 2. Reading strategies used by participants while reading text 1 (no support), text 2 (audio support), text 3 (video with sound support)

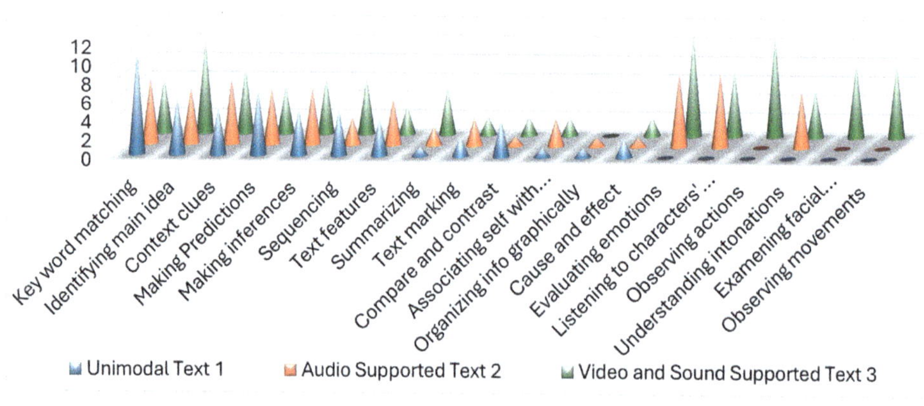

Just to clarify, the most frequently used strategies reached the highest. It can be also clearly seen in Figure 2 above that *Texts 2* and *3* supported by the features of multimodality more frequently reach the highest planks. Out of the two texts supported with the features of multimodality, it most frequently applied to *Text 3*, which was supported by a combination of different multimodal features. This important finding supported the data from the participants' interviews, where all students expressed their ideas about helpfulness of video with sound, which assisted them the most with their meaning making of print-based *Text 3*.

PATTERNS IN CHOICE OF STRATEGIES

Importantly, the data collected through the *After-Reading Reflective Questionnaires* indicated that the whole sample of research participants implemented **233 reading comprehension strategies**, both text-based and multimodal ones when working on all three texts within this project. Yet, imperatively, when working with the conventional print-based text supported by the video with sound, my participants employed the largest number of diverse strategies. In addition to 56 text-based strategies, these students utilized 50 more multimodal reading strategies per the whole sample when their reading was supplemented with the video with the sound. Conclusively, this number was practically **twice** as high.

Naturally, while working with the different types of unimodal and multimodal texts, my participants implemented different reading strategies. With addition of different types of multimodal support, the usage of some of the text-based strategies decreased (e.g., *Key-word Matching*, *Compare and Contrast*), while utilization of some other unimodal strategies (e.g., *Summarizing*, or *Sequencing*) increased (See *Table 1* below for reading strategies most and least frequently implemented by participants on different texts).

Table 1. Strategies implemented by participants in the process of working with text 1 (no support), text 2 (audio support), and text 3 (video support)

#	Strategies implemented by participants	Text 1	Text 2	Text 3	Total
1	Key-word matching	11	7	6	**24**
2	Identifying the main idea	6	6	10	**22**
3	Evaluating emotions of the characters	0	8	11	**19**
4	Using context clues	5	7	7	**19**
5	Making predictions	7	6	5	**18**
6	Making inferences	5	6	6	**17**
7	Listening to the character's speeches	0	8	7	**15**
8	Sequencing the events	5	3	6	**14**
9	Text features	4	5	3	**12**

continued on following page

Table 1. Continued

#	Strategies implemented by participants	Text 1	Text 2	Text 3	Total
10	Observing actions of the characters	0	0	11	**11**
11	Understanding the intonation of the speeches	0	6	5	**11**
12	Examining facial expressions	0	0	8	**8**
13	Observing the movements and gestures of characters	0	0	8	**8**
14	Summarizing	1	2	5	**8**
15	Text marking strategy	2	3	2	**7**
16	Compare and contrast	4	1	2	**7**
17	Associating oneself with a character while watching and/or reading	1	3	2	**6**
18	Cause and effect	2	1	2	**5**
19	Organizing the information graphically	1	1	0	**2**
	Total amount of strategies	**54**	**73**	**106**	**233**

Interestingly, when working with the supported by the multimodal features *Texts 2* and *3*, participants did not use *Key-Word Matching* as often as they did when working with the unimodal print-based *Text 1*. Yet, during reading *Text 1* with no multimodal support, all students chose usage of *Key-Word Matching* for answering comprehension questions, where they could match the corresponding words or expressions encountered in the questions with the ones in the print-based text. During interviews, all students recognized that when they were reading print-based texts and answering questions on some real-life tests or quizzes, *Key-word Matching* was one of the major strategies they strongly relied on.

Consequently, addition of multimodal support significantly reduced the need to use *Key-Word Matching* because reading comprehension in students strongly improved due to addition of multimodalities. Thus, availability of visual support eliminated the need in *Organizing* the print-based *Information Graphically.* Additionally, the need in *Comparing and Contrasting* both the events and characters in the story was also reduced thanks to addition of plentiful multimodal features. So, as reported by participants, availability of multiple additional resources helped them to make the meaning more efficiently.

It is important to emphasize that the major purpose for the above-described investigation was to help generations of educators and their students. This research identified, which exactly reading strategies, as perceived by the students-participants, were most prevalently relied on during their working on this project's tests. It was equally important to understand which of those strategies appeared to be most effective in terms of reading comprehension of the unknown to the participants texts. So, this research found that when working on unimodal, conventional print-based *Text 1* (no support), these students most frequently used *Key-Word Matching*. Nevertheless, this strategy was rejected by them and was not used for answering the comprehension test questions.

Imperatively, this research found that most of the participants failed *Test 1,* where they strongly relied on *Key-Word Matching*. Thus, *Key-word Matching*, though widely used for test taking, cannot be considered an effective strategy in test-taking contrary to the students' initial belief in its helpfulness.

Further, when working with the video- and sound-supported *Text 3*, my participants more actively used *Identifying Main Idea* strategy. These students explained in their interviews that the video with sound allowed them to strongly rely on this strategy, since they could more easily visualize "the whole picture," as they called it, meaning the setting, the epoch, and the social and societal atmosphere in the story as shown in the video. All the above notions may be unified within one term coined with Mikhail Bakhtin (1981), which is *chronotope*.

Using Context Clues appeared to be more helpful when the hints were obtained from the visual and auditory sources, rather than from the print-based text. It was also easier for participants to *Make Inferences* and *Sequence Events in the Story* while being exposed to the video with sound. *Summarizing* strategy was also utilized significantly more often in the case with the video- and sound-supported *Text 3*. As the results of the comprehension assessment to *Text 3* were the highest for the whole sample, this strategy appeared to be one of the most efficient ones when utilized by the participants on *Text 3*.

It needs to be noticed that some students found that addition of auditory mode and utilization of some strategies based on listening to the audio support also assisted them with their meaning making. Though to a lesser degree, than the video with the sound, this audio support was found "*pretty helpful*" by five people (45% of the sample). Nevertheless, the participants were noticeably more enthusiastic about the video compared to the audio support. Three students (27%) said that the audio-recording helped them "*a very, very small amount,*" two other people (18%) believed "*it helped, but not that much,*" and one person (9%) stated "*it helped only at some moments.*" These ideas expressed by participants supported the findings based on the results of the comprehension assessment to the texts. Definitely, the video with sound allowed students to utilize significantly more of both: reading comprehension and test-taking strategies. The above facts explained to me why my participants perceived the audio support as less helpful versus the video with sound support, which they strongly perceived as most helpful to them for both their reading comprehension and test taking.

When working with the two multimodally-supported texts, my participants utilized more strategies, which can be explained by several naturally-occurring factors (e.g., increase in available resources, greater interest in multimodal reading, and their higher internal motivation in comprehending the multimodal texts).

Importantly, the interview data supported these findings from the questionnaires: all participants believed that the multimodal, especially, visual reading strategies were most interesting, attractive, and helpful to them with their meaning making.

STRONG PREFERENCE OF VISUALS

As it was reported above, all participants in this study expressed their high appreciation of addition of a video with sound to the print-based *Text 3*. Yet, these statements alone were not enough to satisfy my researcher's curiosity. For getting a fuller picture, I needed to most importantly understand *why* and *in what ways* multimodality was so helpful. So, I decided to talk about it more with my research participants. When discussing their preference of visual support, all students emphasized the role and significance of the visual mode. Imperatively, the results on the text-comprehension assessments were the highest on the video supported *Text 3*.

Subsequently, the latter fact made it especially important for me to understand in what ways the visual mode of multimodality assisted these students with their meaning making of *Text 3*, as well as with their answering the comprehension test questions to this text. In the following chapter, I will further discuss my participants' perceptions and their own understanding of why they considered the visual means of multimodality most helpful to their reading comprehension and test-taking purposes. Meanwhile, I will sum up that all of them (100%) answered that multimodality helped their reading comprehension. It was interesting that two of the students (18%) stressed that it was exactly the visual component that they needed to correctly make the meaning. In response to my next question, which was concerned with my participants' answering the comprehension test questions, all students (100%) confirmed that multimodality was helpful to them for the test-taking purposes as well. And in response to my question, "If you were offered another text with test questions to answer, would you prefer to be exposed to supporting multimodal features in the form of a video with the sound or not?" all participants (100%) unanimously answered *yes*.

Further, the students explained that watching the video strongly facilitated their deeper understanding of both the traditional print-based text and the test questions to this text, while availability of visual support reduced the need for the students to match the key-words in the comprehension questions with the ones in the print-based *Text 3*. The results from the comprehension assessments administered within this project strongly supported the students' words about helpfulness of multimodality, especially in the form of a video with the sound added to the print-based text.

Amazingly, during the interviews, the female participants stressed importance of visual support more actively rather than the male students. This fact may be explained with a greater interest in females in the romantic nature of the content of Romeo and Juliet's story. Regardless of some variations by gender, all participants advised that it was important for educators to include features of multimodality, especially visuals, in addition to traditional print-based texts for the purpose to assist their students with forming their deeper connections of the content of the course readings. That connection, as follows, might also facilitate a deeper engagement of students via the highly attractive and more comprehensible visual means.

The above portions from the interview data supported the ones from surveys and questionnaires All participants strongly relied on multimodal support, and primarily on the visual mode in combination with the auditory one. Some of the students stated they strongly relied on the combination of diverse visual resources. Lesser number of students made the meaning while relying on the spatial and gestural modes. Least of all, as reported by the students, was reliance on making the meaning through listening to the auditory texts. Importantly, all participants stressed that it was more imperative for them ***to see*** rather than to hear. I believe the visual representation of my participants' ideas supplemented with some numeric information could be very helpful to my readers in forming their visualizable picture of these research results (See Figure 3 below for numbers of cases of usage of different modes of multimodality by participants in the process of performing this project's tasks.)

Figure 3. Frequency of usage of different modes of multimodality by participants

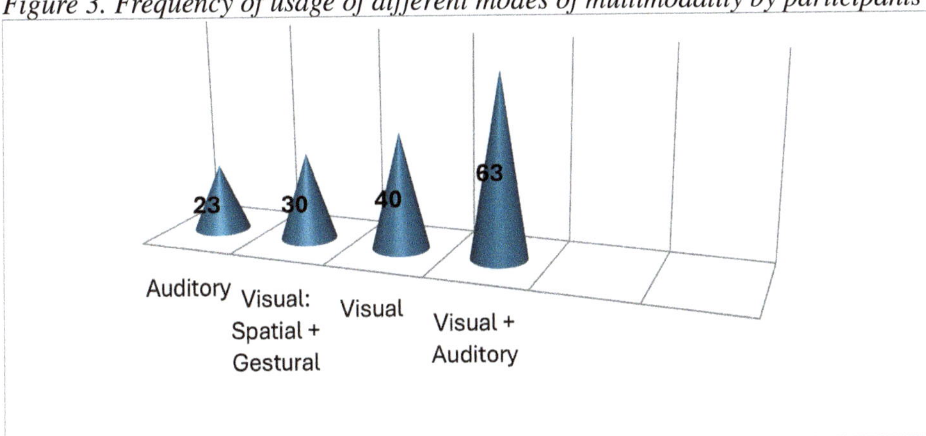

In sum, in the process of analyzing the data obtained from my participant observations, surveys, after-reading reflective questionnaires, and interviews, I understood how exactly my participants perceived the complexity level of each text offered within this project. These data also added to the knowledge of how these students perceived complexity levels of their working on this project tests. Importantly for this research goals, I found that students utilized diverse reading strategies more actively while working with multimodal text and subsequently succeeded in meaning making and test-taking at significantly higher rates. The latter finding was one of the greatest and most significant objectives of this project.

REFERENCES

Bakhtin, M., Holquist, M., & Emerson, C. (1981). *The dialogic imagination: Four essays by M.M. Bakhtin*. University of Texas Press.

Shakespeare, W. (1597). *Romeo and Juliet*.

Chapter 10
When Numbers Speak Louder Than Words

ABSTRACT

In Chapter 10, I will discuss and visually demonstrate the results of all three comprehension tests to Text 1 with no support added, Text 2 with audio support, and Text 3 with multimodal support in the form of a video with the sound. For this purpose, the information will be presented both in a narrative and multimodal forms. As the focus of this entire publication is strongly on multimodal reading, I will be richly using tables, charts, and figures to assist my reading audiences with visualization of this research findings. In this chapter, the numeric information is assembled in several tables. Additionally, affordances of color are used to assist readers with faster distinguishing between the correct and incorrect answers on the comprehension test questions. Separate tables were created for the results of the tests for Text 1 (with no support), Text 2 (with audio support), and Text 3 (with video and audio support). As some differences in working by gender were found in this study, this information will also be shown in a separate table.

ASSESSMENT SCALE

After having discussed this research participants' perceptions of their working experiences with this projects' texts, (as a reminder, these were three scenes from *Romeo and Juliet* by Shakespeare, 1597), I will share more information on the assessments to these texts. Each of the three tests had six comprehension questions. This number of questions was chosen so that the result of each test might be either "*Pass*" or "*Fail*," based on the 50/50 ratio, where the score of 3/6 or 50% and any result below this score was considered a failure. In many real-life classrooms, as well as within this project, all six correct answers to the comprehension test questions counted as 6/6, or a 100%, or a letter-grade *A*, or its equivalent, or verbal feedback

DOI: 10.4018/979-8-3373-3426-4.ch010

Excellent. Five correct answers would count as 5/6, or 83%, or a letter-grade *B*, or its equivalent, or verbal feedback *Good.* Four correct answers would count as 4/6, or 67%, or a letter grade *C,* or its equivalent, or verbal feedback *Satisfactory.* Three correct answers might count as 3/6, or 50%, or a letter-grade *D*, or its equivalent, or verbal feedback *Poor*. Two correct answers might count as 2/6, or 33%, or a letter-grade "*F*," or its equivalent, or verbal feedback "*Very Poor*." A letter-grade "*F*" would be also given for only one correct answer, which would make 1/6, or 17% numerically. Verbally this low achievement would be addressed as "*Unacceptable.*" The same letter grade "*F*" would be also given for a test with no correct answers or 0/6, or 0%.

To sum up, for this project's purposes, only the scores of a 100%, 83%, and 67% were considered passing scores, while 50%, 33%, 17%, and 0% would mean failing the test. It is important to state that no letter-grades were issued, ***though not disclosed,*** to the research participants, and no verbal feedback was provided with regards to their performance on the tests. I was the only person who had access to and the knowledge of the test results. It needs to be clarified that the tests performed by the participants were assessed in percentages and letter grades with the only purpose for this research, i.e., to receive the individual and a whole-group outcomes for shaping a fuller research picture through the data on student-achievement.

Additionally, the analysis of the assessment outcomes on all the three tests allowed me to look at these data from a position of a classroom teacher, who would be not only responsible for evaluating and grading her students' work, but also interested to see whether the newly implemented multimodal approach to education brought fruitful results. Later in this chapter, I will demonstrate every student's and a whole-group test score assembled in tables, so my readers could get an entire picture of the results of the assessment on each comprehension test comparatively and practically at a glance.

Another important clarification that needs to be provided is that the comprehension test questions were numbered from 1 to 6 and had four multiple-choice answers to each of the six questions. In the tables, they were marked with the lower-case letters as follows: option answer *#1 – a,* option answer *#2 – b*, option answer *#3 – c*, and option answer *# 4 – d* (to not be confused with the letter grades, which were marked with the upper-case letters, *A*, *B*, *C*, *D*, and *F).* Students were supposed to mark their answer to each question via circling the corresponding letter (*a*, *b*, *c*, or *d*) standing in front of each of the four option answers.

TEXTS

Text 1 (No Support): Test 1 Results

In this section, I will share the data from the very first comprehension test to *Text 1*, which had no support. As a reminder, *Text 1* was offered to every research participant on Day 1 within this project, where each student arrived to the designated research site at his or her own scheduled time. As this print-based *Text 1* was not supported by any multimodal features, right upon completion of reading this text, each student was offered to answer six comprehension questions to the text. Looking at the assessment results for the entire sample, I found that out of 66 possible answers (100%), the whole sample of students provided 24 correct answers and 42 incorrect answers, which was 36% and 64% respectively.

Breaking the above data by the lowest and highest results, I found that one student (9% of the sample) provided five correct answers (which was 83%), three other students (27% of the sample) gave 3 correct answers (which was 50%). The other four students (36% of the sample) answered 2 questions correctly (which was 33%). And the remaining two students (18% of the sample) were able to answer only 1 question correctly (which was 17%). Unfortunately, one person (9% of the sample) was not able to answer correctly any of the comprehension test questions to the print-based *Text 1* (See Table 1 below for *Test 1* results).

Table 1. Results of comprehension test to text 1 (no support)

Participant	Students' answers						Total correct answers	Total incorrect answers
Question #	1	2	3	4	5	6		
Sanjay 1m	b[1]	~~a~~[2]	~~d~~	c	~~a~~	c	3	3
Prem 2m	~~e~~	d	~~d~~	c	~~a~~	~~b~~	2	4
Vijay 3m	~~e~~	~~e~~	~~d~~	c	d	c	3	3
Ting 4f	b	~~e~~	~~a~~	~~b~~	~~a~~	c	2	4
Miyuki 5f	b	~~b~~	~~d~~	c	~~a~~	~~b~~	2	4
Kumar 6m	~~a~~	~~e~~	~~d~~	~~b~~	~~a~~	~~a~~	0	6
Mei 7f	b	~~e~~	~~d~~	~~d~~	~~a~~	~~b~~	1	5
Eun 8f	b	~~e~~	~~b~~	c	d	~~a~~	3	3
Anjali 9f	~~e~~	~~a~~	~~b~~	c	~~a~~	c	2	4
Sang 10m	b	~~e~~	c	c	d	c	5	1
Faiz 11m	~~a~~	~~b~~	~~d~~	~~a~~	d	~~b~~	1	5
Total correct	6	1	1	7	4	5	24	
Total incorrect	5	10	10	4	7	6		42

Table Convenience: [1] Correct answers are marked in blue: test question 1 – **b**; question 2 – **d**; question 3 – **c**; question 4 – **c**; question 5 – **d**; question 6 – **c**. [2] Incorrect answers are marked in red as a crossed out letter (e.g., a). The letters in this table are signifiers of four option answers to each multiple-choice comprehension test question.

As my readers can perceive, the results of the comprehension test to *Text 1*, which had no support, were not very high for the entire sample. Importantly, according to this project's evaluation system, only one student (9% of the sample) passed the first test; thus, would have received a passing grade in a real-life situation. The rest of 10 students (91% of participants in the sample) failed the comprehension test to the print-based *Text 1*, which was not supported by any means of multimodality (See Table 1 above for the results of the comprehension test to the print-based *Text 1*, which was not supported by features of multimodality).

Text 2 (Audio Support): Test 2 Results

Importantly, the picture of the second assessment results changed on the same day. This was when each student was offered to read *Text 2*, which was supported by features of multimodality in the form of an audio-recording of the same text. The results of the comprehension *Test 2* to *Text 2* appeared to be higher compared to the first test, when students attempted to read *Text 1* with no support and answered six comprehension questions of *Test 1* to the print-based *Text 1*.

So, on the second assessment of Day 1, out of 66 possible answers to the comprehension *Test 2* to the print-based *Text 2* supported by an audio, the students as a whole group provided 48 correct answers and 18 incorrect ones, which was 73% and

27% respectively. This means that the number of correct answers to the questions of comprehension *Test 2* was twice or 50% higher, than the number of the correct answers to comprehension *Test 1*.

Two of the eleven students (18% of the sample) answered all six questions (100%) correctly. Three other students (27% of the sample) answered 5 questions (83%) correctly. Four students (36% of the sample) provided four correct answers (67%). Two students (18% of the sample) still failed the test according to this project evaluation system. One of them (9% of the whole group) answered only half of the test questions correctly (50%), and another participant (9% of the sample) could provide only 2 correct answers (33%). Nevertheless, there were only two failing scores on comprehension *Test 2*, which made only 18% of the sample versus that extremely high 91% of failing scores on the comprehension *Test 1*. (See Table 2 below for the results of comprehension *Test 2* to the print-based *Text 2* supported by features of multimodality in the form of an audio).

Table 2. Results of comprehension test 2 to text 2 (audio support)

Participant	Students' answers						Total correct answers	Total incorrect answers
Question #	1	2	3	4	5	6		
Sanjay 1m	d[3]	c	a	c	d	b	6	0
Prem 2m	d	d[4]	b	b	a	b	2	4
Vijay 3m	d	d	a	c	b	b	4	2
Ting 4f	d	c	a	b	a	b	4	2
Miyuki 5f	d	c	a	a	a	b	4	2
Kumar 6m	d	c	a	c	d	b	6	0
Mei 7f	d	d	a	c	d	a	4	2
Eun 8f	d	c	a	c	a	b	5	1
Anjali 9f	d	c	a	c	a	b	5	1
Sang 10m	d	c	a	c	a	b	5	1
Faiz 11m	d	d	d	c	e	a	3	3
Total correct	11	7	9	8	3	10	48	
Total incorrect	0	4	2	3	8	1		18

Note: [3] Correct answers are marked in blue: test question 1 – **d**; question 2 – **c**; question 3 – **a**; question 4 – **c**; question 5 – **d**; question 6 – **b**. [4] Incorrect answers are marked in red as a crossed-out letter (e.g., d). The letters in this table are signifiers of four option answers to each multiple-choice comprehension test question to the texts.

Importantly, the findings based on the comprehension assessments supported the ones from the students' interviews. Practically all participants believed that addition of an audio helped them to make a deeper meaning of the print-based *Text 2*. Only one person did appreciate the audio support.

There was a conclusive thought, which I, as a researcher and as an educator would like to bring to the table for my readers. It is worth to notice that on *Test 1*, ***all*** students made mistakes when answering comprehension questions to *Text 1* (no support). Nevertheless, during the second assessment *Test 2* for the (audio-supported) *Text 2*, two students made no mistakes at all. Three other students made only one mistake; so, altogether, this group of five high achievers formed about a half of the sample. Thus, multimodal support in the form of the audio made a significant difference for this group of students. Later, these numeric findings were echoed during the interviews with participants, where many of these students expressed their appreciation of the audio support.

Text 3 (Video with Sound Support): Test 3 Results

On the second day within this research project, the participants reported to the research site each at their individually scheduled time again. On Day 2, participants were offered to read *Text 3*, which had video with sound support and completed comprehension *Test 3* to this text. The results of the comprehension *Test 3* appeared to be significantly higher than the results of the comprehension *Test 1* and *Test 2*. Imperatively for this research, six participants (55% of the whole sample) provided 5 correct answers (83%) to the comprehension test questions to *Text 3* supported by features of multimodality in the form of a video with an audio, while the rest of the sample, 5 students (45%) answered **all** test questions correctly (See Table 3 below for the results of comprehension *Test 3*).

Table 3. Results of comprehension test to text 3 (video and audio support)

Participant	Students' answers						Total correct answers	Total incorrect answers
Question #	1	2	3	4	5	6		
Sanjay 1m	a[5]	c	b	a	c	b[6]	5	1
Prem 2m	a	c	b	a	a	a	5	1
Vijay 3m	a	d	b	a	c	a	5	1
Ting 4f	a	d	b	a	c	a	5	1
Miyuki 5f	a	c	b	a	a	a	5	1
Kumar 6m	a	c	b	a	c	a	6	0
Mei 7f	a	c	b	a	c	a	6	0
Eun 8f	a	c	b	a	c	a	6	0
Anjali 9f	a	c	b	a	c	a	6	0
Sang 10m	a	c	b	a	c	a	6	0
Faiz 11m	a	c	b	a	c	e	5	1
Total correct	11	9	11	11	9	9	60	
Total incorrect	0	2	0	0	2	2		6

Table convenience: [5] Correct answers are marked in blue: test question 1 – **a**; questions 2 – **c**; question 3 – **b**; question 4 – **a**; question 5 – **c**; question 6 – **a**. [6] Incorrect answers are marked in red as a crossed letter (e.g., d). The letters in this table are not to be confused with letter-grades. These letters are signifiers of four option answers to each multiple-choice comprehension test question to the texts.

Victoriously, none of the participants failed the comprehension *Test 3* to the print-based *Text 3*, which was supported by multimodal features in the form of a video with the sound. Significantly, five students, which was almost a half in the sample, made no mistakes at all. Each of the other six students made one mistake only. Thus, it is possible to conclude that in a real-life situation, all these students would have received either a letter grade *A* or *Excellent* and a *B* or *Good* correspondingly as per the assessment system adopted for this project.

Positively, the above increase in correct answers between comprehension *Test 3*, where the print-based text was supported by a video with an audio versus *Test 2*, where the print-based text was supported by an audio made 25%. Importantly, the increase in correct answers appeared to be even greater when the results of *Test 3* were compared to the results of *Test 1*. That increase in correct answers between *Test 1* and *Test 3* made **75%** in favor of the print-based Text 3, supported with an entire ensemble of multimodal features.

As an extremely passionate educator and educational researcher, I might have started celebrating the victory of the multimodal approach in education as it was found in my current research. Nevertheless, I had to harness my excitement and continue my work as too many questions were to be answered yet. So, with the internal and ever-gleaming fire of passion enlightening my endeavors, I saddled my impatient soul, settled my galloping mind, and continued my scrupulous work on the further tasks of this project.

VARIATIONS BY GENDER

Interestingly, in the process of the test data analysis, I found some variations by gender (See Table 4 below for raw numbers of correct and incorrect numbers to comprehension test questions to *Text 1* (No support), *Text 2* (Audio Support), and *Text 3* (Video with sound support) by gender).

Table 4. Numbers of correct and incorrect answers to comprehension test questions to text 1 (no support), text 2 (audio support), and text 3 (video support) by gender

	Text 1 (No Support)		**Text 2 (Audio Support)**		**Text 3 (Video Support)**	
Answers	Correct	Incorrect	Correct	Incorrect	Correct	Incorrect
6 males	**14**	**22**	**26**	**10**	**32**	**4**
5 females	**10**	**20**	**22**	**8**	**28**	**2**
Total	**24**	**42**	**48**	**18**	**60**	**6**

At a first glance at Table 4 above, it might seem that the six male participants outscored five female students on each of the three tests. Nevertheless, I offer my readers to have a deeper insight into the results of each test. All five females participating in this study provided 10 correct answers to the comprehension *Test 1*, which was 2 correct answers on average, while six male students gave 14 correct answers to the same test, which was 2.3 correct answers on average. Next, when working on the comprehension *Test 2*, the five females answered 22 comprehension questions correctly, which was 4.4 correct answers on average, while six male students answered 26 questions to the same test correctly, which made 4.3 correct answers.

The results of comprehension *Test 3* revealed that five female students provided 28 correct answers to the comprehension *Test 3* correctly, which made 5.6 correct answers on average. Six male students gave 32 correct answers to the same test, which made 5.3 correct answer on average.

Now, I offer my readers to look at the same data conveniently placed into another table. This different type of calculation, i.e., calculating the averages, will open to the readers a slightly different, yet realistic picture (See Table 5 below to see average numbers provided by female and male research participants to each of the three comprehension tests).

Table 5. Average numbers of correct answers to comprehension test questions provided by female and male participants

Gender	Test 1	Test 2	Test 3
Males	2.3	4.3	5.3
Females	2	4.4	5.6
Difference / Females	15% behind	2% ahead	5% ahead

So, as one can see now, in Table 5 above, the increase in the average numbers of correct answers provided by each group of participants, females and males, is obvious. Yet, these were the female participants who outscored the male students on *Tests 2* and *3*. It is interesting that upon the results of comprehension *Test 1* to the print-based *Text 1*, which was not supported by features of multimodality, the female participants fell 15% behind the male students. When working on *Test 2* upon reading *Text 2* supported by and audio, the female participants did 2% better than the male students. And when working on comprehension *Test 3* to the print-based *Text 3* supported by a video with the sound, females did 5% better than their male counterparts.

Conclusively, according to the data in Tables 2, 3, 4, and 5 above, the male students made a 130% improvement between *Test 1 / Text 1* (no multimodal support) and *Test 3/ Text 3* (supported by multimodal features in the form of a video with the sound). Impressively, the female participants made 180% improvement on the same tasks. Thus, it was not only the participants' perception of helpfulness from addition of multimodality. Moreover, this was the fact documented via the participants' assessment results. With the above said, my readers might agree with my decision to engage in calculating the numeric outcomes in addition to listening to my participants' speeches, as advocated by Maxwell (2010) in his publication in defense of numbers in qualitative research.

LOOKING AT THE MEANS

Besides calculating the averages, I also decided to count the means. As I mentioned before, in this study, the tests results were not shared with the participating students. I tried my best to not sadden nor frustrate my participants. Nevertheless, for this research purposes, I assessed each individual student's work and the outcome by the whole sample. The data in Table 6 below demonstrates the means of the correct and incorrect answers to the comprehension test questions for each of the three comprehension tests to each of the texts, *Text 1* (No support), *Text 2* (Audio support), and *Text 3* (Video with the sound support).

Table 6. The mean of correct and incorrect answers to comprehension test questions to text 1 (no support), text 2 (audio support), and text 3 (video with the sound support) in numbers and percentages

All participants	Text 1 (No support)	Text 2 (Audio support)	Text 3 (Video with sound support)
Mean of correct answers	24	48	60
Mean of incorrect answers	42	18	6
Percentage of correct answers	36%	73%	91%

As one can see, utilization of only 54 unimodal text-based reading strategies by these research participants resulted in only 36% of correct answers. In a real-life classroom, this score of 36% would be considered a failing or very poor performance not only by the students, but also by their teacher. Yet, addition of the auditory resources to the conventional print-based text allowed my study participants to use 76 of both unimodal and multimodal reading strategies. This addition helped the whole group of participants to complete the task with the score of 73% of correct answers. Thinking of a real-life classroom, this would be most likely considered an average achievement for the students and their teacher.

Moreover, utilization of the total of 106 reading strategies, 50 of which were multimodal reading strategies in addition to the 56 unimodal print-based ones, helped these research participants to answer 91% of comprehension test questions correctly when they received an ensemble of multimodal resources in the video with sound, which supported the print-based text. Thus, when having 106 multimodal and unimodal reading strategies at their disposal, while working with the text supported with a video including sound, my participants reading comprehension increased dramatically and allowed them to complete the comprehension test at a high rate of 91%. It is needless to prove, as it is self-evident that in a real-life situation, the students and their teacher would be considered extremely high achieving were they demonstrating the above results on their midterm or final tests.

REFERENCES

Maxwell, J. A. (2010). Using numbers in qualitative research. *Qualitative Inquiry, 16*(6), 475–482. DOI: 10.1177/1077800410364740

Shakespeare, W. (1597). *Romeo and Juliet.*

Section 3
Nonchalant Accounts of AI

Chapter 11
MAXQDA-Portrayed Speech

ABSTRACT

Chapter 11 will allow my readers to evaluate the affordances of the Artificial Intelligence (AI) used for the qualitative analysis of the interview data. In this chapter, I will continue discussing my findings from the first round of the individual interviews with each of my research participants. I will endeavor to practically let my readers "hear" each individual voice. And via the affordances of the visual means of Artificial Intelligence, I will assist my readers with their visualization of the major topics and themes emphasized by each person and by the whole sample of participants within this project. For this purpose, I will share with my audiences Portraits, which I developed with the help of the MAXQDA software for qualitative data analysis.

MAXQDA PORTRAITS OF DAY 1 INTERVIEW 1: AUDIO VERSUS NO SUPPORT

As I shared with the readers of this book, I am a part of the studied population of Polylingual English as an Additional Language speakers in academe. My belonging to the selected for this research cohort opened an invisible gate for a sincere and genuine Bakhtin (1981) dialogue during my meetings with participants. So, the interviews did not have the character of an interrogation, but instead, looked, sounded, and felt as an extremely open tête-à-tête literature-, arts- and the reading science-based conversations between the researcher and each participant. All students were asked the same sets of questions concerning their experiences with the Shakespeare (1597) and Zeffirelli (1968) *Romeo and Juliet* texts during Interview I on Day 1 and Interview II on Day 2. Nevertheless, each person was given as much freedom as possible via the affordances of the open-ended questions. So, the responses to

DOI: 10.4018/979-8-3373-3426-4.ch011

the questions differed and provided many unique and, often, unpredictable ideas, as every person focused on the topics of his or her highest significance and priority, as they perceived it. Amazingly, the unique logic I tracked in every person's reasoning echoed the ideas of the other people participating in this study. Upon having noticed those occurrences, I was able to identify some categories which further shaped into common themes.

The data collected in this research appeared to be so plentiful that I decided to utilize some type of the available on the market software for qualitative data analysis. To my great and almost unbelievable luck, I was granted a license to a package of software for qualitative data analysis by the MaxQda company during my attendance and presenting at the powered by Norman Denzin (1941 – 2023) International Congress of Qualitative Inquiry (ICQI). In this chapter, I will share with my readers the MaxQda-processed and visually represented data from each participant's interview. Those will be the individual color-coded portraits, which were generated via processing the transcribed interview speeches. For my readers' convenience, I will list the color-coded themes in Table 1 below.

Table 1. Color-coded themes most frequently addressed by participants in their interviews

Orange	Multimodality reduces necessity of repetitive re-readings
Lime	Multimodality involves cooperation of multiple brain functions
Pine	Powerful effect of color
Red	Multimodality makes content stick to memory
Azure	Addition of multimodality did not hinder
Navy	Multimodality enhances interest and motivation
Lilac	Visuals preferred
Yellow	Multimodal support helped with this project tasks
Turquoise	Multimodality has the potential to assist with comprehension

Additionally, I will explain that the phrases and sentences in Table 1 above are the major themes which emerged from interviews with each participant. I selected and assigned a certain color to each of these major themes. My readers will soon see the color-coded individual interview portraits, which will distinctly show by the prevalence of some specific colors which exactly themes and topics mattered the most for each interviewee.

And of course, I will comment on every portrait and verbally interpret the themes encoded in each participant's interview.

Quick Guide to Reading Portraits

Prior to introducing my readers to the MaxQda software-generated visual graphic representations of participants' speeches during their interviews or so-called portraits I will add some clarifications which might be very handy for the first-time viewers. So, every color-coded zone in each portrait below will represent a certain theme and topic, just as shown in Table 1 above. The wider the zone marked by a certain color, the longer each student contemplated aloud on that particular topic. For example, zone 1 in *Portrait 1a* was coded in lime color. Checking with Table 1 above, one can notice that the lime color represents the following idea: "Multimodality involves cooperation of multiple brain functions." Next, in *Portrait 1a* in the *First Interview* of Day 1, this lime-colored zone 1 takes approximately a quarter (25%) of this image. This means that a quarter of the entire time in the *Interview 1* on Day 1 was spent by this participant discussing this very topic of how multimodality may activate multiple brain zones in humans. Importantly, as the researcher, I did not cater the themes and topics to my participants' attention. On the contrary, the identified themes were raised by each student without any leading from the side of the researcher.

Next important moment, when some specific colors appear in the interview portraits of several or all participants, this means that all those subjects, independently from each other, raised the same questions and discussed the same topic. The width of the zones within each graphic interview portrait will vary, since different participants were discussing these themes with different longevity due to having a greater or a lesser interest in each of these topics.

It also needs to be explained that the color-coded portraits of Day 1 interviews were comprised of the columns built off the tiny colorful squares, which represented the time units. Also, when participants gave their first Day 1 interviews and shared their experiences concerning their working with the audio-supported text and test versus the unimodal ones, the visual portraits of their speeches were marked with a lower-case letter *a*, which stands for *audio* support, for example, *Portrait 1a*, *Portrait 2a*, etc.

On Day 2, the interview portraits were generated with the columns comprised of colorful circles. On the second day in the project, the participants largely discussed their experiences with multimodal support in the form of a video with sound. So,

Day 2 interview portraits were marked with letter *v,* which stands for *video* next to each participant's number, for example, *Portrait 1v*, *Portrait 2v*, and so on.

With the above clarifications provided, my readers may now attend to viewing the AI-processed and visually represented voices or speeches of this research' participants.

Day 1. Interview 1

Sanjay #1 M

Figure 1. Portrait 1a. Sanjay's perceptions of effects of addition of an audio to conventional print-based text 2

(MaxQda, 2021)

During the first interview, participant #1m Sanjay expressed his appreciation of multimodal auditory support in addition to the print-based *Text 2*. He stressed the fact that the organs of senses of a human tend to cooperate; so, as Sanjay believed, it is necessary to provide the condition for this cooperation. Sanjay clarified his idea saying that, "If you are looking at something with your eyes, your ears are cooperating automatically. When you hear some text, but your eyes are looking at something else, you get distracted."

Sanjay talked about the need in evaluating several multimodal resources, such as sounds, intonations, pitch of voice, etc., rather than just any one unimodal textual resource. This participant clarified that multimodal texts activate different zones in the brain of a reader (See *Portrait 1a*, zone 1). Further, Sanjay extrapolated that simultaneous reading a verbal text with one's eyes and double-processing the same text via listening to it provides great assistance to the reader with his or her comprehension processes, due to increase in focus (See *Portrait 1a*, zone 2).

Moreover, Sanjay explained that he had previously read some positive information on how a human brain can process multiple sources of information, such as a plain print-based text in combination with color, sound, movement, and action, etc. Sanjay assigned his ability to better understand *Text 2* to addition of the audio (*Portrait 1a*, zone 4). He also stated that audio did not hinder his work at all (*Portrait 1a*, zone 5).

According to this participant, multimodality might also enhance interest in reading (*Portrait 1a*, zone 3). Concluding his interview, Sanjay suggested that a video might be of a great service to him for his meaning making of the print-based test supported with visuals.

Prem #2 M

Figure 2. Portrait 2a. Prem's perceptions of effects of addition of an audio to conventional print-based text 2

(MaxQda, 2021)

Participant #2m, Prem characterized himself as a skilled and highly internally motivated reader. Essentially, the primary topic he was developing in his Day 1 interview was concerned with potential helpfulness from diverse multimodal features in addition to a print-based text to student meaning making (see *Portrait 2a*, zone 1). Importantly, this participant specifically stressed that the audio support needed to be true to life, which means dramatized or performed by skilled actors.

Just as Sanjay, Prem suggested that video support might be more powerful thanks to the impact of color on humans' ability to intake, process, and retain visual information (*Portrait 2a*, zone 2). Prem supported his statement on importance of supplemental resources with an example from his academic experiences, "In my field, in Math, and in technical fields, everything [physical phenomena and objects] speaks to us. Words do not matter that much." Prem decided to verbally illustrate his idea, "If I show you numbers in columns, like, 30%, 40%, 50%, they are just numbers. But if I show to you the same data in the form of colorful graphs, you will get it thousand times faster." This idea expressed by Prem, a doctoral scholar, even stronger confirmed my decision to use the multimodal AI-generated interview portraits for visually communicating my research findings to my audiences (as in the MaxQda-created portraits).

Just as Sanjay, Prem had also had prior access to publications on effectiveness of multimodal visual representations of information for faster understanding the content without the need in repetitive re-readings (*Portrait 2a*, zone 4). Prem believed that multimodality might assist with more efficient memorization (*Portrait 2a*, zone 5). He furthered this idea saying that, "Color is really powerful. Your mind grasps the color faster… It is a very, **very** important tool and it is very important **in any language**." (The words in bold print were the ones emphasized by the speaker's tone and intensity of his voice.)

Just as Sanjay, Prem would strongly prefer having visual support in addition to the print-based text supported by an audio (*Portrait 2a,* zone 3). When asked to clarify why visuals would be better, Prem shrugged his shoulders and made a wide, opening gesture with his hands as if he were opening a double window, "What do we have to discuss here if that's where it is." Prem's posture and his opening gesture spoke louder than his words and helped this student express his thoughts about his strong preference in seeing the events discussed in the text for getting the picture of what was happening in the story. This person also found visuals helpful for better memorization. Further Prem clarified,

> *Hypothetically, demonstration of throwing a pencil would be an easier way to show how I throw a pencil. Of course, it is better with animation or videos; just the audio would not help us that much. If it is a video that shows real life, I can remember real life longer. (Prem)*

Vijay #3 M

Figure 3. Portrait 3a. Vijay's perceptions of effects of addition of an audio to conventional print-based text 2

(MaxQda, 2021)

Participant #3, Vijay believed that multimodality had a great potential to assist students with their reading comprehension (see *Portrait 3a*, zone 1). He did not take addition of multimodality as distraction and believed it was extremely helpful to him (see *Portrait 3a*, zone 2 & 3). Vijay made this conclusion based on his own experiences with reading *Text 1* without any support and, later on the same day, *Text 2* supported with an audio. The audio helped this participant to better comprehend *Text 2* via evaluating the actors' intonations, pitch, and tone of their voices, etc. Vijay also assumed that a video might assist him with comprehension of the project texts better than the audio (see *Portrait 3a*, zone 4).

This participant shared that in the process of learning English as an Additional Language, which in his case was language number four, he used to watch multiple *Hollywood* movies with subtitles. Then, Vijay noticed how greatly it worked for him when he could simultaneously match the print-based text in the subtitles with the actors' speeches in the films and with the events on the screen.

Vijay mentioned importance of multimodalities for memorization processes. This student frankly shared, "In my case, I remember more things when I look at them or hear, but not when I read."

Ting #4 F

Figure 4. Portrait 4a. Ting's perceptions of effects of audio support added to conventional print-based text 2

(MaxQda, 2021)

Participant #4f, Ting, generously shared how powerfully multimodality helped her to better understand the print-based *Text 2* offered in this project (see *Portrait 4a*, zone 1). Based on her own experiences in this project, Ting suggested that addition of multimodality might greatly assist students with their comprehension of print-based texts (see *Portrait 4a*, zone 2). In Ting's case, her interest in the text was enhanced by the sounds in the audio, such as the voices of actors, their intonations, tone, pitch, breath patterns, etc. All these factors appealed to the emotional side of Ting's perception, thus ignited her motivation in understanding the content of text in a greater detail (see *Portrait 4a*, zone 3).

Ting also explained that she usually had to re-read again, and again, when she needed to deeper understand her readings. But when she received the auditory support to the print-based *Text 2*, she felt it was not necessary for her to re-read the print-based *Text 2* multiple times (see *Portrait 4a*, zone 4). It started turning into a pattern, which recurred in several interviews, including the one by Ting, when participants expressed their preference of a video with the sound in addition to the print-based text, rather than just an audio (*Portrait 4a*, zone 5).

Miyuki #5 F

Figure 5. Portrait 5a. Miyuki's perceptions of effects of audio support added to conventional print-based Text 2

(MaxQda, 2021)

Participant #5f, Miyuki contemplated in her first interview over the ways in which multimodality might be helpful to students' meaning making in the process of their reading print-based texts supported by multimodal features (*Portrait 5a*, zone 1). Addition of the audio to the conventional print-based *Text 2* was of great service to Miyuki and greatly assisted her with comprehension of this text (*Portrait 5a*, zone 2).

Nevertheless, just as the other participants in this project, Miyuki expressed her strong preference of multimodal support in the form of a video with the sound (*Portrait 5a*, zone 3). This student suggested, "If I had both the audio and a visual text, maybe a video would be more effective for me." Importantly, in the sentence above, Miyuki named visuals *a visual text*. This wording shows that this student was aware of a possibility to *read* visual texts rather than simply observing some events in a video or real life. She was positive about humans' ability to read and obtain information from the observable texts.

Per Miyuki's words, the audio did not hinder her in the process of meaning making of *Text 2* (*Portrait 5a*, zone 4), but it was insufficient for this student, as she perceived it. When talking, Miyuki thoughtfully evaluated every utterance she produced. After having matched her own experiences within this project to her prior classroom observations, she shared,

> *I think if we have only text, a written text, I am sure it is hard to concentrate on reading. I do not know why, but when listening, students may be more focused on listening. I also feel I can listen more than just be reading. (Miyuki)*

Kumar #6 M

Figure 6. Portrait 6a. Kumar's perceptions of effects of addition of audio support to print-based text 2

(MaxQda, 2021)

Kumar, participant #6m, shared with the expression of great relief showing both in his face and posture that addition of multimodality was of good service to him within this project and might be highly helpful to other students as well (*Portrait 6a*, zones 1 & 2). It can be seen from the prevalence of the first two larger zones out of the three available in the visual *Portrait 6a*, where each column represents one specific topic of high interest for this participant, that Kumar dedicated a very significant share of his time in this interview to discussing predominantly two topics. This student talked mostly about the ways in which addition of multimodal features assisted him and might assist other students with their reading comprehension of print-based texts supported by features of multimodality.

Kumar's case was extremely interesting for this project as he appeared to be a voracious reader in his mother-tongue who read a lot of historic nonfiction in English as well. Nevertheless, this student had had no prior exposure to any information about Shakespeare or Shakespearean poetry. Kumar shared that he struggled to identify the genders of Romeo and Juliet as these European names were new to his ear. Interestingly, Kumar shared and stressed that this was the piece of information on the characters' gender he got exactly from the audio, but not from the print-based text.

When recollecting many other moments touched in *Text 2*, Kumar emphasized that addition of a video with the sound would help him even better than just the audio. He disclosed his perceptions stressing, "I had to **guess** rather than **know**… A presentation with pictures or a video would be helpful" (*Portrait 6a*, zone 3).

The above statement by Kumar made it very clear that seeing and hearing simultaneously would give him a more precise picture or *knowledge*, as he put it, of the context and the situation versus just hearing the sounds in the audio.

Mei #7 F

Figure 7. Portrait 7a. Mei's perceptions of effects of audio support added to conventional print-based text 2

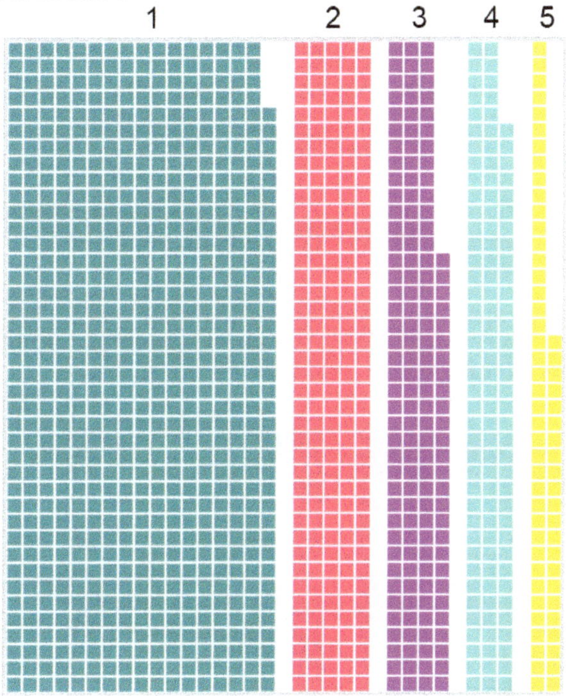

(MaxQda, 2021)

Mei, participant #7f, expressed her appreciation of multimodal support in the form of an audio on Day 1 in this project. This student had had some prior experiences with multimodalities in her own classroom as a teacher. Mei had multiple opportunities to observe the "hypnotizing" effects multimodality produced on her young learners. This participant shared she knew how helpful multimodalities might be to students in the process of their mastering different academic fields (*Portrait 7a*, zone 1). With the strongly pronounced assertiveness in the tone of her voice, this participant made her clear statement, "If I had an audio for the first text, it could have been very much helpful, because the first one, I just couldn't understand at all."

Several times during the first interview, Mei complained about her problems with memorizing information in general. In connection to the above, this participant stressed positive effect of multimodality on her memorization processes (*Portrait 7a*, zone 2). Mei explained,

It [multimodality] sticks to memory. I forget very quickly. Lots of texts I had read in the first semester, I have, probably, forgotten by now. I would have to read them again, and again. But this audio feels like it's got stuck to my mind now. (Mei)

This student reported being used to exploring the public domain online and searching for multimodal support to her academic texts and assignments. She added that visual support worked much better for her (*Portrait 7a*, zone 3). No way did she find multimodality hindering her in the process of working with the *Text 2* (*Portrait 7a*, zone 4). On the contrary, as Mei reported, it was of great help to her (*Portrait 7a*, zone 5).

Eun # 8 F

Figure 8. Portrait 8a. Eun's perceptions of effects of addition of an audio to conventional print-based text 2

(MaxQda, 2021)

Eun, participant # 8f, spoke mostly about how greatly multimodality might enhance students' interest and motivation in reading (*Portrait 8a*, zone 1). This student shared that multimodal resources might be of a good service to students in terms of assisting them with their meaning making in the process of their reading print-based texts supported by features of multimodality (*Portrait 8a*, zone 2). Interestingly, this participant's opinion was shaped during her studies in her home-country, where one of her professors, who was native to that country but educated in the United States, utilized lots of diverse methods and techniques based on employment of multimodality in her college classroom. Eun shared she was greatly impressed by that educator's teaching style. This student believed she appropriated her former professor's multimodal approach in education and was dedicated to conduct her own classroom teaching in the same style.

Further, Eun recognized that addition of the audio to the print-based *Text 2* was of great service to her (*Portrait 8a*, zone 3). She clarified that listening to the audio support to the print-based *Text 2* ignited her imagination. Eun revealed, "I could use my imagination in an easier way. I could sympathize with the characters. When I listened to the audio clip, I could easily read how characters were feeling." Similarly to the other participants in this study, Eun expressed her opinion about greater helpfulness of multimodality, in the form of technology-assisted visual aids in combination with textual and auditory ones (*Portrait 8a*, zone 4).

This participant compared two generations: the one of her age and the other of the children of today. Eun concluded based on her own real-life observations,

> *These days, people, youngsters, get used to media. That is how they get information. When they get information from articles and from academic books, they are not using technology. But that is how they get information usually: they usually use technology. (Eun)*

Importantly, Eun believed that teaching college students might be more efficient if some habitual for them multimodal technology-based readings were widely employed for teaching and learning purposes. Conclusively, this participant also confirmed that multimodality did not hinder her understanding, but made her more focused on the content of the text (*Portrait 8a*, zone 5).

Anjali #9 F

Figure 9. Portrait 9a. Anjali's perceptions of effects of addition of and audio to conventional print-based text 2

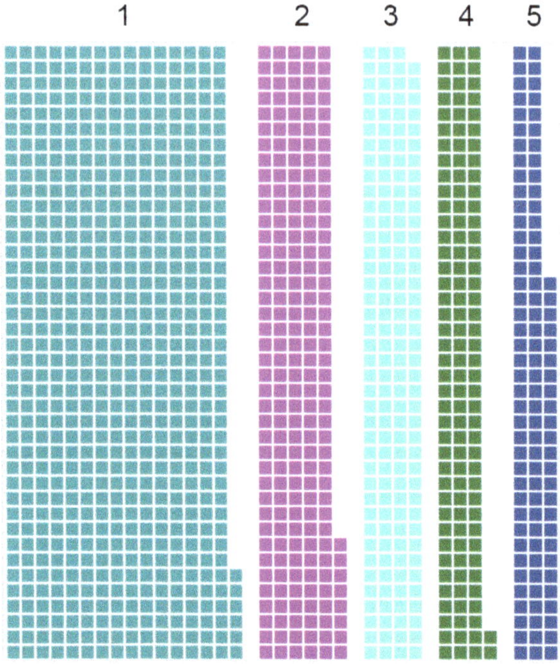

(MaxQda, 2021)

Anjali, participant #9f, strongly believed that multimodality had a great potential in assisting students with their meaning making of their readings (*Portrait 9a*, zone 1). This participant shared how unexpectedly, with the help of one of her friends, she discovered enjoyment of reading fiction in the form of voluminous novels both in her native languages and in English. Yet, regardless of being an internally motivated reader, Anjali had problems with comprehending texts in the English language due to presence of unknown to her terminology in most of the readings. This student genuinely believed that visuals had a greater potential to assist meaning making, rather than an audio (*Portrait 9a*, zone 2).

Obviously, Anjali did not view addition of an audio as a hindering factor (*Portrait 9a*, zone 3). Nevertheless, this participant shared she would prefer some visual support in addition to the print-based text instead of, or in addition to the audio. Speaking about books, Anjali suggested, "If they want us to have interest, there should be pictures in readings. It is universal knowledge: if there are pictures, they make it more attractive to read." After having expressed the above idea, Anjali added with emphasis, "In color."

This participant, similarly to her Indian country-fellowmen, had had some prior knowledge on the positive effects from different colors on humans' ability to learn (*Portrait 9a*, zone 4). Anjali strongly believed that addition of colorful still images or animated videos might help students to get deeper emotionally connected to the content of their readings. This student believed that visuals might enhance reader interest and motivation in reading, while facilitating a deeper understanding of the content. Importantly, Anjali suggested that enhanced internal motivation in students might also trigger their interest in further exploration of the topics of their readings (*Portrait 9a*, zone 5).

Sang #10 M

Figure 10. Portrait 10a. Sang's perceptions of effects of addition of an audio to conventional print-based text 2

(MaxQda, 2021)

Sang, participant # 10m, was raised and schooled in the United States since his early age, though he was born and started his schooling in Vietnam. In his early childhood, Sang was taught how to read and write in his mother tongue, which was Vietnamese. Upon having immigrated to the USA, this student successfully adjusted to his new life in America. Thus, Sang perceived and positioned himself as a Domestic college student, though of an International decent.

As it can be seen from *Portrait 10a*, zone 1, Sang generously shared his opinion on how helpful multimodality could be to students with their meaning making of print-based texts supported by multimodal features. In particular, Sang recollected how addition of auditory support helped him with mastering the Spanish language during his high school years.

When offered the second text, this participant was the only person in the sample who put the print-based *Text 2* aside and allowed himself to get deeply absorbed in listening to the audio version of the same text. At some moment, Sang produced the impression of a person who accidentally blacked out during listening. Yet, this would be a completely wrong assumption because, after having listened to the audio, Sang engaged in discussing multiple aspects of the audio-text in detail. For example, Sang stated that the audio helped him greatly with both meaning making of the text and later with identifying the answers to the comprehension test questions to the text (*Portrait 10a*, zone 2). Sang explained,

> *The first question asked about discourse. I did not change my answer, because I got stuck. But hearing the audio, hearing how Romeo said that whole series of sentences, I think really helped me out. Just for that particular passage, it definitely helped me. It did contribute to my understanding the tone and what the characters were saying. (Sang)*

Later, when contemplating aloud about his experiences with multimodality within this project, Sang indirectly characterized himself as an auditory learner and confirmed that addition of the audio-text did not distract him (*Portrait 10a*, zone 3) but, on the contrary, greatly assisted him with his meaning making of the conventional print-based *Text 2*.

Faiz #11 M

Figure 11. Portrait 11a. Faiz's perceptions of effects of addition of an audio to conventional print-based text 2

(MaxQda, 2021)

Participant # 11m, Faiz was the only person in this study who chose to abstain from pre-reading the print-based *Text 2* and decided to start directly from listening to the audio version of the same text. *Portrait 11a*, zone 1 represents the major topic of the first interview with this participant where Faiz focused on the power of multimodalities to enhance readers' interest and motivation (*Portrait 11a*, zone 1).

As Faiz shared, his opinion was greatly influenced by one of his American professors at the times of his Master's program. That educator generously included multimodal support in the form of audios and videos in addition to the print-based texts and discussions she offered in her classes. So, Faiz had had a chance to witness and experience in person how greatly multimodality assisted himself and the other students in his class with their reading comprehension (*Portrait 11a*, zone 2). In particular, Faiz valued addition of a video with sound support higher rather than only an audio (*Portrait 11a*, zone 3).

In his own teaching, as a college educator, Faiz implemented video support in addition to the texts he offered his students to read. As he found out from his students' evaluation forms upon completion of the most recent semester, "About 90% said they would watch it [video support offered by Faiz]. And I was happy to see that."

This participant also stated that addition of the audio to the print-based *Text 2* helped him with his meaning making of the content of this text; although there were multiple words in *Text 2* which this student had never encountered before and thus did not know at all (*Portrait 11a*, zone 4).

Contemplating on his own experiences from the point of view of an EAL speaker, Faiz shared,

> *Let us say, there was a sentence that I did not understand, or a line that I did not understand at all... The tone of the person who was reading the play gave me additional information that I could use for comprehension. (Faiz)*

By the end of Day 1 in this project, Faiz expressed his frustration with his own erroneous decision to not pre-read the print-based *Text 2* prior to listening to the audio support. Through his experience on Day 1 in this study, this student developed the understanding that pre-reading might have helped him with his meaning making during listening to the audio support to the text. Faiz expressed his intention to verify his assumptions on Day 2 in this research.

REFERENCES

Bakhtin, M. M. (1981). Discourse in the novel. In Holquist, M. (Ed.), *The dialogic imagination: Four essays by M. M. Bakhtin* (pp. 259–422). University of Texas Press.

MAXQDA. (2021). MAXQDA 2022 [computer software]. Berlin, Germany: VERBI Software. Available from maxqda.com.

Shakespeare, W. (1597). *Romeo and Juliet.*

VERBI Software. (2021). MAXQDA 2022 [computer software]. Berlin, Germany: VERBI Software. Available from maxqda.com.

Zeffirelli, F. (1968). *Romeo and Juliet.* Paramount Pictures. Retrieved from public domain: https://www.youtube.com/watch?v=VCe0nzdD76k

Chapter 12
AI and Day 1 Group Accounts

ABSTRACT

In Chapter 12, I will further discuss my AI-powered analysis of the participants' interview speeches. Yet, now, via the multimodal affordances of MaxQda, I will visually demonstrate and verbally explain the patterns in the interviews by the entire group. I will also address the differences by gender found in this research. Each AI-generated Matrix will show the largest and less focused topics raised by each participant in their interviews. Collectively, these data will be available in the MaxQda matrixes. These matrices provide an opportunity to view all interviewees' speeches and their major ideas in the summarized and concise multimodal representation of ideas.

INTERVIEW I: PERCEPTIONS OF AUDIO

With all that commotion around the usage of Artificial Intelligence (AI), its affordances may be highly useful to qualitative researchers. Apparently, the problem, which concerns so many minds today is not with the AI per se, but with dishonesty of its usage by some members of the global academic community. Nevertheless, modern days' technology may be equitably and honestly utilized for transcribing, processing, and analyzing extensive amounts of data, such as lengthy interview speeches, to provide just some examples. Though I transcribed all the interviews manually with the purpose to enhance my memorization of every speech, the AI software assisted me with creating the data displays, the purpose of which was to show to my audiences at a glance everything or the major ideas extracted from the hours of interview recordings and pages of transcripts.

Additionally, thanks to the technology, I was able to approach my sets of data from multiple positions. Nevertheless, it is important to notice that utilization of software did not nullify, nor contradict, or eliminate the need for me to double-process all my

DOI: 10.4018/979-8-3373-3426-4.ch012

research data manually and via affordances of my own, human intellect. For this purpose, I created large, whole-wall coded data displays in my home office. All the information was securely encoded with the help of stickers, sticky notes, signs, and symbols known only to myself. Breach of security of identity of my participants was totally excluded; so, upon entrance, an intruder, such as a colleague, a student, would only spot a colorful mosaic with no meaning visibly attached.

Nevertheless, using the AI for creating data displays appeared to be significantly more reliable security-wise. Thus, with the help of MaxQda Code Matrix Browser, I developed different types of matrices, which helped me and might also assist my reading audiences with visualization of the codes in those sets of transcribed participant interviews. Yet, the primary reason for which I created the visual graphic matrices was to save my verbal reports in the form of the almost instantly observable and easily readable visual representations of the topics addressed and frequently emphasized by the individual participants, a whole sample, or a group of students. These matrices helped me to instantaneously grasp such phenomena as frequency and, most importantly, the intensity of my participants' unique individual or patterned utterances.

Quick Guide to Reading Matrixes

Just as I have done with the AI-generated interview portraits, I will provide my readers with a quick guide to reading the AI-developed matrices. These visual representations of human speeches assisted me not only with more efficient data processing and analysis, but also helped me identify major themes and topics, which were most frequently and intensively discussed by the entire sample of participants. So, prior to demonstrating these matrices to my readers, I will briefly comment on the code system within these visual representations. I offer my readers to first have a look at *Figure 2 Matrix 1* below, specifically at the first left-hand column. This is where all the major topics discussed by participants are listed. So, these major topics were as follows: Multimodality has the potential to:

- Assist students with their reading comprehension when added to the print-based text. This topic is referred within the matrixes as "*Has the potential to assist with comprehension*" (See *Figure 2 Matrix 1* below).
- Eliminate necessity to repeatedly re-read texts multiple times to be able to comprehend their content. This theme is marked in the matrices as "*Eliminates the need in multiple re-reading.*"
- Enhance motivation and interest in the content of texts in students. This topic is referred to as "*Enhances interest & motivation.*"

- Activate multiple brain zones due to processing different modes, each of which is being processed by a certain specific zone in the human brain. This topic is marked as "*Activates multiple brain zones.*"
- Assist faster and more efficient memorization processes in readers. This theme is marked as "*Assists with memorization.*"
- Benefit student engagement via affordances of color. This theme is referred as "*Benefits via effects of color.*"

Also, as per the participants responses, multimodal visual support:

- Was reported to be more helpful, thus, strongly preferred versus the auditory support. This theme is referred as "*Visuals are strongly preferred.*"
- Was not perceived as hindering each student's working processes within this project. This topic is marked in the matrixes as "*Did not hinder this task.*"
- Assisted research participants with their meaning making and helped them with working processes and completion of project tasks within this project. This topic is referred as "*Helped with this task.*"

In the first left-hand column in every matrix, one can see the colorful dots located next to each of the themes within the matrices and listed above. This configuration means that the themes in the matrices were color-coded with the same colors as the color-coded zones in the interview portraits (See *Figures 1 to 10* above and *Figures 11 to 21* below for the Day 1 and Day 2 interview portraits correspondingly). To provide an illustrative example, the theme "*Multimodality assists with reading comprehension*" is marked with the same turquois color in both interview portraits and the matrices; the color of the dot in the matrix next to this theme is the same as the corresponding zone in the interview portraits. Same color-code correspondence between every theme in matrices and the color-coded theme zones applies to all interview portraits.

Another important reminder may help my audiences to read the visual representations more efficiently. The matrices, which graphically represent the interview speeches concerned with the audio support were comprised of different size squares. The larger is the size of these squares in each matrix, the more substantially a particular participant discussed a certain topic listed in the first left-hand column of each matrix.

Importantly, the matrices, which visually represent the information from the interviews on Day 2 and were largely concerned with the video and sound support to print-based texts were comprised of circles. The larger is the size of each circle, the more substantially a certain participant focused on that particular topic in his or her interview.

DATA IN THE MATRIXES

Now, when my readers have familiarized with the guide on reading the information encoded in the AI-generated matrices, they can proceed with *viewing* my participants' speeches. Yet, no worries, I will continue providing my verbal clarifications and explanations to all the data comprised in these matrices.

For example, from *Matrix 1* below, one can conclude that the most frequently discussed theme during Day 1 interviews was the potential of multimodality to assist students with their reading comprehension. It was addressed in 38 turns by the whole sample of participants. The second important topic appeared to be helpfulness of the audio support in this project (23 turns) (See *Figure 1 Matrix 1* below for coded themes emerged in all participants' interviews on Day 1 combined).

Figure 1. Matrix 1: Participants 1 to 11: Coded themes emerged in all participants' interviews on day 1 (combined)

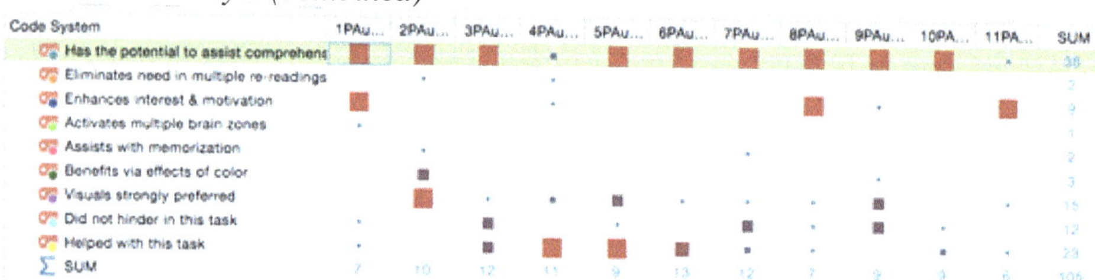

(MaxQda, 2021)

As one can perceive from the visually represented data in *Figure 1* above, practically all participants stated that addition of the audio to the print-based *Text 2* helped them to cope with the two tasks: 1. understand the text and 2. answer the comprehension questions to this text.

The third most frequently addressed theme (15 turns) was the participants' preference of multimodal support in the form of a video in addition to the provided auditory support to the print-based *Text 2*. Importantly for this research conclusions, the fourth important topic discussed by the participants quite frequently was that addition of multimodality did not hinder their working processes with the print-based *Texts 2* (12 turns). Participants were also discussing how multimodality might enhance readers' interest and motivation in reading when added to print-based texts (9 turns).

Less frequently yet notably, during the first interview on Day 1, the participants addressed such topics as potential benefits of addition of visual information in color (3 turns), the potential of auditory support to assist students with their memorizations processes (2 turns), reduced need in repetitive re-readings (2 turns), and activating multiple brain zones when processing multimodal information (1 turn).

Importantly, with the help of the MaxQda-generated matrices, my readers received not only my researcher's statements, but also the evidence, which was nonchalantly presented by the disinterested and unbiased analyst, the robotic intellect of AI.

INTERVIEW I: VARIATIONS BY GENDER

It was interesting for me to conclude that not only the test, but also interview data analysis conducted with the help of MaxQda Code Matrix Browser, resulted in some variations by gender. As it can be seen in Figure 2 *Matrix 2* below, all female participants (Ting, #4f, Miyuki, #5f, Mei, #7f, Eun, #8f, and Anjali, #9f) most often discussed the potential of multimodal support to assist students' comprehension when added to print-based texts (15 turns) and, also, how the audio-recording helped them to better understand the print-based *Text 2* within this project (11 turns).

Figure 2. Matrix 2: Females. Audio. Participants Ting, #4f, Miyuki, #5f, Mei, #7f, Eun, #8f, and Anjali, #9f: Coded themes emerged in all female participants' interviews on day 1 (combined)

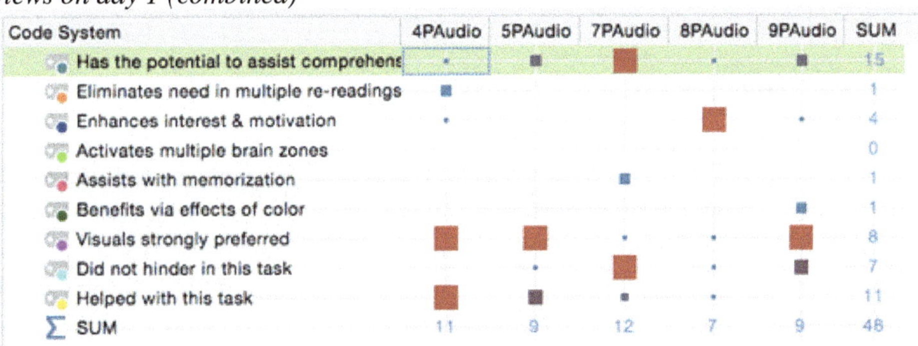

(MaxQda, 2021)

Additionally, the female group quite frequently addressed the topic of their strong preference of visuals, which they believed needed to be added to the print-based *Text 2* along with the audio (8 turns). The female students also quite frequently mentioned that the audio recording did not hinder their working with *Text 2* (7 turns). The group of female participants also discussed how the audio support might enhance interest in readers if it were added to practically any print-based text (4 turns). The other topics were mentioned only once during the first interview with the female participants.

There were some differences in the choice of topics in the male students. Figure 3 *Matrix 3* below was created to help me better visualize all the data combined, obtained from all male research participants' interviews on Day 1. As it appeared, the male participants more powerfully addressed the topic of potential of multimodality to assist students with their reading comprehension of print-based texts (23 turns versus 15 turns by females) (See Figure 3 *Matrix 3* below to visualize combined data from all male research participants' interviews on Day 1).

Figure 3. Matrix 3: Males. Audio. Participants Sanjay, #1m, Prem, #2m, Vijay, #3m, Kumar, #6m, Sang, #10m, and Faiz, #11m: Coded themes emerged in all male participants interviews on day 1 (combined)

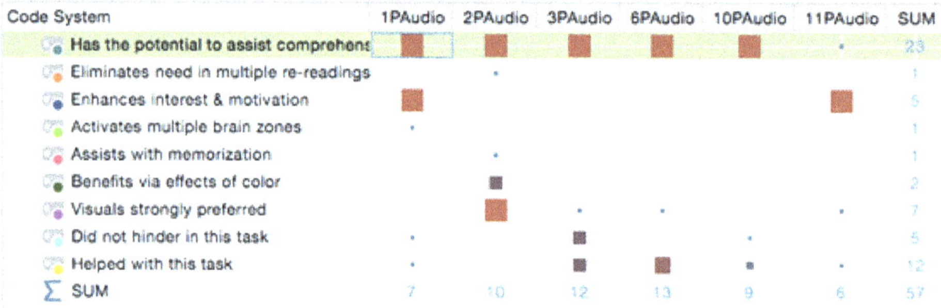

(MaxQda, 2021)

Further, the male participants reflected on how addition of the audio assisted them with their working on *Text 2* within this project (12 turns). Fewer male participants (7 turns) expressed their suggestion that visual support, in addition to the auditory one, might have helped them to deeper understand the print-based *Text 2*.

Though less frequently, the male participants addressed the fact that addition of the audio did not hinder their work with *Text 2*, but enhanced their interest in the reading (5 turns in each case). Some male students also mentioned some potential benefits of addition of colorful visual multimodal support to print-based texts (2 turns). The other topics, such as potentially reduced need in repetitive re-readings, activation of multiple brain zones when processing multimodal resources, and assistance with memorization were also addressed by the male participants, but only once in each category.

REFERENCES

Bakhtin, M. M. (1981). Discourse in the novel. In Holquist, M. (Ed.), *The dialogic imagination: Four essays by M. M. Bakhtin* (pp. 259–422). University of Texas Press.

MAXQDA. (2021). MAXQDA 2022 [computer software]. Berlin, Germany: VERBI Software. Available from maxqda.com.

Shakespeare, W. (1597). *Romeo and Juliet.*

Zeffirelli, F. (1968). *Romeo and Juliet.* Paramount Pictures. Retrieved from public domain: https://www.youtube.com/watch?v=VCe0nzdD76k

Chapter 13
More Truths Unveiled

ABSTRACT

In Chapter 13, I will continue introducing my readers to the AI-generated portraits developed on Day 2 in this project. Just as a reminder, all participants were interviewed for the second time when they were asked to share their perceptions of their work with the video-supported Text 3 versus the audio-supported Text 2. This is the major topic discussed in this chapter. Importantly, this portion of my research report verbally and visually delivers the major ideas of my research participants on helpfulness of the visual mode of multimodality. Moreover, this chapter contains several highly significant ideas on different working styles and reading practices as described by the participating students. Just as chapters XI and XII above, this Chapter XIII is rich in visuals. So, multimodality in the forms of shape, size, and color in the figures, and portraits, aims to help readers to more efficiently evaluate the intensity of every idea discussed by the participants.

PORTRAITS OF DAY 2 INTERVIEW 2: VIDEO VERSUS AUDIO SUPPORT

On the second day of this project, each participant was offered to read print-based *Text 3* supported by a video with the sound and attempt a comprehension test to this text from Shakespeare's (1957) *Romeo and Juliet*. When completed, the students were asked to give another interview and share their perceptions of using the video with sound support versus working with the audio-supported text and test. Though each individual participant's opinions were quite unique, there were found some patterns in all speeches. To be more specific, all students, unanimously, though

DOI: 10.4018/979-8-3373-3426-4.ch013

independently from each other, expressed their preference of multimodal support in the form of a video with the sound.

Just as in the previous chapter, I will display every individual participant's focus topics within the color-coded AI-generated interview portraits. Every colorful column in each of the portraits represents some certain topic discussed by the speaker. Additionally, I will also interpret these data. Importantly, I will discuss the themes moving from left to right within each color-coded MaxQda-created interview portrait. Just as a reminder, the lower-case letter *v* standing next to each participant's name indicates that the second interview was mostly concerned with the effects from the video.

Sanjay #1 M

Figure 1. Portrait 1v. Sanjay's perceptions of effects of addition of a video with sound to conventional print-based text 3

(MaxQda, 2021)

Sanjay, participant #1m, in his second interview expressed his great appreciation of addition of multimodality in the form of a video with the sound to the print-based *Text 3.* This student stated that this was exactly the type of multimodal support he wanted in addition to any print-based texts, so he was able to make the meaning correctly (*Portrait 1v*, zones 1 & 2). Sanjay shared, "It [video] helped a lot better than the audio. In comparison to an audio, a video is better."

Further, this participant shared his point of view on how and why a video might assist viewing audiences with their faster and better memorization of the content (*Portrait 1v*, zone 3) due to involvement of multiple organs of reception of information. Sanjay clarified his idea (*Portrait 1v*, zones 4 & 5) saying that,

> *It is a basic thing: any child or any person can remember what was happening in a movie. We can remember the context because video involves more of sensory organs. More of them are involved at the time of watching... I feel that videos are better in terms of understanding the idea. And information gets right there [Sanjay pointed to his head with his hand gesture] because of high interest. (Sanjay)*

Importantly, Sanjay did not see any negative effects from addition of the video to the print-based *Text 3* which might hinder his reading processes (*Portrait 1v*, zone 5). Neither could he presuppose any disadvantages from addition of a video with the sound to a print-based text. Sanjay stated directly, "The video was pretty much helpful. That way, it would make people realize the situation better... There are no disadvantages. It is mostly advantages."

Prem #2 M

Figure 2. Portrait 2v. Prem's perceptions of effects of addition of a video with sound to conventional print-based text 3

(MaxQda, 2021)

Prem, participant #2m, briefly and powerfully expressed his positive attitude towards addition of the video with the sound to the print-based *Text 3*. He also believed in helpfulness of video support to many other students. This participant stated that videos have a great potential to captivate students and grasp their attention (*Portrait 2v*, zone 1). Powerfully ignited interest might allow educators to keep their students strongly motivated in further studying the topics discussed in the readings, on condition those texts were supported with both video and sound (*Portrait 2v*, zones 2 & 3).

Though Prem did not struggle with the print-based *Text 3* in this project, he believed that the video helped him to fully understand the meaning of this text (*Portrait 2v*, zone 4). Prem also shared that the video did not hinder his meaning-making processes (*Portrait 2v*, zone 5). This student put it directly,

The video helped me to understand the questions. It helped me with visualization of the scene and made it more comfortable for me to answer the questions. Compared to the audio, this video was really amazing, and it didn't hinder me at all when I was answering the questions. The video did not distract me. (Prem)

Vijay # 3 M

Figure 3. Portrait 3v. Vijay's perceptions of effects of addition of a video with sound to conventional print-based text 3

(MaxQda, 2021)

Vijay, participant #3m, spoke mostly about how helpful multimodality might be to students in terms of their reading comprehension when added to print-based texts (*Portrait 3v*, zone 1). He also shared at which exactly instances the video added to the print-based *Text 3* assisted him with his meaning making (*Portrait 3v*, zone 2). Vijay evaluated several types of usage of additional features of multimodality in combination with the print-based text. His first suggestion for any readers was to read a text and, simultaneously, listen to an audio. Vijay's second working strategy was to pre-read a text and then, watch a video with the sound. This student also came out with another strategy to first pre-read a text, then watch a video while going back and forth between the video and corresponding sections of the print-based text.

Though this participant believed that addition of all types of multimodal support could be helpful, he confessed that a video would work better for him anyway (*Portrait 3v*, zone 3). Vijay shared,

I prefer a video. But before a student goes to the video, he must have an idea about it, which might be right or wrong. But he can check with the video. If he has any doubts, he can clarify them by watching the video. (Vijay)

Interestingly, this student revealed that he was not able to watch the video support and read simultaneously. Still, when asked to comment on his multimodal reading practices, he shared that he did not perceive that the video hindered his understanding of the content of *Text 3,* nor distracted him from focusing on his work (*Portrait 3v*, zone 4). Vijay stated, "It [the video] did not distract me, but it helped me in finding the answers… And while watching the video, I've got the perspective of what was going on there, in the text."

Later, in the same interview, Vijay chose to return to the above topic once again. He re-stated the idea he had previously uttered, "No, it [video] did not distract me. When I read the text, I could not understand every part of it. But while watching the video, I had a clear understanding." And by the end of this interview, Vijay added that in the future, when he starts teaching his own college students in the field of Engineering, he would try to assist their understanding of difficult topics via enhancing their interest (*Portrait 3v*, zone 5) with the help of videos in support of class readings and discussions.

Contemplating over his future teaching approach, Vijay suggested,

I would ask them [students] to read the text first, then, go for a discussion… Then, after the discussion, I would go for a video and give them the explanation about the machine. It will be better for them to see the animation of that machine and how it works. (Vijay)

This participant in his interview demonstrated his vision of multiple potential benefits of multimodality for himself and for many other college students in general. Moreover, Vijay shared how, as a future college instructor, he was pre-planning to use visual support in addition to print-based texts and in-class discussions for his future college students.

Ting # 4 F

Figure 4. Portrait 4v. Ting's perceptions of effects of addition of a video with sound to conventional print-based text 3

(MaxQda, 2021)

Ting, participant #4f, talked most generously about how multimodal visual and auditory support helped her with reading comprehension of the print-based *Text 3* (*Portrait 4v*, zone 1). On both days, Day 1 and Day 2 within this project, this participant complained about having difficulties with understanding the accents [speech peculiarities] by the actors in the audio (on Day 1) and in the video (on Day 2). This student greatly appreciated addition of visual aid in combination with the sound to the print-based *Text 3* on Day 2.

Ting also reported that her own interest was strongly enhanced when she could observe events in the story while watching the video (*Portrait 4v*, zone 2). This student explained, “This was a play I have not heard of before. It was hard for me and very abstract. The video looked like a movie. It was entertaining! It attracted me!” Besides the emerged interest in the events in the story, this participant shared she realized how helpful the video with the sound was for her meaning making (*Portrait 4v*, zones 3 & 4).

Ting clarified,

I prefer the video. Just as I mentioned before, it looked like a movie. I could relax and I could really engage with the text. I also could perceive what was happening from their facial expressions and from the characters' phrasing. And I also could see whether they were nervous, or whether they were angry. It also helped me to understand the full meaning of this text. (Ting)

Ting did not consider addition of the video to the print-based *Text 3* to be distracting (Portrait 4v, zone 5). On the contrary, this student expressed her highly positive attitude towards implementation of multimodal support to print-based texts. This person illustrated her statement with an example from her recent academic experiences.

Ting shared,

I think people are more visual. They prefer to see visuals. In my major, we have a course for data analysis. In some videos, scientists try to relate their data with some visual image. For example, they relate their data with Barbie dolls showing how many women get breast cancer surgery every year. It shocked me. And I can remember it. (Ting)

In this revelation, Ting indirectly implied the idea about positive effect of visuals on human memorization processes. This idea had been previously expressed by some other participants in this study as well.

Miyuki # 5 F

Figure 5. Portrait 5v. Miyuki's perceptions of effects of addition of a video with sound to conventional print-based text 3

(MaxQda, 2021)

Miyuki, participant #5f, dedicated most of the time in her interview to developing the following two topics: she contemplated about the ways in which addition of the video to the print-based *Text 3* assisted her with meaning making (*Portrait 5v*, zone 1) and how it could also be useful to some other students (*Portrait 5v*, zone 2).

This student shared,

Although I could see the [print-based] text, I could not understand all the words. But when I saw the picture [the video] and listened to the sound, I could see the characters' emotions, I could see them moving. The movements and emotions I could identify through the video. (Miyuki)

Miyuki pointed to a certain part of the print-based *Text 3*, which she could not understand from reading alone. She said, "This part (she touched a paragraph in the hard copy of *Text 3*), this text says, 'They whisper.' But who are **they**? I am not sure." This participant stated that she was able to gain understanding of that particular portion of *Text 3* only when watching the video with the sound.

Positive effects of visual means of multimodality on memorization processes (*Portrait 5v*, zone 3) were also mentioned by this participant. Miyuki contemplated,

I am not sure whether it is only me, but I can focus on a movie more than just on reading a text… And even later, after I have watched the movie, I can remember the scene. It made it easier for me to answer the [test] questions. (Miyuki)

Miyuki strongly preferred multimodal support in the form of a video with the sound (*Portrait 5v*, zone 4). In her opinion, it is the enhanced interest in the viewers that keeps them better focused on the content of multimodal texts (*Portrait 5v*, zone 5). This participant expressed her opinion, saying, "I think it [video] definitely helps students to understand more. Some students are not that good with reading, but they can focus on visuals, movements, or voices. They might enjoy watching movies."

As it can be understood from Miyuki's statement above, she viewed an enhanced internal motivation as a crucially important factor for both: students' engagement with the text and their deeper comprehension of the content of the multimodal and print-based texts due to their forming a stronger emotional connection with the content of the text.

Kumar #6 M

Figure 6. Portrait 6v: Kumar's perceptions of effects of addition of a video with sound to conventional print-based text 3

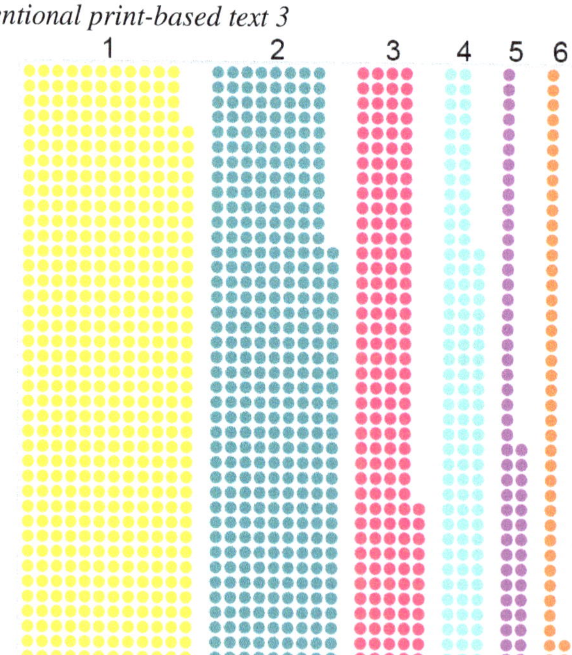

(MaxQda, 2021)

Kumar, participant #6m, similarly to the previous participant Miyuki, #5f, expressed his appreciation of multimodal video support to print-based *Text 3* (*Portrait 6v*, zone 1) and suggested addition of video with sound might also help many other college students with their deeper comprehension of print-based texts (*Portrait 6v*, zone 2). He stated directly, "The video was very helpful."

When questioned in what ways the video was helpful to him, Kumar clarified that it helped him to better memorize the details in the story (*Portrait 6v*, zone 3). Then, he furthered, "It was easy to remember the video. In comparison to the text, video is easier. I could recollect the emotions of the characters when they said something... I recollected everything in the video, and then, answered the questions." This participant also found it necessary to provide more details about his experiences with the multimodal texts he read on Day 2 in this project.

Kumar explained,

> *The [print-based] text itself [Text 3] was* **difficult** *[stressed with his voice] compared to the previous texts. Addition of the characters in the play [in the video] helped me in understanding the situation and what was happening... It is more pronounced in the video. The relations between the people, and how they try to communicate was also clear to me during watching the video. The video helped me in understanding the situation, and the context in this scene. (Kumar)*

When questioned, Kumar explained that he did not find addition of multimodal features to the print-based *Text 3* distracting (*Portrait 6v*, zone 4). On the contrary, he believed video with the sound would make more sufficient support to complicated print-based texts (*Portrait 6v*, zone 5). This participant expressed his opinion saying, "Since in this text number three, the things were difficult, I would prefer a video for a difficult text compared to an audio." Further, Kumar added, "First, going through the text, and understanding the words, and then, going to the video, actually, helped me the most."

When asked in what ways a video might assist with meaning making of a text, Kumar briefed on his vision of cooperation of multiple resources within a multimodal ensemble. This participant suggested that it was a range of modes and resources that might help viewers with their meaning making. Kumar shared,

> *Comparing positioning of the people: whether they were facing each other, or how far apart they were, was not evident from the [print-based] text. From the video, you can see what is happening. That is a nice thing about a video. And again, emotions were very helpful in answering the questions. (Kumar)*

As Kumar perceived it, video support might reduce necessity for readers to repeatedly re-read the text (*Portrait 6v*, zone 6). Kumar related this fact to the potential of visuals to be longer and more efficiently retained in the memory.

Mei # 7 F

Figure 7. Portrait 7v: Mei's perceptions of effects of addition of a video with sound to conventional print-based text 3

(MaxQda, 2021)

Mei, participant #7f, expressed her strong preference of addition of visual support to print-based texts (*Portrait 7v*, zone 1). "I think video is much better than an audio. For me, contact with people matters. I prefer video," stated Mei. Her major point was that visuals enhance readers' interest (*Portrait 7v*, zone 2).

As a devoted early-childhood educator, Mei often reflected on her professional experiences. Just as she did on Day1, in her second interview, Mei provided an example from her own classroom teaching practices. This participant offered,

> *Compare: 'We are going to watch a video,' and 'We are going to read a text.' The feeling is different for me: video is for fun, and a text feels different, 'Ok (she imitates tired and disappointed expression in her young learners' faces), I am going to do it.' (Mei)*

Enhanced interest and internal motivation were exactly the factors, which, from Mei's point of view, had a powerful potential to engage students, so that they persisted in their attempt to make a deeper meaning (*Portrait 7v*, zones 2 & 3).

Addition of the video with sound helped Mei to deeper understand the print-based *Text 3,* as she perceived it (*Portrait 7v*, zone 4). Multimodality did not hinder nor distract this participant (*Portrait 7v*, zone 5). On the contrary, it helped her to longer retain some details from the text in her memory (*Portrait 7v*, zone 6). This factor, as Mei believed, assisted her with answering the comprehension test questions to the text.

Notably, during both interviews, on Day 1 and Day 2, Mei complained about her problems with memorization. From the position of a learner habitually struggling with the problems connected to both memorizing and recollecting information, Mei confirmed her view of importance of visual aid for such students as herself, who lack the ability to easily memorize print-based texts or new to them verbal information.

During the second interview with this participant, it became obvious how video assisted her. This student shared how visuals resolved her problems with memorization. Additionally, they also helped her to not get confused about some new and unknown to her information.

Mei described her own perceptions saying that,

The part where Romeo is trying to hide… that part I really did not get from the [print-based] text, but it was very obvious in the video. In the [print-based] text, it is just said that he was in his enemies' house. But I was confused about how he would get into his enemies' house. Then, in the video, I could see that he was wearing a mask: he knows he is in the house where he is not supposed to be… At first, I thought, 'Why is he there?' So, observing their dresses, their facial expressions, his eyes were running away; this all made more sense to me. (Mei)

Though quite a young person in her 20's, Mei shared some unique moments of her past life and revealed that in the place where she was born and raised, there were no TV sets in the house of her parents, nor in the other families like her own. Thus, watching films in a movie theatre was quite a big event. This occurred in her home country since vast layers of populations during those times were poorly paid. So, children grew up without any luxuries which are taken by the American people for granted. Instead of enjoying the modern technologies, Mei and her friends were just playing active games together outside. As for new information, they learned it from their schoolteachers and books.

Mei recollected,

When I was a child, I did not have a TV at home (she chuckled with embarrassment)… I remember books were very important to us; but still, all kids loved cartoon films. Cartoon films were a great part of our life. (Mei)

Subsequently, Mei made connections between her younger years memories and her current observations in her own early-childhood classroom in America. As she had noticed, attention span and focus of her students improved greatly when the content of her lessons was supported by videos. When observing her own students,

Mei had identified some patters. When given a free choice, her students would be reluctant to take part in some educational activities. Nevertheless, practically all of them showed great interest in the classroom events which involved viewing videos. So, as concluded by Mei, based on the above observations, preference of visuals is inherent to human nature.

Eun # 8 F

Figure 8. Portrait 8v: Eun's perceptions of effects of addition of a video with sound to conventional print-based text 3

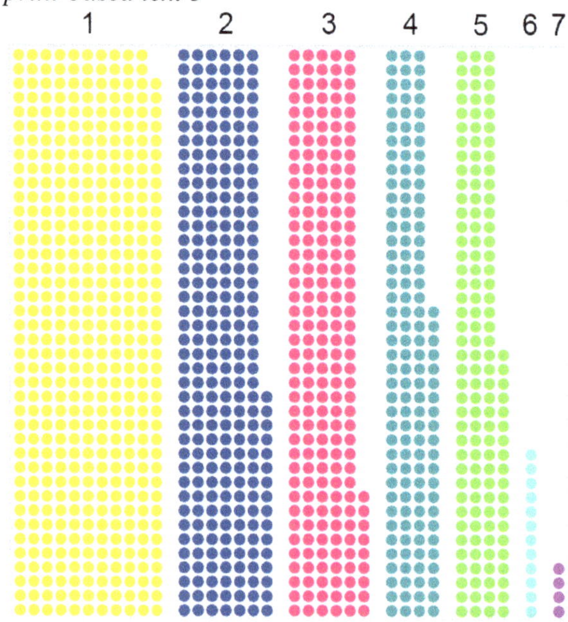

(MaxQda, 2021)

Eun, participant #8f, similarly to the other research participants above, shared how greatly multimodality assisted her meaning making of the print-based *Text 3* (*Portrait 8v*, zone 1). As she believed, the major impact of videos on her reading comprehension occurred thanks to her enhanced interest in the watched content due to observing the events in the video with sound (*Portrait 8v*, zone 2). This participant illustrated her opinion about some positive effects of visuals on memorization processes (*Portrait 8v*, zone 3) via providing the following example from her academic life.

Eun addressed to me saying,

I remember your presentation for the class [Intercultural Communication in Education] we took together. You also talked about multimodality. You talked about the culture of Turkmenistan. You compared the text without multimodality with the text plus multimodality. It was very eye-opening for me because with the multimodality that you provided, it was very engaging. And they [classmates] really enjoyed that text more. And I still can remember it the way you presented. (Eun)

When questioned about the ways in which multimodality could be helpful to different student populations, Eun replied "I think the advantage is that it gives you a lot of information that you can't even realize while you are working on those test questions" (*Portrait 8v*, zone 4).

Subsequently, Eun indirectly implied the idea of multimodal ensembles activating multiple brain areas. When describing the effects of a video on her meaning-making processes, this participant shared her point of view on why exactly a multimodal video might be more effective for reading comprehension, rather than a unimodal auditory or print-based text. Eun declared, "Because it is multiple representations, rather than an audio. It is visual information" (*Portrait 8v*, zone 5).

Eun was very laconic in her answers to the interview questions, while her statements were brief but to the point. When asked whether the video distracted her (*Portrait 8v*, zone 6), this participant powerfully stated, "**No. No**." And when questioned about her preferences in multimodal support (*Portrait 8v*, zone 7), Eun provided a short shot-like statement strongly stressed by her voice, "**Video**."

Anjali # 9 F

Figure 9. Portrait 9v. Anjali's perceptions of effects of addition of a video with sound to conventional print-based text 3

(MaxQda, 2021)

Anjali, participant #9f, expressed her preference of video with sound type of support to print-based texts from the very beginning of her second interview (*Portrait 9v*, zone 1). She clarified, "In the video, we can connect to what is happening. Sequence of events matters." This participant genuinely believed that addition of a video could be also helpful to any other college students (*Portrait 9v*, zone 2), just as it was helpful to herself (*Portrait 9v*, zone 3).

Anjali strongly believed in positive effects of color (*Portrait 9v*, zone 4) on student learning processes. This participant shared that as an educator, she would include images in color to support the print-based texts she would offer to her prospective students in her future classroom. When asked to explain why, as she believed, color would produce positive effects on her students' learning, Anjali expressed her idea about a strong potential for the colorful images to ignite a greater interest in learners. This participant clarified, "Because it is attractive, students get stuck to it. Otherwise, if it is black and white, it is not that attractive. If I have a provision of showing a video, I will opt for that."

In addition to enhancing interest in readers, visuals might assist students with their memorization of new information, as stated by Anjali. Afterwords, this participant furthered, "... Video is visual. It remains in your memory for a longer time. So, for answering questions, it is helpful. Characters' actions and facial expressions help you to answer the questions."

Importantly, Anjali did not perceive the video added to the print-based *Text 3* as distracting. On the contrary, she confirmed multiple times during this interview that the video with sound helped her with this project's tasks.

Sang # 10 M

Figure 10. Portrait 10v. Sang's perceptions of effects of addition of a video with sound to conventional print-based text 3

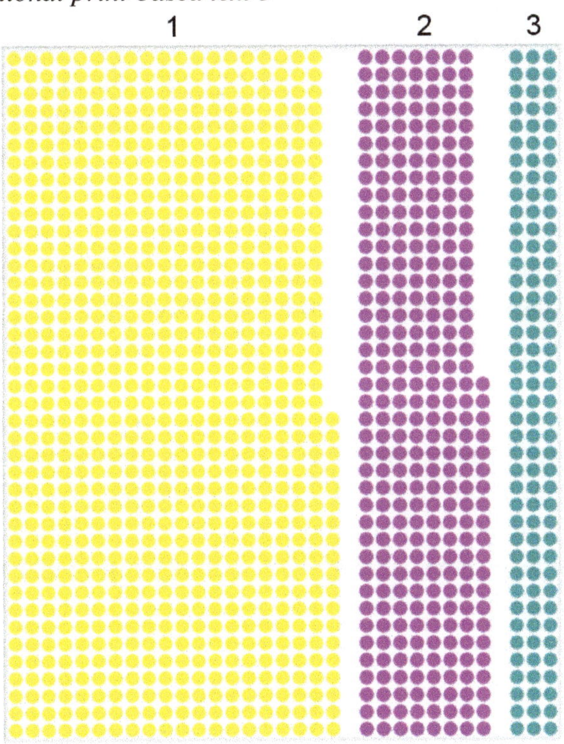

(MaxQda, 2021)

Sang, participant #10m, generously spoke about how multimodal support helped him with his meaning making of the print-based *Text 2* supported by an audio and *Text 3* supported by a video with the sound *Portrait 10v*, zone 1). In his reply to the question whether addition of the video with the sound to the print-based *Text 3* helped him to better understand the text, this participant confirmed that it did. The largest width of the first zone in this participant's interview portrait above indicates that this student considered this topic most important to him.

When questioned about helpfulness from the video, Sang stated directly,

I will say, yes, it [video] did [help]. It helped me in understanding the subtleties, the emotions. It is interesting, but I was following the emotions in the text I was trying to read at the same time… It did give me another dimension to look at the text… I think it helped to show especially Juliet herself, how she was a teenager in love, like she was. I did not necessarily get it from the text itself. (Sang)

When asked to compare addition of a video versus an audio to the print-based *Texts 2* and *3,* Sang shared his point of view stating, "I would say, if I had to compare, I would say, video would be a lot more advantageous. A very well-done video would be a lot better than a well-done audio" (*Portrait 10v*, zone 2).

When asked to compare all his experiences within this project, Sang replied with confidence,

I would say that the text by itself was least effective. But in terms of audio versus video, it's very tight. I would say, video gave a lot more information than the audio itself. It gave me information that I did not get from the text, while the audio merely supplemented. (Sang)

Further, this student described his own experience with the multimodal support in this project and attempted to evaluate in what way the video appeared to be most helpful to him. Sang developed his initially expressed idea,

I would say the video did give me the stuff that I didn't get from the text or from the audio… It was nice seeing characters' interactions. I definitely could see the things that made sense later on, when the [print-based] text did not make sense. (Sang)

Linking his utterances with his internal perceptions, Sang confirmed that addition of visuals in combination with the sound to conventional print-based texts might also be helpful to many other students with their reading comprehension (*Portrait 10v*, zone 3).

Faiz # 11 M

Figure 11. Portrait 11v. Faiz's perceptions of effects of addition of a video with sound to conventional print-based text 3

(MaxQda, 2021)

Faiz, participant #11m, expressed his preference of multimodal support in the form of a video with the sound in addition to print-based texts right away at the start of the second interview (*Portrait 11v*, zone 1). From this student's point of view, "Video is the best thing that has been invented! It's really great to have it."

Faiz confirmed that video helped him a lot (*Portrait 11v*, zone 2). Being a professional educator with several semesters of college teaching experiences and, simultaneously, a Graduate student, this participant suggested a specific technique he would implement when working with a multimodal text.

Faiz thoughtfully explained his proposed multimodal reading strategy,

I think, if I had an option, if I did that individually, independently, I would go a couple of times through the video: first time, to see the video, to see the play going, and then, the second time, following the text. (Faiz)

This participant believed addition of a video with the sound to a print-based text might be also helpful to many other students (*Portrait 11v*, zone 3). Later, during his interview, this student added some more insightful details and clarified his strong preference of video support in combination with the sound.

Faiz contemplated,

I think this (pointed to the video at the computer screen) works best because it puts you in the scene more. Even if you do not understand exactly what the words mean, the context will tell you something from the actions in the play and from the people playing the characters. (Faiz)

During the second interview on Day 2, this participant contemplated about why a video might be of a greater service compared to an audio.

Faiz clarified his position (*Portrait 11v*, zone 4) saying,

I think video is more engaging for people. If you think in general about TV, for example, I think TV is a way more widely accepted means of receiving information than an audio, than a radio, for example. Personally, if I had the choice of a radio or a TV, I would certainly go for TV because there is a lot more stimulation going on, than just with the sound. (Faiz)

In addition to that, this student noticed that multimodality appeals to multiple organs of reception of information (*Portrait 11v*, zone 5); thus, a video with the sound, as he believed, becomes more memorable (*Portrait 11v*, zone 6), more understandable, and more meaningful.

Faiz's further words sounded like a confession,

I think with the video, you use more senses, rather than just when you are just reading. You also hear sounds, the tones of the people in the play, and you see the scene overall, that context. It is totally different, especially in the text like that. When I read it first, with no support, it was just this plain thing with no idea. I almost felt frustrated with the words there. It was just "grey." And I am going to see Shakespeare tomorrow in the park! (Faiz)

At that moment, Faiz looked deeply saddened by his memories of his work with the print-based *Text 3* prior to his exposure to the video with sound. After a brief pause, this person continued, "And I've got so much into the scene because of this video! I think if I had to create as many videos in my life as I could, I would certainly do that."

REFERENCES

MAXQDA. (2021). MAXQDA 2022 [computer software]. Berlin, Germany: VERBI Software. Available from maxqda.com.

Shakespeare, W. (1597). *Romeo and Juliet*.

VERBI Software. (2021). MAXQDA 2022 [computer software]. Berlin, Germany: VERBI Software. Available from maxqda.com.

Chapter 14
Triangulating With AI:
Day 2 Group Accounts

ABSTRACT

Chapter 14 will talk about in summary the participants' perceptions of video support. To be more exact, I will dig deeper into their perceptions. The affordances of Artificial Intelligence will help me again with generating the concise visual displays for the extensive interview data. So, long hours of the audio-recorded interviews and multiple pages of their transcripts will be organized in the MaxQda-developed whole-group products, the matrices. To not let my readers ponder and decipher each matrix, I will interpret the visual data verbally. Importantly, in addition to the diverging individual reading peculiarities, this Chapter XIV will also discuss some differences by gender, by culture, and by learning abilities, and practices which were found within this project. Some of the traits appeared characteristic of the entire group of the participating students.

INTERVIEW II. PARTICIPANTS' PERCEPTIONS OF VIDEO SUPPORT

Upon having completed all interviews with my participants, I had all my data processed through the AI for qualitative research analysis. Now, I will present the matrices, which were developed with the help of MaxQda Coded Matrix Browser. These technological affordances enabled for me to analyze and gain a deeper understanding of my research picture. So, in the following sections below, I will not only verbalize, but also show to my readers how exactly AI helped me, as a researcher, to better visualize the extensive portions of the combined data from all participants' interviews.

DOI: 10.4018/979-8-3373-3426-4.ch014

Joint Data in Matrices

During the second set of individual interviews, my participants densely discussed their perceptions of their experiences working with the video- and sound-supported print-based *Text 3*. In particularly, they addressed their strong preferences of multimodal support in the form of a video with sound to *Text 3*, which, per their words, outweighed the audio support, which was added to the print-based *Text 2*.

As it can be seen from Figure 1 *Matrix 4* below, all participants strongly believed that addition of the video with sound helped them to cope with the tasks on Day 2 in this project. Altogether, the entire group of participants made 51 turns discussing this topic (See Figure 1 *Matrix 4* below).

Figure 1. Matrix 4: Video. Participants 1 to 11: Coded themes emerged in all participants' interviews on day 2 (combined)

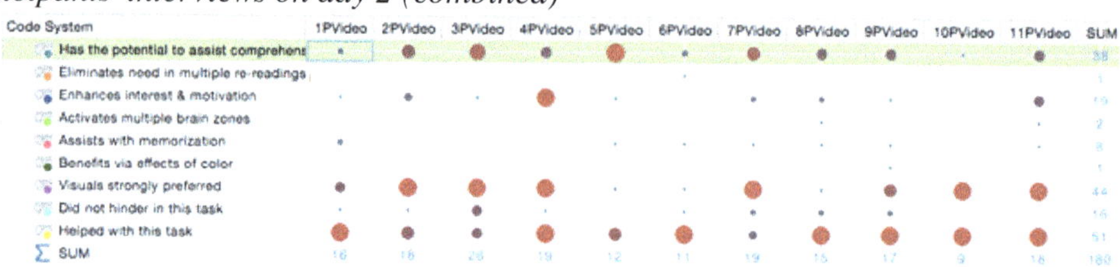

(MaxQda, 2021)

In 44 turns, which made a quarter of all cases, the students stated with confidence that they would strongly prefer visual support in addition to conventional print-based texts to be able to deeper understand the content of the readings. In about 38 turns, the students confirmed the idea that multimodality has a strong potential to assist readers with their comprehension. Further, in 19 turns, participants addressed the topic of a potential for multimodality to enhance readers' interest and motivation. And, in 16 turns, these students shared that addition of multimodality did not hinder them when they were working on this project's tasks. Additionally, in 8 turns, the students addressed the topic of multimodality as a helpful means to assist people with memorization of the read materials. Less frequently, but still, important, some of the students with their background knowledge in brain research, discussed a potential for multimodality to activate multiple brain zones in the process of reading multimodal texts (2 turns). One student also mentioned an eliminated or reduced need in repetitive re-readings (1 turn), while another one touched the topic of benefits of colors (1 turn).

Interview II. Variation by Gender

After having deeper scrutinized the visual data generated by MasQda compared to my researcher's observations, I found some variations by gender in the transcripts of the second-round interviews and in the matrices. I should state how important the results of this triangulation between the AI- and human mind-produced analyses were for this project!

So, the female research participants, Ting, #4f, Miyuki, #5f, Mei, #7f, Eun, #8f, and Anjali, #9f, shared how video with the sound helped them to deeper understand the print-based *Text 3* and answer the comprehension test questions (22 turns). In another 19 turns, the female students discussed a potential of multimodality to assist students with their reading comprehension. In 17 more turns, the female participants expressed their strong preference of the visual support (See Figure 2 *Matrix 5* below to visualize combined data from female research participants' interviews on Day 2).

Figure 2. Matrix 5: Females. Video. Participants Ting, # 4f, Miyuki, #5f, Mei, #7f, Eun, # 8f, and Anjali, #9f: Coded themes emerged in all female participants' interviews on day 2 (combined)

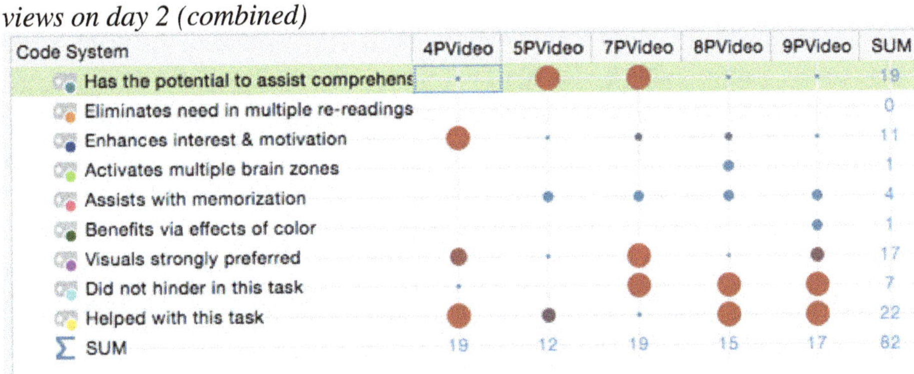

(MaxQda, 2021)

Additionally, the female participants believed that video with sound has a strong potential to enhance interest and motivation in reading (11 turns). In 9 turns, female students discussed that addition of the video support did not hinder their working processes. With less frequency (1 turn in each category), female participants addressed such topics as activating several brain zones during processing many different multimodal resources and benefits of color for learning processes.

Notably, the male participants most often addressed the theme of how addition of the video with sound helped them cope with the tasks on Day 2 in this project (29 turns versus 22 in females) (See Figure 3 *Matrix 6* below to visualize combined data from male research participants' interviews on Day 2).

Figure 3. Matrix 6: Males. Video. Participants Sanjay, #1m, Prem, #2m, Vijay, #3m, Kumar, #6m, Sang, #10m, and Faiz, #11m: Coded themes emerged in all male participant interviews on day 2 (combined)

(MaxQda, 2021)

The male students expressed their preference of the visual support in 27 turns (versus 17 turns by females). In 19 turns, males expressed their idea of the potential for a video plus sound to assist students with their meaning making. Nine turns (1 turn in each category) made by the male students addressed the topic of how addition of a video with sound did not hinder their working processes with the print-based *Text 3* (versus 7 turns made by females).

Further, eight turns were made by the male participants to clarify how multimodality might enhance student interest and motivation (the females addressed this topic in 11 turns). Four turns were concerned with some positive effects of multimodality on memorization processes. The facts that processing multiple resources of multimodality might activate several brain zones and that multimodal support has the potential to reduce the need in repetitive re-readings were addressed only once in each of the categories.

DAY 1 AND 2 COMBINED

Whole Sample: Perceptions Multimodal Effects

Looking at the data obtained from an entire sample allowed me to draw the final conclusions in my data analysis. These data were also AI-processed through the MaxQda Matrix Browser, where all interview transcripts were loaded in the system with the purpose to extract the major themes, which were most often and most powerfully addressed by a whole sample of participants during their individual interviews.

The highest concentration of brown squares in Figure 4 below shows the topics which all participants addressed most frequently and prosodically. This fact might be explained with these students' high interest in these topics (See Figure 4 *Matrix 7* below for perceptions of addition of multimodalities to traditional print-based texts by all participants).

Figure 4. Matrix 7: Perceptions of addition of multimodalities to print-based texts by all participants

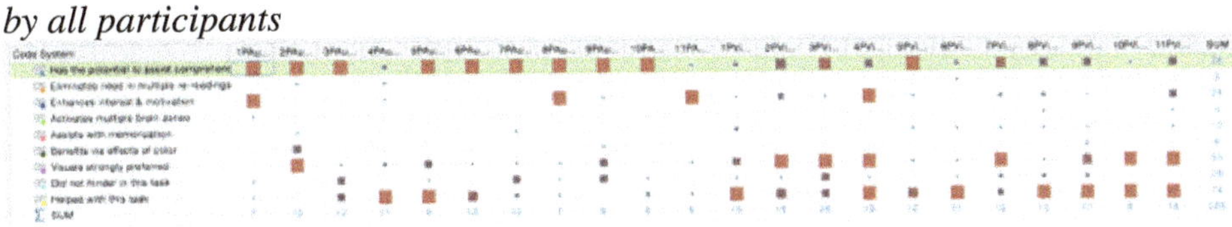

(MaxQda, 2021)

As one can see in Figure 4 *Matrix 7* above, the whole sample most frequently focused in their interviews on the potential of multimodalities to assist students with their reading comprehension when added to print-based texts (76 turns). All participants came to this conclusion based on their own experiences on Day 1 and Day 2 when they had a chance to compare their working processes with the different types of multimodal support. Through their own practice within this project, the students realized that addition of multimodal features to print-based *Texts 2* and *3* helped them to deeper understand both texts (74 turns).

It is obvious from the data in Figure 4 *Matrix 7* that, in great majority of cases in this project, the students expressed their preference of visual support in addition to the print-based texts (59 turns). Many participants confirmed that additional multimodal features did not hinder them, but, on the contrary, enhanced their interest in the content of the texts and triggered their motivation to deeper comprehend these texts (28 turns in each of the cases). Additionally, the students expressed their opinions about a strong potential for multimodalities to positively affect readers' interest and motivation.

Several students addressed the topic of multimodalities assisting them with memorization of the content of the read materials (10 turns). Four turns made by the participants were concerned with the power and some positive effects from colors on students' learning processes. Some people found that addition of multimodalities to print-based texts might reduce or eliminate the necessity in repetitive re-readings (3 turns). Several students shared their background knowledge on the positive effects of multimodality due to its potential to activate multiple brain zones (three turns), which they explained with the opportunity to process multiple multimodal resources through multiple sources of information when reading multimodally.

CONCLUSIVE THOUGHTS

Summarizing my contemplations over the usage of AI for qualitative data analysis and display, I concluded that the AI-generated visual data representations helped me to better visualize the differences between Day 1 and Day 2 interview topics raised by participants. For this purpose, I assembled all the AI-created visual portraits of Day 1 interviews side by side to the ones of Day 2. Having memorized the color codes for the major topics allowed me to clearly see all similarities and, most importantly, the differences just at a glance (See Figure 5 below). Yet, for my readers' convenience, I included the color codes and their signified topics at the bottom of Figure 5 (see below)

Figure 5. Day 1 (audio) and day 2 (video with sound) interview portraits with the color-codes listed underneath

(MaxQda, 2021)

As it appears in Figure 5, turquois, yellow, and lilac color zones can be more frequently seen across all the interview portraits on both days. Importantly, the zones marked in these colors appear to be noticeably larger, rather than the other color-zones. Thus, the interviewees most frequently and most intensively discussed such topics as *Multimodality Assists with Reading Comprehension*, *Multimodal Support*

Helped Students with Project Tasks within this Study, and *Visual Support Strongly Preferred*, as perceived by these project participants.

Notably, the shift in the width of majority of color zones is significantly stronger pronounced in Day 2 interview portraits. More, these differences can be clearly seen now, when the portraits of both interviews have been placed in one figure and side by side. Conclusively, the main finding in this data analysis was that during Day 1 interviews, after having experienced working with audio-supported *Text 2* versus unimodal, conventional print-based *Text 1* without any support, the participants suggested that multimodality had the potential to assist students with meaning making.

Yet, the Day 2 portrait set shows that after having experienced video and sound support to *Text 3*, all participants stated that the video helped them the most with their reading comprehension. Importantly, all students stated the video with the sound helped them the most with working on the comprehension tests as well.

Another significant finding was that all participants strongly appreciated and preferred multimodal support in the form of a video with the sound.

WHOLE SAMPLE: VARIATIONS BY GENDER

As my previous portions of data analysis helped me identify some variations by gender, I needed to have a deeper insight into this topic. In the process of my multimodal data analysis, where my researcher's observations were backed up with the MaxQda Matrix Browser products, I found some more variations by gender in my participants' perceptions of effects of multimodal features added to the print-based *Texts 2* and *3*. Id est, all female participants, Ting, #4f, Miyuki, #5f, Mei, #7f, Eun, #8f, and Anjali, #9f, strongly stressed the potential for multimodality to assist college students with their reading comprehension (34 turns). Additionally, the female students shared that supplementation with multimodal features, as for the print-based *Texts 2* and *3* within this project, helped them to deeper understand these texts (33 turns).

Moreover, the female participants expressed their preference of visual support in addition to conventional print-based texts (25 turns). The female students stated that multimodal features did not hinder their understanding of the texts and the tests to the texts (14 turns), but helped them due to their enhanced interest and motivation in reading *Texts* 2 and 3 (15 turns). Some female participants shared that the multimodalities added to the print-based texts, assisted them with their faster and more reliable memorization of the read, heard, and viewed information (5 turns). Two turns were made by two female students mentioned their background knowledge on some positive effects of color on learning processes.

Importantly, one female participant shared her prior knowledge on the potential of multimodalities to activate several brain zones due to necessity to process multiple resources and sources of information, which, as this participant understood, had many positive and beneficial effects. One female participant believed that addition of an audio or a video with sound might reduce or even eliminate the need in repetitive re-readings of complicated texts (See Figure 6 *Matrix 8* below for all female participants' perceptions of effects of addition of multimodalities to conventional print-based texts).

Figure 6. Matrix 8: Multimodalities. Female participants' Ting, #4f, Miyuki, #5f, Mei, #7f, Eun, #8f, and Anjali, #9f perceptions of effects of multimodalities

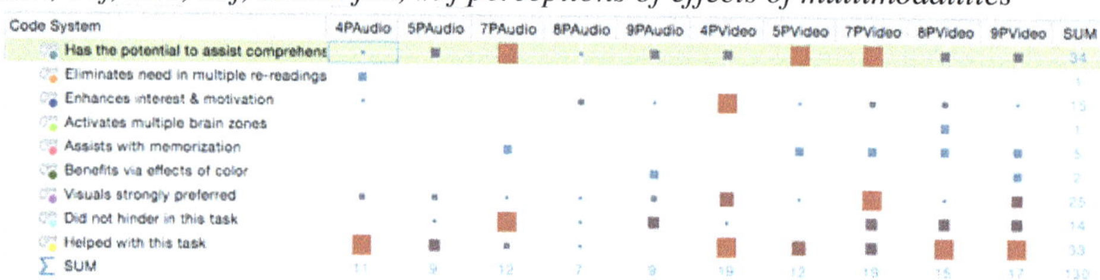

(MaxQda, 2021)

Some shift in the degree of importance of these topics can be perceived from viewing the visually represented data on the male students' interviews. The male participants, Sanjay, #1m, Prem, #2m, Vijay, #3m, Kumar, #6m, Sang, #10m, and Faiz, #11m, made 42 turns (versus 34 made by females) describing their perceptions of potential of multimodality to assist college students with their reading comprehension. All males made 41 turns (versus 33 by females) describing how additional features of multimodality helped them to deeper understand the texts in this project. In 34 turns (versus 25 by females), male participants expressed their strong preference of visual support in addition to print-based texts.

Overall, the male group made 14 turns to state that addition of multimodal features to the print-based *Texts 2* and *3* did not hinder their working with these texts, but enhanced their interest in the content and supported their motivation in a deeper comprehension of these texts (13 turns). Five turns were made to share the opinion that addition of multimodal features has the potential to assist readers with their memorization of content of readings.

Some male students also shared their background knowledge on positive effects of color on learning processes. Some other participants addressed the topic of activating several brain zones due to processing multiple multimodal resources when reading multimodal texts. Some of the participants stressed that it is not only activation of multiple brain zones, but the cooperation between those activated brain zones that mattered. They also discussed a reduced need in repetitive re-readings thanks to the beneficial effects of multimodalities (2 turns in each of the cases) (See Figure 7 *Matrix 9* below for all male participants' perceptions of the effects of addition of multimodalities to conventional print-based texts).

Figure 7. Matrix 9: Multimodalities. Male participants' Sanjay, #1m, Prem, #2m, Vijay, #3m, Kumar, #6m, Sang, #10m, and Faiz, #11m perceptions of effects of multimodalities

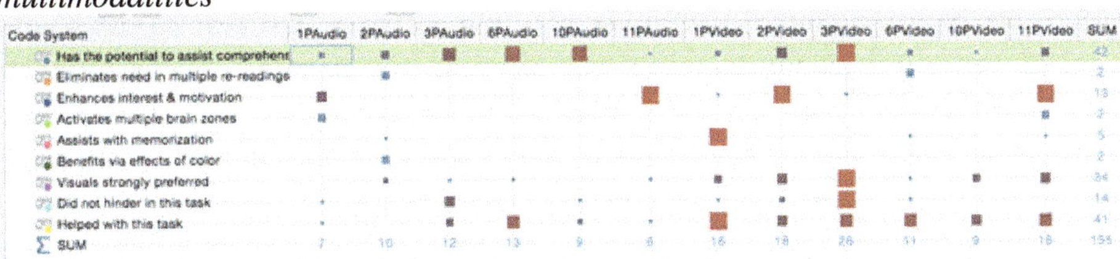

(MaxQda, 2021)

Having scrutinized the matrices by different gender, I proceeded with using the AI for generating a whole sample matrix. Figure 8 *Matrix 10* below gave me a compressed view that represented the major topics, which were most frequently and powerfully addressed by ***all*** participants in their interviews on Day 1 and Day 2 (See Figure 8 *Matrix 10* below for compressed view of the most frequently and powerfully addressed topics by all participants in this study).

Figure 8. Matrix 10: Perceptions of multimodality by all participants expressed in all interviews (compressed view)

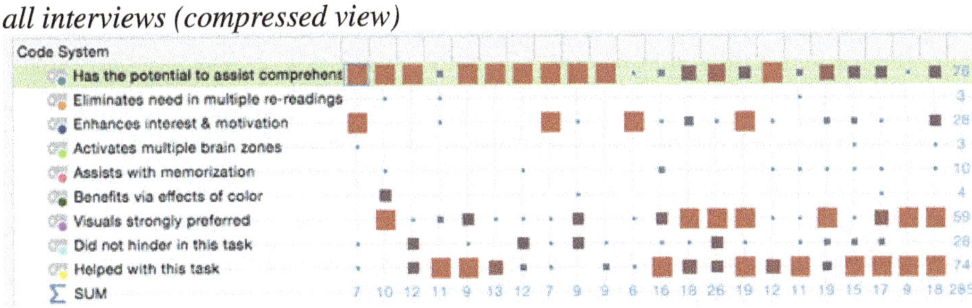

(MaxQda, 2021)

Three main themes are absolutely observably prevailing in *Matrix 10* above. Yet, the total of five major topics were most frequently and powerfully addressed by the whole sample of the participants in all their interviews combined. In the descending by frequency order, these topics were: *Potential of Multimodality to Assist Students with Reading Comprehension, Helpfulness of Multimodality with the Task in this Project, Strong Preference of Visual Means of Multimodality, Potential of Multimodalities to Enhance Interest and Motivation in Reading*, and *Little to no Hindering Affect from Addition of Multimodal Features to Print-Based Texts within this Project.*

Conclusively, my analyses of all the research participants' interview data via listening to their audio-recorded speech, reading and memoing their interview transcripts, and examining the AI-generated visual representations of the data in the form of the individual interview portraits and group matrices, confirmed my researcher's assumption about the shift that occurred in my participants' perceptions of effects of multimodality between *Text 2* (audio support) and *Text 3* (video with sound support). In particular, during Day 1, when students were discussing their experiences working with the audio supported *Text 2*, they were most frequently talking about *the potential* of multimodality to assist readers with their meaning making. Yet, after having worked with the video- and audio-supported *Text 3* on Day 2, all participants discussed more intensively how multimodal support ***helped them*** with Day 2 tasks. All students also stressed significance of visual means of multimodality.

Additionally, on Day 2, my participants more often addressed the topic of a strong power of multimodality to engage them and keep them motivated in making the meaning of *Text 3*. In comparison to Day 1 interviews, the participants more vigorously denied the potential of multimodal features to distract readers. It was also obvious from the Interview 2 data analysis that all participants strongly preferred and appreciated video with the sound support and considered this type of multimodal support most helpful for their reading comprehension and answering comprehension questions to the texts within this project.

Some final thoughts to conclude this Chapter 14, as well as the previous three chapters, ask to be uttered and put on paper. As a researcher with years of experiences, I fully realize that it may not be enough to state, to say, or even explain the state of things while discussing one's project results. It is clearly imperative to be able to show the evidence in support of one's words. Most definitely, the AI, so belittled and denigrated these days due to its frequent misuse, appeared to be highly helpful to me, as both an analyst and a presenter, with enabling my own and my audiences' visualization of the participants speeches. So, gratefully, I close this case.

REFERENCES

MAXQDA. (2021). MAXQDA 2022 [computer software]. Berlin, Germany: VERBI Software. Available from maxqda.com.

Shakespeare, W. (1597). *Romeo and Juliet.*

VERBI Software. (2021). MAXQDA 2022 [computer software]. Berlin, Germany: VERBI Software. Available from maxqda.com

Section 4
How Multimodalities Work

Chapter 15
Multimodal Analysis 1:
Attempting to Understand Role, Position, and Significance of Visuals Within Multimodal Ensembles

ABSTRACT

In Chapter 15, I will detail on my initial multimodal analysis. As my research participants strongly relied on the visual texts for making the meaning from the verbal texts supported by multimodality, it appeared highly significant to me to switch my focus on the affordances of exactly the visual mode of multimodality. Apparently, life situations with the visual mode as an only asset rarely happen. Most naturally, in the real-life world, as well as in the videos, whole ensembles of modes are available to a multimodal reader. Nevertheless, the Multimodal Analysis 1 purpose was to help me as a researcher to gain a more profound understanding of the role of precisely the visuals, which formed multimodal ensembles within this project's video and were noted as extremely helpful by all students. More precisely, I focused on the visually assessable behaviors of the actors in the scene under investigation; particularly, I scrutinized their postures, gazes, gestures, positions of the head.

ANALYSIS 1: INTRODUCTION

Though the world we live in is extremely multimodal, humans have stored and shared information predominantly via the means of verbal: oral or written language. Nevertheless, people are also able to correctly make the meaning and convey ideas through the affordances of the non-verbal language. For example, from observing events of a real life or the ones broadcast on a screen, it is oftentimes possible to

DOI: 10.4018/979-8-3373-3426-4.ch015

understand the happenings without an audio component being available. Thus, I conclude about development of some hereditary or learned skills by humans, which allow us to read different modes within multimodal ensembles, just like we read alphabetical, print-based verbal texts. Moreover, when we observe non-verbal interactions, which involve two or more participants, we evidently realize that those actors can correctly understand each other via exchanging information in non-verbal ways; for example, via gazes, gesture, nods or positions of head, facial expressions, postures, etc. Similarly, people can understand the meaning conveyed via pictures, photos, paintings, and book illustrations, even when those have no captions.

Interestingly, while children are being largely taught how to read and understand the print-based verbal language, they seem to not be schooled on how to comprehend non-verbal texts. Yet, humans seem to have and use that knowledge. So, it ignited my researcher's interest to understand how exactly people learn or teach themselves metacognitively to read and share information in a range of multimodal ways.

With this purpose, I engaged myself in this current analysis of an excerpt from Zeffirelli's (1968) movie production of *Romeo and Juliet* based on the Shakespeare's (1597) play, while aiming to understand how different means of the non-verbal language, a.k.a., modes of multimodality (e.g., positions of actors and objects in the space, their movements, postures, gestures, facial expressions, the available colors, the space by itself, and the usage of its dimensions) may allow viewers to correctly construct the meaning based on their observations.

Specifically, I analyzed how the resources of the multimodal non-verbal language (e.g., postural behavior / body position, head position, gaze, and color) might assist readers with their meaning making in the absence of the verbal, print-based or orally produced texts. I also considered the instances when verbal language is minimally present in the video episode under the investigation. Further narrowing the focus, I aimed to understand the role of the position in space, as the means for making meaning within a larger multimodal ensemble. I narrowed the focus of my investigation to test my hypothesis of whether or not, in the presence of a broad spectrum of available modes of multimodality, a reader may need only a few of them for reading and constructing the meaning, while the rest of the resources might appear either secondary or unnecessary for meaning making.

ANALYSIS 1: RATIONALE

It needs to be explained that this analytical work was of high significance for my research purposes. Most importantly, the results of my study might be helpful to many educators, especially the ones who teach English as a Foreign or an Additional language. Having served a half of my professional life in the capacity of an EAL schoolteacher or higher education instructor in the language-focused and all-inclusive classrooms, I noticed that multimodality, especially in its visual forms, had a great potential for assisting students with their meaning making on all grade levels. In addition to my own professional educator and researcher experiences (e.g., Gould-Yakovleva, 2023a, 2023b), my conclusions were confirmed through extensive readings on this topic (e.g., Archer, 2025; Baildon & Damico, 2009; Binder & Kotsopoulos, 2011; Breuer & Archer, 2016; Brown & Eskildsen, 2024; Ericson & Häikiö, 2025; Gellevij et al. 2002; Giampapa, 2010; Huang, 2012, 2023; Kaur, 2012; Pütz & Mundt, 2018; Wang, 2011, 2022), where my colleagues and predecessors developing the field of multimodality stressed the potential for the multimodal language to serve the communicative goals.

The major goal of my current analysis though was to understand how exactly and in what ways the visual mode of multimodality assisted the multimodal readers, including but not limited to myself and my research participants, with our meaning making in the process of watching a video clip from Zeffirelli's (1986) production of Shakespearian *Romeo and Juliet*, which was offered in support of the print-based text.

ANALYSIS 1: THEORY AND LITERATURE OVERVIEW

Importantly, the works by Franks and Jewitt (2001), such as *The Meaning of Action in Learning and Teaching* as well as *Colour as a Semiotic Mode: Notes for a Grammar of Colour* by Kress and van Leeuwen (2002) served as theoretical framework foundation for this analysis. I used the analyses conducted by Franks and Jewitt (2001) and Kress and van Leeuwen (2002) as guidance for my multimodal analysis of the selected episode from Zeffirelli's *Romeo and Juliet*. I feel it necessary, though, to recognize contributions of my highly valued predecessors in the field of multimodality, for example Callow and Zammit (2012), whose works helped me extend my knowledge and understanding of multimodal reading of visual texts, precisely, making the meaning from non-verbal information.

For instance, Kress, the founding father in the field of multimodality noticed that in order to make the meaning, a person needs to be able to decode multimodal messages comprised of ensembles of different modes (2011). Precisely, visual, spatial, sensory, gestural, and, if available, auditory resources in their combination may be orchestrated by an author of a message so that they gain the power to deliver the exact message. Amazingly, this work may influence, shape, or even change the addressee's thinking. With the above knowledge, one question persists, though: how exactly do the readers receive information non-verbally and make the correct meaning? Moore-Russo & Shanahan attempted to answer this question. In their 2014 publication, these researchers suggested that it is an entire ensemble of resources that needs to be processed by a reader to make the meaning. Considering the instances when at least some verbal texts are present, Moor-Russo and Shanahan delivered, “The choice of color, placement of text and images, inclusion of illustrations, font selection and size are all clues that readers can and should use to help make meaning of visual representations” (2014, p. 528). Even though it might be hard to counter the above idea, the posed by myself research question for this analysis remains unanswered: we need yet develop understanding of how multimodal meaning making occurs.

Notably, as if placing the conclusions by the latter researchers in juxtaposition, Callow righteously noticed, “Written text has always held and will continue to hold a key place in our cultures” (2014, p. vii). Nevertheless, Callow further admitted, “So many texts today are multimodal” (2014, p. 13). These mentioned by this researcher multimodal texts appear as representations of meaning, in the form of messages, which have been composed with the help of multiple multimodal resources and created with the help of specific non-verbal grammar, structure, and design. Multiple researchers in the field of multimodality echoed the above ideas and noticed that to be literate today, it is important to possess multimodal literacy (e.g., Callow, 2014; Goodwin, 2000; Franks & Jewitt, 2001; Goldin-Meadow, 2000; Hostetter & Alibali, 2008; Kress, 2011; Kress & van Leeuwen, 1996, 2002; Shanahan, 2013; Unsworth, 2006). The above researchers pioneered studying meaning-making processes in the scenarios when readers could strongly rely on the information they could acquire through visual mode. Thus, the findings by the above cohort implied the idea that the visually readable texts might include such components as behaviors of actors, their gestures, movements, gazes, postures, positioning in the scene, etc. Additionally, meaningful non-verbal language might include such elements as colors or objects, which might be either naturally present or intentionally brought into a situation by the actors with the purpose to create or emphasize a certain meaning.

Conclusively, I weighed a range of perspectives on significance or prevalence of certain features of multimodality for meaning making (e.g., Ainsworth et al., 2023; Moore-Russo & Viglietti, 2012; Rahmanu et al., 2020; Roth, 2001; Sindoni 2023; Stein, 2008, 2012; Shanahan & Flury-Kashmanian, 2014; Włodarczyk et al., 2023). Yet, my choice of a paradigm for this analysis strongly shifted towards the one postulated by Kress (2011) who pronounced that all modes and resources of multimodality are equally important.

ANALYSIS 1: METHODOLOGY

Artifact

Returning to the film episode I selected to analyze, I need to clarify that it was enactment of Act I Scene IV of Shakespeare's play *Romeo and Juliet* in Franco Zeffirelli's (1968) production. The major characters taking part in this scene were: Juliet, Juliet's nurse, Romeo, and Tybalt. Additionally, many guests of the House of Capulet were distantly present in the scene under analysis. At some short instances, Juliet's fiancé Paris and her father appeared on the screen, while the background setting of this event was the rich and spacious palace of the Capulets. Apparently, this episode was one of the most significant ones in the entire story because it depicted the moment when Romeo received the news about the lady he fell in love with, Juliet precisely, of her belonging to the family of Capulet, the mortal enemies of Romeo's clan, the House of Montague. Importantly, during this very scene, both in the play and in the film, Juliet also found out that the young man who fascinated her at the ball in her house belonged to the clan of her family's bloodiest foes.

Type of Analysis

So, I chose to engage in this multimodal analysis of an ensemble with a strong emphasis on its visual language. Following the guidelines by Franks and Jewitt, I focused on the body language, head positions, postures, movements, positions of actors in the space, and their gazes. Specifically, I used Franks and Jewitt's (2009) report on the meaning of action as a guiding framework for my analysis.

These researchers described the following steps in their study,

> *First, focusing on the human body as material for making meaning, we look at the ways in which pupils [students] as groups of individuals make and reveal meaning through gesture, 'face-work' and so forth. Second, we examine how pupils [students] arrange themselves in relation to each other and objects in the... room, and how they move in and through the space and time. (Franks & Jewitt, 2001, p. 205)*

Having also grounded my analysis in the work by Kress and van Leeuwen (1996, 2002), I scrutinized the colors present in the film episode under investigation. So, besides analyzing postures, positions in the space (in relation to the other actors in the film and to the viewing audiences), the characters' movements through the space and time, their head positions, and gazes, I paid close attention to the moviemaker's (Zeffirelli's) choice of colors. My decision was guided by Kress and van Leeuwen (2002) who stated, "Colour is also used to convey 'interpersonal' meaning. Just as language allows us to realize speech acts, so colour allows us to realize 'colour acts'" (p. 347).

So, I analyzed the meanings that the author of this multimodal composition attempted to convey through affordances of color as one of the meaning-conveying modes of multimodality. My researcher's decision was also shaped by the following clarification by Kress and van Leeuwen (2002), "Starting with the ideational function, color clearly can be used to denote specific people, places and things as well as classes of people, places and things, and more general ideas" (p. 347). These eye-opening findings by these researchers and the founding fathers of multimodal meaning making served me as guidelines for investigating the meaning-baring colors used by the grand master of visual arts, Gian Franco Corsi Zeffirelli (1968).

There was also another valuable note, which saliently sounded in Kress and van Leeuwen's 2002 publication, "Ideas have been expressed by color for a long time, for instance in Medieval colour symbolism, in which black stood for penance, white for innocence and purity, red for Pentecostal fire, and so on" (p. 347). With the above ideas, most definitely known, studied, and considered by Zeffirelli, I scrutinized such aspects of his production as color, its salience, consonance, dissonance, complementarity, or its contrast in relation to some other colors present in the same scene. I also analyzed the correlation and coherence of the colors with the context of the investigated episode.

Procedures

Prior to conducting my multimodal analysis of the visual language present in the scene under investigation, I collected synchronic multimodal data and organized them in charts (See *Appendix C 1* in the *Appendices* section of this paper to examine the synchronic multimodal data). For these data collection purposes, I broke the whole excerpt from the video under investigation into several meaningful units. The condition for "cutting" off each small chunk of the video was: the meaningful changes occurring in the screen; for example, change in number of characters in that specific short chunk of the video, or transformation of the background, or shifts in actions, or positions of people, variations in color, progress in postures, variance in gazes, turns in head movement or position, etc.

It is crucially important for understanding the results of this work to explain that while examining each of those shorter chunks of the video, I chose to pay close attention to the following questions:

- What character(s) is (are) present in the scene?
- What is the position of each character in the space?
- In what relation to each other are the characters positioned?

- What is the position of each character towards the viewing audiences?
- Where and how do the characters move through the space?
- What are the postures of the characters?
- What is the direction of each actor's gaze? What is the intensity of each gaze?
- What emotions can be read in the gazes?

It was equally important to find answers to the following questions:

- Do the available means of multimodality complement the context of the scene?
- Do the available means of multimodality enhance the meaning, which I, as a part of the viewing audiences, am making from the verbal text?
- What is the meaning of the whole picture during each shorter scene?
- What images are on the screen?
- What colors are present in each shorter scene?
- What was the symbolic meaning of the colors in each scene in Medieval Europe?
- In what ways, if at all, did the ensemble of all available modes in each shorter scene reveal, imply, or convey the meaning?
- Do my perceptions as a viewer and findings as a researcher correlate with the findings in the reviewed literature and theoretical framework underpinning this analysis?

Subsequently, I scrutinized the multimodal ensemble of visuals present in the video and attempted to address each of the aspects listed above with the purpose to answer my research question and to better understand the role of visual language in the process of meaning making while reading multimodal texts. I am presenting the findings of my multimodal analysis in the section below. (See also the *Appendices* section, *Appendix C 1* to find complete transcript of the video episode under investigation used for this analysis).

ANALYSIS 1: FINDINGS

I have analyzed one 1-minute-long episode from Act I Scene IV of Zeffirelli's (1968) production *Romeo and Juliet* filmed after the play by William Shakespeare (1594). In my analysis, I focused on postural behavior and body positions, as well as positions of the head, gaze directions and expression, and the meaning of the available colors. My major purpose was to understand whether and, if yes, then how the elements of the non-verbal language present in this episode contributed to my meaning making, while I regarded myself as a part of the viewing audiences. The main characters participating in this episode were: Juliet, her nurse, and Tybalt. In the background, there was the crowd of guests leaving the ball. Among them, in the farthest back stood Romeo. I will report my findings in the four consecutive subsections below.

Postural Behavior and Body Positions

So, in the episode under investigation, there were present two women: Juliet and her nurse. While conversing with each other, they were cowering their bodies and lowering their heads in an attempt to keep their secretive dialogue less visible and less noticeable for the crowd in the house. These actors' fearful body postures as well as their hiding positions indicated a lower status of women in the society in that historic chronotope (Bakhtin, 1981). On the contrary, Tybalt, Juliet's cousin, who was present in this scene, and who was also hiding, behaved in a distinctly different manner. Precisely, this pronounced masculine character avoided attention for a reason: he was watchfully observing and guarding the happenings in the House of Capulet, as if, and most obviously feeling in charge. Despite his trying to stay unnoticed for any potentially present enemies of his family, this young man was not cowering. Tybalt's body posture was full of power, dignity, and self-confidence, which made a strong contrast to the behaviors by Juliet and her nurse.

Importantly for this analysis' conclusions, there was another character in this scene who also tried to hide. It was Romeo, who secretly visited the ball in the house of his enemies. This young man had his life-important reasons to hide his identity and to not be discovered, nor even noticed by the hosts of this grand event. Nevertheless, at this extremely dangerous for Romeo moment, this young man was not cowering either. His behavior did not indicate any internal fear. These observations of the body postures of the main characters in this scene confirmed my idea of a higher position of men and a lower significance of women in that specific chronotope.

Another finding based on my reading the actors' body positions allowed me to conclude that the nurse was in a very close relationship with each of the young members of the Capulet's clan: Juliet and Tybalt. I have drawn this conclusion based on my observations of the proximity between these three actors. Precisely, the nurse positioned her body very close to both Juliet and Tybalt. This observation allowed me to read beyond the scene and helped me to also understand that the older woman perceived these clan's members as children, who she had been raising and watching grow up. This person cherished her feelings to these youths, regardless of the fact of their becoming adults by and at the moment in the scene and in the story.

Returning to reading Juliet's posture, I have drawn the conclusion that she had little energy left to withstand the hardships of her life. This young lady was visibly exhausted by her troublesome life circumstances, which consisted in an endless, thus, excruciating anticipation of severe troubles which awaited her and her loved ones at any moment in their lives. Same fearful expectation rose as an unavoidable obstacle in Juliet's imagination of her developing a close relationship with Romeo. Precisely, from observing Juliet's body posture, gazes, and facial expressions, I was able to read this girl's anticipation of the forthcoming tragic turn in her life. Most likely, Juliet formed these expectations based on her previous experiences and her background knowledge about the histories of continuous animosity and periodic bloodsheds between both families: the Capulets and the Montagues.

From my reading Juliet's non-verbal language, I could also conclude that this young lady survived more than one tragedy during her short life time. Just as most of the multimodal reading audiences, my meaning making was based on my prior knowledge. As of a viewer with the Associate's degree in Medicine, which preceded my Bachelorette in Education, and was followed by Master's, and topped with the Doctoral scholarship, my background knowledge had also included research in the field of psychology. So, the combination of all the above prior knowledges and experiences allowed me to evaluate and correctly read the non-verbal language of Juliet's body posture. Conclusively, I could nearly sense this girl's being emotionally and physically exhausted. And her exhaustion was readably caused by the prolonged stresses and living in the constant state of fear. Obviously, this emotional devastation in a young girl was constantly fueled by the ever-lasting hatred between two Houses of the mortal enemies.

More of my observations of the actors' behaviors in this scene supported my initial guesses and led to the further findings. In contrast to Juliet's, her nurse's postures signified that this woman had yet lots of energy and a lot of enjoyment of life protuberating out of her personality. For example, at the beginning of the investigated episode, and prior to attending to Juliet's secretive messages, the nurse's posture was straight and laid back. This observation allowed me to understand that this woman, though felt "at home" in the house of Capulet, belonged to a different world, her internal world where she had no one to hate and no one from whom she would need to hide. Observably, this woman's shoulders were wide open, at times, she leaned freely and comfortably backwards while stretching her body. This character felt obviously pleased with the given moment and, probably, with her current life quality.

Significantly, during several seconds following that beginning episode, the posture of the nurse changed dramatically. This change occurred as soon as Juliet made her nurse a part of her own, tense, and secretive world. Even though the young lady had no knowledge yet about the stranger who sparked her interest during this ball, she felt shy and scared to reveal her feelings. This behavior on the young woman confirmed my previously expressed idea about the limited rights women enjoyed in the Capulet family.

Besides examining the body language of Juliet and her nurse, I tried to understand why was it needed to position Tybalt so that he would look at Juliet over his shoulder, but not straight. This daring young man could have positioned himself (or be positioned by the producer, as the ensemble creator) face-to-face with Juliet. Yet, as I found through my preparatory to this investigation readings of Callow (2014), this type of one-third or three-quarter positioning of actors in the space is often used for creating more tension in the image or scene. Hence, Tybalt's ¾ body position to the audiences was arranged by Zeffirelli with the purpose to let the viewers feel and fear the escalating tension in this scene as well as in the anticipated events. Additionally, the above idea could be confirmed through listening to the sounds of music, selected by the producer for this menace-bearing episode. Though, I was not analyzing the effects of music, it was impossible to disregard the malicious and alarming crescendo of French horns and trombones, which enhanced the threatening meaning of the verbal texts and the dramatic effect of the visual images moving on the screen.

Positions of the Head

Further, very thoughtfully, the producer utilized multiple elements of the non-verbal language. In the discussed episode, my observations of the actors' head positions and movements assisted me with my deeper meaning making of this scene. One could perceive that, in the atmosphere full of danger and secrecy, Juliet needed to explain to her nurse who in the crowd of guests attracted her special attention, and whose exactly name she prompted the nurse to find out. Though, the young lady used a deictic gesture of her right hand and pointed to Romeo with her forefinger, she, more often, used a deictic movement of her head, rather than her hands. This choice of the non-verbal communication can be explained with Juliet's wish to not attract the attention of other people present in the room to the object of her attention. Pointing to Romeo with her finger might have fully disclosed her cherished secret. So, I would describe Juliet's behavior as a deictic *position* rather than a deictic *movement* of her head since Juliet was pointing to the object of her interest in a very cautious and practically unnoticeable to the other characters way.

Importantly, the head movements of Juliet's nurse at the beginning of the episode were quite the opposite to the ones made by the young lady. Initially, the nurse moved freely, as I described in the previous chapter section. She openly turned her head to the left and to the right, then up and down while she was staring at the guests and visibly examining them from head to foot. This type of unrestricted behavior in this woman gave away her naïve and undisguised curiosity, the trait of a simple-hearted commoner. Yet, when talking to Juliet, the nurse positioned her head very close to Juliet's face, which indicated their very close, family-like relationship.

When nurse found out the name of Romeo and reported it to Juliet, this woman positioned her head right in front of Juliet's face, which indicated her wish to deliver the major secret and warning message to the girl, whose well-being was entrusted to the nurse by the Capulet family. This message was that Romeo was the one of the enemies' clan, the Montague. Following this disclosure, the nurse read Juliet's body language and realized that her warning message was powerless and not able to stop Juliet's fascination with Romeo. In response, the woman moved her chin down for gathering more of powerful energy within herself; then, she lifted her chin up in a strong and brisk motion, which aimed to remind the teenage child of the need to act thoughtfully and obediently.

Nevertheless, the nurse instantly realized that her efforts gave no result. So, she withdrew her head away from Juliet's face to have a better look at this girl and reevaluate her emotional state. The sight of Juliet's emotionally moved face confirmed the older woman's worst guess: she understood that Juliet fell in love with her family's enemy, Romeo. More, this was the moment when the nurse realized that it was a deep and serious feeling which took over Juliet's soul and her physical being. Subsequently, the nurse turned her head backwards over her left shoulder to look at Romeo. Her head froze for a moment. This posture gave away the nurses being stunned with her blood-chilling discovery: she realized that the feelings of both young people, Romeo and Juliet, were deeply mutual and interconnected.

Gazes

Importantly, gaze direction and intensity was another means for the producer as the author of the multimodal composition to convey his ideas, which could not be found in the verbal texts in the episode under investigation. Besides Juliet's gaze, which was fixed on Romeo only, I, as a part of the viewing audiences, could also read the situation from observing the gazes of the other actors, i.e., the nurse and Tybalt. Significantly, the gaze of the nurse indicated how deeply shaken this older and emotionally rich and intelligent woman was when she realized the deep feelings shared by Juliet and Romeo.

Apparently, this was the moment in this short film episode when reading the gaze of the nurse allowed me to correctly construct the meaning and anticipate the dramatic development of the future events in this story. Another evidence of the nurse's deeply shaken state was her gaze directed straight towards the viewers of the film. As per the social semioticians, the direct gazes have a strong power to engage audiences in the situation on the screen. Moreover, a direct gaze demands an internal co-action from the audience; thus, it may deeper engage the viewers into the events in the scene.

Further scrutiny of the episode under investigation allowed me to conclude that it was not only the nurse who discovered the beginning romantic relationship between Romeo and Juliet. Importantly, another participating character in this video was Tybalt. He was the person who delivered to the nurse the horrifying news about the enemies' secret intrusion into the Capulets' house. Having visually read the situation, which developed at that moment in front of his watchful eyes, Tybalt switched his gaze from observing the secretive actions by the Montague clan members intermixed with the crowd of the invited guests. Now, Tybalt was closely examining his cousin's, Juliet's behavior while reading her facial expressions. Subsequently, this young man quickly gained understanding of the emotions engulfing the two young people, Romeo and Juliet. Quite understandably, this member of the House of Capulet had a very negative attitude rooted in the history of feud between both families. At the end of the investigated episode, Tybalt looked over his right shoulder straight into the eyes of the viewing audiences. His direct gaze demanded the viewers' reaction and called to co-mistrust, co-hate, and be prepared for his and his family's guaranteed response whenever provoked.

At these instances, it was clearly readable that Tybalt's prolonged steady gaze meant a promise of no good. His ripening decision reflected in this young man's look and was confirmed by his next action. Overwhelmingly gradually but promptly, Tybalt's eyes gained the look of two glowing pieces of coal. Further, he tightened his mouth and slowly moved his chin and head down. Then, energetically and powerfully, Tybalt turned his back to the audience in a confident and malevolent move of a leader who owned the field. Promptly he left the scene walking away in powerful strides, demonstrating his readiness to act on his own or raise his entire clan, even prior to and not waiting for being challenged. For a long time, after watching this episode, the vindictive expression of Tybalt's glistening gaze and darkening eyes stayed imprinted in my memory like a saved screenshot.

Following the above moment, Juliet stayed on the screen alone. As I have discussed this character's body positions and postures in the previous chapter sections, I will proceeded with my further analysis of her gazes.

Juliet's gaze had undergone multiple changes following the emotions, which were taking over this young lady's mind and soul. At the described moment in this short episode, Juliet stood still and looked through the air as if envisioning the development of the tragic events, which followed. Most obviously, her logical reasoning was based on her previous experiences as well as her background knowledge about the two families: her own, the Capulet, and their enemies', the Montague. Juliet's gaze allowed me to read her being tired of the life full of endless feud.

Though, I had never personally witnessed the dramatic and tragic events similar to the ones which took place in the life of the two clans, I could read with sympathy from Juliet's face her unspoken story scarred with the outbreaks of cruelty and severity, and filled to the rim with feelings of misery and helplessness. During my scrutinizing this episode, and through my feeling of deep compassion, I realized that, as a multimodal reader, I was able to perceive this information through the non-verbal visual language, to be more exact, through the constantly changing expressions of sadness, exhaustion, and fear reflecting in Juliet's gazes.

Finally, by the end of this scene, Juliet closed her eyes in a visibly protruding emotional and, quite possibly, physical pain and desperation. Yet, even several previous seconds were enough for me to read the gaze of her eyes, which silently, but "loudly" transmitted the information through which I constructed the meaning about her feeling in this scene, the predicaments, and the anticipated events, which should unavoidably follow.

Color

Importantly, the dramatic meaning of the events, which started developing from this turning point in the story was also being conveyed by the director, Gian Franco Zeffirelli, through the affordances of the mode of color. In terms of usage of color by Zeffirelli (1968), the film *Romeo and Juliet* presented quite a unique case. Notably, the objects present in every scene in the movie conveyed rich information, besides the verbal one. Interestingly, this informational stream was available not only through the symbolism of the objects, but also through the means of different colors and their symbolic meanings as perceived in Medieval Europe and today.

To start with, the red color symbolized passion and danger at that historic period, as reported by Hall (1994). So, looking at the bright red outfit of Juliet through the lens of the European symbolism in art, one might conclude that the red color of her dress made Juliet's image the most salient in the episode under investigation. Through the affordances of this color, I could also perceive the meaning that Juliet was the one in great danger. Though some other red garments were worn by some other women present in the episode, the shades and the levels of salience of their reds were significantly less standing out compared to the red of Juliet. Yet, the colors of the women's outfits might also indicate their greater vulnerability, which also positioned them as characters under some kind of threat in that chronotope. Thus, my next task was to identify the source of that threat depicted somewhere in the scene.

According to the Medieval art canons, the black color symbolized threat. Most male guests in the scene were dressed in dark and / or black. As a part of the viewing audiences, I could conclude that the threat was emitted not from the females in that cultural-historical chronotope, but from the male population. Romeo was also dressed in dark and black, which made him emit the same threat. Thus, the affordances of color also conveyed the meaning that, were it possible to remove the romance theme from this story, in that cultural-historical context, Romeo's input into the feud between the two clans would have been nothing less, but equal compared to any other participant in the bloodsheds described by Shakespeare in his play.

On this, mostly dark background of the crowd, the white headgear of the nurse was highly salient in every image where she appeared. In medieval times, the white color symbolized purity and innocence (Kress & van Leeuwen, 2002). Comparing and contrasting the colors of the outfits of the friends and enemies in the crowd at the House of Capulet, I have drawn the conclusion that the nurse was the person who did not belong to any of the clans, which were mercilessly fighting and aiming to finally destroy each other. Moreover, the nurse was almost the only innocent and pure of hatred character among that crowd, many of who were symbolically dressed in the outfits of predominantly dark and black colors.

Multiple shades of purple, burgundy, and maroon chosen by Zeffirelli (1968) for the costumes of guests in the House of Capulet also attracted attention with their signifiers. Apparently, production of the purple textile dye in Medieval Europe was a life-threatening process due to presence of deadly poisonous elements in some of the ingredients used for dying fabrics. Due to this fact, production of fabric dyed in the shades of purple was extremely rare, expensive, and limited in quantity. It is a well-known historic fact that the purple garments were available, first, solely for Royalty, and later, for the rich only. Importantly, this historic fact allowed me to make the meaning about the immeasurable wealth of the guests of the House of Capulet. I made this conclusion while observing the colors of the guests' outfits present in the scene under investigation.

Returning once again to Tybalt, it needs to be noticed that at different times and in different episodes, some certain colors, as applied to different contexts, might be loaded with different meanings. For example, the color of Tybalt's costume could add to this personality's image. Further, the color of this young man's eyes, face, and hands was unusually dark for the North-Italian setting. All these colors in their combination made Tybalt look uniquely different from the rest of the characters present in the episode. To be more exact, the deep colors of Tybalt's eyes, face, as well as his clothes made this character look gloomy and as if glittering with evil.

Next, after having read the available visual texts within the episode under investigation, I attempted to interpret the meaning conveyed by the entire large ensemble of multimodal resources. So, having closely observed Tybalt's image, I perceived him as an insider to many tragic events in this story. Yet, Tybalt was also able to construct his meaning via his observations. Presumably, this young man spotted his family's worst enemies who secretly trespassed into their house. Moreover, one of the enemies succeeded in gaining attention of Tybalt's innocent young cousin,

Juliet. From Tybalt's perspective, Romeo could have planned to seduce the young girl. If succeeded, what could be the consequences, which might have followed the seduction of this young girl by the member of the clan of foes? Following this logical path, I inferred that Tybalt might have anticipated of Romeo a game of revenge to the clan where Juliet might have appeared an innocent, pure, and trustful victim. Thus, from Tybalt's deepening gaze as well as his darkening face one could read his decision to act and protect.

In this way, usage of the dark colors allowed the director to create a gloomy image not only of Tybalt's personality, but the depth of his reasoning, which unrested on his prior knowledge. Additionally, when Tybalt swiftly turned away from the audience, his grim, darkening face with the threatening gleaming coal-like eyes stuck with the audience. Though this character rushed away with his black cloak swaying behind his shoulders, the gaze of his dark eyes left an indelible impression of the promised war. Overall, the combination of Tybalt's gaze, posture, action, body and head movement, and the colors present in this figure helped to convey the meaning of maliciousness and mercilessness of his intention. To sum up, this multimodal ensemble created by the film director totally disheartened and scared me. Most importantly, it had me deeply engaged as a viewer. It made me feel as a co-participant in this story, positioned me as an insider in the turbulent accounts on the screen; thus, prompted me to further read and deeper understand the observable and anticipated events.

To conclude with, the analysis of the symbolic meaning of colors, their salience, coherence, contrast, or dissonance allowed me to make the meaning, which I would not be able to construct from reading or listening to the verbal texts in this specific episode. Thus, I read and gained more understanding from viewing, rather than from listening to the scarcely-available audible language or from the print-based texts in the subtitles, which I chose to disregard in favor of the visuals. These findings of my analysis are coherent with the ones by Kress and van Leeuwen (2002), who believed that humans can make the meaning via reading information encoded in the non-verbal visual language, such as body position, postural behavior, position of the head, posture, gaze, and color.

ANALYSIS 1: DISCUSSION

Upon having analyzed the multimodal language with a strong emphasis on its visual means present in the short video episode and having mostly focused on gazes, head positions, body postures, positioning in the space, and the colors, I have drawn several imperative for my study conclusions. First, reading the non-verbal visual language allowed me, as a part of viewing audiences, to receive a significant amount of non-verbally produced information, which I was able to link to the current, assumed, or anticipated events in this story.

Next, though the multimodal texts I read could be broken into shorter units with the purpose to scrutinize each of them, the major factor, which contributed to my meaning making was the interconnection of the modes, which formed meaningful multimodal ensembles. Importantly, as I perceived, it was the interactions between different units of visual langue, such as proxemics, body position is space, posture, gaze, head movements, and color combined with the audible language (e.g., speeches and music), which helped me construct the meaning. Altogether, the available modes created a rich environment for me within the cohort of viewers to process all modes or focus on the one, which carried the major idea in each snapshot and the entire episode.

So, regardless of some limitations of my multimodal analysis, where I was the only self-analyzing participant and investigator, I concluded that the interplay of different modes within multimodal ensembles has the power to enable for readers constructing the meaning in the scene and go beyond its frames.

Next, thanks to the meaningful and readable ensembles of resources present in the investigated video, I could construct the meaning not only about the present, but also about the past and the future development of the events and life-stories of the participating characters. While relying on reading the rich multimodal information, as a viewer and as a researcher, I also need to state that to fully confirm one's understanding, reading the verbal texts might be highly beneficial when and if available. Yet, in their absence, making the meaning from reading visual texts is also an option.

Conclusively, considering the role and position of the visual mode, it needs to be recognized that, as visuals are highly significant for meaning making purposes, there is the need in a thorough instruction in reading the visual language, just as it is done when teaching and learning any other languages. Thus, educators need to teach their students how to correctly make the meaning of the resources of multimodal ensembles present in a still image, a painting, a book illustration, or a video composition. Based on my findings, I also conclude that the multimodal language, including but not limited its visual mode, has a great potential for assisting diverse learners, including the focus population of my study, the Polylingual EAL-speaking university students, with their meaning making. Yet, mastering it needs to be viewed as a new science, which can be taught to students as one of the forms of linguistic, historical, cultural, artistic, and emotional forms of literacy.

REFERENCES

Ainsworth, S., Griffiths, D., Macrory, G., & Pahl, K. (2023). *Multimodality and multilingualism: Towards an integrative approach.* Multilingual Matters.

Archer, A. (2025). Multimodality and the affordances of co-presence for inclusion in higher education. *Designs for Learning, 16*(1), 1–8. DOI: 10.16993/dfl.230

Archer, A., & Price, C. (2021). Assessment, recognition and the contact zone: How much is 'enough'? *Education as Change, 25*, 1–18. DOI: 10.25159/1947-9417/8741

Baildon, M., & Damico, J. S. (2009). How do we know?: Students examine issues of credibility with a complicated multimodal web-based text. *Curriculum Inquiry, 39*(2), 265–285. DOI: 10.1111/j.1467-873X.2009.00443.x

Bakhtin, M. M. (1981). Discourse in the novel. In Holquist, M. (Ed.), *The dialogic imagination: Four essays by M. M. Bakhtin* (pp. 259–422). University of Texas Press.

Binder, M., & Kotsopoulos, S. (2011). Multimodal literacy narratives: Weaving the threads of young children's identity through the arts. *Journal of Research in Childhood Education, 25*(4), 339–363. DOI: 10.1080/02568543.2011.606762

Breuer, E., & Archer, A. (2016). *Multimodality in higher education.* Brill Academic Publishing. DOI: 10.1163/9789004312067

Brown, A., & Eskildsen, S. W. (2024). *Multimodality across epistemologies in second language research.* Routledge. DOI: 10.4324/9781003355670

Callow, J. (2014). *The shape of text to come: How image and text work.* PETAA.

Callow, J., & Zammit, K. (2012). "Where lies your text?" ("Twelfth Night" act I, scene V): Engaging high school students from low socioeconomic backgrounds in reading multimodal texts. *Engineers Australia, 47*(2), 69–77.

Ericson, K., & Häikiö, T. K. (2025). Visuality and multimodality as tools for learning in geography and art education. *Journal of Aesthetic Education, 59*(2), 50–73. DOI: 10.5406/15437809.59.2.05

Franks, A., & Jewitt, C. (2001). The meaning of action in learning and teaching. *British Educational Research Journal, 27*(2), 201–218. DOI: 10.1080/01411920120037144

Gellevij, M., van der Meij, H., de Jong, T., & Pieters, J. (2002). Multimodal versus unimodal instruction in a complex learning context. *Journal of Experimental Education, 70*(3), 215–239. DOI: 10.1080/00220970209599507

Giampapa, F. (2010). Multiliteracies, pedagogy and identities: Teacher and student voices from a Toronto elementary school. *Canadian Journal of Education, 33*(2), 407–431.

Goldin-Meadow, S. (2000). Beyond words: The importance of gesture to researchers and learners. *Child Development, 71*(1), 231–239. DOI: 10.1111/1467-8624.00138 PMID: 10836578

Goodwin, C. (2000). Action and embodiment within situated human interaction. *Journal of Pragmatics, 32*(10), 1489–1522. DOI: 10.1016/S0378-2166(99)00096-X

Gould-Yakovleva, O. (2023a). Seeking remedy for improving international college students' reading comprehension: A qualitative case study on using multimodality for English language learning. *International Journal of Higher Education Pedagogies, 4*(4), 33–54. DOI: 10.33422/ijhep.v4i4.599

Gould-Yakovleva, O. (2023b). Voices from university classrooms on effects of multimodality on polylingual EAL college students' meaning making. *International Journal of Second and Foreign Language Education, 2*(2), 1–19. DOI: 10.33422/ijsfle.v2i2.450

Hall, J. (1994). *Illustrated dictionary of symbols in Eastern and Western art*. Westview Press.

Hostetter, A. B., & Alibali, M. W. (2008). Visible embodiment: Gestures as simulated action. *Psychonomic Bulletin & Review, 15*(3), 495–514. DOI: 10.3758/PBR.15.3.495 PMID: 18567247

Huang, Y. (2023). Open learning environment for multimodal learning based on knowledge base technology. *International Journal of Emerging Technologies in Learning, 18*(11), 38–51. DOI: 10.3991/ijet.v18i11.39397

Huang, Y. H. (2012). EFL students' views on writing with pictures, sound, and music. *English Teaching & Learning, 36*(2), 79–123. DOI: 10.6330/ETL.2012.36.2.03

Jewitt, C. (2009). *The handbook of multimodal analysis*. Routledge.

Kaur, S., Ganapathy, M., & Sidhu, G. K. (2012). Designing learning elements using the multiliteracies approach in an ESL writing classroom. *Southeast Asian Journal of English Language Studies, 18*(3), 119–134.

Kress, G. (2011). *Multimodality: A social semiotic approach to contemporary communication*. Routledge.

Kress, G., & van Leeuwen, T. (1996). *Reading images: The grammar of visual design*. Routledge.

Kress, G., & van Leeuwen, T. (2002). Colour as a semiotic mode: Notes for a grammar of colour. *Visual Communication, 1*(3), 333–354. DOI: 10.1177/147035720200100306

Moor-Russo, D., & Shanahan, L. (2014). A broader vision of literacy: Including the visual with the linguistic. *Journal of Adolescent & Adult Literacy, 57*(7), 527–532. DOI: 10.1002/jaal.282

Moor-Russo, D., & Viglietti, J. M. (2012). Using the K_5 connected cognition diagram to analyze teachers' communication and understanding of regions in three-dimensional space. *The Journal of Mathematical Behavior, 31*(2), 235–251. DOI: 10.1016/j.jmathb.2011.12.001

Pütz, M., & Mundt, N.-F. (2018). *Expanding the linguistic landscape: Linguistic diversity, multimodality and the use of space as a semiotic resource*. Multilingual Matters.

Rahmanu, E. D., Altun, L., & Kariati, N. M. (2020). Case study on multimodality perception in the higher education classroom. *Journal Sosial dan Humaniora. Journal of Social Sciences and Humanities, 10*(3), 1–11. DOI: 10.31940/soshum.v10i3.2091

Roth, W.-M. (2001). Gestures: Their role in teaching and learning. *Review of Educational Research, 71*(2), 365–392. DOI: 10.3102/00346543071003365

Shakespeare, W. (1597). *Romeo and Juliet*.

Shanahan, L. E. (2013). Composing "kid-friendly" multimodal text: When conversations, instruction, and signs come together. *Written Communication, 30*(2), 194–227. DOI: 10.1177/0741088313480328

Shanahan, L. E., & Flury-Kashmanian, C. (2014). Orchestrating semiotic resources in explicit strategy instruction. *Pedagogies, 9*(2), 99–115. DOI: 10.1080/1554480X.2014.899484

Sindoni, M. (2023). *Multimodality and translanguaging in video interactions*. Cambridge University Press.

Stein, P. (2008). Rethinking resources in the ESL classroom. Rethinking resources: Multimodal pedagogies in the ESL classroom. *TESOL Quarterly, 34*(2), 333–336. DOI: 10.2307/3587958

Stein, P. (2012). *Multimodal pedagogies in diverse classrooms: Representations, rights and resources*. Routledge.

Unsworth, L. (2006). Toward a metalanguage for multiliteracies education: Describing the meaning-making resources of language-image interaction. *English Teaching, 5*(1), 55–76.

Wang, M. (2022). The cultivation of students' multiple practical ability under the multimodal blended teaching mode. *International Journal of Emerging Technologies in Learning*, *17*(12), 106–120. DOI: 10.3991/ijet.v17i12.32087

Włodarczyk, M., Tyrkkö, J., & Adamczyk, E. (2023). *Multilingualism from manuscript to 3D: Intersections of modalities from medieval to modern times*. Routledge. DOI: 10.4324/9781003166634

Zeffirelli, F. (1968). *Romeo and Juliet.* Paramount Pictures. Retrieved from public domain: https://www.youtube.com/watch?v=VCe0nzdD76k

Chapter 16
Analysis 2:
Visual Language Intermodal Relations Data Analysis

ABSTRACT

Upon having gained a deeper understanding of how each or several different modes of multimodality help readers make their meaning, I realized the need in a more profound insight into the ways in which intermodal relationships of visual language contribute to the reading comprehension processes in readers, including the population in the focus of my larger study discussed in this book, i.e., Polylingual EAL-speaking college or university students. In this Chapter XVI, I will detail my second analysis. This Analysis 2 was conducted with the purpose to understand the intermodal relations within multimodal ensembles. The latter work asked to be done, as, most often, viewers, or multimodal readers, are exposed to whole inclusive ensembles of resources in a range of real-life situations or within a video with the sound. Interestingly, even an audio without any visuals available is practically never unimodal, due to such affordances of a human voice as tone, pitch, intensity, intonation, etc. Yet, in this chapter, I will continue discussing intermodal relations.

ANALYSIS 2: INTRODUCTION

And so I made the decision to go further and conduct my second analysis with the purpose to understand the complex intermodal relations of different modes of multimodality within multimodal ensembles. Again, I sought to understand in what ways these relations affect humans' meaning making. For this purpose, I chose to analyze another excerpt from Franco Zeffirelli's (1968) film *Romeo and Juliet* based on Shakespeare's (1597) play. The length of this second video episode was about three minutes. So, I narrowed the focus of this second multimodal analysis of this

DOI: 10.4018/979-8-3373-3426-4.ch016

video to the purpose to understand in what ways the ensembles of multiple modes, which are present in this video episode, assisted myself and my research participants with our meaning making of the visual, verbal, audible, or print-based text. More specifically, I sought to understand whether the visible features of multimodality complemented the verbal text. Another question of my researcher's interest was whether the available in this video features of multimodality were coherent with the verbal texts produced by the actors in the scene in the episode under analysis. Importantly for this research results, I, as a multimodal reader, was a part of the studied cohort of the Polylingual EAL speakers in academe. Thus, this fact allowed for my role within both of my analyses as the one of the researcher-participant.

Prior to proceeding with my report on the processes and findings in this second analysis, I will share some highlights about the video-episode I used for my analytical work. As I mentioned before, this nearly 2 minutes-short episode was a portion of Gian Franco Zeffirelli's (1968) *Romeo and Juliet* production. For my current analysis, I counted minute 36:36 in this movie as the starting point of my analysis and I will refer to it as 0:01 further in this chapter. While the last minute of the episode, 38:30 within this film will be referred to as 1:54 and will be considered the end point of the video episode under investigation.

ANALYSIS 2: RATIONALE

I will explain why I have chosen this artifact. As I needed to deeper understand how multimodal ensembles function and affect humans' perceptions and thinking, and how they might assist my students-participants' and my own meaning making of verbal and visual texts, I decided to stick to the same type of visuals and texts, to which I exposed my subjects within this project. So, I attempted to understand how Zeffirelli (1968), as the experienced, talented, and highly educated artist, orchestrated different modes, such as sounds of music, tones of human speech, movements of actors through the space, their position in the space, their postures, gestures, facial expressions, the verbal texts they produced, the space itself, and its dimensions, as well as objects, their colors, and symbols. Precisely, I analyzed the objects and their potential to carry symbolic meanings. Specifically, I was interested to see how the changes in selection of modes arranged by the director in every micro-snapshot within this episode may affect a reader's meaning making.

My claim, rested upon the findings of my first analysis, was that thoughtfully orchestrated in multimodal ensembles modes of multimodality have a strong potential to assist audiences with their more efficient and correct meaning making of verbal or print-based text in combination with the features of multimodality. Additionally, my researcher's assumption was that availability of features of multimodality, thoughtfully orchestrated by the director into ensembles to accompany the verbal texts in this film were meant to be sent to the viewers as the encoded, but easily decodable messages, each of which was designed to carry its specific meaning.

My best understanding was and is that the artist's thought purposefully worked on selecting exact multimodal resources for every episode during the entire creation process. Thus, the interrelated combinations of those resources were shaped to assist vast viewing audiences with their meaning making of every scene in the movie. Importantly, Zeffirelli, as the highly creative and well-educated in his field artist, not only aimed, but desired his messages to be understood; thus, this director must have been working to help his potential viewers with their understanding of the meaning of not only Shakespearean, but also multimodal texts, which this director thoughtfully created for better conveying both: Shakespeare's and his own ideas. The outcome of these fine-grained orchestrations of different modes merged with the technology-aided multimodality, which interplayed with the verbal Shakespearian texts produced by the movie actors, aimed to not only be understandable, but also targeted to shape the meaning made by the viewing audiences.

ANALYSIS 2: THEORY AND LITERATURE

Upon having considered several different paradigms, I narrowed my choice of theory to the fundamental works by Bezemer and Kress (20160, Franks and Jewitt (2001), Kress and van Leeuwen (1996, 2002), and Norris (2004). So, the postulates of the above theorists formed the ground for my second analysis of intermodal relations within visual ensembles, and I will further explain my choice.

In their 2001 publication, Franks and Jewitt reflected on the meaning-making processes they observed in their research participants. These researchers noted, "Different meanings were realized through the pupils' [students'] actions and speech: here action is the main stuff of meaning, speech is a commentary on the detail of the action. (p. 214). Thus, it may be concluded that oral, verbal speech per se might be secondary, while the non-verbal language of the actions might serve as the primary means for developing the correct understanding.

Further, armed with the above realization, I focused on analyzing the actors' face-work, gestures, postures, positions in the space, and in relation to the other people and objects in the film episode. I also regarded the actors' positioning towards the viewing audiences as well as their movements through the space and time. Additionally, I paid close attention to the colors selected by Zeffirelli for the scenery, costumes, and other objects. To sum up, I tried my best to decipher the meanings, which the director of the multimodal compositions attempted to encode and convey via the affordances of action and color.

Moreover, I delved into analysis of the image-to-text relationship. For this work, I used as guidance the publications by the prominent researchers in the field of multimodality and social semiotics (e.g., Ainsworth et al. 2023; Jewitt & Oyama, 2001; Lee et al., 2024; Marsh & White, 2003a, 2003b; Martinec & Salway, 2005; Maula & Awwalia; 2025; Reyes-Torres et al., 2025; Serafini, 2011, 2014; Sindoni, 2023; Włodarczyk et al., 2023). Per these authors' guidelines, I paid close attention to such aspects of color as its salience, consonance, dissonance, complementarity, or contrast in relation to the other colors present in the same scene. I also analyzed the relationship and coherence of the colors with the verbal texts in every short snapshot within the excerpt under investigation. Most importantly, I investigated the symbolic meaning of color of the objects present in the scenes. Next, I also took in consideration the symbolic meanings of the objects by themselves, as they were perceived in Medieval Europe. For this purpose, I examined the encyclopedic sources of information (e.g., Hall, 1994).

ANALYSIS 2: METHODOLOGY

Artifact Under Analysis

The film episode I analyzed represented Act I Scene IV of Shakespeare's play *Romeo and Juliet* in Gian Franco Zeffirelli's (1968) production, where the main characters in this scene were Juliet, Romeo, and Juliet's nurse. Music and voices of the guests of the House of Capulet could be heard in the far background in this short video, as the setting was the palace of the Capulets. At that moment in the story, Juliet's family gave the ball, and celebrated openly, and without fear or necessity to hide after a long period of being oppressed by their enemies, the Montagues. Yet, the investigated scene took place in a room with a richly laid table in the center. Needless to describe, how richly this table was adorned with gorgeous and treasurable goblets and vases with fruit, and carafes of wine. Obviously, all the richly garnished delicacies were served to not only treat, but also impress the guests via demonstrating the hosts' wealth, rather than generosity.

What made this episode in the film highly significant was that at this very moment, Romeo questioned Juliet's nurse about this young lady. So, this was exactly that meaningful moment when this young offspring of the House of Montague fell in love with Juliet, the daughter of the Capulets. Most importantly, that was also the moment when Romeo realized that this lady was the member of the House of his family's worst enemies.

Type of Analysis

So, while watching this episode, I engaged in my multimodal visual language analysis, to be more exact, I investigated the intermodal relations of the available language or, more precisely, the languag**es**. Following the postulates by Franks and Jewitt (2001), I focused my attention on the actors' body language, face work, gestures, movements, their positioning, and the positions of objects in the space. Via this work, I sought to identify the relations between the non-verbal and verbal languages present in the scene under investigation, where a strong emphasis of my study was on the role of the visuals within this ensemble.

Data Collection and Analysis Processes

For a greater clarity, I need to describe how I collected the synchronic sets of multimodal data. Upon making multiple screenshots of the video under analysis, I placed them in charts. For data collection and its further analysis, I broke the whole multimodal ensemble within the selected video into several meaningful units or *micro-chunks*. For this purpose, I stopped the video and "cut" off each new micro-chunk every time when some meaningful changes occurred on the screen. For example, this was an increase or decrease in the number of characters in the new micro-chunk, or some changes in the background scenes, or variations in the background sounds, or relocation, or any new actions, or positions of actors; these also were some new utterances and responses to them produced by the characters, etc.

It is highly important for understanding the results of this work to explain that while examining every micro-chunk of this video episode, I scrutinized the following details:

- Who acts in the scene, and what relations between these people can be identified via their positioning towards each other in the space?
- How are the actors interconnected with the viewers via their positions on the screen and towards the audience?
- How do the actors move through the space in relations to each other and the viewers?
- What types of gestures are the actors using for communication with each other?
- What meaning do the actors convey via their face work?
- What auditory texts are they exchanging with each other?
- Are the auditory texts coherent with the visual ones?
- Do visual means compliment the audible texts?

- Do the available means of multimodality enhance the meaning of the verbal texts?
- How do different resources comprise in a whole picture in each micro-shot?
- Are the present colors interrelated and form a text?
- What might be the encoded meaning and symbolism of colors present in each micro-scene?
- What objects were placed in every micro-shot by the artist, and how can these objects relate to the events in the episode?
- In what ways might the whole intermodal ensemble of all available resources in every micro-shot reveal, imply, or directly convey the meaning?
- Do my perceptions as a viewer and findings as a researcher correlate with the theory and research findings by Franks and Jewitt (2001) and Kress and van Leeuwen (1996, 2002)?

As one can perceive from the listed above questions, which I posed for myself as the viewer, researcher, and an analyst, I strongly focused my second analysis on interrelations of the available modes. With this objective in mind, I watched every micro-chunk of the given excerpt multiple times. And every time I watched it, I paid attention and recorded the data on every specific mode: visual, spatial, auditory, etc. while attempting to understand their intermodal relations. Further, I organized all the collected in this way data in the chart cells broken by the specific categories (See the *Appendices* section, *Appendix C 2* for multimodal transcript of the video with sound excerpt). This process allowed me to envision and track the inter-relations of the visual and audible languages in this short video.

Next, during my examination of every micro-chunk, I decoded the meanings of small physical objects, their modes, or resources. Then, I attempted to bring all the available details into a bigger mosaic picture, which was comprised of the interrelated multimodal features. Once the Big picture was ready, I also focused on the interplay of all the available modes and resources within each multimodal ensemble. In doing so, I endeavored to understand the purpose for their presence, as well as importance of every feature for conveying and making the meaning.

ANALYSIS 2: FINDINGS

As the result of my scrupulous work, I came out with three major findings upon completion of my second visual language intermodal relations data analysis. Below, I will report what I found and understood.

First, I found that, as discovered by Franks and Jewitt (2001), humans' body language, their movements through the space and time, their postures, gestures, and facial expressions may strongly add to the readers' meaning making. Second, just as noticed by Kress and van Leeuwen's (2002), colors and their combinations in the objects present in multimodal compositions do carry the meaning and add to the viewing audiences' deeper understanding of the verbal texts and implied ideas. Third, actors develop meaningful relationships between themselves and the objects while interacting within each scene. Importantly, certain objects, via their presence in a multimodal composition, may carry the meaning. Moreover, when purposefully brought to attention, they are aimed to help in delivering specific encoded messages through the affordances of their symbolic color and the symbols culturally or universally assigned to those objects.

Relationships of Face-Work and Body Language

With all my strong desire to celebrate my findings in the first analysis, I had yet to understand the relations between different modes and their importance for meaning making. With this purpose, I continued focusing on several shorter episodes within the selected fragment of the film. Strategically named for this research as Episode 0:01 - 0:07 and, further, Episode 0:07 - 0:19, these micro-chunks showed the scene of the ball party in the House of Capulets (See the transcript of this episode in *Appendix C*).

In the brief episode under investigation, merry music and chatter of the excited happy crowd could be heard in the background. Shortly, Juliet's nurse ran into the room in an open towards the viewing audiences move. This jolly woman was looking for Juliet to report to the girl that her mother was willing to talk to her. At this moment, the nurse's face and eyes shone with happiness and excitement. Yet, Juliet stood looking down; her posture indicated her feeling embarrassed. This young lady looked overwhelmed, while her eyes and facial expressions gave out her being concerned. Juliet's appearance revealed her secret thoughts and feelings. Prior to this scene, this young lady had just met Romeo and fell in love with him. Juliet fixed her hair with a quick gesture of her hand before she left this scene to meet with her mother. This gesture showed that the young lady felt obligated to look neat and nice in front of her parents. So, this girl checked every small detail: her behavior, her garment, and her looks prior to meeting her mother.

Further, in episode 0:20 - 0:25, the nurse's gaze made a prompt and sneaky inspection of the room and found no witnesses in the proximity to self. Next, this character clumsily tiptoed towards the table; her manners revealing her being a commoner. Nurse targeted the richly laid table, topped with a huge vase full of fruits. Yet, this woman ignored these treats. Instead, her gaze was strongly fixed on the carafe with wine, which she promptly and greedily grabbed with her right hand. The woman pored the wine in generous portions into the glass she was holding in her left hand, repeatedly emptying it adding some more wine into her glass. These actions and movements by the nurse revealed the behind-the scene story, which was not verbalized: this woman jumped on the opportunity to sneak some expensive, thus, rare for her treat, the wine, which she most definitely could not afford to purchase. This sneaky behavior indicated that, though the nurse was a part of the House, she was not a part of the family, as she had to secretly use the treat prepared for the family guests. Nurse devoured the wine in strong gulps, which revealed her greed and craving for a good earthly life.

In the next episode, 0:26 - 0:38, Romeo who was present in the back of the room and observed Juliet's interaction with her nurse, addressed this older woman and asked her who the mother of the young lady was. Having covertly intruded his enemies' house, Romeo had to hide his upper face behind the mask of an animal, while the lower part of his face was showing from under his mask. While the nurse kept adding and drinking the wine with a greedy expression in her eyes, she bragged to Romeo that she was nursing the daughter of the House of Capulets. This woman's crude manners in this episode confirmed to the readers the fact of her not being a person of a noble heritage, unlike the Capulets and their guests.

In the following episode, 0:39 – 0:44, Romeo's reaction showed when this young man learned the frightening for him news: the young lady, with who he had fallen in love, appeared to be the member of the family of his mortal enemies. Having received this information, Romeo moved towards the back of the scene and behind the large and expensive vase with overabundant fruits. In this way, he repositioned himself in a significantly different setting. Astonishingly contrasting to the previous jolly scene, his current setting included several dimly burning candles and an empty goblet, which stood right in front of Romeo's devastated figure. Though the fruits still were visible within the viewing audiences' reach, their position within the scene was meant to be noticed out of the corner of one's eye. Importantly, these symbols of the cornucopic abundance of life were positioned away from Romeo, as the main character and the only actor within this micro-chunk. Importantly, this rearrangement of the objects and actors made the empty goblet and the candles the most salient symbols acting in this picture, with their presence and position in front of Romeo changing the meaning of this scene. Obviously, the dimness of the candle-light and the emptiness of the goblet created a strong contrast to the gorgeous in its overabundance and richness previous scene.

As for Romeo, he hurriedly shielded his face under his mask. Now, he also covered the lower part of his face behind his wrist. These movements indicated that this character was not only hiding his identity as he did before, at the start of this scene, but also attempted to hide his shaken feelings.

Following the above, in episode 0:45 – 0:52, the nurse continued bragging with the wealth of her masters. She talked and drank full-throttle. This allowed the audiences to assume that this might be the way this common person lived her life: taking from this world all she could take. Meantime, Romeo remained standing motionless, nearly killed with the bad news. This strong and meaningful difference between the two actors and two different settings within the same room served to enhance the viewers' perceptions of the contrast. Obviously, the sight of the jolly nurse, the rich heavy curtain behind her, and the huge vase of fruits, and the carafes with wine in front of this character, all added to the dramatic contrast with Romeo's image, which was framed by the large burning candles, an empty goblet, and the barren vault-like wall behind his back. This contrast enabled reading the conveyed by the director message: the drastic change in the setting promised no good for Romeo.

During 0:53 – 1:05 episode, the nurse hurriedly and happily rushed out of the room and disappeared behind the rich curtain. Following that, Romeo's hand holding the mask started slowly and helplessly moving down to his chest. In despair, this young man whispered, "Is she a Capulet? O dear account? My life is my foe's debt." At this moment, Romeo's facial expression showed desperation, sadness, and helplessness. All his postures and slowed movements within the 0:45 – 1:53 episode revealed that Romeo surrendered his good hopes.

By the end of the 0:53 – 1:05 episode, Romeo caught himself losing self-control; so, he promptly hid his face behind the mask again. Simultaneously present in the background merry music and happy chatter of the crowd of guests strongly stressed the contrast to Romeo's shattered inner world.

Following that, in episode 1:06 – 1:19, the rich, merry, and dressed-up crowd of guests of the House of Capulets started leaving the ball heading to their homes. Juliet's father gave a farewell speech to his departing friends and allies. All happy people in the crowd smiled, laughed, and talked to each other with excitement, while their postures and positions showed their happiness and their pleasurable exhaustion with eating, drinking, and dancing at the ball.

Further, between 1:20 and 1:32, Juliet joined her nurse again. Prior to leaving, Juliet's cousin Paris kissed her hand, gave her one single brisk smile, and said good-bye. Beyond this brief moment, the face of Juliet's fiancé remained cold. Noticeably, the nurse looked down with a disapproving expression in her face when Paris kissed Juliet's hand. For one second, the corners of this older woman's mouth went down showing disgust. Yet, next very moment, the nurse's face lit up again, as soon as Paris left. Gradually, the music in the background slowed down and sounded ever softer and farther, indicating the hired musicians leaving the house after the ball ended.

In the next scene, between 1:33 and 1:42, as soon as Paris left, Juliet leaned forward towards the nurse and asked her to find out the name of the young man she had talked to during the ball. She pointed to Romeo secretly, while using the nurse as a shield against the other people around. Juliet hoped the man of her interest was not married yet. This girls' gaze was focused and fixed on this one person only; yet, she did not know his name nor his origins yet. At this time, Romeo was standing still in the far-right corner of the room; he did not move. While moving towards the exit off the house, the Capulets' happy guests were passing by, and the music could not be heard anymore. Soon, the sounds of the crowd faded away as well.

Next, in the following episode 1:44 – 1:48, the nurse rushed to Tybalt to find out the name of the young man in the mask, as requested by Juliet. Tybalt positioned himself by the far wall of the hallway; it could be inferred that he was on guard. This young man was watchfully observing the crowd; his face showed tension, suspicion, and mistrust. Tybalt was fully aware of the troubles the Montagues could cause to his family in their own home. Thus, the secretive presence of the uninvited and unwanted Montague family members in the Capulets' house alerted and simultaneously infuriated this guard. Tybalt's face turned dark and gloomy when he reported to the nurse that the young man she questioned about was the only son of the Montagues. In response, the nurse froze in fear for a moment. Then, she rushed back to share this frightening news with Juliet.

In the following episode 1:49 - 1:54, the nurse shared the horrifying news with Juliet. The woman looked very scared; she evidently knew about all the endless deaths and tragedies connected to the feud between the two families. Visibly, the nurse's fear showed in her posture: she cowered while walking back to Juliet. When the young lady got the news, she made a little step backwards and leaned onto the wall in a desperate attempt to withstand the blow, and not to faint and fall. At this moment, Juliet's posture indicated her lack of hope and faith. Obviously, this disheartening news visibly hurt her both emotionally and physically. Observably, the excruciating pain showed through the young lady's facial expression and body language. Almost simultaneously, viewers could see Romeo. Being also strongly emotionally affected, this character finally regained his ability to move and headed towards the exit, hiding behind the people in the crowd.

During and after analyzing the visual language in intermodal relation of the described above visuals in their combination with scarcely-present verbal texts performed by the characters in the scene, I have drawn the conclusion that the non-verbal visual language in rich inter-relationships of different modes, i.e., facial expressions, gazes, postures, gestures, movements of actors through time and space, their positions towards each other and towards the viewers, as well as the characters' verbal interactions assisted me, as a part of the viewing audiences, with my meaning making of the verbal and non-verbal texts. Evaluating the interrelationships within the ensembles allowed me to correctly understand the ideas, which I would not be able to fully reach if exposed to the verbal, print-based texts only. Thus, my findings about the power of the ensembles of the visual language and its importance for meaning making strongly corresponded with the ones by Franks and Jewitt (2001).

Understanding Relationships Between Actors and Colors

In terms of usage of color by Zeffirelli (1968), his production *Romeo and Juliet* was rich in the means serving to convey vast layers of additional information through affordances of color and its symbolism, predominantly the way it was used in Medieval Europe. Thus, I proceeded with my analysis of the colors assigned by Zeffirelli (1968) to Juliet, Romeo, the Nurse, the objects, the settings, and members and guests of the House of the Capulets, just as I did in my *Multimodal Analysis 1* (See *Chapter XV* above). In both of my analyses, I paid close attention to the meaning and symbolism of every available color and their combinations present in the video episode under investigation. Yet, in my second analysis, I will go further with my scrutinizing the relationships between the colors and the actors.

To start with, I will examine the meaning of the colors chosen to characterize Paris, Juliet's fiancé. This young man was a character whose clothes of light-blue color stood saliently out in the episodes where he could be spotted in the scenes of the ball party in the House of the Capulets. Notably and importantly for meaning making, Paris was wearing a costume of a cold shade of blue. Presence of this color created a conflict in the scene between all the available colors: precisely, the fiery-red dress of Juliet and this cold-blue outfit of Paris. Besides the contrast in the colors and their shades, the viewing audience could perceive the undiscussed incompatibility of temperaments of these two young people: the passionate nature of Juliet and the reserved character of Paris. This strong disagreement of colors in Juliet's and Paris' attires allowed viewers to predict the scale of the internal personality conflict between these two opposing natures. As one can perceive, through the affordances of artistic expression, viewers may gain significantly more information from reading the meaning of colors in their relation to the persons adorned with the thoughtfully selected fabrics.

Returning to the episode where Romeo found out from the nurse that Juliet belonged to the House of Capulets, it needs to be noticed that this young man was moved by the director from one setting and color spectrum within the same room into a completely different one, and that was arranged for a purpose. At that moment, Romeo froze in the space while being emotionally devastated with desperation and helplessness. This was the moment, when the setting in the scene changed from colorful and joyful to the washed-off, dim, and dull shades. Apparently, the sight of the nearly colorless, empty, barren, vault-like wall in the background of Romeo's devastated figure helped the director emphasize the feeling of desperation. Further enhancing this shared emotion between Romeo and the viewing audiences was this young man's position. Romeo stood straightly facing the viewers, which served to evoke co-action, co-feeling, and compassion in the audiences. Yet, examining exactly the effects from the change of colors in relation to this character, evidently enabled me, as a viewer to construct understanding of the current and predict development of the further events in this story through affordances of the colors in their interrelationships with the objects and the character on the screen. Importantly for my research findings, I would not be able to read these meanings from the verbal, oral of print-based texts available in the *Romeo and Juliet* play and in the production.

To conclude with, the symbolic meaning of colors, their salience, coherence, or their yelling contrast may allow readers to make the correct meaning, which might add to their deeper understanding of the events discussed via the verbal, orally produced or print-based texts. Thus, the above findings in my analysis were coherent with the ones by Kress and van Leeuwen (2002). Importantly, as an educator, I drew the conclusion that students need to be taught or get self-educated to understand the symbolism of colors. It might happen that some parts of the viewing audiences may be able to intuitively read and construct the meaning correctly from the audible speeches and visuals. Yet, with my deep respect to any kind of learning prodigy, I suggest that students need to be taught how to read and interpret the multimodal language. Mastering this language through studying the meanings and the symbolism of colors in multiplicity of their shades may be further used for both constructing and delivering ideas.

Understanding Relationships Between Actors and Objects

In the process of my second multimodal analysis, I understood that presence of different modes of multimodality and their interrelationships present in the artistically orchestrated scenes are seldom a simple coincidence. As I found, different modes of multimodal ensembles (e.g., sounds of music, tones of human speech, movements through the space, and position in the space, color, posture, gesture, and facial expressions) in their interplay and interrelation, compliment the available verbal text or serve in the lieu of verbatims. As a part of the viewing audiences, I also perceived that the changes in selection of the interrelated modes in every micro-snapshot within the brief episode I analyzed assisted me with my meaning making of the verbal texts performed by actors in the scene and at the times the speeches were not available. I also understood that thoughtfully orchestrated in multimodal ensembles, intertwined modes of multimodality had the potential to assist readers with their deeper meaning making of the verbal or print-based text in combination and in interrelation with the features of multimodality.

Yet, I also realized there might be more interrelations, rather than those I scrutinized. Thus, there is a potential for viewers to use and rely on even greater modes and ensembles for multimodal meaning making. With this hypothetical thought, I proceeded with my studies of the relationships between the characters present in the scene and the objects, which were thoughtfully placed in each setting by the director, as the knowledgeable cinematic artist.

So, in this section, I will focus on the objects and their symbolic meaning. Here, I will return to the scene where Romeo moved deep behind and away from the richly laid table and stood still, with his back to the barren wall. During that moment, the candles burning in front of Romeo might have been used by Zeffirelli as they were "widely used as a symbol in the ritual, especially funerary, of many religions" (Hall, 1994, p. 60). Thus, presence of candles in the scene implied the idea of the nearing tragic end for this character.

In the following moment, Romeo tightened his mask to cover his face more securely. This was a mask of some canine animal: either a dog, or a wolf, or a jackal. As stated in Hall's (1994) publication on symbolism, a wolf was considered "an animal of mainly ill-repute. In western allegory it is a symbol of anger…" (p. 53). Thus, the symbolic meaning of Romeo's mask allowed viewers to draw conclusion that Romeo was hiding his identity under the symbolically aggressive mask. This young man's belonging to his extremely malicious clan, explains the choice of the mask. It also shows that this Montague clan member had, most likely, appropriated not only the aggressive looks of the wolves, but also merciless behaviors symbolically assigned to these predators. Another important connotation of the wolf's mask was that, according to the same source of information, four temperaments of human nature were each assigned some certain symbols, where a canid was a symbol of melancholy (Hall, 1994). These two symbolic meanings in their inter-combination gave me, as the reader, a deeper understanding of Romeo's quite controversial position among his immediate surroundings and the other actors in this story.

Next present in the scene symbolic object, the meaning of which I analyzed was the fruit. For example, green grapes were the symbol of youth and hope in Medieval Europe. Notably, upon having learned the sad news about Juliet's belonging to the clan of Romeo's mortal enemies, this character moved away and completely out of the setting with the green grapes and immediately appeared inside the new setting with the burning candles and an empty goblet. Meaningfully, the empty goblet, as any empty vessel, symbolized vain efforts, vain endeavors, or vain hopes in many European cultures. So, presence of this object in the scene allowed viewers to correctly anticipate the sad outcome of the story of the two lovers. Furthermore, according to Hall (1994), wine was the symbol of eternal life. Yet, once again, as Romeo's goblet in this scene was empty, the multimodal readers might conclude that his days were counted.

ANALYSIS 2: DISCUSSION

Upon completion of *Analysis 2*, I drew the conclusion that the intermodal relationships between different objects in their relation to the characters in the scene carried the meaning, which I was able to read via relating those objects and their symbolic meanings to the actors in each snapshot within the episode. I also concluded that multiple relationships, for example, between colors and actors, also helped me with my meaning making and strongly contributed to my understanding of the texts encoded in the visual texts in the absence of their verbal analogues. Besides, combinations of symbolic meanings of the objects present in the scene under investigation also allowed for reading the non-verbal texts. Thus, multiple modes within multimodal ensembles were powerful tools to be used by viewers or multimodal readers for making the meaning. My findings of this current analysis supported the ones by the founding fathers of the field of semiotics, Franks and Jewitt (2001), Kress and van Leeuwen (1996, 2002), Bezemer and Kress (2016) and Norris (2004) as well as the ideas by their followers, the researchers in the field of multimodality (e.g., Archer, 2025; Callow, 2014; Callow & Zammit, 2012; Cloonan, 2011; Goldin-Meadow, 2000; Gould-Yakovleva, 2023a, 2023b; Hostetter & Alibali, 2008; Lemke, 1998; Marsh & White, 2003; Miller & McVee, 2012; Moor-Russo & Viglietti, 2012; Moor-Russo & Shanahan, 2014; Mora et al., 2024; Reyes-Torres et al., 2025; Saint-Georges & Weber, 2013; Shanahan & Flury-Kashmanian, 2014; Unsworth, 2006; Yusra et al., 2025; Zarobe & Querol-Julian, 2025).

As for some limitations to this analysis, for quite a while, I entertained the idea that in certain cultural contexts, thinking of humans might be strongly culturally and historically affected and shaped; thus, the perceptions by these diverse readers or viewers might differ. Nevertheless, through my research as the researcher-participant in this *Analysis 2*, as well as via my larger study discussed in this book, I found the unbeatable evidence in favor of my assumption that multimodal language of the resources of modes in their interrelationships may be correctly read by the readers and viewers from diverse backgrounds. My belief in the power of the commonly understandable language of multimodality stemmed from the fact that all participants in my study discussed in this book as well as myself, as the researcher-participant, were able to construct the correct meaning from reading the visual texts. Thus, assumably, larger Domestic and International audiences, including but not limited to the investigated populations, might make the correct meaning via reading multimodally with the strong emphasis on decoding the resources of the visual language.

In conclusion, I am restating that my second multimodal analysis helped me to better understand how and through which means the ensembles of multiple modes in their interrelation might assist my research participants with their meaning making of the texts I offered them to read within this project. I was also able to understand which features of multimodality in the video under investigation complemented the verbal texts, and in what ways they were coherent with the utterances produced by the actors, as orchestrated by the director. Through my own perceptions and experiences with multimodal reading, I, as the part of the polylingual EAL speaking audience in academe, gained a significantly deeper understanding of how multimodal ensembles function and affect human perceptions, thinking, feelings, and meaning making of the verbal and non-verbal texts in their interrelationship.

Additionally, my second multimodal analysis also allowed me to understand the importance of reading the multimodal compositions, which have ben thoughtfully orchestrated by their authors. Besides, I realized that not all students might possess the knowledge and the skills useful for multimodal reading, Thus, learners need to be taught how to read such meaningful modes as the expressive means of music, or sounds, tone, and pitch of human speech, and actors' movements through the space, their positions in the space, the character's postures, gestures, facial expressions, as well as the objects and their colors, etc.

Further, I also gained a deeper understanding of how decoding the available symbols might add to the meaning-making process. Even the unspoken and unuttered ideas still can be read via the symbolic meaning of colors and objects, which are strongly interrelated with many other modes and resources within multimodal ensembles. My findings supported my initial claim, where I stated that the thoughtfully orchestrated in multimodal ensembles and interrelated modes of multimodality have a strong potential to assist audiences with their meaning making of the verbal oral or print-based text in their combination with the features of multimodality. Finally, and most importantly, both of my multimodal analyses resulted in my significantly deeper understanding of perceptions of multimodality by my research participants. More to that, these analyses helped me realize that, regardless of its easy comprehensibility, the Multimodal language needs to be taught to students in the multiplicity of all its aspects, for the learners' great benefit.

REFERENCES

Ainsworth, S., Griffiths, D., Macrory, G., & Pahl, K. (2023). *Multimodality and multilingualism: Towards an integrative approach.* Multilingual Matters.

Archer, A. (2025). Multimodality and the affordances of co-presence for inclusion in higher education. *Designs for Learning, 16*(1), 1–8. DOI: 10.16993/dfl.230

Bezemer, J., & Kress, G. (2016). *Multimodality, Learning and Communication: A Social Semiotic Frame.* Routledge.

Callow, J. (2014). *The shape of text to come: How image and text work.* PETAA.

Callow, J., & Zammit, K. (2012). "Where lies your text?" ("Twelfth Night" act I, scene V): Engaging high school students from low socioeconomic backgrounds in reading multimodal texts. *Engineers Australia, 47*(2), 69–77.

Cloonan, A. (2011). Creating multimodal metalanguage with teachers. *English Teaching, 10*(4), 23–40.

Franks, A., & Jewitt, C. (2001). The meaning of action in learning and teaching. *British Educational Research Journal, 27*(2), 201–218. DOI: 10.1080/01411920120037144

Goldin-Meadow, S. (2000). Beyond words: The importance of gesture to researchers and learners. *Child Development, 71*(1), 231–239. DOI: 10.1111/1467-8624.00138 PMID: 10836578

Hall, J. (1994). *Illustrated dictionary of symbols in Eastern and Western art.* Westview Press.

Hostetter, A. B., & Alibali, M. W. (2008). Visible embodiment: Gestures as simulated action. *Psychonomic Bulletin & Review, 15*(3), 495–514. DOI: 10.3758/PBR.15.3.495 PMID: 18567247

Jewitt, C. (2009). *The handbook of multimodal analysis.* Routledge.

Jewitt, C., & Oyama, R. (2001). Visual meaning: A social-semiotic approach. In van Leeuwen, T., & Jewitt, C. (Eds.), *Handbook of visual analysis* (pp. 134–156). Sage.

Kress, G., & van Leeuwen, T. (1996). *Reading images: The grammar of visual design.* Routledge.

Kress, G., & van Leeuwen, T. (2002). Colour as a semiotic mode: Notes for a grammar of colour. *Visual Communication, 1*(3), 333–354. DOI: 10.1177/147035720200100306

Marsh, E. E., & White, M. D. (2003a). A system for image-text relations in a new (and old) media. *Visual Communication*, *4*, 337–371.

Marsh, E. E., & White, M. D. (2003b). A taxonomy of relationships between images and text. *The Journal of Documentation*, *59*(6), 647–672. DOI: 10.1108/00220410310506303

Martinec, R., & Salway, A. (2005). A system for image-text relations in new (and old) media. *Visual Communication*, *4*(3), 337–371. DOI: 10.1177/1470357205055928

Miller, S. M., & McVee, M. B. (2012). *Multimodal composing in classrooms: Learning and teaching for the digital world*. Routledge.

Moor-Russo, D., & Shanahan, L. (2014). A broader vision of literacy: Including the visual with the linguistic. *Journal of Adolescent & Adult Literacy*, *57*(7), 527–532. DOI: 10.1002/jaal.282

Moor-Russo, D., & Viglietti, J. M. (2012). Using the K_5 connected cognition diagram to analyze teachers' communication and understanding of regions in three-dimensional space. *The Journal of Mathematical Behavior*, *31*(2), 235–251. DOI: 10.1016/j.jmathb.2011.12.001

Mora, R. A., Tian, Z., & Harman, R. (2024). *Translanguaging and multimodality as flow, agency, and a new sense of advocacy in and from the global south*. Routledge.

Norris, S. (2004). *Analyzing Multimodal Interaction: A Methodological Framework*. Routledge. DOI: 10.4324/9780203379493

Reyes-Torres, A., Brisk, M. E., & Lacorte, M. (2025). *Multiliteracies, multimodality, and learning by design in second language learning and teacher education*. Routledge. DOI: 10.4324/9781032620497

Saint-Georges, I., & Weber, J.-J. (2013). *Multilingualism and multimodality: Current challenges for educational studies*. Brill Academic Publishing. DOI: 10.1007/978-94-6209-266-2

Serafini, F. (2011). Expanding perspectives for comprehending visual images in multimodal texts. *Journal of Adolescent & Adult Literacy*, *54*(5), 342–350. DOI: 10.1598/JAAL.54.5.4

Serafini, F. (2014). *Reading the visual: An introduction to teaching multimodal literacy*. Teachers College Press.

Shakespeare, W. (1597). *Romeo and Juliet*.

Shanahan, L. E., & Flury-Kashmanian, C. (2014). Orchestrating semiotic resources in explicit strategy instruction. *Pedagogies*, *9*(2), 99–115. DOI: 10.1080/1554480X.2014.899484

Unsworth, L. (2006). Toward a metalanguage for multiliteracies education: Describing the meaning-making resources of language-image interaction. *English Teaching*, *5*(1), 55–76.

Włodarczyk, M., Tyrkkö, J., & Adamczyk, E. (2023). *Multilingualism from manuscript to 3D: Intersections of modalities from medieval to modern times*. Routledge. DOI: 10.4324/9781003166634

Yusra, S. R., Hanifa, R., Wardana, A., & Fahmiati, M. (2025). Leveraging instructional multimodality for enhanced English grammar learning of undergraduate students: A higher education perspective. *International Journal of Information and Education Technology (IJIET)*, *15*(6), 1172–1181. DOI: 10.18178/ijiet.2025.15.6.2320

Zarobe, Y. R., & Querol-Julian, M. (2025). Multilingualism and multimodality in the CLIL/EMI classroom. *Journal of Multilingual and Multicultural Development*, *46*(5), 1397–1415. DOI: 10.1080/01434632.2025.2482734

Zeffirelli, F. (1968). *Romeo and Juliet.* Paramount Pictures. https://www.youtube.com/watch?v=VCe0nzdD76k

Section 5
Quest for Lingua Franca

Chapter 17
Jakovlev's Search for a Commonly Understandable Language

ABSTRACT

In this chapter, I will justify importance of studies and implementation of multi-modalities in classrooms. Importantly, I will explain significance of multimodal teaching and learning for students and their teachers on all grade levels, including college and university. I will deliver the idea of multimodal support as a highly helpful educational means for the educators who put their strong effort towards aiming to assist their learners with a deeper and more efficient comprehension of complex academic or fiction texts. Additionally, I will illustrate with the help of the verbal and non-verbal languages how exactly the means of multimodality may help readers grasp diverse aspects of the visual information at a glance. Finally, I will summarize the results of my research and draw my major conclusions.

JAKOVLEV'S AID TO *'RAZNOYAZYCHIE'*

The idea of necessity of a commonly understandable language in service of a deeper understanding between speakers of different tongues is not new and has been intensively researched and promoted over the recent centuries. In this chapter, I will share about contribution to this endeavor made by my ancestor. In 1924, Pavel F. Jakovlev, my grandfather who was one of the founders and the President of the Association of Esperanto in Russia, then Soviet Union, stressed the necessity of

DOI: 10.4018/979-8-3373-3426-4.ch017

establishing a language, which could be easily mastered and understood by people of practically any cultural and linguistic backgrounds.

Figure 1. Pavel F. Jakovlev

Note. Photo-portrait of Pavel F. Jakovlev (Paŭlo Teodoroviĉ Jakovlev as appears in the Esperanto language in the primary source, in Jung's (1926) article) published in the periodical Heroldo de Esperanto [Esperanto Herald], 38(266), 16.05.1925. Retrieved from the Österreichischen Nationalbibliothek [National Library of Austria]: https://anno.onb.ac.at/cgi-content/anno?aid=e2j&datum=19250516&seite=2&zoom=33 on March 16, 2025.

Just like myself, my grandfather, Jakovlev P. F., was a polylingual speaker of several languages (his last name, which is also our family name, is spelled here the way it appeared in his publications in German and in the artificially created language Esperanto). Being a Native speaker of Ingrian Finnish, my grandfather used Esperanto, Ingrian, German, and Russian (listed alphabetically) in his professional and personal communication. He also utilized these languages for publishing. Additionally, Jakovlev hosted radio programs which were broadcast in all the four languages at the Komintern Radio station in Moscow and Saint Petersburg (S.E.U. 1924, 1925).

As early as in 1924, which was over a century ago, my grandfather could have foreseen the nearing era of Globalization, which would involve a rapid increase in international travel and evolving telecommunications. In one of his publications, my grandfather clarified,

> *Every invention unavoidably leads to the effects, which serve as a launching ground for development of new demands. Existence of railways, sea-liners, and airplanes turned human-beings into space rulers, who know no borders; usage*

of telegraph, which transmits a human word from country to country and from one part of the world to another in a flash – all this has long ago raised the necessity for a common language for international communication to the level of highest significance. (Jakovlev, 1924b, p. 71)

This idea of an urgent need in a commonly understandable means of communication in the era of globalization expressed by Jakovlev in 1924 later found support in the publications by the New London Group (1996, 2000), while Kalantzis and Cope (2008) furthered and expanded this notion. Yet, long time before, Jakovlev (1924a, 1924b) emphasized the need in the Lingua Franca for speakers of different languages.

Moreover, linking the progress of technologies with the growing process of global communicative and cooperative proliferation, Pavel Jakovlev advocated for expansion of international relations and unification of humankind through the means of borderless communication. Yet, this passionate cosmopolitan could have clearly foreseen the obstacle, which Jakovlev relentlessly worked to eliminate and free the way to the global inter-collaboration. In his speeches and publications, Pavel Jakovlev claimed, "New technologies, while speedily progressing, destroyed multiple segregating borders between people and peoples, except for the one: *raznoyazychie* (Rus) [*heterolingualism* (Eng)]" (Jakovlev, 1924b, p. 71).

With regards to the latter term, it is important to clarify that this Russian-language word *raznoyazychie* translated into the English language as *heterolingualism*, though sounds very close to Bakhtin's (1935, 1979) *raznorechie* or *heteroglossia* still significantly differs in its meaning from the Bakhtinian term. The word *raznorechie* (Russian) or *heteroglossia* (English), as used by Bakhtin (the work started in 1935, published in 1979) indicates the phenomenon of existence of multiple different types of discourse within one single language. As suggested by Shields in her publication *Bakhtin Primer*, *heteroglossia* or *raznorechie* might be defined as follows, "Heteroglossia – the presence of two or more voices or discourses, generally expressing alternative or conflicting perspectives" (2007, p. 33).

Nevertheless, the word *raznoyazychie,* as used by Jakovlev (1924b), or its English analogue *heterolingualism,* as used by English-speaking authors, for example, Meylaerts (2011) or Grutman (1996) indicates "co-presence" of different languages (Grutman, 1996) or "the use of foreign languages or social, regional and historical language varieties" (Meylaerts, 2011, p. 4).

Both Bakhtinian (1935, 1979) *raznorechie* (*heteroglossia*) and Jakovlev's (1924b) *raznoyazychie* (*heterolingualism*) may cause different degree hindrance to humans in their attempt to develop a deeper understanding. Moreover, the lack of the mutual linguistic grounds for communication may strongly interfere or even obstruct collaboration. Importantly, Jakovlev worked to promote establishment and usage of such means of communication, major service and benefit of which would be in its purpose to mediate and assist all and any polylingual, multilingual, and heterolingual populations with their deeper and more definite understanding of each other's ideas via usage of the mediational tools of a commonly understandable language.

Throughout my professional life, I have been seeking identical solutions for my students, many of whom represented the cohort of Polylingual EAL speakers in academe. My decision to further the ideas cherished by my grandfather lead me to my research work and scholarly publishing for disseminating the found. I feel now on the mission to find that solution, that means, that commonly understandable language, utilization of which might assist people in building commonly shared platforms for more efficient communication.

Via this publication, I attempted to attract attention of wide educational, academic, and scientific audiences to the great potential of the multimodal language. A range of my research studies found the capacity of multimodalities to powerfully support and enhance communication. Moreover, further studies and practical usage of Multimodality as Lingua Franca might significantly contribute to the efficacy of learning. Specifically, usage of multiple modes in support of readings or listening to speeches has a great potential to assist audiences with their meaning making of all types of texts in their verbal, oral, and print-based forms. Thus, large and diverse populations of speakers of different languages, including but not limited to polylingual EAL speaking college students and their educators, may strongly benefit if multimodalities were included in educational curricula and, further, in professional communication.

Naturally, the multiple modes of multimodality, such as visual, auditory, spatial, gestural, and others as well as the resources of multimodal ensembles, or, putting it brief, the Multimodal language, have been used by humans for different communicative purposes over millennia. Such multimodal communication started prior to and continued after invention of print. Thus, using multimodal means of communication has historically been not only natural, but also habitual, readable, and understandable by practically all humans. Moreover, reading via a range of multimodal affordances has been inherently embedded in human communication, regardless of their culture, nationality, race, ethnicity, or locality of the bearers of one or more languages and dialects.

Furthermore, humans have been inevitably and habitually utilizing the multimodal language in its diverse forms. For instance, gestures, facial expressions, body postures, sounds, gazes, touches, shapes, colors, sizes, and more have been eternally used for communicating ideas or enhancing their meaning. The above means of the multimodal language has a great potential to assist people with their meaning making in heterolingual environments. Conclusively, the Multimodal language may strongly help reduce or eliminate the hindering effects from *raznoyazychie* (Jakovlev, 1924b) or *heterolingualism* (Grutman, 1996; Meylaerts, 2011), which, otherwise presents a significant obstacle to making the meaning and developing a mutual understanding between the interlocutors.

Further, in the events where one commonly-shared language is not available for the purposes of international communication or in the case when its mastery levels in different speakers are not sufficient for developing a deeper comprehension between all the actors within the given event, it might be Multimodality, the commonly understandable language which may be successfully used to support understanding of the conventional verbal, oral, or print-based texts.

MULTIMODALITY AS AN INTERMEDIATE LANGUAGE

So, combining my grandfather's thoughts with my own with regards to a commonly understandable language, the Lingua Franca, I concluded that the language of multimodality may serve as an additional language for both: communicating and receiving ideas. As discussed above, practically all people communicate while unavoidably using both verbal and non-verbal means of communication. Thus, the ability to read and comprehend both types of language is crucial for making the meaning. More, it is known that the non-verbal multimodal language had been used by the human beings long prior to the historic turning point when humankind started using the verbal languages. Nevertheless, initially, the non-verbal multimodal means of communication were vocal sounds, gestures, gazes, et cetera. These have been widely utilized by humans long before they began using the oral verbal speech in addition to these multimodal non-verbal texts. Importantly, the non-verbal language was not abandoned, as an archaism, after development of the verbal speech. Moreover, humankind elaborated this multimodal means of communication, so that many gestures, gazes, facial expressions, and such may be universally understood. Some of them laid the ground for such theatrical arts as pantomime, dance, or ballet, none of which is based on verbal communicating ideas, yet is globally understood.

Importantly, not only in the Fine or Performing Arts, but in a range of everyday cases, multimodal texts may be read independently from their verbal equivalents. More, multimodality is called to support and enhance the verbal texts in books, many of which initially existed only as oral stories, and only later in history were saved in their print-based forms. Nevertheless, not only in the past, but also today, humans widely employ gestures, many of which are assigned specific meanings instead of and just like the words. Some of these gestures, for example, the emblematic ones (e.g., waving one's hand instead of saying hello or good-buy, and such) may be successfully used and understood without the words. Some other gestures and movements assist their users with more definite expression of their ideas. An example of these might be the iconic gestures; for instance, showing one's thumb up indicates positivity and approval. Some other gestures may serve for enhancement of the meaning of statements. One example of such might be the manipulatory gesture of a mother who is shaking her forefinger in front of her child promising him some consequences for his mischief. There are also some specific gestures, which help the addressee(s) with their visualization of the discussed objects or content. For instance, showing how small or big is an object, an apple, for example, or how tall or short is one's child, who is not present at the moment of the conversation.

The above were only a few examples of the habitual usage of multimodality in people's daily life. Subsequently, utilization of the multimodal communication extended from accompanying oral speech in everyday communication to its print-based forms when book printing was invented. After this big turn in the way of storing and sharing information, some print-based texts were often accompanied with images; for example, initially hand-painted or drawn illustrations, and later, gravures, then, photos, graphs, charts, etc. Most recently in the history, the digitalized verbal print-based texts have been also supplemented with still and moving images, animations, videos, etc.

Significantly, during real-life situations or during reading visual texts available in the books or on the screens, humans often find themselves able to comprehend the non-verbal messages quite correctly. This comprehension occurs thanks to their hereditary ability to share information multimodally, for example via producing or receiving multimodal messages. Interestingly, many non-verbal visual texts may be read and correctly understood by speakers of different languages with practically equal success in meaning making, regardless of their cultural and linguistic belonging.

MULTIMODALITY AS AN ALTERNATIVE LANGUAGE

What matters the most for an educator is that the above discussed phenomenon of multimodal meaning making may be used for classroom teaching and learning. More, it is crucially important for language instructors to keep in mind that their students' classroom learning will be soon followed by practical implementation of the newly-acquired knowledge. Importantly, in the era of the rocketing processes of globalization, development of international businesses, educational and cultural exchange programs, trade, and tourism, the efficiency of communication and mutual understanding play the key role. Moreover, in accordance with Jakovlev's (1924b) predictions of the future, which, most definitely, came true, the processes of inter-globalization rapidly increase the numbers of people who travel across the world.

What is the most imperative for the above fact in combination with my research findings is the perception of the international, intercultural, and interlingual sojourners. If questioned, these global trackers would be the people who confirm importance of successful communication. However, many of them might also express their regret with the lack of sufficient knowledge of the shared language(s) in themselves or in other participants of dialogue.

Anticipating the question about the English language as the currently used linguistic affordance for international communication, it is important to explain and fully understand that it was exactly the difficulties in mastering it, as perceived by both instructors and students, that resulted in this research. It is almost needless to state how hard this task appears for millions of language learners. Both teachers of English as a new or an additional language and their students of English might confirm their facing a range of challenges and frustrations on their way to achieving the mastery.

So, moved with compassion to the struggles in so many classrooms, I posed the question: How can mastering English as an Additional Language be facilitated? In response to this inquiry, my research found a solution to offer, the name of which is Multimodality as the intermediary or an Intermediate language between the known and the learned languages, whatever they are.

Through activating their memories about studying a language, users or, at least, attempters of more than one tongue would most probably remember the challenges and the levels of such in their own prior experiences. And speakers of only one language, trusting the word of the above populations or through their imagination might perceive the additional language learners' sincere attempts to understand and to be understood in a dialogue. Many new language learners might recognize in a mutual agreement that what helps them to correctly read the orally produced verbal messages is the non-verbal language. To provide just examples in support of the above statement, utilization of deictic gestures, which are commonly used to point to the objects or to show directions, are often of great help for finding one's way in a new country, city, or practically any geographical setting. Another means for convey and facilitating comprehension are facial expressions, which may quite clearly illustrate the expressed ideas. Thus, many elements of the visual language may be used as an Additional language in service of more efficient communication between bearers of different tongues united by one major intention: to better comprehend each other in the dialogue.

To further the above ideas, I will provide below a highly illustrative example in support of multimodality-assisted communication. Presumably, many modern day readers have some background knowledge about the early era of cinematograph, where films were made with only the visual component, but had no sound yet. At those times, acting by actors on the screen was largely accompanied with live performances by musicians, usually, a pianist, or a theatre organist. In many of those silent films, print-based subtitles were often scarce or even not available. If present, those scarce verbal captions appeared on the screen quite randomly and seldom, with long intervals between them filled with silent pantomimic actions. If subtitles were used at all.

Nevertheless, viewers were able to correctly make the meaning of the content of the films without the verbal language. Imperatively important for my research results, it needs to be emphasized that the movies without any verbal texts might have been filmed in different countries (e.g., Great Britain, France) and shown to users of different tongues. Nevertheless, these silent, but full of the non-verbal language films were easily understood by most of the international viewers within and outside of the countries where they produced. Thus, the most important conclusion from the above is that comprehensibility of the visual texts occurred in users of any tongues due to the high readability of the non-verbal, visual means of multimodality. So, if the Multimodal language was used in the lieu of the verbal one and was successfully understood, Multimodality may be viewed as not only an Intermediary, but an Alternative language.

VIEW FROM A COUNTERARGUMENT

Countering the omni-comprehensibility of the non-verbal Multimodal language, the verbal texts composed in different languages can be comprehended only by those audiences who can either speak or understand those tongues. Logically, in the absence of any universally-known words, so-called cognates, or any other helpful clues, a new language remains an enigma. Most of the verbal utterances sound (in an oral speech) or look (in writing) practically undecipherable for the non-speakers or non-users. For instance, a speaker of German needs at least some initial knowledge of the Russian language to be able to comprehend the information, which is verbally expressed in Russian. And vice versa, a speaker of Russian needs at least some knowledge of the German language to be able to comprehend the oral or print-based texts in German. To illustrate the above idea, I am providing the following examples (See the examples in *Figure 2* below to compare the same sentences in the German, Russian, English, Hindi, and multimodal visual languages).

Figure 2. Three sentences in different languages: German, Russian, English, Hindi, and a multimodal image

German	Russian	English	Hindi	Multimodal visual language
Das ist ein Hund.	Это собака.	This is a dog.	यह एक कुत्ता है।	
Es ist ein kleines weißes Hündchen.	Это маленькая беленькая собачка.	It is a white little dog.	यह एक सफेद छोटा कुत्ता है.	
Das Hündchen trägt ein rotes Kleid.	Собачка одета в красное платье.	The little dog has a red outfit on.	छोटे कुत्ते ने लाल पोशाक पहन रखी है।	

A person who cannot read the print-based texts in any of the languages used in Figure 2 above, most likely, will not be able to correctly understand the meanings of the sentences. Importantly, the major condition to consider while evaluating the discussed here notion is that the above verbal statements presented in different languages and different alphabetical systems need to be viewed separately from the image, which is provided in Figure 2 above and prior to having learned any of these languages. Importantly, the language learning includes the studies of such resources as a new alphabetic system, vocabulary, grammar, sentence structure, etc.

Though, as a polylingual speaker, I assume that knowledge of one of the two Latin-based languages in Figure 2 might help the users of Latin script with their meaning making due to availability of some linguistic similarities in the tongues of this language family. For instance, the close alphabetical systems may help speakers of different languages with reading the above sentences with at least some share of correctness. Another helpful feather for readers of different languages with a shared linguistic family, for example the English and the German, is a trackable correspondence in the grammatical structures and vocabulary similarities of these sentences with some phonetical divergence in the above languages, where "Das ist [+ the object/subject (e.g., ein Hund)]" in German may be compared to "*That is* [+ the object/subject (e.g., a dog]" in English. Moreover, the English word *hound* meaning a *dog* is a cognate, a very close vocabulary word, in its appearance and sound, to its German equivalent *Hund.*

Nevertheless, the other two verbal languages in Figure 2, Russian and Hindi, use different alphabetic systems, punctuation, and sentence structure. So, it will be impossible for a non-user of any of these languages to read and understand the verbal messages in either of these tongues. Conclusively, the difficulty of the deciphering task will significantly increase when readers face scripts used in some other nations or cultures, where not only the alphabets, but also the directions of the writing differ. For example, they write from right to left in Arabic, Hebrew, or Persian, while in Chinese Mandarin, Japanese, Korean, or Vietnamese, the writings descend from top to bottom.

Hopefully, the above examples and explanations helped my readers to visualize themselves in the role of a new language learners. Imperatively, for many of these scholars, the task of language learning is stressful due to such facts as the urgency and significance of the outcome. To provide just some examples, the language learners might face some important deadlines, such as exams, college enrollment, the need to relocate to a new country, and to a new school, to name just a few. Upon arrival to the new linguistic environment, these new language learners may face such frustrating challenges as reading street signs, maps, or directions on a medication package, official documents, or letters from the authorities of the host country, and many other life-important messages. For the cohort of the International students, just like the ones who participated in my research, the major challenges consisted of their academic readings.

Nevertheless, reading multimodally may significantly simplify many reading tasks. For evaluating this statement, it is necessary to return to the content of Figure 2 above. While looking at the image included with it, one can perceive that the multimodal reading presents a significantly easier task. Contrary to reading alphabetically in the four verbal languages within this figure, one may look at the picture of a small fluffy white dog dressed in a red outfit and understand this non-verbal visual text practically instantaneously. Naturally, the reader will not even need to think about how to read this multimodal ensemble comprised of a wide range of visual resources, including color, texture, facial expression, dimensions, etc. This easiness can be explained by the fact that, unlike reading in the verbal languages, with their unique alphabets, grammar, stylistics, and structure, the multimodal visual reading mostly does not require the extensive studies due to the multimodal reading ability being inheritable in humans.

Importantly, it is impossible to mistakenly take this image of a dog for an image of a reptile or a bird. With an exception of a color-blindness case, the white and red colors in the image will be read as *white* and *red* by readers and speakers of any verbal languages. Whichever shades and variations of red and white an artistically skillful person might be able to distinguish in this image, the dog in this picture is neither black nor brown; it is a white dog. As for its outfit, it is not green, yellow, or purple, but it is clearly and most definitely red. So, all general audiences of multimodal viewers, whatever languages they speak, when exposed to the above picture will be able to correctly read the available visual non-verbal information via the affordances of the resources of the given multimodal ensemble.

To conclude the above exemplification, Figure 2 containing the sentences in four different alphabetical languages and the image in the Multimodal language served the purpose to clarify and support my idea about high readability of multimodal non-verbal texts. This example also confirms that the Multimodal language can be understood by both speakers and non-speakers of other verbal tongues. Thus, the Multimodal language may be utilized as the Lingua Franca, that long-sought and coveted commonly understandable language to be used in any linguistic environment, where utilization of one verbal tongue is not possible or is not sufficient for the present audiences to gain a deeper understanding of the verbal texts, be those the oral ones or the conventional print-based texts.

MULTIMODALITY THROUGH HISTORIC LENSE

Though the term *multimodality* is relatively new and its meaning is often tied to digitality, humans have been habitually reading diverse multimodal visual texts without and long before the invention of the modern technologies, but over the centuries and even millennia during and even before the era of print. Nowadays, in many highly technologically developed societies, people have almost forgotten their old traditional culture-specific communication practices, which were richly based on utilization of different meaning-filled symbols, which precluded development of alphabetical systems. These practices of the non-verbal communication with the help of signs and symbols have been extensively studied and described by such authors as Bogatyrev (1971), van Leeuwen (2004), and Zaczeck and Phillips (2014).

Importantly, in some countries and nations, the multimodal language formed by some specific traditional signs and symbols, which had been developed and used in the far past, can still be found today. Though nearly lost, those multimodal communication systems still exist, and carry and convey the encoded in them meanings. Importantly, many bearers of those cultures can decipher and understand those unwritten messages, especially if they were taught how to read them.

To provide just some examples, types of non-verbal messaging include the tartans of different colors and styles of the kilts and shawls, which indicate their owners' belonging to very specific Irish or Scotch clans. Another example would be Slavonic embroidery patterns, which provide rich information on their bearers' locality, language, or dialect. Some other examples are decorative elements of garments and objects used by the Northern nations of Russia, including but not limited to the Ingrian cultures from which my immediate and extended family of the Jakovlevs / the Yakovlevs stem. Those cultural symbols have the power to convey quite detailed information about a life story of their bearers. Some of the costume embroidery works are so detailed, that they may be considered practically equal to a verbally represented narration about the owner, and might serve nearly as their resume (Bogatyrev, 1971; Iskenderov, Iskenderov, & Kostina, 2008; Knapp, Brimner, & White, 1959; Martin 1996; Pietikainen & Pitkanen-Hunta, 2013; van Leeuwen, 2004; Wilton, 2014; Zaczeck & Phillips, 2014). So, the external looks of a person in many cultures are often intentionally loaded with specific non-verbal semiotic signs, which are applied to their garments to carry portions of significant biographic information about their owner.

Interestingly, there is even more to the usage of semiotics in the lieu of the verbal language. For instance, in the culture of the Chuvashes, the ethnos residing in the Ural Mountain region, some specific patterns and ornaments may contain non-verbal messages, which are equivalent to sentences, such as proverbs, advice, or sayings of a teaching or educational character. Those are encoded in the embroidered signs and symbols (Iskenderov, Iskenderov, & Kostina, 2008; Trofimov, 1977, 2007). Similarly to that, as mentioned by van Leeuwen (2004), some Slavonic traditions, for example, the Moravian Slovaks, profoundly and extensively studied by Bogatyrev (published in 1971, though written in 1937), and further discussed in van Leeuwen (2004, p. 37), load the bearers' attire with the non-verbal, patterned texts with rich information on the geographic region, ethnic, and linguistic belonging, and many other historical, and biographical facts.

All the above examples serve to support the idea of the historic roots of the humans' ability to read multimodally. Thus, this ability needs not be forgotten, but, on the contrary, widely used, and further explored, developed, and implemented.

MULTIMODALITY AS AN ADDITIONAL LANGUAGE

So, concluding the contemplation about creation of "talking" images, it is worth to consider that many of them included scenes of everyday life, where many depicted some actions. With regards to reading actions, Franks and Jewitt (2001) noticed, "Action takes place in specific contexts; it is always located in particular settings and in specific histories, both on micro-level... and a macro level" (p. 204).

This idea of helpfulness of reading actions by actors, in addition to the verbal texts was furthered by the above authors who declared, "We see action as a partially articulated semiotic system, which, in reciprocal and dialectical relation, continually both realizes and constructs the social world in both thought and deed" (2001, p. 204).

So, linking the social semiotics perspectives by Franks and Jewitt, intertwined with socio-cultural constructivism postulates by Vygotsky (1978, 1987, 2000), I drew my conclusions about my research participants in this current study. Obviously, these students constructed the social worlds of and around the characters on the screen through their observably readable actions. Importantly, this work helped these participants to further construct the meaning of the other non-verbal and verbal texts they read. Imperatively for this research findings, the characters' actions in the video with the sound helped these culturally diverse Polylingual Domestic and International EAL college students to deeper and more precisely construct the meaning and translate the unknown to them 15th-16th century English into the modern English as the new to them additional language.

Thus, my research participants were able to correctly construct the meaning while cognitively linking the observable actions to the orally produced and print-based texts. As per these students' interview confessions, this work helped them to better envision the smaller and the greater contexts in the episode and in the entire story. Imperatively, prior to the exposure to multimodal support, these students failed to correctly construct the meaning of the unimodal print-based texts.

As follows from the interviews, participants confirmed my hypothetic thoughts when they shared how the actors' movements and positions in the space, as well as their gestures, and postural behaviors assisted them with their understanding first, of the contexts in the story and finally, the content of the text. So, these findings of the current study correspond with the ideas by Franks and Jewitt (2001), who suggested that "…the body, as material and vehicle of action, is fundamental to understanding the meaning of action" (p. 208). The above quote by Franks and Jewitt (2001) also corresponds to my research participants' revelations, when they shared how strongly they relied on their observations of the actors' physical behaviors and their body language, using this material for making the meaning, just as found by Franks and Jewitt (2001, p. 205).

Further, as all participants strongly and prevalently relied on the information received through the visual means of multimodality, they considered that multiple visual resources (e.g., actors' gazes, facial expressions, colors present in the scene) were very helpful for their meaning making. These findings also support the ones by Kress and van Leeuwen (2002); in particularly, where these social semiotics theorists concluded about meaningfulness of color (p. 347).

Thus, the findings in my current study add to the above notion by Kress and van Leeuwen (1996, 2002) and also support the ideas by Franks and Jewitt (2001). My conclusions also correspond with Vygotsky's socio-cultural constructivism theory postulates; i.e., participants constructed their meaning about the historic Shakespearian (1597) chronotope (Bakhtin, 1981) depicted in the video while relying on the ideational function; i.e., scrutinizing the present colors, which were used by Zeffirelli (1968) to denote certain types of personalities, cultural, and historical context, and other meaningful for a deeper understanding of the depicted context phenomena.

The above allows me to conclude that, based on postulates by Kress and van Leeuwen (2002) and my current research findings, the verbal, oral or print-based language is not the only language that humans efficiently and habitually implement for communication. Thus, the Multimodal non-verbal language may and needs to be viewed as an Additional language, as it is widely utilized and largely understood by people.

Yet, in connection to the above statement, I am trying to deliver a highly important idea: just as any new or additional tongue, the Multimodal language deserves to be taught to students. Just as learners at schools on all grade levels are being taught how to read and write in any verbal language(s), they need to be schooled on the Multimodal one(s). Nevertheless, the art and skill of reading, understanding, and expressing one's ideas via the means of the non-verbal multimodal languages is not necessarily taught in-depth in the classrooms of today. Yet, closing this educational gap might significantly benefit students on all grade levels, including higher education classrooms. Thus, learners need to be taught how to read the non-verbal texts in a large variety of their forms and domains, starting off the structure of book illustrations, and proceeding with reading the real-life via examining the meanings of gestures, emotions, revealed via facial expressions and body language, etc.

It needs to be recognized that some elements of reading, decoding, and utilizing non-verbal multimodal language is taught to Fine Arts students. These future artists need to have the knowledge and understanding of the structure of a visual composition in a piece of art. It is equally important for painters to feel and be able to correctly depict space and its dimensionality within a composition. Additionally, the growing talents need to know anatomy and its functions; for example, they need to be able to envision, looking deep through the skin, the configurations of facial muscles in connection to the underlying. Some of the emotions need to be shown through the body language affordances; for example, positions or gestures.

Unfortunately, in the general education classrooms, the above sets of knowledge are not being taught, regardless of all the benefits from multimodalities found by the research (see the literature discussion above in this book). Thus, curriculum developers in practically any education system need to develop such programs and courses, the purpose of which would be to provide students with the knowledge on the rules, grammar, stylistics, and structure of the Multimodal language. These courses might consider both cultures-specific and global aspects. For example, American educators might consider developing programs, which serve for familiarizing diverse International English as an Additional Language speaking students with some very specific to the American culture(s) information on the meaning of gestures, which can be observed and used in everyday life for conveying or enhancing the meaning. The above aspects are equally relevant to real-life situations and to the ones in the films produced in the United States, or on the stage in the U.S. theatres.

Interestingly, this current research's participants confirmed the idea of the non-verbal Multimodal language not being taught in educational institutions. Moreover, these students believed they might strongly benefit were they introduced to some multimodal reading strategies in their American university language classrooms. Yet, when listening to my research participants' revelations about their habits, skills, and preferences in reading, I came to the conclusion that reading multimodally, though not taught to these students, appeared to be highly habitual in them. Further, as noted by all my research participants, one of the drawbacks in their past educational histories was the lack of specific education in reading and decoding multimodal texts. Importantly, some of these students expressed their regret about lack of the multimodal educational experiences and suggested that multimodalities need to be further studied, taught, and implemented in the classrooms. What is important for this research findings, the above revelations by my research participants confirmed the finding in my previously conducted studies in the field of multimodality (e.g., Gould, 2015, 2016, 2017; Gould-Yakovleva, 2023a, 2023b).

SIGNIFICANCE OF MULTIMODAL READING

After having considered all my research participants' ideas on the benefits from using the multimodal language and the rich and expressive ensembles of the multimodal resources, I concluded that utilization of multimodalities in classrooms appeared to be underestimated, thus, limited. Though many teachers implement visual and auditory modes to support and enhance their language-learning students' comprehension, not too many of them teach their learners ***how*** to read and understand the meanings encoded in the non-verbal language. One explanation to this lack of teaching multimodal literacy skills rests in the fact that many instructors had never received any education in the field of teaching with multimodality.

Ironically, as noticed by James Gee in his *Foreword* to Frank Serafini's (2014) publication *Reading the Visual: An Introduction to Teaching Multimodal Literacy*, educators have been assisting their students with their meaning making of conventional verbal print-based texts with the means of *additional verbal print-based texts*. Gee clearly formulated:

> *School has long been about print, words on a page and lectures that sound like print. We give students texts, and when they do not understand them, we give them more texts. If they do not understand a word, we give them more words, such things as definitions, explications, and lectures. (Gee, 2014 in Serafini, 2014, p. xi)*

Importantly, Gee (2004, 2007) righteously believed that a word cannot be understood by its definition, but gains its genuine meaning in every given context. Upon completion of my current research, I draw the conclusion that teachers need to enable their students to view the contexts if they want to assist their learners with their more efficient, faster, and more profound understanding of the meaning of the words. Verbal texts, though, need to be regarded as only some of the meaningful resources within rich and expressive multimodal ensembles. Importantly, the verbal, oral, and print-based texts need to be combined with the other available modes for assisting readers with their more accurate meaning making.

Imperatively, my research findings discussed in this book support the ones by Serafini (2011, 2014). This author contemplated, "From the time humans first painted images on the cave walls… to the present day, when images stream across our computer screens, we have used visual images to help understand ourselves and make sense of the world around us" (p. 1). More, in my current research, all students-participants echoed these ideas when they shared about their habitual use of diverse informational technologies for a range of their academic and non-academic purposes. My subjects' words sounded very logical as, due to development of new and ever-evolving technologies, modern days' humans need to be able to speedily process enormous volumes of multimodal information, large portions of this brain work occur subconsciously. Moreover, practically unnoticeably to selves, all people habitually read and decode the meanings encoded in multiple non-verbal texts in addition to or instead of the information delivered via the verbal means of communication, such as road signs, street signs, and all sorts of labeling inside buildings. Thus, the multimodal reading used by everyone on the intuitive or amateur level, needs to be academically studied and professionally taught for a great benefit of all learners.

More Than One Use

Significantly, there may be more ways to use multimodal reading, rather than for assisting students with their meaning making of the print-based texts. One of the multiple implications of my current research, to which I am willing to attract special attention of wide academic, researchers, and professional audiences, goes beyond implementation of multimodalities for teaching and learning in public schools, universities, or college, in EAL, Arts, Language Arts, Engineering, or Science, etc. classrooms. Additionally, it is crucially important that profound knowledge of multiple functions and aspects of non-verbal multimodal language (e.g., head and body positions, facial expressions, gazes) has a strong potential to help study human behaviors in different kinds of Human Psychology and Applied Psychology classrooms. For example, teaching the non-verbal language reading strategies and skills to the students who prepare to serve in professional surveillance and security organizations may help those future safety officers to learn how to read the hidden ideas and intentions.

Though not an easy task, multimodal analysis of the observable traits may allow professional readers to look through the misleading pretense appearances and read the scarcely available and disguised non-verbal texts, readable through human behaviors. This knowledge may help the guards to promptly understand and calculate vectors of intention, which might be thoroughly and even professionally disguised behind the neutral or friendly facial expressions. This knowledge may help recognize and correctly interpret the malicious and intensive brainwork, which still shows as a visual text in its owner's body language and gaze.

Further, this ability to decipher the non-verbal language and make the meaning of the available visual texts in real-life situations may help to tell between good and evil intentions in individuals or whole or dispersed groups of people. Moreover, the taught knowledge and the learned ability to read non-verbal clues might help professionals to further develop their skills metacognitively and operate on a level significantly higher than meager intuition. Thus, the knowledge of the rules and grammar of the non-verbal multimodal language, when applied in real-life situations, would be of a great benefit for all local communities and global societies in terms of prevention of the unwanted behaviors and actions (e.g., criminal acts or terrorist attacks).

Conclusively, including studies of the Multimodal language may help the professionals to reduce, prevent, or eliminate possible severe damage to wide and diverse populations at different sites, such as schools, businesses, travel facilities, or entertainment events, to name just a few. Absolutely imperatively, the knowledge and mastery of the Multimodal language will help save lives, and that is where the highest significance of its affordances resides. With the above statement, I rest my case.

REFERENCES

Bakhtin, M. M. (1935, 1979). *Эстетика словесного творчества* [The aesthetics of verbal art]. Moscow: Iskusstvo.

Bakhtin, M. M. (1981). Discourse in the novel. In Holquist, M. (Ed.), *The dialogic imagination: Four essays by M. M. Bakhtin* (pp. 259–422). University of Texas Press.

Bogatyrev, P. (1971). *Вопросы теории народного искусства* [Questions of the theory of the volk art]. Iskusstvo.

Franks, A., & Jewitt, C. (2001). The meaning of action in learning and teaching. *British Educational Research Journal, 27*(2), 201–218. DOI: 10.1080/01411920120037144

Gee, J. P. (2004). *What video-games have to teach us about learning and literacy.* Palgrave.

Gee, J. P. (2007). *Social linguistics and literacy: Ideology in discourses.* Routledge. DOI: 10.4324/9780203944806

Gee, J. P. (2014). Foreword. In Frank Serafini (2014 Ed.). *Reading the visual: An introduction to teaching multimodal literacy.* New York and London: Teachers College Press.

Gould, O. (2015, December). *How multimodal features influence college-level International students' reading comprehension of traditional print-based texts.* Paper presentation at the 65th annual meeting of Literacy Research Association (LRA), San Diego, CA.

Gould, O. (2016, February). *How multimodal features influence polylingual EAL speaking college students' reading comprehension of traditional print-based texts.* Research Component paper presented at the12th Midwinter meeting of National Council of Teachers of English Assembly for Research (NCTEAR), University of Eastern Michigan, Ypsilanti, MI.

Gould, O. (June 12, 2017). *'Please, tell them!': Voices from university classrooms on the effects of multimodality on polylingual EAL speaking college students' meaning making.* (Doctoral dissertation). ProQuest LLC.

Gould-Yakovleva, O. (2023a). Seeking remedy for improving international college students' reading comprehension: A qualitative case study on using multimodality for English language learning. *International Journal of Higher Education Pedagogies, 4*(4), 33–54. DOI: 10.33422/ijhep.v4i4.599

Gould-Yakovleva, O. (2023b). Voices from university classrooms on effects of multimodality on polylingual EAL college students' meaning making. *International Journal of Second and Foreign Language Education*, *2*(2), 1–19. DOI: 10.33422/ijsfle.v2i2.450

Grutman, R. (2006). Refractions and recognition: Literary multilingualism in translation. *Target*, *28*(1), 17–47. DOI: 10.1075/target.18.1.03gru

Iskenderov, F. V., Iskenderov, & E. F., Kostina, E. F. (2008). Азбука чувашских орнаментов и эмблем: Учебно-наглядное пособие для изучающих чувашскую культуру и краеведение [Alphabet of Chuvash ornaments and emblems: Educational and visual aid for students of Chuvash culture and local history]. Russian Federation: Ulyanovsk.

Jakovlev, P. F. (1924a). Radio-kroniko Sovetlanda [Radio-chronicles of Soviet country]. *Radiolyubitel* [Radio-Amateur], *1*(4), p. 2. http://archive.radio.ru/web/1924/04/001/

Jakovlev, P. F. (1924b). Радиотелефония и международный язык [Wireless telephony and international language]. *Radiolyubitel* [Radio-Amateur], *1*(5), p. 71. http://archive.radio.ru/web/1924/05/008/

Jung, T. (May 16, 1925). Paŭlo Teodoroviĉ Jakovlev: Prezidanto de Sovetlanda Esp. Unuiĝo [Pavel Feodorovich Jakovlev: President of the Soviet Esperantist Union]. *Heroldo de Esperanto* [Esperanto Herald], *38*(266), p. 2. https://anno.onb.ac.at/pdfs/ONB_e2j_19250516.pdf

Kalantzis, M., & Cope, B. (2008). *New Learning: Elements of a science of education*. Cambridge University Press. DOI: 10.1017/CBO9780511811951

Knapp, R., Brimner, J., & White, M. (1959). Educational level, class status, and aesthetic preference. *The Journal of Social Psychology*, *50*(2), 277–284. DOI: 10.1080/00224545.1959.9922002

Kress, G., & van Leeuwen, T. (1996). *Reading images: The grammar of visual design*. Routledge.

Kress, G., & van Leeuwen, T. (2002). Colour as a semiotic mode: Notes for a grammar of colour. *Visual Communication*, *1*(3), 333–354. DOI: 10.1177/147035720200100306

Martin, R. (1996). *Scottish clans and family names*. Mainstream Publishing.

Meylaerts, R. (2006). Heterolingualism in/and translation: How legitimate are the Other and his/her language? An Introduction. *International Journal of Translation Studies*, *18*(1), 1–15. DOI: 10.1075/target.18.1.02mey

New London Group. (1996). A pedagogy of multiliteracies: Designing social futures. *Harvard Educational Review*, *66*(1), 60–92. DOI: 10.17763/haer.66.1.17370n67v22j160u

New London Group. (2000). A pedagogy of multiliteracies: Designing social futures. In Cope, B., & Kalantzis, M. (Eds.), *Multiliteracies: Literacy learning and design of social futures* (pp. 9–38). Macmillan.

Pietikainen, S., & Pitkanen-Hunta, A. (2013). Multimodal literacy practices in the indigenous Sami classroom: Children navigating in a complex multilingual setting. *Journal of Language, Identity, and Education*, *12*(4), 230–247. DOI: 10.1080/15348458.2013.818471

Serafini, F. (2011). Expanding perspectives for comprehending visual images in multimodal texts. *Journal of Adolescent & Adult Literacy*, *54*(5), 342–350. DOI: 10.1598/JAAL.54.5.4

Serafini, F. (2014). *Reading the visual: An introduction to teaching multimodal literacy*. Teachers College Press.

S.E.U. (1924). Radio-kroniko Sovetlanda [Radio-chronicles of Soviet country]. *Radiolyubitel* [Radio-Amateur], *1*(4), p. 2.

S.E.U. (1925). Radio-kroniko Sovetlanda [Radio-chronicles of Soviet country]. *Radiolyubitel* [Radio-Amateur], *2*(3), p. 2.

Shakespeare, W. (1597). *Romeo and Juliet*.

Trofimov, A. A. (1977). *Орнамент чувашской народной вышивки: Вопросы теории и практики* [Ornaments of the Chuvash ethnic embroidery: Theoretical and historic questions]. Chuvashia, Cheboksary: Chuvash Publishing House.

Trofimov, A. A. (2007*). Искусство чувашской народной вышивки в музеях России* [The art of Chuvash ethnic embroidery in museums of Russia]. Chuvashia, Cheboksary: Chuvash State University of Humanities.

van Leeuwen, T. (2004). *Introducing social semiotics*. Routledge. DOI: 10.4324/9780203647028

Vygotsky, L. S. (1978). *Mind in society: The development of higher psychological processes*. Harvard University Press.

Vygotsky, L. S. (1987). *The collected works of L. S. Vygotsky: Vol. 1. Problems of general psychology, including the volume thinking and speech* (R. W. Rieber & A. S. Carton, Eds., Trans. N. Minick). New York: Plenum.

Vygotsky, L. S. (2000). *Psychology*. EKSMO-Press.

Wilton, B. (2014). *Collins little book of clans and tartans*. Harper Collins Publishers.

Zaczeck, I., & Phillips, C. (2014). *The illustrated encyclopedia of tartan: A complete history and visual guide to over 400 famous tartans*. Southwater Publishing.

Zeffirelli, F. (1968). *Romeo and Juliet*. Paramount Pictures. https://www.youtube.com/watch?v=VCe0nzdD76k

Chapter 18
Post Scriptum

ABSTRACT

Chapter 18 is the final and conclusive piece in this book. In this chapter, I will explain why it is important to teach students how to read texts comprised of different modes of multimodality. I will tie the findings of this research to their possible practical implementation in the classrooms and ground my conclusions in the Vygotskyan socio-cultural constructivism theory. Importantly, in this chapter, I will try to deliver my idea of an urgent need in reconceptualizing modern days' classrooms and turning the unimodal verbal text-based learning into multimodal exploration, which was found suitable for a great majority of diverse learners. In this chapter, I will also provide some implications for further research. Additionally, I will position my current publication in the field of multimodal teaching and learning. My final conclusive message to the wide educational, academic, researchers, and student audiences will conclude this chapter and my entire book.

NEED IN RECONCEPTUALIZATION

Considering all my work in the field of multimodality and concluding my current monograph, I came out with understanding of the role and status of the Multimodal language being in needs of reconceptualization. My conclusion rests on the findings in my own studies and the ones by many world-renowned researchers and theorists in the fields of multimodality and social semiotics, such as Callow, Franks, Gee, Jewitt, Kress, Norris, van Leeuwen and their forerunners, supporters, and followers, whose unique, innovative, and insightful works have been discussed throughout this publication. Combining all the above knowledge, I am willing to attract attention of wide academic and researchers' audiences to the great potential of the rich affordances of multimodalities. Yet, their structure, grammar, and semiotic rules need to be taught to students just like the rules of any language. Significantly, the global and local educational systems may not rely on the amateurish input made by

DOI: 10.4018/979-8-3373-3426-4.ch018

some prominent amateurs-enthusiasts. Instead, professionally developed programs and courses on teaching and learning the Multimodal language as an Additional or an Alternative language need to be offered to students on all grade levels, including colleges and universities, where these classes need to be offered minimum as electives and for some majors as core requirements. At this point, the number of educational opportunities concerning studies of multimodalities, specifically, its non-verbal component is insufficient. Yet, the status quo of Multimodality as the Lingua France can be and needs to be changed for the benefit of students, their educators, and the society at large.

Looking back through the history of humankind, one can perceive how many great ideas, inventions, or innovations were set aside waiting for the stars to come together so their developer could step out of shade and gain attention and recognition, not for themselves, but for the ideas they knew were beneficial to humankind. For example, there was the time when the American Sign Language (ASL) was not recognized nor widely implemented, but had to struggle its way to the public arena for a great relief and joy of its learners and users. For a long period of time, it was regarded as just a set of some gestures, which might be used by deaf, hard of hearing, and mute people for communicative purposes within their circle. And it was only as late as in 1960, and thanks to enthusiastic efforts by William Stokoe, that the American Sign Language became officially recognized as the ASL language, but not only "the visual communication systems of the American deaf" (Stokoe, 1960, p. 1). Linking the history of development of this newly recognized language to that of the Multimodality, it needs to be said that the multidimensional Multimodal language may have as long a story on the way to its becoming officially recognized as an Additional or an Alternative Language for international, intercultural, and interlinguistic communication. Yet, with the endeavors of caring (Bain, 2004) educators, this language may be taught to students in schools on all grade-levels, including colleges and universities.

Nevertheless, regardless of its current status, the Multimodal language, especially its visual resources, when added to conventional print-based texts, appeared to be extremely helpful to the polylingual EAL university students. Importantly, all readers within this current project, as well as in my preceding studies of multimodal reading (e.g., Gould, 2015, 2016, 2017; Gould-Yakovleva, 2023a, 2023b) stated that approaching the challenging texts multimodally significantly helped them with their meaning making. According to the statements by my research participants, usage of multimodal support needs to be recommended for active implementation in the American and international classrooms. Further, students need to be made aware of the benefits of usage of such resources of multimodal ensembles as actors' movements, gestures, postures, gazes, sounds, actions, and the colors present in their settings, in addition or in the lieu, when unavailable, of such resources of the verbal languages as orally produced or print-based words, phrases, or sentences. Conclusively, as the result of studies of Multimodalities, and as the effect of having developed the multimodal reading skills, the current students, as future professionals, may strongly benefit from this knowledge and achieve higher, first academically in their schools, further, professionally, at their work places.

IMPORTANCE OF TEACHING THE MULTIMODAL LANGUAGE

I recognize and acknowledge those of my book readers who find themselves in the solicitudinal stance, the state in which people sympathize with the struggles of the student populations (Gould-Yakovleva, 2023a, p.35). Yet, I still feel the need in emphasizing the idea of importance of teaching multimodality as an Additional Language. With this purpose, I would remind my reading audiences on Vygotsky's Zone of Proximate Development and Scaffolding notions. Although some of the multimodal reading skills are naturally acquired by children through observations of the surrounding environments, the process of mastering reading and decoding more complex texts is yet a task to accomplish. According to the Vygotskyan postulates (1978, 1987, 2000), the above might be more efficiently achieved with the help from the educated, trained, and experienced professional educators.

Importantly, to be effective, studies of Multimodalities need to be started as early as in the primary classrooms. Further, the multimodal education needs to be consistently continued throughout the middle and high school, and then be furthered in colleges and universities. Additionally, as noticed by this project's participants, the multimodal teaching materials need to be thoughtfully designed, created, or selected for instruction. Imperatively, this work may be started even before the directive from the above. And the change towards the Multimodal approach to teaching and learning may be powered by classroom teachers and higher education instructors. So, the re-conceptualization of teaching Multimodality and its language is in the hands of caring educators.

Caring for All Language Learners

Talking about the International and Domestic, multicultural, multilingual, and polylingual English as an Additional Language students, it is important for educators to understand that many of them enter the language and the content area classrooms while having large gaps in their knowledge. Most often, these new to the country and culture learners fall not only due to their insufficiently yet developed skills in reading, writing, or educational technology, but also in many cultural aspects of the new to them social environment.

According to Vygotsky's (1978, 1987, 2000) socio-cultural constructivism theory, these populations of students may and need to be mediated through their Zones of Proximal Development (the ZPD) by more experienced, knowledgeable, and more skilled others, the educators. When mediated, these learners may more efficiently progress through their ZPDs and gain a fuller understanding of both the taught scientific content and the cultural aspect of the life in the new to them country. Importantly, the level of retaining information in their long-term memory might be significantly higher due to the thoughtful and skilled mediation and scaffolding (Vygotsky, 1978, 1987, 2000), which may be achieved with implementation of highly understandable language of multimodalities. Additionally, the attractive means of multimodality may ignite genuine internal motivation in the learners.

In support of the above idea, it is important to emphasize here that all participants in this study, without being prompted, unanimously advocated for multimodality to be embedded in classroom instruction. All these students expressed the idea that it should be arranged by professors that both classwork and homework are supplemented with and facilitated by multimodalities.

With regards to the above ideas, I recollect some extremely meaningful moments during my interviews and informal conversations with my research participants. When I mentioned my intention to present the findings in this study at the National and International conferences and further publish my research reports to reach wide pedagogic, educational, academic, and researchers' audiences, my research participants celebrated the news. More to that, they were happy their voices could be heard. Needless to say how greatly I treasured the input from my participants, their opinions, thoughts, and contemplations. So, I asked them whether the findings in my study with their participation are of importance to educators, as they believed. Amazingly, all my participants answered **yes**, while some of them passionately exclaimed, **"Oh, yes! Please, please, tell them!"** [stressed by the voices and intonations] (Gould, 2017, p. 201).

So, drawing the parallels of teaching and learning the verbal languages and the Multimodal language, my participants' ideas about the role of multimodality in education appeared quite salient. Let us consider the simple fact that all children, who are taught how to understand, then speak, then read, and write in any verbal and print-based language in their native tongues or in their country's official language, receive years of in-depth instruction. Nevertheless, when it comes to reading or expressing ideas multimodally, students are left to employ their intuition. Thus, it is vitally important for all educators to attend to Vygotskyan (1978, 1987, 2000) postulates of ZPD and scaffolding and understand that it is not enough to own a piano to master playing it. More, orienting towards all, but not most exclusive and prodigious learners, it sounds self-explainable that mastery in the performing arts, e.g., in musicianship, can be more efficiently achieved with the help of a trained and highly experienced teacher. Further, the more profound is the learned effort, the higher is the achievement. Thus, both the multimodal readers and the creators of multimodal compositions may reach higher proficiency in their field be they taught by trained, experienced, and knowledgeable educators. So, it is time to start to professionally train the future teachers, giving them the knowledge and skill to share with their prospective learners.

I have one more, final message concluding this book. As educators, we can set our learners to persevere the way we did during our times of being students. Yet, the idea, "We have survived, so they should" sounds careless to me and, also, somewhat cruel. We can have them work hard on their own, like we did. Yet, upon having listened to the students' revelations, we may conclude that this one qualitative study's participants might have expressed the perceptions of many. This understanding urges educators to attend to the needs of those innumerous learners whose silenced needs have been voiced by the ones who selflessly enrolled in this study to give their helping hand to all that are in need. These students came to help and advocate for the millions of learners who, though struggling, might feel too embarrassed to ask for help. They still often achieve, somewhat lower or higher, through a chain of failures, peaking frustrations, and exacerbating feeling helpless and lonely in their academic battles.

So, concluding my quest for the Lingua Franca, I pose here my final question of ***Why?*** - Why is that needed to have learners go through the intellectual and emotional torments? Instead, educators can multimodally facilitate their students' learning, so they study and take their challenging but multimodally-assisted work as the intellectual pleasure, to their instructors' great joy! Thus, I invite my readers to undertake this caring and welcoming endeavor, in addition to all their hard and relentless teaching work, much of which might be eased with the inclusion of the Multimodal and universally understandable language in the classroom instruction, for a great benefit to students' academic and further professional success.

REFERENCES

Bain, K. (2004). *What the best college teachers do*. Harvard University Press.

Callow, J. (2014). *The shape of text to come: How image and text work*. PETAA.

Franks, A., & Jewitt, C. (2001). The meaning of action in learning and teaching. *British Educational Research Journal, 27*(2), 201–218. DOI: 10.1080/01411920120037144

Gee, J. P. (2004). *What video-games have to teach us about learning and literacy*. Palgrave.

Gee, J. P. (2007). *Social linguistics and literacy: Ideology in discourses*. Routledge. DOI: 10.4324/9780203944806

Gould, O. (2015, December). *How multimodal features influence college-level International students' reading comprehension of traditional print-based texts*. Paper presentation at the 65th annual meeting of Literacy Research Association (LRA), San Diego, CA.

Gould, O. (2016, February). *How multimodal features influence polylingual EAL speaking college students' reading comprehension of traditional print-based texts*. Research Component paper presented at the12th Midwinter meeting of National Council of Teachers of English Assembly for Research (NCTEAR), University of Eastern Michigan, Ypsilanti, MI.

Gould, O. (June 12, 2017). *'Please, tell them!': Voices from university classrooms on the effects of multimodality on polylingual EAL speaking college students' meaning making*. (Doctoral dissertation). ProQuest LLC.

Gould-Yakovleva, O. (2023a). Seeking remedy for improving international college students' reading comprehension: A qualitative case study on using multimodality for English language learning. *International Journal of Higher Education Pedagogies, 4*(4), 33–54. DOI: 10.33422/ijhep.v4i4.599

Gould-Yakovleva, O. (2023b). Voices from university classrooms on effects of multimodality on polylingual EAL college students' meaning making. *International Journal of Second and Foreign Language Education, 2*(2), 1–19. DOI: 10.33422/ijsfle.v2i2.450

Jewitt, C. (2009). *The handbook of multimodal analysis*. Routledge.

Jewitt, C., & Kress, G. R. (2003). *Multimodal literacy*. P. Lang.

Kress, G. (2011). *Multimodality: A social semiotic approach to contemporary communication*. Routledge.

Kress, G., & van Leeuwen, T. (1996). *Reading images: The grammar of visual design*. Routledge.

Kress, G., & van Leeuwen, T. (2002). Colour as a semiotic mode: Notes for a grammar of colour. *Visual Communication, 1*(3), 333–354. DOI: 10.1177/147035720200100306

Norris, S. (2004). *Analyzing Multimodal Interaction: A Methodological Framework*. Routledge. DOI: 10.4324/9780203379493

Stokoe, W. C. (1960). *Sign language structure: an outline of the visual communication systems of the American deaf*. Department of Anthropology and Linguistics, University of Buffalo.

van Leeuwen, T. (2004). *Introducing social semiotics*. Routledge. DOI: 10.4324/9780203647028

Vygotsky, L. S. (1978). *Mind in society: The development of higher psychological processes*. Harvard University Press.

Vygotsky, L. S. (1987). *The collected works of L. S. Vygotsky: Vol. 1. Problems of general psychology, including the volume thinking and speech* (R. W. Rieber & A. S. Carton, Eds., Trans. N. Minick). New York: Plenum.

Vygotsky, L. S. (2000). *Psychology*. EKSMO-Press.

Appendices

APPENDIX A. SURVEYS AND QUESTIONNAIRES

A1. Demographic Informational Survey

Protocol: The demographic informational survey (DIS) was administered to participants in written form. Participants read the DIS survey and responded. The DIS survey was administered before reading the stand alone (no support from audio/video) text.

Directions: Please, complete with brief answers.

Demographic Informational Survey Questions:

1. Where are you from?
2. What is your mother tongue?
3. How many languages do you speak? Please, list these languages.
4. What is your highest degree?
5. Where did you get your education?
6. What is your major?
7. How often do you read in English?
8. What types of texts do you read in English?
9. How easy is it for you to read the texts you want to read in English?
10. Are there texts you cannot read or struggle to read in English? Please, briefly describe.
11. How much do you like reading in English?

A2. Reflection Questions After Reading Text 1 (No Support)

Protocol: This post-reading reflection was administered to participants in written form. Participants read this questionnaire and responded on their own. The post-reading assessment was administered after reading the stand alone (no support from audio / video) Text 1.

Directions: Please, complete with brief answers.

Reflection Questions After Reading Text I (No Support):

1. How difficult was it for you to understand the print-based text? (Circle one that applies).
   a. No work at all
   b. Very easy
   c. Easy
   d. A bit hard
   e. Hard
   f. Very Hard
2. If you were offered another text with the test questions to answer, what type of support would you prefer?
   a. Video
   b. Audio
   c. Both
   d. None of the above
3. What strategies did you implement when reading the text and answering the test questions? Choose all that apply from the list below (Please, mark **ONLY** those ones that **YOU USED** while working at the text and the test questions):
   a. Text features
   b. Key-word matching
   c. Making predictions
   d. Identifying the main idea
   e. Compare and contrast
   f. Cause and effect
   g. Using context clues
   h. Making Inferences
   i. Text marking strategy
   j. Organizing the information graphically
   k. Sequencing the events
   l. Summarizing
   m. Observing actions of the characters
   n. Examining facial expressions

o. Listening to the character's speeches
p. Understanding the intonation of the speeches
q. Observing the movements and gestures of the characters
r. Evaluating emotions of the characters
s. Associating yourself with a character while watching and/or reading

A3. Reflection Questions After Reading Text 2 (AUDIO)

Protocol: This post-reading reflection was administered to participants in written form. Participants read this questionnaire and responded on their own. The post-reading assessment was administered after reading Text 2 (with audio support).

Directions: Please, complete the questionnaire. Circle the answer that applies.

Reflection Questions After Reading Text 2 (AUDIO):

1. How difficult was it for you to understand the print-based text? (Circle one that applies).
   a. It was no work at all
   b. Pretty easy
   c. Not hard
   d. A bit hard
   e. Hard
   f. Very Hard
2. Has the addition of audio helped you to better understand the text or not
   a. Quite the opposite! It did not help at all!
   b. Not that much.
   c. It helped a very, very small amount.
   d. Helped at some moments.
   e. Was pretty helpful.
   f. Helped a lot!
3. How much did the audio prevent you from focusing on the content of the text or distracted you?
   a. Quite the opposite! It kept me focused.
   b. It did not distract me at all.
   c. It did not distract me that much.
   d. Distracted at some moments.
   e. Was pretty distracting.
   f. Was extremely distracting!
4. If you were offered another text with the test questions to answer, what type of support would you prefer?
   a. Video

b. Audio

c. Both

d. None of the above

5. What strategies did you implement when reading Text 2 and answering the test questions? Choose all that apply from the list below (Please, mark **ONLY** those ones that **YOU USED** while working at the text and the test questions):

   a. Text features
   b. Key-word matching
   c. Making predictions
   d. Identifying the main idea
   e. Compare and contrast
   f. Cause and effect
   g. Using context clues
   h. Making Inferences
   i. Text marking strategy
   j. Organizing the information graphically
   k. Sequencing the events
   l. Summarizing
   m. Observing actions of the characters
   n. Examining facial expressions
   o. Listening to the character's speeches
   p. Understanding the intonation of the speeches
   q. Observing the movements and gestures of the characters
   r. Evaluating emotions of the characters
   s. Associating yourself with a character while watching and/or reading

A4. Reflection Questions After Reading Text 3 (VIDEO & AUDIO)

Protocol: This post-reading reflection was administered to participants in written form. Participants read this questionnaire and responded on their own. The post-reading assessment was administered after reading Text 3 (with video and audio support).

Directions: Please, complete the questionnaire. Circle the answer that applies.

Reflection Questions After Reading Text 3 (VIDEO & AUDIO):

1. How difficult was it for you to understand the print-based text?
   1. It was no work at all
   2. Pretty easy
   3. Not hard
   4. A bit hard

5. Hard
6. Very Hard

2. Has the addition of video helped you to better understand the text or not?
    1. Quite the opposite!
       It did not help at all!
    2. Not that much.
    3. It helped a very, very small amount.
    4. Helped at some moments.
    5. Was pretty helpful.
    6. Helped a lot!
3. How much did the video prevent you from focusing on the content of the text or distracted you?
    1. Quite the opposite! It kept me focused.
    2. It did not distract me at all.
    3. It did not distract me that much.
    4. Distracted at some moments.
    5. Was pretty distracting.
    6. Was extremely distracting!
4. If you were offered another text with the test questions to answer, what type of support would you prefer?
    a. Video
    b. Audio
    c. Both
    d. None of the above
5. What strategies did you implement when reading Text 3 and answering the test questions? Choose all that apply from the list below (Please, mark **ONLY** those ones that **YOU USED** while working at the text and the test questions):
    a. Text features
    b. Key-word matching
    c. Making predictions
    d. Identifying the main idea
    e. Compare and contrast
    f. Cause and effect
    g. Using context clues
    h. Making Inferences
    i. Text marking strategy
    j. Organizing the information graphically
    k. Sequencing the events
    l. Summarizing
    m. Observing actions of the characters

n. Examining facial expressions
o. Listening to the character's speeches
p. Understanding the intonation of the speeches
q. Observing the movements and gestures of the characters
r. Evaluating emotions of the characters
s. Associating yourself with a character while watching and/or reading

APPENDIX B. INTERVIEW QUESTIONS

B1. Day One. First Interview Questions (NO SUPPORT / AUDIO)

Protocol: First Interview was administered individually with each research participant as the final task on Day 1 in the project. In the first interview, students were asked to reflect on their experiences working with print-based *Text 1* (with no support) and *Text 2* (audio support), and answering comprehension questions to these texts.

Directions: Please, answer the interview questions.

Section A:

1. What brought you to the United States?
2. Tell me a little about what it feels like to be attending an American college.
   a. What do you feel is different?
   b. What seems the same or similar?
   c. What is the greatest challenge for you in attending an American college?
3. Do you have to read much? Tell me, please, about what you have to read in English and for what purposes.
4. Can you share your experiences with reading:
   a. Do you like reading? Why or why not?
   b. What do you enjoy about reading?
   c. Are there some parts of reading you do not enjoy?
   d. Is reading ever a struggle?
   e. When is reading a struggle?
5. How familiar are you with the story of Romeo and Juliet?
6. How do you feel about the *Text 1* offered you to read? Was it hard to work with the *Text 1* and the test questions? Please, tell me about your perceptions during your work with the print-based *Text 1*.

7. What strategies did you implement to answer the comprehension questions to the *Text 1*?
8. Could you tell me what strategies and methods, if any, did you use when looking for the answers to the test questions, please?
9. Is that the way you always work with the test questions to the texts? Tell me what usually works best for you, please.
10. Could you recollect your studies in your home-country: What were the strategies, if at all, your teachers advised you to implement while working at the test-questions to the text when you studied in your home-country?

Section B:

1. Have you ever been taught how to use multimodal features with the purpose to better understand texts? (Multimodal just means using those features like images, color, sound, and so on). If yes, what would be your best advice to a learner who is new to multimodality?
2. Do you believe addition of audio to the print-based *Text 2* helped you to better understand the text or not? Please, tell me how the sound helped or hindered your understanding of the print-based *Text 2*.
3. Tell me, please, what exactly information, if any, have you got from the audio rather than from the print-based *Text 2*?
4. If you were a teacher, what support, if any, would you add to the text to help your students better understand the content?
5. Do you believe the addition of audio to the print-based *Text 2* distracted you from focusing on the content of the text at some point rather than helped you understand it? Please, tell me about your perceptions.
6. Do you believe addition of audio to print-based texts could be helpful or not? What are the advantages, if any, and disadvantages, if at all, of addition of audio to print-based texts?

B2. Day Two: Second Interview Questions (VIDEO)

Protocol: Second Interview was administered individually with each research participant as the final task on Day 2 in the project. In the second interview, students were asked to reflect on their experiences working with print-based *Text 3* (video with sound support) compared to their previous experiences working with print-based *Text 1* (with no support) and *Text 2* (audio support), and answering comprehension questions to these texts.

Directions: Please, answer the interview questions.

Section A:

1. How do you feel about the *Text 3* offered you to read? Was it hard to work with the *Text 3* and the test questions?
2. Please, tell me about your perceptions during your work with *Text 3*.
3. Could you tell me what strategies and methods, if any, did you use when looking for the answers to the test questions, please?
4. Do you believe addition of video to the print-based *Text 3* helped you to better understand the text or not? Please, tell me more about how video helped or hindered your understanding of the print-based *Text 3*.
5. Tell me, please, what exactly information, if any, have you gotten from the video rather than from the print-based *Text 3*?
6. What did you find more helpful: text only, audio, or video? Can you explain why?
7. Do you believe addition of the video to the print-based *Text 3* distracted you from focusing on the content of the text at some point rather than helped you understand it? Please, tell me about your perceptions.
8. Do you believe addition of video to print-based texts could be helpful or not? What are the advantages, if any, and disadvantages, if at all, of addition of video to print-based texts?
9. If you were a teacher, what support, if any, would you add to the text to help your students better understand the content?

Section B:

1. In previous interview, we talked a little about what you read. Can you tell me about what format you read most often (e.g., printed books, articles, phone, tablet, computer)?
2. What are the main resources for you to get information if you need it?
3. How do you usually read? Tell me a little bit about your daily readings.

APPENDIX C. TRANSCRIPTS TO MULTIMODAL ANALYSES 1 AND 2

C1. Transcript to Multimodal Analysis 1: Attempting to Understand Role, Position, and Significance of Visuals within Multimodal Ensembles

Episode of a video under analysis: Franco Zeffirelli Romeo and Juliet, Act I, Scene IV. Utterances produced by actors in the episode:

1:25 – 1:42
Juliet: Come hither, nurse. What is yond gentleman?
Nurse: Who? Paris?
Juliet: No, What's he that follows there?
Nurse: Ah… Oh, I know not.
Juliet: Go ask his name.
1:44 – 1:48
Tybalt: Hm, Romeo, from the House of Montague.
Nurse: What?!
1:49 – 1:54
Nurse: His name is Romeo. And he's a Montague;
The only son of your great enemy.
1:55 – 2:12
Juliet: My only love sprung from my only hate!
Too early seen unknown, and know, and known too late.
Prodigious birth of love it is to me,
That I must love a loathed enemy.
2:25 – end of the episode
(Shakespeare, 1597)

Transcript conventions: "Same" – means: the image lasts. Texts in red print – Juliet. Texts in dark blue print – Nurse. Texts in purple print – Tybalt.

Table 1.

Time	Character speech	Character position	Head movement	Gaze
1:25	Line 1 Juliet: ***Come hither, nurse.***	Leaning towards the nurse, slightly cowering	Pulls her head into her shoulder.	Fixed on Romeo
1:28	Line 2 **Nurse:** ***Um?***	Open, straight, leaning backwards, laid back	Leans her head towards the nurse's shoulder.	Looks at someone from top to down and backwards. Quick look at Juliet, then keeps roaming the room to find the person Juliet points to.
1:29	Line 3 **Juliet:** ***What is yond gentleman?***	Slightly leans to the nurse.	Moves her head as close to the nurse's head / ear as possible.	Fixed on Romeo
1:30	Line 4 **Nurse:** ***Who?***	Stands straight.	Keeps her head up.	Gaze is roaming the room.
1:31	Line 5 **Nurse:** ***PARIS?***	Leans towards Juliet to be able to better follow the direction of her gaze.	Nurse leans her head very close to Juliet's head.	Gaze examines people from head to foot.
1:32	Line 6 **Juliet:** ***No,***	Is cowering more towards the nurse.	Bends her head down, as if pulls her head into her shoulders.	Gaze fixed on Romeo.
1:33	Line 7 **Juliet:** ***What's he that follows there?***	Cowers and leans towards the nurse.	Bends her head very low down as if trying to be less noticeable.	Gaze fixed on Romeo only.
1:35	Line 8 **Nurse:** ***Ah...***	The nurse stands straight.	Nurse's head is facing Romeo.	Examines directly and straightforwardly the person Juliet points to with the deictic gesture of her for-finger.
1:37	Line 9 **Nurse:** ***Oh...I know not.***	Leans backwards in the posture that indicates surprise.	Nurse's head is turned to her right to look directly into Juliet's face.	Then, looks down to her right into Juliet's face to tell her she has no knowledge. Then looks at Romeo (prior to going to ask his name).
1:39	Line 10 **Juliet:** ***Go ask his name.***	Makes some tiny steps backwards.	Head is positioned straight towards Romeo.	Gaze fixed on Romeo.
1:40	Juliet (Stays alone)	Slowly moves backwards in tiny steps, ½ to audience.	Head is in fixed position, faces straight in front of herself.	Juliet is steadily looking at Romeo.
1:43	**Line 11 Nurse: *(Her whispering is inaudible).***	Leans very close to Tybalt. Cowers to keep secrecy.	The nurse pulls her head into her shoulders and turns toward Tybalt.	Looks at Romeo, then into Tybalt's face questioning him.
1:43	Line 11 **Tybalt:** ***Hm...***	Stands as if hiding under the wall.	Bends his head down, his chin almost to the chest observing Romeo.	Instant looks at Romeo.
1:44	Line 12 **Tybalt:** ***Romeo.***	Stands as if in ambush, hiding, trying to be unnoticeable.	Turns his head to his left to the nurse, bends his head down, as if hiding.	Then immediately back to the nurse to his right, directly into her face.
1:45	Line 13 **Tybalt:** ***From the House of Montague***	Turns his body towards the nurse.	Confirms the nurse's understanding with the firm nod of his chin.	Then, watchfully, returns to his "job" - to observing Montague's actions.
1:46	Line 14 **Nurse:** ***WHAT?!***	First frizzes on her spot. Then, runs back cowering very low. Tries to be less visible.	Bends her head very low down, pulls her head into her shoulders.	Freezes for a moment looking over her shoulder at Juliet. Then looks down.
1:48	Line 15 **Nurse:** ***His name is Romeo.***	Bends forward towards Juliet.	Face-to-face with Juliet	Looks straight into Juliet's eyes.

continued on following page

Table 1. Continued

Time	Character speech	Character position	Head movement	Gaze
1:49	Line 16 **Nurse:** ***And he's a Montague;***	Withdraws herself from Juliet.	Chin down and then up – this movement adds power to the words.	First, she looks into Juliet's face with the eyes full of fear, then looks down to gather more power, and has a much stronger look into Juliet's eyes.
1:50	Line 17 **Nurse:** ***The only son of your great ENEMY. Ah!..***	Turns around and freezes with fear again at the sight of Romeo. Body position open to the audience, ½ to Juliet.	Head turned to her left to be able look over her shoulder.	Straight into the eyes. Looks backwards at Romeo with fear and gasps for air.
1:55	Line 18 **Juliet:** ***Ah…My only love sprung from my only hate!***	Slowly steps backwards.	Head faces front. Frozen position.	Looks straight in front of her as if through the air.
2:06	Line 19 **Juliet:** ***Too early seen unknown,***	Body is lifeless.	Head faces front.	Looks straight in front of her as if through the air.
2:07	Line 20 **Juliet:** ***and know, and know too late.***	Body leans forward towards audience.	Slowly moves her head from side to side.	Looks straight in front of her as if through the air.
2:13	Line 21 **Juliet:** ***Ah!.. Prodigious birth of love it is to me,***	Helplessly leans backwards towards the wall. As if losing the energy.	In a strengthless motion moves her head up and backwards.	Closes her eyes.
2:18	Line 22 **Juliet:** ***That I must love a loathed enemy.***	Leans backwards towards the wall.	Moves her head from side to side face upwards in despair.	Eyes are closed.
2:20	Tybalt (in silence with dreary music in the background)	Turns ¾ to his right towards Juliet (who stands behind his back).	Turns his head to his far right.	Looks intensively at Juliet to verify his guess.
2:22	Juliet (Sighs out; mourning sound of French horns and trombones in the background)	Stands almost positioned up front towards the audiences.	Head is leaning backwards.	Eyes are closed.
2:25	Tybalt (silent, with threatening gloomy music in the background). Shakespeare (1597).	Is turning away from the audiences ready to go away.	The chin of his head goes forward and down.	Malicious look in his eyes.

C2. Transcript to Multimodal Analysis 2: Visual Language Intermodal Relations Data Analysis

Multimodal analysis of a video snapshot from F. Zeffirelli's (1968) production of Shakespeare's play *Romeo and Juliet.* Minutes: 36:36 to 38:30 (in the excerpt used for this paper: 0:01 – 1:54.

Table 2.

Time	Actors	Verbal Text	Color	Image	Action/Position/ Movement in the Space	Facial Expression	Gesture	Background Sounds	Framework
0:01- 0:07 – 0:07- 0:19	Nurse and Juliet	N: Juliet? Lady Juliet! J: Nurse N: Your mother craves to have a word with you.	Reds and golds in Juliet's garment. White headgear and dark maroon dress of the nurse. Dark red-gold of the curtain.	The nurse, lots of fruits in gorgeous vases, wine in goblets and carafes, heavy rich curtain, lots of large candles in chandeliers	Nurse: faces the audience. Juliet: Looks down, fixes her hair behind her neck with her right hand very quickly. Nurse turns her back to the audience, is leaving the space.	Nurse: Excited, happy. Juliet: Embarrassed, overwhelmed.	Nurse: calling Juliet up with her right hand. Juliet: Fixes her hair shyly with her left hand.	Merry music, excited chatting crowd.	Franks, A., & Jewitt, C. (2001). The meaning of action in learning and teaching. *British Educational Research Journal*, *27*(2), 201-218.
0:20- 0:25	Nurse stays, Juliet leaves promptly.	N: Make haste! Make haste!	Reds, golds, cognac, bronze, greens and plum colors of fruit.	Lots of gorgeous fruits and wine in the front. The crowd of guests of the Capulet's house in the back.	Juliet: runs away to the left behind the curtain. Nurse: Returns to the front of the screen, sneaky looks around, and pores some wine in a large goblet and drinks greedily.	Nurse: sneaky, excited.	Nurse moves the fingers of her right hand with excitement over her idea to sneak some expensive wine from the masters' table. Pores if with her right hand, the goblet in her left hand.	Merry music, excited chatting crowd.	Franks, A., & Jewitt, C. (2001). The meaning of action in learning and teaching. *British Educational Research Journal*, *27*(2), 201-218.
0:26- 0:38	Romeo and Nurse	R: Who is her mother? N: Um?.. Merry bachelor, Her mother is the lady of the house, And a good lady, and wise and virtuous. I nurs'd her daughter that you talk'd withal. Um!	Black metallic mask and dark costume of Romeo. Black and maroon dress and white headgear of the Nurse.	Romeo: from torso up. He hides his face behind the mask, but the lower part of his face can be seen. Nurse: keeps poring wine.	Nurse is ¾ towards the audience. She keeps adding some more and a bit more wine. Looks up front at the audiences several times repeatedly. Romeo leans front towards the audiences.	Nurse: bragging, proud, happy, excited.	Romeo hides his face behind the mask with his left hand. Nurse makes some left-hand-up gesture.	Merry music. Excited chatting crowd.	Franks, A., & Jewitt, C. (2001). The meaning of action in learning and teaching. *British Educational Research Journal*, *27*(2), 201-218.

continued on following page

Table 2. Continued

Time	Actors	Verbal Text	Color	Image	Action/Position/ Movement in the Space	Facial Expression	Gesture	Background Sounds	Framework
0:39-0:44	Romeo	Romeo moves silently.	Black metallic mask and dark costume of Romeo. Greens, yellows, and plum colors of fruits. Plain color of the wall.	The scene changes drastically: from the rich and multiple fruits and wines of bright colors Romeo moves to the spot with barren vault-like walls at the background. Empty goblet in front of him (symbol of vain endeavor), burning candles.	Romeo hides his face behind the mask. The lower part of his face is now also hidden behind his wrist. He moves to a contrasting different background to the left.	Right hand in front of his face holding the mask steadily.	Merry music. Excited chatting crowd.		Kress, G., & van Leeuwen, T. (2002). Colour as a semiotic mode: Notes for a grammar of colour. *Visual Communication*, 1(3), 333-354.
0:45-0:52	Nurse and Romeo	N: I tell you, he that can lay hold of her Shall have the chinks.	Black metallic mask and dark costume of Romeo. Black/maroon dress and white headgear of the Nurse. Barren-brown wall.	Nurse is greedily drinking wine and talking to Romeo. Romeo stands in the farthest end of the space.	Nurse ¾ to the audience. Shows the sign of a coin forming a circle with the thumb and the for-finger of her right hand.	Speaks as if giving out a secret. Nurse winks with her right eye.	Shows the sign of a coin forming a circle with the thumb and the for-finger of her right hand.	Merry music. Excited chatting crowd.	Franks, A., & Jewitt, C. (2001). The meaning of action in learning and teaching. *British Educational Research Journal*, 27(2), 201-218.
0:53-1:05	Nurse and Romeo	R (whispers): Is she a Capulet? O dear account? My life is my foe's debt.	Dark, black.	Nurse's back. Romeo facing front.	Nurse is leaving the scene, running away behind the curtain. Romeo's stays alone. Romeo shakes his head while speaking.	Romeo's face is sad and pale and still. Disappointed, shocked.	Nurse removed the curtain with her left hand while running away. Romeo's hand holding the mask helplessly goes down to his chest. Then, he promptly puts his mask back on.	Merry music. Excited chatting crowd.	Franks, A., & Jewitt, C. (2001). The meaning of action in learning and teaching. *British Educational Research Journal*, 27(2), 201-218.

continued on following page

Table 2. Continued

Time	Actors	Verbal Text	Color	Image	Action/Position/ Movement in the Space	Facial Expression	Gesture	Background Sounds	Framework
1:06-1:19	Guests of the house of Caplets. Juliet's father.	Ha-ha-ha! Capulet: Oh! Watch out my mistresses! Nay, gentlemen, prepare not to be gone; We have a trifling foolish banquet towards. Is it e'en so? why, then, I thank you all I thank you, honest gentlemen; good night. More torches here! Come on then, let's to bed. Ah, sirrah, by my fay, it waxes late: I'll to my rest.	Bright reds, golds, bronze.	Happy, laughing, talking guests of the House of Capulets are leaving the ball.	People are moving up front towards the audience. Everybody stops and looks backwards at Juliet's father. At the end of his speech, ladies laugh leaning backwards and bending forwards. A page crosses the stage from rig ht to left carrying the lights.	Happy, laughing, smiling, excited.	A lady is waving her left hand to cool her face down. He partner is gesticulating while speaking to convey his idea.	Merry music. Excited chatting crowd.	Franks, A., & Jewitt, C. (2001). The meaning of action in learning and teaching. *British Educational Research Journal, 27*(2), 201-218.
1:20-1:32	Juliet, Nurse, Paris	Paris: Good night.	Reds and golds in Juliet's garment. White headgear and black/maroon dress of the nurse. Cold blue and silver of Paris' outfit.	Juliet ¾, almost her back to the audience, the nurse farther behind her, also, ¾ to us. Paris ¾ to the audience but facing front and towards Juliet.	Paris kisses Juliet's hand. Juliet and the nurse at the left of the screen, Paris stands at the right of the screen, then, he leaves to the right. Nurse makes a couple of steps forward, smiles to someone to the right.	Juliet looks lost and overwhelmed. Paris's face looks cold, but he gives a brief smile to Juliet. Nurse looks at Paris with negative attitude, almost disgust.	When saying goodbye, Paris lifts Juliet's hand up, to his lips.	Sounds of the excited happy crowd. Same music slows down and the sound is remote.	Kress, G., & van Leeuwen, T. (2002). Colour as a semiotic mode: Notes for a grammar of colour. *Visual Communication, 1*(3), 333-354.

continued on following page

Table 2. Continued

Time	Actors	Verbal Text	Color	Image	Action/Position/ Movement in the Space	Facial Expression	Gesture	Background Sounds	Framework
1:33-1:42	Juliet, Nurse, Romeo	J: Come hither, nurse. What is yond gentlemen? N: Paris? J: No, What's he that follows there? N: Oh, I know not. J: Go ask his name: If he be married, my grave is like to be my wedding bed.	Reds and golds in Juliet's garment. White headgear and black/maroon dress of the nurse. Heavy, velvety, rich dark reds, bronze, and golds of the crowd. Men wear black.	Leaving guests all over the back of the screen. Nurse and Juliet at the front, the closest to the audiences in the left front corner. Romeo is at the Back right corner.	Nurse makes two steps back to Juliet. Romeo ¾ to us at the very back of the scene looking back towards the audiences, at Juliet. Juliet is ½ to the audience looking at Romeo only. Juliet leans back to the wall.	Juliet is very focused on Romeo, her look is very serious. Nurse looks puzzled.	Nurse's hands are hidden under her apron. Juliet point to Romeo with her fore finger.	Sounds of the excited happy crowd. Same music slows down, its sound is remote.	Franks, A., & Jewitt, C. (2001). The meaning of action in learning and teaching. *British Educational Research Journal*, *27*(2), 201-218.
1:44-1:48	Nurse, Tybalt	T: Hm, Romeo, from the House of Montague. N: What?!	Black and dark of Tybalt's outfit. White headgear and black/ maroon dress of the nurse.	Tybalt at the back wall, the farthest from the audience. Nurse leans forward and towards Tybalt while secretly conversing with him.	Both: Nurse and Tybalt stand at the farthest back of the stage. Nurse bends down as if hiding while whispering to Tybalt. Tybalt stands straight, but in the shadow as if observing and guarding. Nurse freezes then runs to Juliet	Nurse looks with curiosity and the look of secret in her face. Tybalt looks gloomy with hatred. Nurse face freezes with fear when she gets the reply about Romeo.	Nurse describes the mask of Romeo with her both hands, then points to Romeo from under her chin, secretly.	Sounds of the excited happy crowd.	Franks, A., & Jewitt, C. (2001). The meaning of action in learning and teaching. *British Educational Research Journal*, *27*(2), 201-218.
1:49-1:54	Juliet, Nurse, Romeo	N: His name is Romeo. And he's a Montague, the only son of your great enemy! (Shakespeare, 1597).	Reds and golds in Juliet's garment. White headgear, black/ maroon dress of the nurse. Heavy, velvety, rich dark reds, bronze, and golds of the crowd.	Nurse is reporting the news she had just learned to Juliet.	Nurse is ½ to the audience on the right, Juliet is ¾ away from the audiences on the left. Juliet is leaning towards the nurse. Juliet makes a half-step backwards.	Nurse looks terrified.	Juliet's arms hang down lifelessly.	Sounds of the excited happy crowd.	Franks, A., & Jewitt, C. (2001). The meaning of action in learning and teaching. *British Educational Research Journal*, *27*(2), 201-218.

Compilation of References

Ainsworth, S., Griffiths, D., Macrory, G., & Pahl, K. (2023). *Multimodality and multilingualism: Towards an integrative approach*. Multilingual Matters.

Ajayi, L. (2008). Meaning-making, **multimodal** representation, and transformative pedagogy: An exploration of meaning construction instructional practices in an ESL high school classroom. *Journal of Language, Identity, and Education*, *7*(3/4), 206–229. DOI: 10.1080/15348450802237822

Ajayi, L. (2009). English as a second language learners' exploration of multimodal texts in a junior high school. *Journal of Adolescent & Adult Literacy*, *52*(7), 585–595. DOI: 10.1598/JAAL.52.7.4

Ajayi, L. (2015). Critical multimodal literacy: How Nigerian female students critique texts and reconstruct unequal social structures. *Journal of Literacy Research*, *47*(2), 216–244. DOI: 10.1177/1086296X15618478

Archer, A. (2025). Multimodality and the affordances of co-presence for inclusion in higher education. *Designs for Learning*, *16*(1), 1–8. DOI: 10.16993/dfl.230

Archer, A., & Price, C. (2021). Assessment, recognition and the contact zone: How much is 'enough'? *Education as Change*, *25*, 1–18. DOI: 10.25159/1947-9417/8741

Baildon, M., & Damico, J. S. (2009). How do we know?: Students examine issues of credibility with a complicated multimodal web-based text. *Curriculum Inquiry*, *39*(2), 265–285. DOI: 10.1111/j.1467-873X.2009.00443.x

Bain, K. (2004). *What the best college teachers do*. Harvard University Press.

Bakhtin, M. M. (1935, 1979). *Эстетика словесного творчества* [The aesthetics of verbal art]. Moscow: Iskusstvo.

Bakhtin, M. M. (1981). Discourse in the novel. In Holquist, M. (Ed.), *The dialogic imagination: Four essays by M. M. Bakhtin* (pp. 259–422). University of Texas Press.

Bakhtin, M., Holquist, M., & Emerson, C. (1981). *The dialogic imagination: Four essays by M.M. Bakhtin*. University of Texas Press.

Bergen, B. K. (2012). *Louder than words: The new science of how the mind makes meaning*. Basic Books.

Bezemer, J., & Kress, G. (2016). *Multimodality, Learning and Communication: A Social Semiotic Frame*. Routledge.

Binder, M., & Kotsopoulos, S. (2011). Multimodal literacy narratives: Weaving the threads of young children's identity through the arts. *Journal of Research in Childhood Education, 25*(4), 339–363. DOI: 10.1080/02568543.2011.606762

Bogatyrev, P. (1971). *Voprosy teorii narodnogo iskusstva*. Iskusstvo.

Bogatyrev, P. (1971). *Вопросы теории народного искусства* [Questions of the theory of the volk art]. Iskusstvo.

Breuer, E., & Archer, A. (2016). *Multimodality in higher education*. Brill. DOI: 10.1163/9789004312067

Bronfenbrenner, U. (1979). *The ecology of human development: Experiments by nature and design*. Harvard University Press. DOI: 10.4159/9780674028845

Bronfenbrenner, U. (1993). Ecological models of human development. In Gauvan, M., & Cole, M. (Eds.), *Readings on the development of children* (pp. 37–43). Freeman.

Brown, A., & Eskildsen, S. W. (2024). *Multimodality across epistemologies in second language research*. Routledge. DOI: 10.4324/9781003355670

Bruce, D. L. (2009a). Reading and writing video: Media literacy and adolescents. In Christenbury, L., Bomer, R., & Smagorinsky, P. (Eds.), *Handbook of adolescent literacy research* (pp. 287–333). The Guilford Press.

Bruce, D. L. (2009b). Writing visual images: Examining the video composition processes of highs school students. *Research in the Teaching of English, 43*(4), 426–450. DOI: 10.58680/rte20097073

Bruce, D. L., & Chiu, M. M. (2015). Composing with new technology: Teacher reflections on learning digital video. *Journal of Teacher Education, 66*(3), 272–287. DOI: 10.1177/0022487115574291

Callow, J. (2012). The rules of visual engagement: Images as tools for learning. *Screen Education*, (65), 72–79.

Callow, J. (2014). *The shape of text to come: How image and text work*. PETAA.

Callow, J., & Zammit, K. (2012). "Where lies your text?" ("Twelfth Night" act I, scene V): Engaging high school students from low socioeconomic backgrounds in reading multimodal texts. *Engineers Australia, 47*(2), 69–77.

Cekaite, A., & Evaldsson, A. (2008). Stating linguistic identities and negotiating monolingual norms in multiethnic school setting. *International Journal of Multilingualism, 5*(3), 177–196. DOI: 10.1080/14790710802387588

Cloonan, A. (2011). Creating multimodal metalanguage with teachers. *English Teaching, 10*(4), 23–40.

Connery, M. C., John-Steiner, V. P., & Marjanovic-Shane, A. (2010). *Vygotsky and creativity: A cultural-historical approach to play, meaning making, and the arts.* Peter Lang. DOI: 10.3726/978-1-4539-0060-4

Creswell, J. W. (2007). *Qualitative inquiry and research design: Choosing among five traditions.* Sage Publications.

de Saussure, F. (1959). *Course in general linguistics.* Philosophical Library.

Duncum, P. (2004). Visual culture isn't just visual: Multiliteracy, multimodality and meaning. *Studies in Art Education: A Journal of Issues and Research in Art Education, 45*(3), 252-264.

Ely, M., Anzul, M., Friedman, T., Garner, D., & Steinmetz, A. M. (1994). *Doing qualitative research: Circles within circles.* The Palmer Press.

Ericson, K., & Häikiö, T. K. (2025). Visuality and multimodality as tools for learning in geography and art education. *Journal of Aesthetic Education, 59*(2), 50–73. DOI: 10.5406/15437809.59.2.05

Exley, B., & Cottrell, A. (2012). Reading in the Australian curriculum English: Describing the effects of structure and organization on multimodal texts. *Engineers Australia, 47*(2), 91–98.

Farrugia, C. A., & Bhandari, R. (2016). *Open doors 2016 report on International educational exchange.* Institute of International Education.

Flesh, R. (1949). *The art of readable writing.* Harper.

Franks, A., & Jewitt, C. (2001). *The meaning of action in learning and teaching.* British Educational Research Journal, 27(2), 201-218.

Franks, A., & Jewitt, C. (2001). The meaning of action in learning and teaching. *British Educational Research Journal, 27*(2), 201–218. DOI: 10.1080/01411920120037144

Gardner (1993). *Multiple intelligences: The theory in practice*. New York, NY: Basic Books.

Gee, J. P. (2014). Foreword. In Frank Serafini (2014 Ed.). *Reading the visual: An introduction to teaching multimodal literacy.* New York and London: Teachers College Press.

Gee, J. P. (2004). *What video-games have to teach us about learning and literacy*. Palgrave.

Gee, J. P. (2007). *Social linguistics and literacy: Ideology in discourses*. Routledge. DOI: 10.4324/9780203944806

Gellevij, M., van der Meij, H., de Jong, T., & Pieters, J. (2002). Multimodal versus unimodal instruction in a complex learning context. *Journal of Experimental Education*, *70*(3), 215–239. DOI: 10.1080/00220970209599507

Giampapa, F. (2010). Multiliteracies, pedagogy and identities: Teacher and student voices from a Toronto elementary school. *Canadian Journal of Education*, *33*(2), 407–431.

Glesne, C. (2010). *Becoming qualitative researchers* (4th ed.). Longman.

Glesne, C., & Peshkin, A. (1992). *Becoming qualitative researchers: An introduction*. Longman.

Goldin-Meadow, S. (2000). Beyond words: The importance of gesture to researchers and learners. *Child Development*, *71*(1), 231–239. DOI: 10.1111/1467-8624.00138 PMID: 10836578

Goodwin, C. (2000). Action and embodiment within situated human interaction. *Journal of Pragmatics*, *32*(10), 1489–1522. DOI: 10.1016/S0378-2166(99)00096-X

Gould, O. (2015, December). *How multimodal features influence college-level International students' reading comprehension of traditional print-based texts.* Paper presentation at the 65th annual meeting of Literacy Research Association (LRA), San Diego, CA.

Gould, O. (2016, February). *How multimodal features influence polylingual EAL speaking college students' reading comprehension of traditional print-based texts.* Research Component paper presented at the12th Midwinter meeting of National Council of Teachers of English Assembly for Research (NCTEAR), University of Eastern Michigan, Ypsilanti, MI.

Gould, O. (June 12, 2017). *'Please, tell them!': Voices from university classrooms on the effects of multimodality on polylingual EAL speaking college students' meaning making*. (Doctoral dissertation). ProQuest LLC.

Gould-Yakovleva, O. (2023a). Seeking remedy for improving international college students' reading comprehension: A qualitative case study on using multimodality for English language learning. *International Journal of Higher Education Pedagogies*, *4*(4), 33–54. DOI: 10.33422/ijhep.v4i4.599

Gould-Yakovleva, O. (2023b). Voices from university classrooms on effects of multimodality on polylingual EAL college students' meaning making. *International Journal of Second and Foreign Language Education*, *2*(2), 1–19. DOI: 10.33422/ijsfle.v2i2.450

Gould-Yakovleva, O. (2024). Demystifying the notion of charisma: Micro-ethnography on a veteran-teacher's classroom practices. *The Qualitative Report*, *29*(4), 1192–1211. DOI: 10.46743/2160-3715/2024.6521

Gould-Yakovleva, O., & Liu, X. (2024). Mutualism as mutual trust: An ethnographic case study on an elementary-school teacher-team participation in a science PD program. *The Qualitative Report*, *29*(4), 915–938. DOI: 10.46743/2160-3715/2024.6440

Gould-Yakovleva, O., McVee, M., & Fronczak, D. (2020). "Ready-ready" to teach: The telling case of a reflective teacher-practitioner. *The Qualitative Report*, *25*(2), 306–319. DOI: 10.46743/2160-3715/2020.4040

Grutman, R. (2006). Refractions and recognition: Literary multilingualism in translation. *Target*, *28*(1), 17–47. DOI: 10.1075/target.18.1.03gru

Halliday, M. A. K. (1978). *Language as social semiotic: The social interpretation of language and meaning*. University Park Press.

Hall, J. (1994). *Illustrated dictionary of symbols in Eastern and Western art*. Westview Press.

Hasty, M. M., & Fain, J. G. (2014). Emergent understandings: Multilingual fourth grade students generating close readings as multimodal responses to global and informal texts. *Perspectives on Urban Education*, *11*(2), 10–20.

Hegelheimer, V. (2006). Helping ESL writers through a multimodal, corpus-based, online grammar resource. *CALICO Journal*, *24*(1), 5–32. DOI: 10.1558/cj.v24i1.5-31

Hostetter, A. B., & Alibali, M. W. (2008). Visible embodiment: Gestures as simulated action. *Psychonomic Bulletin & Review*, *15*(3), 495–514. DOI: 10.3758/PBR.15.3.495 PMID: 18567247

Huang, Y. (2023). Open learning environment for multimodal learning based on knowledge base technology. *International Journal of Emerging Technologies in Learning*, *18*(11), 38–51. DOI: 10.3991/ijet.v18i11.39397

Huang, Y. H. (2012). EFL students' views on writing with pictures, sound, and music. *English Teaching & Learning*, *36*(2), 79–123. DOI: 10.6330/ETL.2012.36.2.03

Institute of International Education. (2024). Enrollment trends. *Open doors.* https://opendoorsdata.org/data/international-students/enrollment-trends/

Iskenderov, F. V., Iskenderov, & E. F., Kostina, E. F. (2008). Азбука чувашских орнаментов и эмблем: Учебно-наглядное пособие для изучающих чувашскую культуру и краеведение [Alphabet of Chuvash ornaments and emblems: Educational and visual aid for students of Chuvash culture and local history]. Russian Federation: Ulyanovsk.

Jacobs, G. E. (2012). Developing multimodal academic literacies among college freshmen. *The Journal of Media Literacy Education*, *4*(3), 244–255.

Jakobson, R. (1981). "Linguistics and poetics" (1960): Poetry of grammar and grammar of poetry. *Selected Writings*, *3*, 18–51.

Jakovlev, P. F. (1924a). Radio-kroniko Sovetlanda [Radio-chronicles of Soviet country]. *Radiolyubitel* [Radio-Amateur], *1*(4), p. 2. http://archive.radio.ru/web/1924/04/001/

Jakovlev, P. F. (1924b). Радиотелефония и международный язык [Wireless telephony and international language]. *Radiolyubitel* [Radio-Amateur], *1*(5), p. 71. http://archive.radio.ru/web/1924/05/008/

Jewitt, C. (2009). *The handbook of multimodal analysis*. Routledge.

Jewitt, C., & Kress, G. R. (2003). *Multimodal literacy*. P. Lang.

Jewitt, C., & Oyama, R. (2001). Visual meaning: A social-semiotic approach. In van Leeuwen, T., & Jewitt, C. (Eds.), *Handbook of visual analysis* (pp. 134–156). Sage.

Jimenez, L. M., & Meyer, C. K. (2016). First impressions matter: Navigating graphic novels utilizing linguistic, visual, and spatial resources. *Journal of Literacy Research*, *48*(4), 423–447. DOI: 10.1177/1086296X16677955

Jung, T. (May 16, 1925). Paŭlo Teodoroviĉ Jakovlev: Prezidanto de Sovetlanda Esp. Unuiĝo [Pavel Feodorovich Jakovlev: President of the Soviet Esperantist Union]. *Heroldo de Esperanto* [Esperanto Herald], *38*(266), p. 2. https://anno.onb.ac.at/pdfs/ONB_e2j_19250516.pdf

Kalantzis, M., & Cope, B. (2008). *New Learning: Elements of a science of education.* Cambridge University Press. DOI: 10.1017/CBO9780511811951

Kaur, S., Ganapathy, M., & Sidhu, G. K. (2012). Designing learning elements using the multiliteracies approach in an ESL writing classroom. *Southeast Asian Journal of English Language Studies, 18*(3), 119–134.

Kincaid, J. P., Fishburne, R. P., Rogers, R. L., & Chissom, B. S. (1975). *Derivation of new readability formulas (automated readability index, fog count, and Flesch reading ease formula) for navy enlisted personnel.* (PDF)*(Report). Naval Air Station Memphis: Chief of Naval Technical Training. Research Branch Report 8–75.* Retrieved March 15, 2024.

Kitson, L. (2011). Reconceptualising understandings of texts, readers and contexts: One English teacher's response to using multimodal texts and interactive whiteboards. *Engineers Australia, 46*(3), 76–86.

Knapp, R., Brimner, J., & White, M. (1959). Educational level, class status, and aesthetic preference. *The Journal of Social Psychology, 50*(2), 277–284. DOI: 10.1080/00224545.1959.9922002

Kress, G. (2011). *Multimodality: A social semiotic approach to contemporary communication.* Routledge.

Kress, G., & van Leeuwen, T. (1996). *Reading images: The grammar of visual design.* Routledge.

Kress, G., & van Leeuwen, T. (2002). Colour as a semiotic mode: Notes for a grammar of colour. *Visual Communication, 1*(3), 333–354. DOI: 10.1177/147035720200100306

Kuo, F. O., Yu, P. T., & Hsiao, W. H. (2013). Develop and evaluate the effect of multimodal presentation system on elementary ESL students. *The Turkish Online Journal of Educational Technology, 12*(4), 29–40.

Lankshear, C., & Knobel, M. (2003). *New literacies: Changing knowledge and classroom learning.* Open University Press.

Lee, S. S. J., Siew, L. L., Tiong, N. D., & Ma, N. (2024). Multimodality in art teacher education in China. *Design, 1*(1), 45–54. DOI: 10.36922/dp.4554

Lenters, K. (2016). Riding the lines and overwriting in the margins: Affect and multimodal literacy practices. *Journal of Literacy Research, 48*(3), 280–316. DOI: 10.1177/1086296X16658982

Lincoln, F., & Rademacher, B. (2006). Learning styles of ESL students in community colleges. *Community College Journal of Research and Practice*, *30*(5/6), 485–500. DOI: 10.1080/10668920500207965

Liu, X., & Qu, D. (2014). Exploring the multimodality of EFL textbooks for Chinese college students: A comparative study. *RELC Journal*, *45*(2), 135–150. DOI: 10.1177/0033688214533865

Lofland, J., & Lofland, L. (1995). *Analyzing social settings: A guide to qualitative observation and analysis*. Wadsworth.

Lysaker, J. T., & Nie, A. Y. (2017). Social and relational aspects of comprehending in one fourth grader's unaided and illustration-aided picturebook retellings: Retelling as co-authoring. *Journal of Literacy Research*, *49*(1), 38–67. DOI: 10.1177/1086296X16684583

Marsh, E. E., & White, M. D. (2003a). A system for image-text relations in a new (and old) media. *Visual Communication*, *4*, 337–371.

Marsh, E. E., & White, M. D. (2003b). A taxonomy of relationships between images and text. *The Journal of Documentation*, *59*(6), 647–672. DOI: 10.1108/00220410310506303

Martinec, R., & Salway, A. (2005). A system for image-text relations in new (and old) media. *Visual Communication*, *4*(3), 337–371. DOI: 10.1177/1470357205055928

Martin, R. (1996). *Scottish clans and family names*. Mainstream Publishing.

Maula, Q. I., & Awwalia, L. (2025). Scrutinizing teachers' practice of multimodality use in elementary English classroom. *KnE Social Sciences*, *10*(12), 69–79. DOI: 10.18502/kss.v10i12.18863

MAXQDA. (2021). MAXQDA 2022 [computer software]. Berlin, Germany: VERBI Software. Available from maxqda.com.

Maxwell, J. A. (2010). Using numbers in qualitative research. *Qualitative Inquiry*, *16*(6), 475–482. DOI: 10.1177/1077800410364740

McNeill, D. (1992). *Hand and mind: What gestures reveal about thought*. University of Chicago Press.

McVee, M. B., Bailey, N. M., & Shanahan, L. E. (2008a). Teachers and teacher educators learning from new literacies and new technologies. *Teaching Education*, *19*(3), 197–210. DOI: 10.1080/10476210802250216

McVee, M. B., Bailey, N. M., & Shanahan, L. E. (2008b). Using digital media to interpret poetry: Spiderman meets Walt Whitman. *Research in the Teaching of English, 43*(2), 112–143. DOI: 10.58680/rte20086774

Meylaerts, R. (2006). Heterolingualism in/and translation: How legitimate are the Other and his/her language? An Introduction. *International Journal of Translation Studies, 18*(1), 1–15. DOI: 10.1075/target.18.1.02mey

Miles, M. B., & Huberman, A. M. (1984). *Qualitative Data Analysis: A sourcebook of New Methods*. Sage Publications.

Millard, J. (May *2006*). *eUSER conceptual and analytical framework*. Part D: e-Government, a deliverable of the European Commission financed eUSER project.

Miller, S. M. (2013). A research metasynthesis on digital video composing in classrooms: An evidence-based framework toward a pedagogy for embodied learning. *Journal of Literacy Research, 45*(4), 386–430. DOI: 10.1177/1086296X13504867

Miller, S. M., & McVee, M. B. (2012a). *Multimodal composing in classrooms: Learning and teaching for the digital world*. Routledge.

Miller, S. M., & McVee, M. B. (2012b). Changing the game: Teaching for embodied learning through multimodal composing. In Miller, S., & McVee, M. (Eds.), *Multimodal composing in classrooms: Learning and teaching for digital world* (pp. 132–152). Routledge.

Mills, K. (2011). "I'm making it different to the book": Transmediation in young children's multimodal and digital texts. *Australasian Journal of Early Childhood, 36*(3), 56–65. DOI: 10.1177/183693911103600308

Mills, K. A. (2007). Access to multiliteracies: A critical ethnography. *Ethnography and Education, 2*(3), 305–325. DOI: 10.1080/17457820701547310

Mills, K. A. (2010). A review of the "Digital Turn" in the New Literacy studies. *Review of Educational Research, 80*(2), 246–271. DOI: 10.3102/0034654310364401

Molle, D., & Prior, P. (2008). Multimodal genre system in EAP writing pedagogy: Reflecting on a need analysis. *TESOL Quarterly, 42*(4), 541–566. DOI: 10.1002/j.1545-7249.2008.tb00148.x

Molyneux, P., & Godinho, S. (2012). "This Is My Thing!": Middle years students' engagement and learning using digital resources. *Australasian Journal of Educational Technology, 28*(8), 1466–1486. DOI: 10.14742/ajet.782

Moor-Russo, D., & Shanahan, L. (2014). A broader vision of literacy: Including the visual with the linguistic. *Journal of Adolescent & Adult Literacy*, *57*(7), 527–532. DOI: 10.1002/jaal.282

Moor-Russo, D., & Viglietti, J. M. (2012). Using the K_5 connected cognition diagram to analyze teachers' communication and understanding of regions in three-dimensional space. *The Journal of Mathematical Behavior*, *31*(2), 235–251. DOI: 10.1016/j.jmathb.2011.12.001

Mora, R. A., Tian, Z., & Harman, R. (2024). *Translanguaging and multimodality as flow, agency, and a new sense of advocacy in and from the global south*. Routledge.

Murray, J. (2013). Composing multimodality. In Lutkewitte, C. (Ed.), *Multimodal composition: A critical sourcebook* (pp. 323–350). Bedford / St. Martin's.

Nelson, M. E. (2008). Multimodal synthesis and the voice of the multimedia author in a Japanese EFL context. *Innovation in Language Learning and Teaching*, *2*(1), 65–82. DOI: 10.1080/17501220802158826

New London Group. (1996). A pedagogy of multiliteracies: Designing social futures. *Harvard Educational Review*, *66*(1), 60–92. DOI: 10.17763/haer.66.1.17370n67v-22j160u

New London Group. (2000). A pedagogy of multiliteracies: Designing social futures. In Cope, B., & Kalantzis, M. (Eds.), *Multiliteracies: Literacy learning and design of social futures* (pp. 9–38). Macmillan.

Norris, S. (2004). *Analyzing multimodal interaction: A methodological framework*. Routledge. DOI: 10.4324/9780203379493

Ntelioglou, B. Y. (2011). 'But why do I have to take this class?' The mandatory drama-ESL class and multiliteracies pedagogy. *Research in Drama Education*, *16*(4), 595–615. DOI: 10.1080/13569783.2011.617108

Pahl, K. (2007). Creativity in events and practices: A lens for understanding children's multimodal texts. *Literacy*, *41*(2), 86–92. DOI: 10.1111/j.1467-9345.2007.00462.x

Paivio, A. (1969). Mental imagery in associative learning and memory. *Psychological Review*, *76*(3), 241–263. DOI: 10.1037/h0027272

Pantaleo, S. (2012a). Exploring grade 7 students' responses to Shaun Tan's "The Red Tree.". *Children's Literature in Education*, *43*(1), 51–71. DOI: 10.1007/s10583-011-9156-x

Pantaleo, S. (2012b). Meaning-making with colour in multimodal texts: An 11-year-old student's purposeful "doing.". *Literacy*, *46*(3), 147–155. DOI: 10.1111/j.1741-4369.2012.00664.x

Pietikainen, S., & Pitkanen-Hunta, A. (2013). Multimodal literacy practices in the indigenous Sami classroom: Children navigating in a complex multilingual setting. *Journal of Language, Identity, and Education*, *12*(4), 230–247. DOI: 10.1080/15348458.2013.818471

Pütz, M., & Mundt, N.-F. (2018). *Expanding the linguistic landscape: Linguistic diversity, multimodality and the use of space as a semiotic resource*. Multilingual Matters.

Rahmanu, E. D., Altun, L., & Kariati, N. M. (2020). Case study on multimodality perception in the higher education classroom. *Journal Sosial dan Humaniora. Journal of Social Sciences and Humanities*, *10*(3), 1–11. DOI: 10.31940/soshum.v10i3.2091

Reyes-Torres, A., Brisk, M. E., & Lacorte, M. (2025). *Multiliteracies, multimodality, and learning by design in second language learning and teacher education*. Routledge. DOI: 10.4324/9781032620497

Roth, W.-M. (2001). Gestures: Their role in teaching and learning. *Review of Educational Research*, *71*(2), 365–392. DOI: 10.3102/00346543071003365

S.E.U. (1924). Radio-kroniko Sovetlanda [Radio-chronicles of Soviet country]. *Radiolyubitel* [Radio-Amateur], *1*(4), p. 2.

S.E.U. (1925). Radio-kroniko Sovetlanda [Radio-chronicles of Soviet country]. *Radiolyubitel* [Radio-Amateur], 2(3), p. 2.

Saint-Georges, I., & Weber, J.-J. (2013). *Multilingualism and multimodality: Current challenges for educational studies*. Brill Academic Publishing. DOI: 10.1007/978-94-6209-266-2

Saldaña, J. (2013). *The coding manual for qualitative researchers*. Sage Publications.

Saldaña, J. (2015). *Thinking qualitatively: Methods of mind*. Sage. DOI: 10.4135/9781071909782

Schunk, D. H. (2008). *Learning theories: An educational perspective* (6th ed.). Pearson.

Seidman, I. E. (2013). *Interviewing as qualitative research* (4th ed.). Teachers College Press.

Serafini, F. (2011). Expanding perspectives for comprehending visual images in multimodal texts. *Journal of Adolescent & Adult Literacy*, *54*(5), 342–350. DOI: 10.1598/JAAL.54.5.4

Serafini, F. (2014). *Reading the visual: An introduction to teaching multimodal literacy*. Teachers College Press.

Shakespeare, W. (1597). *Romeo and Juliet*.

Shanahan, L. E. (2013). Composing "kid-friendly" multimodal text: When conversations, instruction, and signs come together. *Written Communication*, *30*(2), 194–227. DOI: 10.1177/0741088313480328

Shanahan, L. E., & Flury-Kashmanian, C. (2014). Orchestrating semiotic resources in explicit strategy instruction. *Pedagogies*, *9*(2), 99–115. DOI: 10.1080/1554480X.2014.899484

Shanahan, L. E., McVee, M. B., & Bailey, N. M. (2014). Multimodality in action: New literacies as more than activity in middle and high school classrooms. In Ferdig, R. E., & Pytash, K. E. (Eds.), *Exploring multimodal composition and digital writing* (pp. 36–53). IGI Global. DOI: 10.4018/978-1-4666-4345-1.ch003

Shih, Y. C. (2014). Communication strategies in a multimodal virtual communication context. *System*, *42*, 34–47. DOI: 10.1016/j.system.2013.10.016

Sindoni, M. (2023). *Multimodality and translanguaging in video interactions*. Cambridge University Press.

Spradley, J. P. (1980). *Participant observation*. Holt, Rinehart and Winston.

Stein, P. (2000). Rethinking resources in the ESL classroom. Rethinking resources: Multimodal pedagogies in the ESL classroom. *TESOL Quarterly*, *34*(2), 333–336. DOI: 10.2307/3587958

Stein, P. (2008). *Multimodal pedagogies in diverse classrooms: Representations, rights and resources*. Routledge.

Stokoe, W. C. (1960). *Sign language structure: an outline of the visual communication systems of the American deaf*. Department of Anthropology and Linguistics, University of Buffalo.

Stone, P. (2012). Learners performing tasks in a Japanese EFL classroom: A multimodal and interpersonal approach to analysis. *RELC Journal*, *43*(3), 313–330. DOI: 10.1177/0033688212463287

Trofimov, A. A. (1977). *Орнамент чувашской народной вышивки: Вопросы теории и практики* [Ornaments of the Chuvash ethnic embroidery: Theoretical and historic questions]. Chuvashia, Cheboksary: Chuvash Publishing House.

Trofimov, A. A. (2007). *Искусство чувашской народной вышивки в музеях России* [The art of Chuvash ethnic embroidery in museums of Russia]. Chuvashia, Cheboksary: Chuvash State University of Humanities.

U.S. Department of Education, National Center for Education Statistics. (2024). *Digest of Education Statistics.* Retrieved from: https://nces.ed.gov/programs/digest/d22/tables/dt22_204.27.asp

Unsworth, L. (2006). Toward a metalanguage for multiliteracies education: Describing the meaning-making resources of language-image interaction. *English Teaching*, *5*(1), 55–76.

Van Leeuwen, T. (2004). *Introducing social semiotics.* Routledge. DOI: 10.4324/9780203647028

VERBI Software. (2021). MAXQDA 2022 [computer software]. Berlin, Germany: VERBI Software. Available from maxqda.com

VERBI Software. (2021). MAXQDA 2022 [computer software]. Berlin, Germany: VERBI Software. Available from maxqda.com.

Vincent, J. (2006). Children writing: Multimodality and assessment in the writing classroom. *Literacy*, *40*(1), 51–57. DOI: 10.1111/j.1467-9345.2006.00426.x

Vygotsky, L. S. (1987). *The collected works of L. S. Vygotsky: Vol. 1. Problems of general psychology, including the volume thinking and speech* (R. W. Rieber & A. S. Carton, Eds., Trans. N. Minick). New York: Plenum.

Vygotsky, L. S. (1978). *Mind in society: The development of higher psychological processes*. Harvard University Press.

Vygotsky, L. S. (2000). *Psychology*. EKSMO-Press.

Walsh, M. (2008). Worlds have collided and modes have merged: Classroom evidence of changed literacy practices. *Literacy*, *42*(2), 101–108. DOI: 10.1111/j.1741-4369.2008.00495.x

Wang, M. (2011). Using multimodal presentation software and peer group discussion in learning English as a Second Language. *Australasian Journal of Educational Technology*, *27*(6), 907–923. DOI: 10.14742/ajet.920

Wang, M. (2022). The cultivation of students' multiple practical ability under the multimodal blended teaching mode. *International Journal of Emerging Technologies in Learning*, *17*(12), 106–120. DOI: 10.3991/ijet.v17i12.32087

Wertsch, J. V. (1991). *Voices of the mind*. Harvard University Press.

Wilton, B. (2014). *Collins little book of clans and tartans*. Harper Collins Publishers.

Włodarczyk, M., Tyrkkö, J., & Adamczyk, E. (2023). *Multilingualism from manuscript to 3D: Intersections of modalities from medieval to modern times*. Routledge. DOI: 10.4324/9781003166634

Yusra, S. R., Hanifa, R., Wardana, A., & Fahmiati, M. (2025). Leveraging instructional multimodality for enhanced English grammar learning of undergraduate students: A higher education perspective. *International Journal of Information and Education Technology (IJIET)*, *15*(6), 1172–1181. DOI: 10.18178/ijiet.2025.15.6.2320

Zaczeck, I., & Phillips, C. (2014). *The illustrated encyclopedia of tartan: A complete history and visual guide to over 400 famous tartans*. Southwater Publishing.

Zarobe, Y. R., & Querol-Julian, M. (2025). Multilingualism and multimodality in the CLIL/EMI classroom. *Journal of Multilingual and Multicultural Development*, *46*(5), 1397–1415. DOI: 10.1080/01434632.2025.2482734

Zeffirelli, F. (1968). *Romeo and Juliet.* Paramount Pictures. https://www.youtube.com/watch?v=VCe0nzdD76k

Zeffirelli, F. (1968). *Romeo and Juliet.* Paramount Pictures. Retrieved from public domain: https://www.youtube.com/watch?v=VCe0nzdD76k

About the Author

Olga Gould-Yakovleva, is an American researcher, author, and educator who earned her Ph.D. in Curriculum, Instruction & the Science of Learning from the State University of New York. Prior to that, she had earned her M.Ed. from Florida Atlantic University. Dr. Gould-Yakovleva holds her initial Dual Bachelor's and Dual Master's degrees in Teaching ESOL & Foreign Languages. This Florida state-certified educator (2008 – 2028) has had her life-long K-12 & university/college teaching experiences in the United States and Internationally. Dr. Gould-Yakovleva's research topics lie in the fields of Educational Research, including Qualitative Methods; Teacher Education; Multimodality; Dialogic Teaching and Learning; Teaching Diverse, Multicultural & International Students; Poverty Reduction through Education.

Index

N

P

Q

R

S

T

U

V

W

www.ingramcontent.com/pod-product-compliance
Ingram Content Group UK Ltd.
Pitfield, Milton Keynes, MK11 3LW, UK
UKHW051038091026
15624UKWH00011B/524

9 798337 334264